Alexander Smith Paterson

A Concise System of Theology

On the Basis of the Shorter Catechism

Alexander Smith Paterson

A Concise System of Theology
On the Basis of the Shorter Catechism

ISBN/EAN: 9783743686700

Printed in Europe, USA, Canada, Australia, Japan

Cover: Foto ©Lupo / pixelio.de

More available books at **www.hansebooks.com**

A CONCISE

SYSTEM OF THEOLOGY,

ON THE BASIS OF THE

SHORTER CATECHISM.

BY

ALEXANDER SMITH PATERSON, A.M.,
AUTHOR OF "A HISTORY OF THE CHURCH."

WITH AN INTRODUCTORY PAPER

By *DUNCAN MACFARLAN, D.D.,*
Renfrew.

London:
T. NELSON AND SONS, PATERNOSTER ROW.
EDINBURGH; AND NEW YORK.

1881.

ADVERTISEMENT.

The Author of the following work, Mr ALEXANDER SMITH PATERSON, was the elder son of the late Rev. Alexander Paterson of Dundee, and nephew of the Rev. Dr Paterson, one of the ministers of Montrose. He was educated at the Grammar School and Marischal College, Aberdeen, where his family resided after the death of his father. Although a singularly laborious student, he evinced no small anxiety in the prospect of appearing before the Presbytery for examination. This apprehension was, in a great measure, the occasion of leading him to draw up very ample notes on the topics connected with Ecclesiastical History, which were afterwards posthumously published under the title, "History of the Church from the Creation of the World to the Nineteenth Century." The present work was composed with a somewhat similar object; and it is supposed that the intensity of mind which he brought to bear on both, in some measure hastened his premature and lamented death, which took place on the 12th of September 1828, in the 25th year of his age.

The "Analysis of the Shorter Catechism" was left by Mr Paterson in a state of entire preparation for the press, but various circumstances have delayed its publication. It is now presented to the public entirely on account of its intrinsic merit. The manuscript was submitted to several distinguished ministers, who expressed their opinions in terms of the most unqualified approbation. In particular, the Rev. Dr Brewster of Craig described it "as being one of the most beautiful, complete, and accurate expositions of the Shorter Catechism which has ever appeared,—unfolding the meaning of the answers to each question, with a clearness and minuteness of detail hitherto unequalled in works of the kind." Another gentleman of great literary experience, stated, that it "had been prepared with such elaborate care, that, after a critical perusal, he could not suggest the addition or diminution of a single word." Strong as these testimonies are, the Publisher confidently anticipates that they will be amply borne out by an examination of the work itself.

The annexed admirable Paper on the History and Arrangement of the Shorter Catechism, by the Rev. Duncan Macfarlan of Renfrew, appeared some time ago in a periodical publication, and is transferred into this volume with the obliging permission of the author.

EDINBURGH, *August* 1841.

NOTE TO THE SECOND EDITION.

In the present edition several important alterations have been made in the typographical arrangement, calculated to make the work more accessible for reference; and, with a similar view, two new indices have been added—the first showing where the illustration of each individual Question in the Shorter Catechism is to be found, and the other indicating alphabetically the various subjects discussed in the work.

EDINBURGH, *January* 1844.

HISTORY AND ARRANGEMENT OF THE SHORTER CATECHISM.

BY THE REV. DUNCAN MACFARLAN,

RENFREW.

CATECHISMS were, at a very early period, drawn up and used by all, or nearly all, of the Reformed Churches of Europe. The earliest which we recollect to have seen mentioned, as used by the Scottish Reformers, had been drawn up by Calvin. But in 1590, we find the General Assembly adopting measures for securing a general and national Catechism. "Anent the examination before the communion," say they, "it is thought meet for the common profite of the whole people, that ane uniform order be keepit in examination, and that ane schort form of examination be set down, be their breither, Messrs John Craig, Robert Pont, Thomas Buchanan, and Andrew Melvine, to be presented to the next Assembly." In 1591, a form was laid before the Assembly by Mr Craig, but it was remitted, with instructions "to contract in some schorter bounds." The abridged form was accordingly laid before the Assembly of 1592, and approved. The following directions were also added :—" Therefore, it is thought needful, that every pastor travel with his flock, that they may buy the samen buick, and read it in their families, quhereby they may be the better instructed; and that the samen be read and learnit in lector's (reading) schools, in place of the little Catechism" (Calvin's). This Catechism, or "Form of Examination," which is commonly called Craig's Catechism, consists of twelve heads or chapters, having the following titles :—" Of our miserable bondage through Adam—Of our redemption by Christ—Of our participation with Christ—Of the Word—Of our liberty to serve God—Of the Sacraments—Of Baptism—Of the Supper—Of Discipline—Of the Magistrate—Of the Table in special (meaning the Protestant mode of observing the Supper)—The end of our redemption." Under each of these are a number of questions and answers, amounting in all to ninety-six; and the latter are remarkably short and pertinent, and usually accompanied with at least one Scripture proof.

When the Solemn League and Covenant was projected, contemplating, as it did, an ecclesiastical union between the three kingdoms, measures were also adopted for preparing a uniform Confession, Directory, and Catechism. And it is important to observe, that the plan afterwards executed by the Westminster Assembly, was first proposed in the General Assembly of the Church of Scotland. Towards the end of 1640, several Scottish commissioners, of whom Henderson was one, went to London to treat on matters then pending between the King and the Presbyterian party. Henderson returned in the July following, and found the General Assembly holding an adjourned meeting at Edinburgh, and anxiously waiting his arrival. He was immediately elected Moderator, and laid before them a letter from the Presbyterians in and about London, in which they complain of the spread of schismatical opinions, and earnestly crave the advice and assistance of the Assembly. In replying to this letter, the Assembly says, among other things, "We have learned by long experience, *ever since the time of the Reformation*, and *specially after the two kingdoms have been*—in the great goodness of God to both—*united under one head and monarch, but most of all, of late*, which is not unknown to you, what danger and contagion in matters of kirk government, of divine worship, and of doctrine, may come from the one kirk to the other; which, beside all other reasons, make us to pray to God, and to desire you, and all that love the honour of Christ, and the peace of these kirks and kingdoms, heartily to endeavour, that there might be in both kirks, *one Confession, one Directory for Public Worship, one Catechism, and one Form of Kirk Government.*" And agreeably to this, we find Henderson suggesting to the same Assembly, only twelve days before the writing of this letter, the propriety of drawing up such a Confession, Catechism, and Directory; thus leaving scarcely any reason to doubt, that the thing itself was projected by Henderson, and first laid before the General Assembly; but that the Assembly had itself been long favourable to such a measure, and was immediately incited to it by what had taken place in England. The Assembly accordingly approved highly of the measure, and urged Henderson to undertake the drawing up of the documents required. And to render this the more easy, they allowed him to refrain from preaching, and to avail himself of assistance. But he declined the task, as being too arduous. The subject is repeatedly mentioned in the Assembly's correspondence during the intervening period; but it does not appear that any thing was done before the meeting of the Westminster Assembly in 1643. This Assembly met under the authority of the English Parliament, but chiefly at the instance of the Scottish Church. It was composed of 121 divines, with 30 lay assessors, and 5 commissioners from the Church of Scotland, and continued its sittings for upwards of five years.

The matters laid before this Assembly were numerous and important, and some of them are detailed with great minuteness. It unfortunately happens, however, that our information respecting the drawing up of the Catechisms is meagre and imperfect. The late Dr Belfrage of Falkirk appears to have been at great pains in collecting whatever was accessible on this point. We have made some further inquiries, but have hitherto found scarcely any thing beyond what he seems to have examined and abridged. The *sum* of what we have been able to gather, either from his work or original authorities, may be stated in a few words. In 1647, while the Assembly was engaged discussing the different articles of the Confession, committees were appointed to reduce these into the form of two Catechisms; a *larger*, which was to serve as a text-book for pulpit exposition, according to a usage of the churches on the Continent; and a *shorter*, for the instruction of children. It appears, however, that before the Confession had been finished, some progress was made in composing the Catechism, and that the reducing of it to a conformity with the Confession was an after-thought. "We made long ago," says Baillie, "a pretty progress in the Catechism, but falling on rules and long debates, it was laid aside till the Confession was ended, with the resolution to have no matter in it, but what was expressed in the Confession." And, accordingly, much curiosity has been excited respecting the author of the *original draft*. Dr Belfrage, after detailing various opinions, and assigning reasons for his own, alleges Dr Arrowsmith to be the most likely person. After weighing the evidence by which this and several other opinions have been supported, we have not been able to come to any other conclusion, than that the matter is altogether uncertain.* After the Catechism had been finished by the com-

---

* "While the Confession of Faith was under discussion in the Assembly, committees were appointed to reduce it into the form of catechisms, one Larger, for the service of a public exposition in the pulpit, according to the custom of foreign churches; the other Smaller, for the instruction of families. It has been generally thought, that a draught or sketch was prepared by some individual of the Shorter Catechism, and laid before the Committee for their revisal. It is not certainly known who this individual was. I have heard it said by a theologian of great research, and now with God, it was his conviction that it was Dr Arrowsmith. Brooke, in his history of the Puritans, says that he united with several of his brethren in drawing up the Assembly's Catechism; and Baillie, in his Letters, says that the Catechism was composed by a committee, of whom Dr Arrowsmith was one. None of the Assembly was more competent to the task. He officiated for some

mittee, it was laid before the Assembly and approved of, first in so many successive portions, and afterwards as a whole. On the 5th of November it was approved of by the Parliament, and would have been licensed by the king, had not certain hindrances occurred. It was next laid before the General Assembly of the Church of Scotland. This was in July 1648. And the following time as one of the University Preachers at Cambridge, where his education had been completed. It was while officiating as a Preacher at St Martin's, Ironmonger's Lane, London, that he was called to sit in the Assembly of Divines. Baillie mentions a circumstance which shows the high estimation in which he was held in that council. He calls him a learned divine, on whom the Assembly had put the writing against the Antinomians. He was promoted to be Master of John's College, Cambridge, where he discharged the duties of his office with exemplary diligence.

"The excellent Dr M'Crie, whose researches have shed so much light on the character, doctrines, and conduct of our Reformers, states, in a communication with which he has favoured me, that from a circumstance mentioned by Baillie, he is inclined to think that Mr Palmer was concerned in the first draught of the Catechism. In volume first of the Letters, page 431, he says, 'It was laid on Mr Palmer to draw up a directory for catechising.' The directory contains no article on this point. In the same volume, page 440, he says, 'Mr Palmer's part about catechising was given in, and though the best catechist in England, did not suit, but was left in our hands to frame according to our mind.' There is a work published by this divine, entitled, 'The Principles of the Christian Religion made Plain and Easy,' in which a considerable similarity to the Shorter Catechism may be traced. Palmer was constituted Master of King's College, Cambridge, and showed the greatest solicitude to promote religion and learning, maintained several poor scholars at his own expense in the College, and when he died, left a considerable benefaction for the same purpose.

"'In running over Wodrow's MSS.,' says Dr M'Crie in his communication, 'I recollect noticing a statement that he had received information from some person, that the Catechism was composed by Dr Wallis. This was the celebrated mathematician of that name, who was one of the Secretaries to the Westminster Assembly. Perhaps the statement may have arisen from his official situation, and his name having been seen appended to the printed copy of that work. It would be a feather in the cap of our little formulary, and no real disparagement to the philosopher, that its draughtsman was Dr Wallis. In one of his works he avows that he obtained much insight from the discussion of so many learned divines, in composing the Confession and Catechisms, but says nothing of his having any hand directly in its compilation.'

"There was another member of the Assembly, Dr Gouge, who may be thought to have some claim to the honour, from his learning and activity, and also from an excellent and comprehensive scheme of divinity, in the form of question and answer, which bears his name. He was minister of Black Friars, London, was appointed a member of the Assembly, and was in such reputation, that he often filled the Moderator's chair in his absence. Amidst claims so varied, I am inclined to think, with all due veneration for the memory of the rest, that the weightiest is that of Dr Arrowsmith. Baillie says, 'We have nearly agreed in private on a draught of Catechism, on which, when it comes in public, we may have little debate.' From the MSS. of Mr George Gillespie, it appears, that after the report had been given in and con-

was the deliverance of the Assembly:—"The General Assembly having seriously considered the Shorter Catechism, agreed upon by the Assembly of Divines sitting at Westminster, with the assistance of commissioners from this Kirk, do find, upon due examination thereof, that the said Catechism *is agreeable to the Word of God, and in nothing contrary to the received doctrine, worship, discipline, and government of the Kirk;* and therefore approve the said Shorter Catechism, as a part of the intended uniformity, to be a Directory for catechising such as are of weaker capacity." The year following it was also ratified by an act of the Scottish Parliament. And from that time it has continued to be in common use, generally in Scotland, and among Presbyterians and several other denominations in England and Ireland; and has latterly obtained a firm footing in the United States, in most of the British colonies, and at not a few missionary stations far hence among the heathen. And it is remarkable, that amidst all the controversies which have occurred, it has been almost universally approved by every party of orthodox believers. "Amidst the jealousy and rivalship of contending parties," says the late pious and judicious Dr Belfrage, "it has been a centre of union, in which the faith and charity of good men have met; and in seasons of innovation, when a veneration for what is ancient is derided as the freak of imbecility or prejudice; when 'the march of intellect' is the pretext for every change, however presumptuous or violent, and when all the foundations of the earth seem out of course, this summary of the truth remains uninjured and revered; and it will continue to be an exhibition and defence of pure religion and undefiled, before God and the Father, to the latest age."

Frequent notice has been taken of the extraordinary simplicity of arrangement and depth of thought observable in the Assembly's Shorter Catechism. Of the former, I have just had a remarkable proof, in reading over Dr Chalmers' preface to the first volume of the new edition of his works. With his usual clearness and analytical acumen, he proposes two methods of studying Theology. According to the one, the first object of contemplation is the Divine Being; and then the history of his

sidered, the Catechism was recommitted, that improvements suggested by the wisdom of the Assembly might be made. I find in the letter of Baillie various hints respecting the progress of the Catechism. 'We made long ago,' says he, 'a pretty progress in the Catechism, but falling on rule and long debates, it was laid aside till the Confession was ended, with the resolution to have no matter in it but what was expressed in the Confession, which should not be debated again in the Catechism.' In another letter of later date, he says, 'We have passed a quarter of the Catechism, and thought to have made a short work with the rest, but we have fallen into such endless janglings about the method and the matter, that all think it will be a long work: the increase of all heresies is very great'"—*Belfrage's Shorter Catechism* vol. I. pp. 14-18.

doings in this world, detailed in natural, if not chronological order. The other fixes at once on some awakened sinner, and accompanying him as he advances in knowledge and holiness, describes progressively the discoveries which he makes, or which are made to him, in the word and works of God. The former considers God abstractly, and follows out the other branches as so many of his works. And divinity taught upon this principle recommends itself to reason, as regularly deductive and capable of systematic arrangement. And accordingly, this is the principle on which catechisms and systems of divinity are usually constructed. The other, instead of the matter observed, takes up the observer; and simply recording what he is supposed to see and feel, as he advances towards perfection, the same subjects pass in review; but they are seen from different points, and under different lights. They are seen, not as abstract truths, but as practical directions. And this, therefore, is the view of divine truth best fitted for the guidance of the heart and conduct. The principles thus referred to, are, if we mistake not, the same with the categories of Aristotle and the first principles of Bacon; the one assuming, as the basis of his arrangement, *being*, or the things about which men think; and the other, the powers of mind by which these are known and enjoyed. Now, it is perhaps new to some of our readers to be told, that the profound distinctions of an Aristotle and a Bacon are employed in the construction of that humble Primer called the Shorter Catechism; and that the prolific mind of a Chalmers could not have selected a finer example of its own original speculations, than is to be found in this directory for catechising *such as are of a weaker capacity*.

The number of Questions in this little manual, is, in all, one hundred and seven. The first three are introductory—God's chief or principal end in creating man; the rule by which man may attain to that end, and the principal branches into which that rule may be divided, are the topics thus introduced.

From the beginning of the fourth question, to the end of the thirty-eighth, we have a system of divinity, regularly constructed according to the first of the two principles explained. Every thing stated under these questions, is laid down speculatively—that is, as a matter of study and contemplation, not of command and direction. Each answer tells us what *is*, and not what *should be*. The arrangement of topics, also, is such as to show their consecutive dependence on each other, so that, like so many links of a chain, they are all sustained from the primary question,—"What is God?" This will be observed in a mere rehearsal of the subjects, of which the questions are composed:—the being and attributes of God—the persons in the Godhead—the divine purposes or decrees—the execution of these in creation—their fulfilment in providence—the special providence of God towards man, in an unfallen state—in the fall and its consequences—in redemption from these—in the character and offices of the Redeemer—in what he did on earth to redeem man, and in what he is raised to in heaven, for the further purposes of redemption—in applying to sinners the blessings of redemption by the Holy Spirit—his operations in effectual calling, justification, adoption, and sanctification—and the fruits of these in life, at death, at the resurrection, and throughout eternity.

From the beginning of the thirty-ninth question, to the end of the book, the topics are strictly practical, and they are so arranged as to furnish an appropriate directory for every stage of Christian advancement. The subjects introduced are not presented speculatively, but as pointing to the conscience and the heart, and as leading forth the mind, and guiding the conduct, into the ways of God. And accordingly, the arrangement, instead of assuming some principle in the *matter* of contemplation, assumes a principle in the *man*, and proceeds to address and direct him in all his advances onward to perfection. It is in this way that the thirty-ninth question commences with what "God requireth of man?" It is thus the first arrow driven from this quiver, is so pointed as to aim at the conscience, *God's witness in man*. And the commandments which follow are as a bundle of these. They are variously pointed, yet all have a point; and this very diversity only fits them the more for the diversified circumstances in which man is found. One, for example, is aimed at the conscience of such as worship strange gods,—another at those who worship even the true God, through the medium of images,—a third at the blasphemer,—a fourth at the Sabbath-breaker,—a fifth at children who are disobedient to parents,—a sixth at murderers,—a seventh at adulterers,—an eighth at thieves,—a ninth at liars,—and a tenth at the covetous. And to render each of these sharp as a "two-edged sword," there is under each, first, what concerns the "want of conformity to," and then, what belongs to the "transgression of;" in other words, a "required," and a "forbidden," with occasional reasons also annexed. Nor does each commandment point only to as many individual sins or duties, but under these, to as many classes of both. It is therefore scarcely possible to conceive of any arrangement better fitted to bring home guilt to every conscience. And it is accordingly followed by other questions, respecting man's inability to keep the commands, the sins of which he thus becomes guilty, and the eternal judgments to which he is exposed. By these he is left helpless and hopeless, under a sentence of condemnation, and is thus driven to inquire, what he must do to be saved. Here the very next question takes him up, tells him how he may escape the wrath and curse of God due by sin, and explains this, under the heads of faith in Jesus Christ, repentance unto life, and the ordinary means of grace. Even in this subordinate arrangement, the condition of the inquirer is kept steadily in view. The only direct answer which can be given to the question, "What must I do to be saved?" is, "repent and believe;" and agreeably to this, the only points immediately explained in the Catechism, are faith in Jesus Christ, and repentance unto life. Repentance is the *turning* of the heart from every thing else to God, as reconciled in Christ; and faith is the *looking* at Christ *believingly*, as the gift of God, and *receiving* him as the salvation of the soul. But this very "looking at Christ," and "turning of the heart" to God, as reconciled in Christ, imply some knowledge of his will, and create a desire for the enjoyment of other ordinances. And these next follow, under the teaching of the Word, the observance of the sacraments, and the exercise of prayer. An awakened and repentant sinner seeks early and earnestly to know the will of God. The Catechism meets him, offering instruction respecting the profitable reading of the Word, and waiting on the ordinance of preaching. But supposing him to be in some measure instructed, he yet desires to receive *seals* of the covenant, and may never before have partaken of any of its *signs*. The nature, use, and proper observance of the sacraments are therefore now unfolded. And last of all comes prayer, not as if the individual were up till this time considered prayerless, but because it is now that he especially requires to be taught how to pray for such things as he ought; and this, because it is now that he declares himself to be an heir of those promises on which prayer rests, and through which it obtains blessings. The prayer of the soul, like breath in the natural body, is essential to life, and, like it, begins properly as soon as we are born anew. But though this be its beginning, its end is unseen. The renewed soul becoming more and more conformed to the will of God, enters more and more into the spirit of prayer, and finds, in the simple but comprehensive example with which the Catechism concludes, materials more and more fitted for guiding its intercourse with the Father of Spirits.

1. By using the Catechism in the right observance of these distinctions and principles, we shall be better able to understand each question in its true and proper meaning; and the reason why such questions as Effectual Calling and Justification are so far separated from Faith in Jesus Christ and Repentance unto Life; and how, in general, the doctrines of the Gospel, as contained in both parts of the Catechism, should not be together. These things happen, simply because we have, in the first, a *speculative system*, and, in the latter, a *practical directory*. The doctrines of the Gospel are necessary to both, but require to be presented in *different forms*, so as the more perfectly to secure the *different ends* contemplated.

2. Each division may thus be turned to its own proper use

Suppose, for example, that I were asked in what book a clear outline of the Christian faith might be found and studied, I would at once say, "In the first thirty-eight questions of the Assembly's Shorter Catechism." But if I were asked for a practical guide, to lead men to Christ, and to train them to holiness, I would say, "Begin at the thirty-ninth question, and be guided with those which follow, onward to the end."

3. Even children might, on these principles, be taught to greater advantage than they usually are. Instead of beginning to instruct a child, respecting the abstract character of God, the distinctions of personality in the Godhead, the doctrine of decrees, and other matters of difficult comprehension, I would begin my attempts to instruct him, with the meaning and application of each succeeding commandment, and onwards to the end; by which time, he would have materials out of which to conceive of God, of his purposes and works; and his mind would be also, in some measure, prepared for more abstract processes of thinking.

4. Much of the apparent abstruseness of this little work would in this way disappear, and on the same principle on which science becomes comparatively easy, when perceived in a proper course and by proper means. Depart from the arrangements of a Linnæus and Jussieu, and the beautiful order observable in botany will appear confused and perplexing; or invert the order in any process of mathematical inquiry, and the evenness of the way along which we find an easy path will be rugged to the master, and impassable to the pupil. And strange were it, indeed, if an arrangement so exact and so well adapted to its own *special ends* as that of the Catechism, should nevertheless leave each question to be taken up, like some cube cast on a gammon board, in any order and with equal intelligence.

5. If these principles and distinctions were more observed, more justice would be done to the merits of the work, and it would be rendered more generally useful.

SYNOPSIS OF CONTENTS.

PAGE

GENERAL INTRODUCTION.
The Chief Design of Man's Creation . . . 19
The Scriptures the only Rule of Faith and Duty . . 22
The two principal topics treated of in Scripture, and explained in the Two Divisions of the Catechism . . 26

PART FIRST.

WHAT WE ARE TO BELIEVE CONCERNING GOD.

CHAPTER I.

CONCERNING GOD CONSIDERED IN HIMSELF.

Nature and Perfections of God 29
Unity of God 40
Trinity of Persons in the Godhead . . . , 42

CHAPTER II.

CONCERNING GOD'S DOINGS WITH RESPECT TO HIS CREATURES.

SECTION I.—Of the Nature and Character of God's Decrees . 47

SECTION II.—Of the Execution of God's Decrees . . 51

In the Creation of the World 52
  ,, Creation of Man 54
  ,, Nature and Character of God's General Providence 56

SECTION III.—Of the Special Providence of God towards Man in his Creation and Fall.

Covenant of Works—its Parties and Terms . . 58
Man's Disobedience and Fall by Sin 62
Nature of Sin in General 63
Nature of Adam's Sin in Particular 65
1. Extent of the Fall 68
2. Consequences of the Fall 70
3. Sinfulness of Man's State by the Fall . . Ib.
4. Misery of Man's State by the Fall . . . 72

SECTION IV.—Of the Special Providence of God towards Man in Redemption.

    Div. 1.—Plan of Redemption 70
        The Person and Character of the Redeemer . 83
        The Redeemer's Assumption of Human Nature 86
        The Offices of the Redeemer . . . 89
          1. Prophetical Office 92
          2. Priestly Office 93
          3. Kingly Office 100

    Div. 2.—The States in which the Redeemer executed his Threefold Office.
        State of Humiliation . . . 104
        State of Exaltation 107

    Div. 3.—Of the Application of Redemption.
        Of the Agent by whom Redemption is applied 112
          " Means used for the Application of Redemption in Effectual Calling . 115
          " Manner and Order of the Application of Redemption in Effectual Calling . 117

    Div. 4.—Of the Benefits of Redemption.
        Benefits of Redemption in this Life . . 122
          1. Of Justification . . . 125
          2. Of Adoption . . . 132
          3. Of Sanctification . . . 135
          4. Additional Benefits . . 139
        Benefits of Redemption at the Resurrection 147

PART SECOND.

THE DUTY WHICH GOD REQUIRES OF MAN.

INTRODUCTION.—Nature of Man's Duty in General . 153

CHAPTER I.

SECTION I.—Of the Moral Law, binding on all rational creatures, as summed up in the Ten Commandments.
        Of the Moral Law 155
        Summary of the Moral Law . . . 162
        Sum of the Ten Commandments . . 166
        Preface to the Ten Commandments . . 169

SECTION II.—The Duties which we owe to God—contained in the first four Commandments of the Law.
    Div. 1.—The First Commandment . . 172
        Duties required . . . . *ib.*
        Sins forbidden . . . 175
        O the expression " Before Me " . 177

	PAGE
Div. 2.—The Second Commandment	178
Duties required	179
Sins forbidden	181
Reasons annexed	184
Div. 3.—The Third Commandment	186
Duties required	187
Sins forbidden	191
Reason annexed	193
Div. 4.—The Fourth Commandment	196
Duties required	ib.
Change of the Sabbath	201
Sanctification of the Sabbath	204
Sins forbidden	207
Reasons annexed	209

SECTION III.—The Duties which we owe to man—contained in the last six Commandments of the Law.

Div. 1.—The Fifth Commandment	212
Duties required	ib.
Sins forbidden	220
Reason annexed	225
Div. 2.—The Sixth Commandment	227
Duties required	ib.
Sins forbidden	228
Div. 3.—The Seventh Commandment	232
Duties required	ib.
Sins forbidden	233
Div. 4.—The Eighth Commandment	236
Duties required	ib.
Sins forbidden	238
Div. 5.—The Ninth Commandment	242
Duties required	ib.
Sins forbidden	244
Div. 6.—The Tenth Commandment	247
Duties required	ib.
Sins forbidden	250

CHAPTER II.

INTRODUCTION.

Man's Inability to keep the Moral Law	253
Different Degrees of Guilt in Breaking the Law	256
Desert of every Breach of the Law	255

SPECIAL DUTIES REQUIRED OF MAN UNDER THE GOSPEL DISPENSATION.

SECTION I —Faith in Jesus Christ	268

	PAGE
SECTION II.—Repentance unto Life	282
SECTION III.—The Diligent Use of the Means of Grace	286

   Div. 1.—Of the Word of God as a Means of Grace.

1. Effects of the Word of God	290
2. Proper Use of the Word of God	294

   Div. 2.—Of the Sacraments as a Means of Grace.

1. Of the Efficacy of the Sacraments	297
2. „ Nature of the Sacraments	300
3. „ New Testament Sacraments	303
4. „ Nature and Use of Baptism	307
5. „ Subjects of Baptism	314
6. „ Nature and Use of the Lord's Supper	320
7. „ Proper Observance of the Lord's Supper	329

   Div. 3 —Of Prayer as a Means of Grace.

1. Of the Nature of Prayer	340
2. „ Rule of Direction in Prayer	347
3. „ Preface to the Lord's Prayer	350
4. „ First Petition in the Lord's Prayer	353
5. „ Second Petition in the Lord's Prayer	357
6. „ Third Petition in the Lord's Prayer	361
7. „ Fourth Petition in the Lord's Prayer	364
8. „ Fifth Petition in the Lord's Prayer	368
9. „ Sixth Petition in the Lord's Prayer	373
10. „ Conclusion of the Lord's Prayer	377

THE ASSEMBLY'S SHORTER CATECHISM
ANALYZED AND EXPLAINED.

GENERAL INTRODUCTION.

SHOWING THE CHIEF DESIGN OF MAN'S CREATION—THAT THE SCRIPTURES ARE THE ONLY RULE OF FAITH AND DUTY—AND THE TWO PRINCIPAL TOPICS TREATED OF IN SCRIPTURE, AND EXPLAINED IN THE TWO DIVISIONS OF THE CATECHISM.

The Chief Design of Man's Creation.

Q. 1.—What is the Chief End of Man?

Man's chief end is to glorify God, and to enjoy him for ever.

ANALYSIS AND PROOFS.

We are here taught,—

1. That the chief design of man's creation, in reference to God, was to glorify him. 1 Cor. x. 31.—"Whether therefore ye eat or drink, or whatsoever ye do, do all to the glory of God."

2. That the chief design of man's creation, in reference to himself, was the enjoyment of God for ever. Ps. lxxiii. 25, 26.—"Whom have I in heaven but thee? and there is none upon earth that I desire beside thee.—God is my portion for ever."

EXPLANATION.

Observation 1.—*The chief end of man's creation, in reference to God, was to glorify him.*

The glory of God is commonly distinguished into his *essential* and his *declarative* glory.

1. God's *essential glory* is what he is absolutely in himself. "I am that I am."—Exod. iii. 14. It is that glory which he has in himself, and which he will not give to another. This glory is infinite, eternal, and unchangeable; and, consequently, it can neither be increased nor diminished.—Job xxxv. 7; Ps. xvi. 2.

2. God's *declarative glory* in his making known his glory to, by, and in, the creatures which he hath made.

The *irrational creatures*, both animate and inanimate, glorify God *passively*, by affording matter of praise to God, their Maker.—Ps. xix. 1. But we, his *rational* creatures, ought to glorify him *actively*,—by setting our hearts wholly upon him,—by making use of all things in subordination to his glory, and only as means more perfectly to show forth his praise,—by being willing to part with every thing dear to us, rather than not maintain and declare his glory,—and by employing for this purpose all the powers and faculties which he hath conferred upon us—(1 Cor. vi. 20; Matt. v. 16)—by obeying his commandments,—and by acknowledging all his perfections.

God is to be glorified in *all things.*—1 Cor. x. 31; 1 Pet. iv. 11. We are to glorify him in all our actions, whether *natural*, as eating and drinking, &c.; or *civil*, as in the common affairs of life; or *moral* and *religious*, in the duties which we owe to God. "There is not a grain of real goodness in the most spacious actions which are performed without a reference to the glory of God. This the world cannot understand; but it will appear highly reasonable to those who take their ideas of God from the Scriptures, and who have felt the necessity and found the benefits of redemption."

We ought to make the glory of God our *chief end* in all our actions. 1. Because it was God's chief end in our creation, preservation, and redemption. 2. Because God hath made us capable of glorifying him. 3. Gratitude should excite us to make this our chief end.—Ps. c. 3; Prov. xvi. 4; Ps. lxvi. 8, 9; 1 Cor. vi. 19, 20; Ps. ciii. 1–5.

We may here observe that no man can glorify God acceptably, until he believes in Jesus Christ; for without faith it is impossible to please him.—Heb. xi. 6. Nor can we of ourselves glorify God, for of ourselves we can do nothing good.—John xv. 5. But seeing

God hath promised the grace of his Spirit, we should not be weary in well-doing.

Obs. 2.—*The chief end of man's creation, in reference to himself, was the enjoyment of God for ever.*

To *enjoy God* is to acquiesce or rest in God as the chief good, with complacency and delight; or it is to feel unspeakably happy in his presence.—Ps. cxvi. 7.

Believers enjoy God in *this* world as well as in that which is to come.—Gen. v. 24; 1 John i. 3; 1 Cor. i. 9. But there is a very great difference between the enjoyment of God *here* and the enjoyment of him *hereafter.* In this world, the enjoyment of God is *mediate;* that is, ordinances intervene: but in the world to come it will be *immediate;* ordinances will be unknown—means shall be done away. Here, the enjoyment of God is only *begun :* there, it will be *completed.* Here, it is *partial:* there, it will be *full.*—1 Cor. xiii. 12; Ps. xvi. 11.

The enjoyment of God in this world consists in *union with God in Christ*, through faith in him. And from this flows *communion* with him in this world.

The *external means* by which we are to seek after this enjoyment, and in which we hold communion with God, are, the *institutions of his appointment*, public, private, and secret; such as prayer, meditation, the reading, and preaching, and hearing of the Word, and the sacraments, &c.

The enjoyment of God here is a pledge of the full enjoyment of him hereafter in glory, when believers shall be admitted into his glorious presence, where they shall have a full sense of his love, and fully and eternally acquiesce and rest in him with perfect and inconceivable delight and joy.—1 Cor. xiii. 12; Ps. xvi. 11.

We ought chiefly to desire and seek the enjoyment of God for ever, because he is the chief good, and in the enjoyment of him consists man's chief happiness; and likewise, because God is but imperfectly and inconstantly enjoyed here, and we cannot be perfectly happy until we eternally enjoy him in heaven.—Ps. iv. 6, 7; 1 Cor. xiii. 9, 10; Ps. xvi. 11.

It may here be observed, that, in the world to come, believers will have communion not only with God in Christ, but also with angels, and with their brethren of mankind redeemed from among the nations.

Obs. 3.—*The glorifying of God, and the enjoyment of him, are inseparably connected.*

The glorifying and the enjoyment of God are here connected as one chief end, because God hath inseparably connected them; and no one can truly design and seek the one, without, at the same time, designing and seeking the other. And we may here remark, that the glorifying of God is here set before the enjoyment of him for ever, to show that the former is the means by which the latter is obtained; that holiness on earth must precede happiness in heaven; and that none shall enjoy God for ever who have no desire to glorify him in this world.—Heb. xii. 14; Matt. v. 8.

INFERENCES.

From this subject we learn,—1. That there is great cause for lamentation, that God and his glory are so seldom the subject of our meditation. 2. The necessity of examining ourselves, whether *we* have ever viewed the glory of God as *our* chief end? whether it is *our* desire to do what he hath commanded, and to abstain from what he hath forbidden? 3. That we ought to be convinced that of ourselves we cannot glorify God, and therefore, that prayer for the Spirit of God is absolutely necessary, to enable us to glorify him in our bodies and in our spirits which are his. 4. That the soul of man is immortal; for, seeing that a desire of happiness is natural to it, and that nothing can satisfy its desire or constitute its chief good but God, it is evident that we must inscribe immortality on this better part of man. 5. The goodly heritage of the people of God beyond the grave. 6. The necessity of holiness. 7. That the believer ought not to be discouraged on account of the difficulties with which he may meet in the way to heaven, seeing that they are but of short duration —that they are but light afflictions.—Rom. viii. 18. *Lastly*, That it ought to be our aim, while we are in this world, in the strength of divine grace, to glorify God in all things, that we may enjoy him for ever in the world to come.

The Scriptures the only Rule of Faith and Duty.

Q. 2.—What Rule hath God given to direct us how we may glorify and enjoy him?

The Word of God, which is contained in the Scriptures of the Old and New Testaments, is the only rule to direct us how we may glorify and enjoy him.

ANALYSIS AND PROOFS.

We are here taught,—

1. The necessity of a rule to direct us how we may glorify and enjoy God. Jer. x. 23.—"The way of man is not in himself: it is not in man that walketh to direct his steps." See also Acts ii. 37.

2. That the Scriptures of the Old and New Testaments are the Word of God. 2 Tim. iii. 16.—"All Scripture is given by inspiration of God." See also 2 Pet. i. 21.

3. That the Word of God is the *only* rule to direct us how we may glorify and enjoy him. Isa viii. 20.—"To the law and to

the testimony: if they speak not according to this word, it is because there is no light in them."

EXPLANATION.

Obs. 4.—*We need a rule to direct us how to glorify and enjoy God.*

The light of nature, and the works of creation and providence, show indeed that there is a God; that this God is infinite in his being, and wisdom, and power, and goodness; and that he is to be worshipped and glorified by his creatures. But they cannot fully and savingly show what God is; they cannot reveal his love and mercy to sinners in his Son; they cannot reveal how he should be glorified and worshipped; and they cannot direct us how we should enjoy him, either here or hereafter.—Rom. i. 20, and ii. 14; 1 Cor. i. 21; Heb. xi. 6; Rom. x. 17; Acts iv. 12.

Obs. 5.—*The Scriptures of the Old and New Testaments are the Word of God, or a revelation from heaven.*

The word *Scriptures* signifies *writings*. And the Word of God is emphatically so called, because he has therein *written* to us the great things of his law and covenant.—Hos. viii. 12.

A *Testament* is a writing or a voluntary act of a person bequeathing legacies on such as are mentioned by the testator, which can never take place until his death.—Heb. ix. 16.

The writings of Moses and the prophets are called the *Old* or *First Testament*, because the Testament or Covenant of Grace which God made with man, is therein revealed in the dispensation of it, in which Christ, the testator and the old mediator of the covenant, is exhibited by types and figures; and many burdensome services and carnal ordinances of the ceremonial law were required.

The writings of the evangelists and apostles are called the *New* or *Second Testament*, because the Testament of God or Covenant of Grace is therein revealed in the new dispensation of it, in which Christ being now come in the flesh, is revealed without types and figures; and because he hath fulfilled and abolished the ceremonial law, and freed his people from that yoke of bondage,—now requiring more spiritual worship in its room.

That the Scriptures are *a revelation from heaven*, may be proved by arguments or evidences, both external and internal.

1. The *external evidences*, which prove that the Scriptures are the Word of God, are these:—Their superior antiquity—the good character of the sacred penmen—the miracles by which they have been confirmed—the exact fulfilment of the prophecies and predictions contained in them—the effects produced by them— the opposition they have sustained and surmounted—and their being prized and esteemed as such by the best of men.

2. The *internal evidences*, which prove that the Scriptures are

the Word of God, are these:—Their whole contents contradict nothing in nature or sound reason, but confirm every rational fact—many important truths are revealed in them which could not be discovered by nature or reason—the strict purity of their doctrines, duties, and precepts, and whole contents—the harmony of their various parts—their suitableness to our condition—the full and perfect discovery which they make of the only way of salvation—the majesty of their style—their power and efficacy to convince and awaken the conscience, to convert and change the heart, to quicken men out of spiritual death, and to rejoice and comfort under the deepest distress—their scope and design to give glory to God, and to debase the sinner—and the experience which real Christians possess of their truth.

That neither *men* nor *angels* could be the *authors* of the Scriptures, will be evident from the following things:—1. *Good men* could not be the authors of them, because they would often arrogate to themselves what is infinitely above their power. 2. *Bad men* could not be the authors of them, because they could not write such language; nor could they have any conception of that heavenly-mindedness which is everywhere discernible in them. 3. *Good angels* could not be the authors of them, because they could have no wish to deceive; and because it is said that they desire to look into their mysteries; and it cannot be supposed that they would write what they did not thoroughly understand. —1 Pet. i. 12. 4. *Bad angels* could not be the authors of them, because they everywhere oppose the kingdom of Satan, and discover the way in which it shall be finally overthrown.

Obs. 6.—*The Scriptures are the only rule to direct us how we may glorify and enjoy God.*

The Scriptures are the *only* rule of faith and duty, because none but God, their author, could show the way in which he himself is to be glorified and enjoyed by fallen sinners of mankind.—Micah vi. 6-9; Matt. xi. 25-28. This will be further evident when we consider,—

1. That they are a *sufficient* rule. The Scriptures alone are sufficient, without the aid or writings of men, to give us that knowledge of God and of his will, which is necessary to salvation. —Gal. i. 8; John v. 39.

2. That they are a *perfect* rule. The whole counsel of God concerning all things necessary for his own glory, man's salvation, faith and life, is either expressly set down in Scripture, or may, by good and necessary consequence, be deduced from Scripture.—2 Tim. iii. 15-17; Gal. i. 8, 9. That not only express Scriptures, but also plain and necessary Scripture consequences, may be admitted as a part of the rule, is evident from the example of our Lord in proving the doctrine of the resurrection against the Sadducees.—Matt. xxii. 31, 32

3. *That they are a clear and perspicuous rule.* There are indeed some things in Scripture hard to be understood, because they have a reference to time and place; and there are mysteries which are beyond the comprehension of created beings. But to those who are under the enlightening influences of the Holy Spirit, the fundamental truths of the Gospel, with respect both to faith and practice, are plain and perspicuous. For every thing necessary to eternal salvation is so clearly laid down in Scripture, that every one who uses the ordinary means, may attain to a sufficient knowledge of them.

The reason why God hath left some parts of his Word *obscure and difficult to be understood,* are the following:—1. That we may be convinced that it is he alone who can make us understand the Scriptures; and that prayer for the Spirit is necessary to open our understandings. 2. That the Scriptures may be our frequent study, if we would know the voice of God speaking therein. 3. That we may be kept humble; and that we may be led to see and to acknowledge that the wisdom of man is but folly. 4. That we may highly esteem the Word,—which, were it all plain and easy to be understood, might be little esteemed. 5. That we may highly value the ministry of the Word, which God hath appointed in his Church, in order that its truths might be made known and inculcated. 6. That the world may see that it is not by the wisdom of man, but by the teaching of the Spirit of God, that sinners are made wise to salvation.

The best interpreter of Scripture is *Scripture itself;* for it is evident that the Spirit of God must be the best interpreter of that which was dictated by him.—1 Cor. ii. 11.

Obs. 7.—*Although the Scriptures are a sufficient, a perfect, and a clear and perspicuous rule of direction, yet they are not sufficient of themselves to make us wise to salvation.*

In order to this end, they must be accompanied with the almighty power of the *Spirit of God;* for without this the reading and preaching of the Word would be in vain.—1 Cor. ii. 14. If the teaching of the Holy Spirit were not necessary, it would follow: That such passages of Scripture as Isa. liv. 13, Jer. xxxi. 34, would be unnecessary,—to assert which would be the height of blasphemy. That those who are most learned in the things of this world, would be best acquainted with the Scriptures; which, however, is not the case.—Mal. xi. 25; 1 Cor. i. 21. That were we able of ourselves to understand the things of God, the promise of the Spirit to open the eyes of the blind, would be to no purpose. That the prayers of the people of God for divine illumination (such as Ps. cxix. 18, &c.) would be in vain.

Obs. 8.—*The Scriptures were originally written in the Hebrew and Greek languages.*

The Old Testament. except a few passages which were written

in *Chaldee*, was originally written in *Hebrew*, the first language in the world, and, at the time of the revelation, the language best known to the Church of God. And the New Testament, with the exception of the Gospel according to Matthew, which is supposed to have been written in *Hebrew*, was originally written in *Greek;* the language which, at the time of writing it, was most common and best known both to Jews and Gentiles. By this we are taught that all nations should have the Scriptures in a language which they understand. The passages of the Old Testament which were written in *Chaldee*, are the eleventh verse of the tenth chapter of the Prophecies of Jeremiah; from the second verse of the fourth chapter of Daniel, to the end of the seventh chapter; and the fourth, fifth, and sixth chapters of Ezra

INFERENCES.

From this subject we learn,—1. The duty and necessity of searching the Scriptures, which are able, through the influence of the Holy Spirit, to make us wise to salvation.—John v. 39. 2. That we must believe that all things contained in them are the word of God. 3. That under a sense of our own ignorance, we should seek after a more extensive knowledge of the saving truths of the Scriptures, than we yet possess. 4. That the practice of the Word must accompany the knowledge of it.—John xiii. 17. 5. The goodness of God in committing to us a revelation of his will. 6. The necessity of divine illumination, that we may see wondrous things out of the Scriptures.—Ps. cxix. 18. 7. That the Word of God is the only rule of faith and obedience; and that it alone discovers the way by which we are to glorify him in this world, that we may come to the full enjoyment of him in a future world.

The Two Principal Topics treated of in Scripture, and Explained in the Two Divisions of the Catechism.

Q. 3.—What do the Scriptures principally teach?

The Scriptures principally teach, what man is to believe concerning God, and what duty God requires of man.

ANALYSIS AND PROOFS.

We are here taught,—

1. That the Scriptures teach us other things besides the knowledge of God, and the duty and happiness of man.—See Matt. xxiii. 23.

2. That they principally teach us what we are to believe concerning God. Deut. xxxi. 12.—"That they may learn, and fear the Lord your God, and observe to do all the words of this law." 2 Tim. i. 13.—"Hold fast the form of sound words,—in faith and love."

3. That they principally teach us what duty God requires of man. Ps. cxix. 105.—" Thy word is a lamp unto my feet, and a light unto my path." See also Luke x. 25, 26.

EXPLANATION.

Obs. 9.—*The Scriptures teach us what we are to believe concerning God.*

To *believe*, is to assent or give credit to truth, upon the authority of another.

To *believe what the Scriptures teach*, is to assent or give credit to the truths therein revealed, upon the authority of God, whose Word the Scriptures are. This is what constitutes divine faith; and it is produced in the soul of man, not by any power of his own, but by the operation of the Spirit of God.—Gal. v. 22; Eph. ii. 8.

The things which the Scriptures teach concerning God, and which are to be believed by us, respect his nature and perfections, the persons of the Godhead, the decrees of God, and the execution of his decrees.—Heb. xi. 6; 1 John v. 7; Acts xv. 14, 15-18, and iv. 27, 28.

We are to believe nothing in point of faith but what the Scriptures teach; because they are the only book in the world of divine authority, and consequently the only one that is absolutely infallible.—Isa. viii. 20.

Obs. 10.—*The Scriptures teach us what duty God requires of man.*

By *the duty which God requires of man*, we are to understand that which is God's due, or that which we owe to God, and are bound to do, as his creatures, his subjects, and his children.

We are bound to do nothing in practice but what is required in the Scriptures; because the laws and commandments of God, revealed therein, are so exceeding broad and extensive, reaching the thoughts and intents of the heart, as well as the actions of the life, that it is not lawful for us to do any thing but what is either directly or consequentially prescribed therein.—Isa. viii. 20.

Obs. 11.—*The Scriptures are said " principally" to teach what we are to believe and practise, because these things are most important, and absolutely necessary to salvation.*

Although all Scripture is the Word of God, and consequently all equally true, and no part of it undeserving our notice, yet all things in it are not equally important, nor equally connected with eternal salvation. Those things which man is bound to believe and do, as necessary to salvation, are the things which the Scriptures *principally* teach. And we may observe, that although the Scriptures teach these things plainly, yet they must be accompanied with the Spirit of God, who alone can teach them effectually to salvation.

Obs. 12.—*Faith or belief is the foundation of obedience.*

This is evident from the order in which they are here stated. *Faith* or *belief* is made the *foundation* of duty or obedience; and not duty or obedience the foundation of faith: or, in other words, the things to be *believed* are set before the things to be *practised.*—Tit. iii. 8. And this is done for the following reason, viz.—that the order of things in the *covenant of grace* may be distinguished from their order in the *covenant of works.* Under the covenant of works, life was promised as the reward of perfect obedience.—Rom. x. 5. But under the covenant of grace, life is promised freely, and to be received freely; and their obedience is to be yielded to the law, from gratitude and love.—Jer. xxxi. 18, 19. Hence, there can be no saving faith, which is not followed by obedience; and no acceptable obedience, which does not flow from faith.

This order of doctrine is farther evinced from the method observed by the Apostle Paul, who informs us, that all true Gospel obedience is *the obedience of faith.*—Rom. xvi. 26. And accordingly, in his epistles, he first lays down the doctrines to be believed; and then, on that foundation, he proceeds to inculcate the duties to be practised.

This order does not make void the law, nor weaken our obligation to comply with its precepts. On the contrary, it establishes the law, by settling our obligation to duty on its proper foundation.—Rom. iii. 31.

When it is said, that, "In keeping of God's commandments there is great reward;" and, "Verily there is a *reward* for the righteous,"—we are to understand by *reward*, here and in similar passages, not a *reward of debt*, but a *reward of grace.* They who shall be rewarded, are believers in Christ. Their persons must first be accepted through union to him, before any of their works can be accepted by God as righteous.—Heb. xi. 6. See also Gen. iv. 4, last clause.

INFERENCES.

From this subject we learn,—1. That we ought to be much exercised in reading the Scriptures. 2. The necessity of prayer for the Spirit, who indited the Scriptures, and who alone can make us understand and practise them. 3. That the works of a man who is void of faith, are dead works; and consequently cannot please God.—Heb. xi. 6. 4. The necessity of being united to Christ by faith, as the branch is to the vine; and of being built upon him as the foundation which God hath laid in Zion.

PART FIRST.

WHAT WE ARE TO BELIEVE CONCERNING GOD

CHAPTER I.

CONCERNING GOD CONSIDERED IN HIMSELF, VIZ. :—IN RESPECT OF HIS NATURE AND PERFECTIONS—HIS UNITY—AND THE TRINITY OF PERSONS IN THE GODHEAD.

Nature and Perfections of God.

Q. 4.—*What is God?*

God is a Spirit, infinite, eternal, and unchangeable in his being, wisdom, power, holiness, justice, goodness, and truth.

ANALYSIS AND PROOFS.

We are here taught,—
1. That God is a Spirit. John iv. 24.—"God is a Spirit."
2. That he is infinite in his being and perfections. Job xi. 7. —"Canst thou by searching find out God? Canst thou find out the Almighty unto perfection?"
3. That he is eternal in his being and perfections. Ps. xc. 2. —"From everlasting to everlasting thou art God."
4. That he is unchangeable in his being and perfections. Mal. iii. 6.—"I am the Lord, I change not." See also James i. 17.
5. That he is infinitely wise. Ps. cxlvii. 5.—"His understanding is infinite."
6. That he is infinitely powerful. Job. xlii. 2.—"I know that thou canst do every thing." See also Rev. iv. 8.
7. That he is infinitely holy. Rev. xv. 4.—"O Lord—thou only art holy."
8. That he is infinitely just. Deut. xxxii. 4.—"A God— without iniquity; just and right is he." See also Zeph. iii. 5.
9. That he is infinitely good and merciful. Exod. xxxiv. 6. —"The Lord, the Lord God, merciful and gracious, long-suffering, and abundant in goodness and truth."

10. That he is infinite in truth. Deut. xxxii. 4.—" A God of truth, and without iniquity; just and right is he."

EXPLANATION.

Obs. 13.—*The first point of religion taught in the Scriptures is, the existence of God.*—Heb. xi. 6.

The existence of God cannot be denied, without at the same time denying our own existence, and that of every thing around us.

The existence of God may be proved,—1. From the works of creation.—Psal. xix. 1, and c. 3. 2. From the preservation of all things, and the regular government of the world. Gen. viii. 22. 3. From the existence of conscience within us, and also from the visible judgments inflicted on the wicked at death, besides the check of conscience. 4. From the wonderful deliverances wrought for the Church in all ages. 5. From the consent of all nations. Whatever is consented to by all mankind, must be a dictate of nature, and, consequently, a truth. 6. From the Scriptures of the Old and New Testaments. 7. From the accomplishment of prophecy, and from God's frequently revealing himself to the sons of men, as Noah, Abraham, Moses, &c.

Obs. 14. *There are various names and titles by which God is known in Scripture.*

Of these, the following are a few:—

1. AL, which expresses the omnipresence of God,—that is, the universal extension of his power and knowledge.—Gen. xvii. 1.

2. ALEHIM, which exhibits him as the real, proper, and only object of worship and praise.—Gen. i. 1.

3. SHADDAI, which denotes him to be almighty and all-sufficient.—Gen. xvii. 1; Exod. vi. 3.

4. ADON, which represents him as the Lord and Judge of all. —Ps. cx. 1.

5. JAH, which expresses his self-existence,—his having existence in himself, and his giving it to all other beings.—Isa. xxvi. 4.

6. JEHOVAH, which denotes his self-existence, independence, unsuccessive or immutable eternity; and his accomplishing the promises which he hath made.

7. EHIEH, " I am," or " I will be what I will be "—denoting his absolute independence and immutable eternity.—Exod. iii. 14.

8. KURIOS and THEOS, the former denoting his self-existence, and his governing power over all things, and the latter representing him as the Maker and Observer of all things.

God is also known in Scripture in several other ways:—

1. He is represented by a variety of terms, such as, a rock, a fortress, a buckler, a sun, a shield, &c. These are figurative expressions, and represent what God is to his people, or those who trust in him.

2. He is exhibited by a variety of names, having a relation to him,—as, the God and Father of our Lord Jesus Christ—The Father of Mercies—The God of Peace—The God of Grace—The God of Patience—The God of Consolation—The God of Hope—The God of Salvation, &c. &c.

Obs. 15.—*God is a Spirit.*

A Spirit is an immortal, an immaterial, a thinking, and an eternal substance.

God is a Spirit,—that is, he is a being or substance, invisible, immaterial, incorruptible, incorporeal, infinite, eternal, immutable, uncreated, &c.—Exod. xxxiii. 20; John i. 18, iv. 24. v. 37, vi. 46; Col. i. 15; Tim. i. 17, vi. 16.

The spirituality of God, and that of angels and souls of men, differ in the following respects :—Angels and souls of men are *created* spirits, and can be reduced to their original non-existence; but God is an *uncreated* Spirit : they are *finite;* but God is *infinite:* they are *dependent;* but God is *independent.*

Although we find that *bodily parts* or *members* (such as eyes, ears, hands, &c.), and *passions* or *affections* (such as desire, hope, love, anger, joy, grief, &c.), are ascribed to God in Scripture,—yet these are only emblems of his spiritual perfections and acts, used in condescension to human weakness. They are ascribed to him, not properly, but figuratively. Thus, when eyes and ears are ascribed to God, they denote his omniscience; hands denote his power; and his face, the manifestation of his favour,—and so of the rest.

All the knowledge which it is possible for us to attain in this world respecting God as a Spirit, may be acquired in the following manner :—1. By removing from him every imperfection which is found in ourselves, we obtain the knowledge of God in those attributes which cannot, in the least degree, be found in created beings,—such as, self-existence, independence, infinity, unsuccessive eternity, immutability, &c. 2. By ascribing to him, in the greatest possible measure and degree, whatever excellence is found in the creature, we obtain the knowledge of God in those attributes which are just visible in the creatures,—such as, knowledge, wisdom, power, holiness, justice, goodness, and truth.

Obs. 16.—*The attributes or perfections of God are commonly distinguished into communicable and incommunicable, or imitable and inimitable.*

1. The *incommunicable* attributes of God are, his infinity,

eternity, and unchangeableness; and they are so called, because no trace of them is to be found in the creatures.

2. The *communicable* attributes of God are, his being, wisdom, power, holiness, justice, goodness, and truth; and they are so called, because some faint but imperfect resemblance of them is to be found among the creatures.

Although we, on account of our weakness and imperfection, must speak and think of the divine attributes or perfections separately, yet we must ever remember, that they are neither distinct from God himself, or the divine essence, nor separable from one another; but that they are altogether *the one infinite perfection* of the divine nature.

Obs. 17.—*God is infinite in his being and perfections.*

The *infinity* of God is that essential perfection of his nature, by which all things in his essence or being are known to be without measure and quantity. And hence his being and perfections are incomprehensible.

God is infinite in respect of his being; for our finite understandings can form no adequate conception of his nature. He is also infinite in respect of all his glorious perfections,—wisdom, power, holiness, justice, goodness, and truth.—Rom. xi. 33; Job xxvi. 14, and xlii. 2; Isa. vi. 3; Rev. iv. 18, and xv. 4; Deut. xxxii. 4; Rev. xv. 31; 1 Chron. xvi. 34; Exod. xxxiv. 6; Ps. cxlv. 9; Numb. xxiii. 19; Deut. vii. 9; Ps. cxix. 89, 90, and cxlvi. 6.

In the infinity of God are included the following things:—
1. His *incomprehensibility;* or his infinitely transcending the utmost or most enlarged capacity of angels and of men, with respect to his essence, or being and perfections.—Ps. cxlv. 3; Job xxxvi. 26. 2. His *immensity;* or that perfection of his nature, by which he is wherever any space or any creature can be. And hence it includes,—3. His *omnipresence;* or that perfection of his nature, by which he is most intimately present with all his creatures in every place; and fills all places at once—heaven, and earth, and hell—with his essential presence.—1 Kings viii. 27.

Although God is essentially present everywhere, yet he manifests his presence in a peculiar manner in *heaven*. He is also peculiarly present with his *Church on earth*, in the institutions and ordinances of his appointment.—Matt. xviii. 20. With his *saints*, by his Spirit dwelling in them, and manifesting to them his gracious favour and support.—Eph. ii. 22. And with the *Church invisible above*, by the bright, and glorious, and immediate displays of his goodness and excellencies. We may here observe, that he is also present in hell, where he displays his awful and tremendous power and justice on devils and wicked men, whom he preserves in endless existence, that they may endure the effects of his wrath for ever.—Matt. xxv. 46.

Obs. 18.—*God is eternal in his being and perfections.*

The *eternity* of God is that perfection of his nature by which he continually exists, without beginning or end, or succession of duration.—Ps. xc. 2, cii. 12–27, and xc. 4; 2 Pet. iii. 8.

God is said in Scripture to be *eternal*, because he had no beginning, and is the same yesterday, to-day, and for ever; and also, because he is the author of eternal duration to others.

The eternity of God, and that of angels and souls of men, differ in the following respects:—The eternity of angels and souls of men means only, that they shall have no end; but the eternity of God means, that he had no beginning, that he has no succession, and that he shall have no end. The eternity of angels and spirits is neither essential, nor absolute, nor independent; but the eternity of God is both essential, and absolute, and independent.—Ps. xc. 2–4, and cii. 27; 2 Pet. iii. 8.

Obs. 19.—*God is unchangeable in his being and perfections.*

The *unchangeableness* or *immutability* of God is that attribute of his nature by which it is impossible for him to undergo the least possible change, but continues always the same.

This perfection of God may be proved both from reason and from Scripture. 1. Reason informs us, that, were God changeable, the change must be either for the better or for the worse. But from each of these suppositions an absurdity arises. If the change were to the better, it would be inconsistent with the perfection of God, who sees the end from the beginning, and all whose works are done in consummate wisdom. If it were to the worse, it would also derogate from his perfection, inasmuch as it would indicate, that he did not know from eternity what would take place in time; to assert which would be the same as to deny his existence. 2. This perfection is proved from Scripture by these and many other passages: Numb. xxiii. 19; 1 Sam. xv. 29; Isa. xlvi. 10; Mal. iii. 6; Heb. vi. 17, 18; James i. 17.

God is unchangeable,—1. In his existence. He cannot cease to be.—1 Tim. i. 17, and vi. 16. 2. In his nature or essence. He cannot cease to be what he is in every perfection. 3. In his purposes.—Isa. xlvi. 10, and xiv. 24. 4. In his promises to his people; in his threatenings against the wicked; and in all his predictions.—Numb. xxiii. 19. 5. In his duration.—Ps. cii. 27.

Although angels and glorified spirits are unchangeable, as well as God; yet their unchangeableness differs from his in this respect,—that they receive it from him, and have it not in their own nature.

It is said, indeed, in several passages of Scripture (such as Gen. vi. 6; Jonah iii. 10; and 1 Sam. xv. 11) that God *repents;* but by *repentance*, in these and similar passages, we are to understand only *an alteration of the outward dispensations of his pro-*

vidence, according to his knowledge of all things in every relation and circumstance respecting them. We are by no means to attribute to him any *change of mind;* for in this respect it is impossible for God to change.—Job xxiii. 13. Every change which the Scriptures attribute to him, is in reality a change only in the creatures.

Obs. 20.—*God alone is infinite, eternal, and unchangeable in his being.*

The *being* or *essence* of God is his glorious and transcendent nature, by which he is what he is—infinitely blessed in himself, and comprehended by none but himself; for finitude cannot comprehend infinitude.

The highest perfection of being is that which can neither be increased nor diminished, and which is independent of any other being whatever.—Job xxxv. 6–8.

Being, in this proper and strict sense of the word, can be ascribed to none but to God alone; for although the heavens and the earth, and angels and men, have a being, yet there is no infinite, eternal, and unchangeable being but God. He alone can say, "I am that I am."—Exod. iii. 14.

Obs. 21.—*God is infinitely wise.*

The *wisdom* of God is that attribute or perfection of his nature, by which he perfectly knows himself, and all things which have been, which are, and which shall be, or can possibly be, together with the reasons of them.

In the wisdom of God are included,—1. His *knowledge,* or *omniscience,* or that perfection of his nature by which he discovers objects, or by which he knows all things.—Prov. xv. 3; Gen. vi. 5. 2. His *wisdom,* properly so called, or that perfection of his nature by which he directs all things to the best ends, and to the very ends for which he gave them existence.—Acts xv. 18.

We may here observe, that God knows things, not as man knows them, by succession of ideas, but by one single intuitive glance, distinctly, comprehensively, in every circumstance respecting them, and infallibly.

The wisdom of God appears,—1. In the works of creation: in the beautiful order and variety of all things.—Ps. civ. 24, and cxxxvi. 5; Prov. iii. 19. 2. In the works of providence: in upholding all things in being; and in so ordering them as to fulfil all his pleasure. 3. In the work of redemption; both in its contrivance, its accomplishment, and its application.

Obs. 22.—*God is infinitely powerful.*

The *power* of God is that perfection of his nature by which he is able to effect all things, or do whatever he willeth or can will; or by which he can do what seemeth good unto him, in heaven, on earth, in hell, in the seas, and in all deep places.—Ps. cxxxv. 6; Dan. iv. 35.

In Scripture, the power is expressed,—1. *Positively.*—Ps. lxii. 11; Gen. xvii. 1; Job xlii. 2, ix. 4, xxxvii. 23; Ps. xxxv. 10. 2. *Negatively;* or by removing from him all imperfection in power, or all weakness.—Gen. xviii. 14; Jer. xxxii. 17; Luke i. 37. 3. *Metaphorically;* by his arm,—Ps. xcviii. 1; right hand,—Ps. lxiii. 8; stretched-out arm,—Exod. vi. 6; arm of strength,—Isa. lxii. 8; and glorious arm,—Isa. lxiii. 12, &c.

The power of God is displayed,—1. In the creation of the world, and of all things in it.—Rom. i. 20; Ps. xxxiii. 9. 2. In providence.—Col. i. 17; Heb. i. 3; Ps. lxxvi. 10. And here we may observe, that God's power has been displayed in erecting a Church in the world, and in preserving it, notwithstanding all the persecutions and sufferings to which it has been subjected. 3. In the work of redemption by Jesus Christ; in his incarnation; in the miraculous union of his two natures in one person; in the numerous miracles which he performed; in supporting his human nature under that load of wrath which was due to us for our transgressions; and in raising him from the dead. 4. In the conviction and conversion of sinners,—for it requires the same power to raise a sinner, dead in sins, to spiritual life, that it required to raise Christ from the dead; and in preserving the graces of his people amidst all the afflictions and temptations to which they are exposed.—1 Pet. i. 5.

We may here also observe, that, although there are some things which God can neither will nor do, yet this implies no imperfection in his power. He cannot do such things as are contrary to his nature; as to cease to exist, or to destroy himself. He can neither will nor do such things as imply weakness or imperfection; as to lie, or to deny himself.—Tit. i. 12; 2 Tim. ii. 13. He cannot do such things as imply a contradiction.

Obs. 23.—*God is infinitely holy.*

The *holiness* of God is that essential perfection of his nature by which he contemplates the untainted purity of his essence, and delights in it; loves righteousness, and hates evil, as that exceeding sinful thing which his soul abhorreth.

This perfection of Deity is largely exhibited in Scripture; for every thing relating to God is called *holy*. *Holiness* is ascribed to each of the persons in the Godhead; and the third person is frequently called the Holy Ghost, or the Holy Spirit.—John xvii. 11; Ps. xvi. 10. Heaven is called God's *holy* habitation, and the habitation of his *Holiness*.—Deut. xxvi. 15; Isa. lxiii. 15. The Sabbath is called *holy*.—Exod. xvi. 23, and xxxi. 14. The Church is called *holy*, under different terms; as the Holy Sanctuary,—Lev. xvi. 33; the Holy House.—Lev. xxvii. 14. God's people are called *holy*.—Dan. xii. 7. His angels are called *holy*

—Matt. xxv. 31. His ministers are called *holy.*—2 Pet. ı. 21. And many other things relating to God are called holy.—Ps. xiv. 5, 17; 1 Sam. ii. 2.

We may here observe, that God puts a peculiar honour upon his *holiness;* for he singles it out as that attribute by which he swears, that he will accomplish whatever he hath spoken.—Ps. lxxxix. 35; Amos iv. 2.

The holiness of God appears,—1. In the works of creation. Every creature capable of holiness was made perfectly holy. Angels were made holy, and man was made holy.—Gen. i. 27; Eccl. vii. 29. 2. In his works of providence: in casting the angels that sinned out of heaven; in thrusting man out of paradise, when he rebelled against him; in the destruction of the old world by water, and of Sodom and Gomorrah by fire and brimstone; in the punishments inflicted on the Israelites in the wilderness, and in the destruction of Jerusalem by the Romans; and in his conduct towards his own people, when they transgress his just and holy commandments. 3. In his Word, or in the Scriptures, which are called the Holy Scriptures.—Rom. i. 2. His Word is holy in its commands, in its promises, and in its threatenings.—Ps. cv. 42; 2 Pet. i. 4. 4. In the work of redemption. All the instances which God hath given of his hatred at sin, are nothing when compared with the display which he hath given of his holiness in the sufferings and death of his only Son, who was his delight from everlasting!

Obs. 24.—*God is infinitely just.*

The *justice* of God is that perfection of his nature by which he is infinitely righteous in himself, and just in all his works and ways towards all the creatures which he hath made.

The justice of God is exhibited in Scripture,—1. *Positively;* when God is expressly called just.—Deut. xxxii. 4; Isa. xlv. 21; Acts vii. 52. 2. *Negatively;* when injustice of every kind. and in every degree, is removed from him.—Rom. iii. 5; Deut. xxxii. 4; Heb. i. 10; Ps. xcii. 15. 3. This perfection is also exhibited when he is said to render to every man according to his works, &c.—Deut. vi. 30; Job xxxiii. 26; Jer. xvii. 10, &c.

The justice of God has been distinguished into various kinds; such as his legislative justice, his distributive justice, his remunerative justice, and his vindictive justice; according to the various ways which he adopts in executing it.

1. God's *legislative* justice is his giving just laws to the rational creation, by which it is bound to obey and to submit to his will in all things.

2. God's *distributive* justice is his constant will and purpose to render to rational creatures their due, according to law, without respect of persons.—Job xxxiv. 11; 1 Pet. i. 17.

3. God's *remunerative* justice is his rewarding the sincere

though imperfect obedience of his people to the law, as a rule of life, with the enjoyment of himself in glory. But then this reward is entirely of free grace, and not of debt. It is not on account of any worthiness in their obedience, but only on account of what Christ has merited by his obedience and sufferings.—Heb. v. 9; 1 Tim. iv. 8; Ps. lviii. 11; Ps. xix. 11; Rom. iv. 4, 5; Ps. cxv. 1; 1 Pet. ii. 5.

4. God's *vindictive* justice is his punishing sin in the sinner, and taking vengeance on all those who disobey his holy and just commandments.

The justice of God is displayed in various ways. 1. It is displayed in providence: in the judgments which he executeth.—Ps. ix. 16. 2. It was displayed in a very striking manner in the sufferings and death of the Lord Jesus Christ. God cannot, in consistency with his perfections, and he will not, pardon sin without a satisfaction. 3. It shall be signally displayed at the general judgment; for he hath appointed a day in which he will judge the world "in righteousness."—Acts xvii. 31. 4. It shall be signally displayed in the everlasting punishment of fallen spirits, and of sinners of mankind condemned at the last day.—Jude 6; 2 Pet. ii. 4.

Obs. 25.—*God is infinitely good and merciful.*

The *goodness* of God is that perfection of his nature by which he is infinitely good in himself, and bestows on all his creatures what they can receive of his goodness in this world.—Ps. cxlv. 9, and cxxxvi. 1.

The goodness of God is commonly distinguished into absolute and relative. 1. His *absolute goodness* is that essential goodness of his nature which can be imparted to none. 2. His *relative goodness* is that which he bestows upon his creatures.

In Scripture the goodness of God is distinguished by different names, according to the manner in which, and the objects about which, it is exercised. As it inclines him to promote the happiness of his creatures, and to delight in them, it is called *love*. As it inclines him to supply their wants, which he is not bound to do, it is called *bounty*.—Ps. cxvi. 7. As it inclines him to manifest himself to the undeserving, or to those who deserve nothing but what is evil, it is called *grace*.—Rom. iii. 24. As it inclines him not to execute judgment immediately on the sinner, but to forbear for a time, it is called *patience or long-suffering*.—Exod. xxxiv. 6; 2 Pet. iii. 9; 1 Pet. iii. 20, &c.

The goodness of God is displayed,—1. In the works of creation: in giving being to so many things, of which he stood in no need, and without which he was infinitely happy. But especially in the creation of man: in making him for his worship and service in this world, and for the enjoyment of him in the world to come. 2. In the works of providence: in respect of which it is either common or special. The *common goodness* of God is that which he bestows on all his creatures, rational and irrational, without distinction.—Ps. xxxiii. 5, and xxxvi. 6; Matt. v. 45. His *special goodness* is that which he manifests to a certain number of lost mankind in their *redemption* through Jesus Christ.—John iii. 16, and xv. 13. 3. The goodness of God will be displayed in a glorious manner at the "day of final retribution."—Ps. xxxi. 19; Matt. xxv. 34; 1 Cor. ii. 9.

Obs. 26.—*God is infinitely true and faithful.*

The *truth* or *faithfulness* of God is that perfection of his nature by which he is true in himself, and by which it is impossible for him not to fulfil whatever he hath promised, or not to bring to pass whatever he hath purposed.—Deut. xxxii. 4; Exod. xxxiv. 6.

We may here observe, that this perfection of God has respect chiefly to the revelation of his will in the Scriptures.—Matt. v. 18.

The truth of God is displayed,—1. In his works of providence. No providential act which strikes the observation of a number of mankind, takes place in the world, but what is founded on the declarations of his Word.—Gen. viii. 22; Ps. xxv. 10, and cxi. 7-9. 2. In his Word; both in its promises and in its threatenings.—Matt. xxiv. 35; 1 Kings viii. 56; Numb. xxiii. 19; Isa. xlvi. 11; Jer. iv. 28; 2 Sam. vii. 28; Isa. xxv. 1; Ezek. xii. 25; Heb. x. 23, and xi. 11; 2 Cor. i. 20. 3. The truth and faithfulness of God will be fully manifested at the last judgment. All his promises to his people in this world, and all his threatenings against the wicked, shall be, as it were, concentred here.

INFERENCES.

From this subject we learn the following things:—

From the spirituality of God we learn,—1. The necessity of worshipping him in spirit and in truth. 2. That we ought to speak of God with reverence. 3. The sinfulness of forming any representation of him, either externally or internally. 4. That God alone can be the chief good of our souls, which are spirits.

From the infinity of God, and the attributes included in it, we learn,—1. That no affliction or temptation can befall the righteous without his knowledge and sympathy. 2. That God is well acquainted with the most secret retirements of the sinner. 3. That if the sinner continue to go on in his sins, God will be present with him in the place of everlasting punishment, displaying his awful justice for ever.

From the eternity of God we learn,—1. That the righteous have reason to rejoice, because their God liveth and reigneth for evermore. 2. That the wicked have great reason to tremble. Eternity is a word which will break the hearts of sinners in that place which mercy never enters.

From the unchangeableness of God we learn,—1. That it is a

source of strong consolation to the righteous, that God rests in his love; that whom he loveth, he loveth to the end. 2. What terror the consideration of the unchangeable purpose of God concerning the wicked may cause to arise in their minds.

From the being of God we learn,—1. That he will assuredly accomplish all his purposes to his people. 2. The necessity of an interest in this God, whose name is "I am," and who remaineth unchangeably the same.

From the wisdom of God we learn,—1. That no evil can befall the righteous which shall not work for their spiritual good. —Job v. 13; Rom. viii. 28. 2. That God is acquainted with the thoughts of the heart, and with the secret wickedness of the sinner, although concealed from the world.—Heb. iv. 13. 3. The necessity of worshipping God in spirit and in truth; seeing he knows whether our hearts are right in his sight or not. 4. Gratitude to God for the wonderful display of his wisdom in the plan of redemption.

From the power of God we learn,—1. That he will perform whatever he hath promised. 2. That the people of God ought to trust in him in the greatest difficulties. 3. To learn to do well; to cease to do evil: God is able to save; he has power to destroy. 4. That sinners ought to take warning to flee from the wrath to come.—Job ix. 4. 5. To beware of abusing the power of God, by "limiting the Holy One of Israel."—Ps lxxviii. 19-41.

From the holiness of God we learn,—1. The contrariety of sin to his spotless nature. 2. The danger to which they expose themselves, who are strangers to holiness, or who love the ways of sin. 3. The necessity of evangelical holiness, without which no man shall see the Lord.—2 Cor. vi. 17. 4. The necessity of hating sin with a perfect hatred, of walking in the ways of God, and of obeying his commandments. 5. The necessity of an interest in Jesus Christ, in whose righteousness alone we can stand with confidence before God.

From the justice of God we learn,—1. That we ought to acknowledge his ways towards us to be faithfulness and truth. 2. That he will not allow sin to pass with impunity. 3. The danger of impenitence. 4. The truth of the general judgment. 5. That we ought to endeavour to imitate God in justice.—Mic. vi. 8; Matt. xxii. 21.

From the goodness of God we learn,—1. That God alone is the portion of the soul. 2. To beware of abusing his goodness. 3. Gratitude to him for the goodness which he bestows upon us. 4. To be resigned to every dispensation of his providence. 5. That we ought to imitate God in this perfection.

From the truth of God we learn,—1. That we have most sure ground to believe, that what God hath said shall be accomplished. 2. That secure and careless sinners have reason to be afraid

3. To beware of hypocrisy in the worship of God, and of deceitfulness in our dealings in the world. 4. That we ought to imitate God in this imitable perfection.—Mic. vi. 8.

From the whole we learn,—1. That the perfections of God are a source of unspeakable comfort to his people, and of indescribable terror to the wicked. 2. That we ought more and more to seek after the knowledge of God as he hath revealed himself in his Word and in his Son Jesus Christ; seeing it is life eternal to know God and his Son whom he hath sent.—John xvii. 3.

Unity of God.

Q. 5.—Are there more Gods than One?

There is but one God only, the living and true God.

ANALYSIS AND PROOFS.

We are here taught,—

1. That there is but one God. 1 Cor. viii. 4.—" There is none other God but one." See also Deut. vi. 4.

2. That he is the only living and true God. Jer. x. 10.— " The Lord is the true God; he is the living God; and an everlasting King."

EXPLANATION.

Obs. 27.—*There is but one God.*

This may be proved both from Scripture and reason:—

1. It is proved from Scripture *positively* or *affirmatively* when the Scriptures expressly declare that there is but one God,—Deut. vi. 4; Gal. iii. 20; Ps. lxxxvi. 10; 1 Cor. viii. 6: and *negatively*, when they declare that there are no other gods but one.—Deut. xxxii. 39; Isa. xliii. 10, xliv. 6–8, and xlv. 5, 6. It is also evident from the *command* in Scripture to worship *one* God only.—Matt. iv. 10. If it were possible that there could be two gods, we could not love both supremely: our love must be divided; and our hearts could not be given to God, according to his commands.

2. Reason informs us, that there is but one cause and ultimate end of all things; and that there cannot be two infinite, eternal, omnipotent, and self-existent beings. If it were possible that there could be more gods than one, no reason can be assigned why there should not be a *million* of gods, or as many as there are sands upon the sea-shore.

Obs. 28. *God is the living and true God.*

1. God is called the *living God*,—(1.) In opposition to everything else that is called God. (2.) Because he is self-existent.

and the author of all natural, spiritual, and eternal life.—Acts xvii. 28; Eph. ii. 2; Col. iii. 3, 4.

2. God is called the *true God*, to distinguish him from false gods. The meaning of the epithet *true* in this place is, that God really exists; that he exists in truth, and not in imagination only; that of him it cannot be said, as of idols, that he is no God; but that he is the only true God, besides whom there is and can be none else.

The epithets *living* and *true* are here connected, because they are inseparably united in the nature of God. He who is the living God is the only true God; and he who is the only true God is the only living God.—1 Thess. i. 9.

In Scripture there are others that are called gods, besides the living and true God.—1 Cor. viii. 5. *Moses* is called a god to Pharaoh, because he was sent to him by the living God, to fulfil his pleasure respecting him; and because he was the instrument of doing what no created being could overturn.—Exod. vii. 1. *Magistrates* are called gods, because they act in God's name in this world, and because we are bound to obey them.—Ps. lxxxii. 6; Rom. xiii. 2. *Idols* are called gods, because idolaters think that they are gods, and worship them as such. The *belly* is called a god, because some regard it more than they regard God.—Phil. iii. 19. And the *Devil* himself is called the god of this world, because of that power which is given him in the world by the living and true God, over the wicked and the children of disobedience.—2 Cor. iv. 4.

INFERENCES.

From this subject we learn,—1. That it is dangerous to hasten after other gods.—Ps. xvi. 4. 2. That, seeing there is but one God, our prayers must be directed to him alone. 3. That we ought to love him above all.—Ps. lxxiii. 25. 4. That we have reason to bless God, that our lot is cast in a land of light, where we hear of the only living and true God. 5. That, seeing God is the living God, his people may rejoice, because he abideth with them for evermore. 6. That we ought to present our bodies living sacrifices, holy and acceptable to him; which is our reasonable service.—Rom. xii. 1. Seeing God hath given us life, it is but reasonable that it should be devoted to him. 7. That, seeing God is the only true God, we ought to worship him in spirit and in truth; for he desires truth in the inward parts, and delights in spiritual worship. 8. That we ought to beware of atheistical sentiments; of denying God in heart or life; and of such opinions as lead to Atheism and to the casting off all fear of God.

Trinity of Persons in the Godhead.

Q. 6.—How many persons are there in the Godhead?

There are Three Persons in the Godhead, the Father the Son, and the Holy Ghost; and these Three are One God, the same in substance, equal in power and glory.

ANALYSIS AND PROOFS.

We are here taught,—

1. That there are Three persons in the Godhead. 1 John v. 7. —" There are Three that bear record in heaven, the Father, the Word, and the Holy Ghost."

2. That the Father is God. John i. 18.—" No man hath seen God at any time; the only begotten Son, which is in the bosom of the Father, he hath declared him."

3. That the Son is God. Heb. i. 8.—" But unto the Son he saith, Thy throne, O God, is for ever and ever."

4. That the Holy Ghost is God. Acts v. 4 (compared with verse 3).—" Thou hast not lied unto men, but unto God."

5. That these Three Persons, the Father, Son, and Holy Ghost, are but One God. 1 John v. 7.—" These Three are One." See also Deut. vi. 4.

6. That the Father, Son, and Holy Ghost, though distinct persons, are the same in nature or substance. John x. 30.—" I and my Father are One." John xv. 26.—" The Spirit of truth proceedeth from the Father." See also 1 John v. 7.

7. That they are equal in power and glory. Matt. xviii. 19.— " Go ye, therefore, and teach all nations, baptizing them in the name of the Father, and of the Son, and of the Holy Ghost." See also John v. 21.

EXPLANATION.

Obs. 29.—*There is a plurality of persons in the Godhead.*
This may be proved from the following passages of Scripture:—

1. Gen. i. 26.—Let *us* make man in *our* image, after *our* likeness." No satisfactory reason can be given, why the word for *God* is so suddenly changed from the singular to the plural number, were we not to consider it as an insinuation of a plurality of persons in the unity of the Divine essence.

2. Gen. iii. 22.—" Behold the man is become as one of *us*." This evidently implies that there is a plurality of persons in the Godhead.

3. Gen. xi. 7.—" Let *us* go down and confound their language." —meaning the language of the builders of Babel. Here it is observable, that in all the context, there is no mention of any. to whom God could thus address himself; which shows that there is a plurality of persons. See also Gen. xix. 24.

4. Job xxxv. 10.—" Where is God my Maker?" or, as it is in the original, *Makers*.

5. Eccles. xii. 1.—" Remember now thy Creator in the days of thy youth;" or, as in the original, *Creators*.

6. Isa. vi. 8.—" Whom shall *I* send, and who will go with *us?*" Here the transition from the singular to the plural number is very observable, and plainly points out a plurality of persons in the Godhead.

Obs. 30.—*There are Three, and only Three Persons, in the Godhead.*

We may here observe, that the *doctrine of the Trinity*, or *of Three Persons in the Godhead*, could never have been discovered by the light of nature or unassisted reason; for it is a doctrine above human comprehension. And hence it is called by the apostle a *mystery*.—Col. ii. 2.

This doctrine, however, is evident from the following passages of Scripture:—

1. Ps. xxxiii. 6.—" By the Word of the Lord were the heavens made, and all the host of them by the breath of his mouth." Here three are distinctly pointed out:—The *Father;* the *Word*, or the Son of God; and the *breath of his mouth*, or, as it is elsewhere expressed (2 Thess. ii. 8), the *Spirit of his mouth*, which can be no other than the *Holy Ghost*. See also Job xxxii. 8, and xxxiii. 4.

2. From the account given of the deliverance of the Israelites from the land of Egypt. If we examine the different parts of this great deliverance; the different messages-of God to Pharaoh, and the threatenings denounced against him; and likewise his promises to his own people; we must conclude that *Three Persons* concurred in bringing them from Egypt to the land of promise.—See Exod. iii. 2, xxiii. 20, and xxxii. 34; where, by the *angel* so often mentioned, we cannot understand any created angel; for such things are ascribed to him as can be said of none but God. See Exod. xiv. 19, compared with chap. xiii. 21. See also Isa. lxiii. 7–10.

3. Isa. lxi. 1–3: where mention is made of *Three* distinct persons,—the *Lord God*, and the *Spirit* sending and anointing *Him*, that is, *Christ*.—Luke iv. 18.

4. Haggai ii. 4, 5: where mention is made of *Three*,—the *Lord of hosts;* the *Word*, or Jesus Christ; and the *Spirit of God*. See Isa. xli. 14; Ps. xlv. 7.

5. Matt. iii. 16, 17: where mention is made of *Three* distinct Persons,—the *Father*, the *Son*, and the *Holy Ghost*, the Spirit of God.

6. Matt. xxviii. 19: where it is to be observed, that the connective particle, *and*, is repeated before each of the Persons mentioned, which clearly discovers a *Trinity* of Persons. The unity

of the Godhead is also here pointed out :—" In the *name*," &c. —not, In the *names*.

7. 2 Cor. xiii. 14: the apostolical benediction, where there is distinct mention of *Three* Persons. The three blessings for which the apostle prays, are significative of the different operations of the Three Persons in the work of salvation;—the love of *God* in contriving and designing it: the grace of the *Lord Jesus Christ* in purchasing the blessings of salvation; and the communion of the *Holy Ghost* in the application of redemption; which things can be applied to none but God.

8. John xiv. 16, 17, 26, and xv. 26: where there is mention made of *Three* distinct Persons,—the *Father*, the *Son*, and the *Comforter*.

9. Eph. ii. 18: where mention is made of the *Father, to whom* we have access; of the *Son* (of whom the apostle is speaking), *through whom* we have access; and of the *Holy Ghost, by whom* we have access. See also Eph. iii. 14, &c.; Gal. iv. 4, &c.

10. Rev. i. 4, 5: where mention is made of the *Father*, who is described by his eternal existence,—" Who is, and who was, and who is to come;" of the *Holy Ghost*, who is described by "the seven spirits which are before his throne," so called on account of his diversity of gifts, and influences, and operations; and of *Jesus Christ*, who is here mentioned last, because the apostle was to enlarge more upon a description of him and his person, as manifested in the flesh, and as one with whom he was so intimate while on earth.

It may be shown, from the work of redemption, that it is absolutely necessary that there should be *Three Persons* in the Godhead. It is necessary that the Mediator between God, and man who has violated his law, should be infinite; and if so, he must be both God and man,—man to die, and God to overcome death; and also, because it is necessary that a mediator should partake of the nature of both parties. But there must also be a third person, to apply the purchased redemption, who likewise must be infinite; because such things belong to this part of redemption as can be ascribed to none but to God.

Obs. 31.—*The Three Persons in the Godhead are distinguished by their personal properties, which are incommunicable.*

1. The personal property of the Father is *to beget* the Son.— Ps. ii. 7; Heb. i. 5, &c.

2. The personal property of the Son is *to be begotten* of the Father.—John i. 14, 18.

3. The personal property of the Holy Ghost is *to proceed* eternally from the Father and the Son.—John xv. 26; Gal. iv. 6; Rom. viii. 9; John xvi. 14, 15, xv. 26, and xiv. 26.

The difference between a *personal* property and an *essential* property is this :—A *personal* property is peculiar to one of the persons only: whereas an *essential* property is common to them all.

It is further evident, that the Three Persons in the Godhead are *distinct* persons, from their distinct operations in the work of redemption. In Scripture, we find the Father contriving and ordaining it, the Son purchasing its blessings, and the Holy Ghost applying them.

The calling of the Father the *first*, the Son the *second*, and the Holy Ghost the *third* person in the Godhead, does not imply any inequality among them; for these are only terms of order, and imply no superiority either of nature, or excellence, or duration. See 2 Cor. xiii. 4, where the Son is mentioned before the Father; and Rev. i. 4, 5, where the Holy Spirit is named before the Son.

We may here remark, that the assertion that there are Three Persons in the Godhead with distinct personal properties, does not in the least infer any separation or division in the divine essence; for the Persons in the Godhead are not separated, but *distinguished* from one another by their personal properties. As the unity of the essence does not confound the Persons, so the distinction of Persons does not imply any division of the essence.

Obs. 32.—*The Father is God, the Son is God, and the Holy Ghost is God.*

That *the Father is God*, is evident from the following things:—

1. In Scripture, all the perfections already considered, which necessarily belong to God, are ascribed to him.—John v. 26· Rom. i. 4, &c.

2. Works are ascribed to him which can be ascribed to none but God.

3. That worship is performed to him which it would be gross idolatry to offer to any created being.—John xi. 41, 42, and xii. 27, 28, &c.

That *the Son is God*, is evident from the following things:—

1. He is expressly called *God.*—Rom. ix. 5. The *true God* and eternal life.—1 John v. 20. The *great God.*—Tit. ii. 13. The *mighty God.*—Isa. ix. 6. The *Lord* or *Jehovah*,—Mal. iii. 1; which is the incommunicable name of God.

2. He is represented as possessed of *Divine attributes*. Eternity is ascribed to him.—Mic. v. 2. Immutability.—Heb. xiii. 8 Omniscience.—John xxi. 17. Omnipotence.—Rev. i. 8. Omnipresence.—Matt. xxviii. 20. Supremacy.—Rom. ix. 5. See also Rev. i. 11; Phil. iii. 20, 21; Rev. i. 32; Ps. cii. 27; Heb. i. 10, and xiii. 8.

3. Works peculiar to God are ascribed to him. The creation and preservation of all things.—Col. i. 16, 17. The purchasing of eternal redemption.—Heb. ix. 12. The working of miracles by his own power.—Mark v. 41. The forgiveness of sins.— Mark ii. 5. The raising of the dead at the last day.—John v 28, 29. The judging of the world.—Rom. xiv. 10.

4. We are commanded to give the same *divine worship* to him which is due to the Father.—John v. 23. To believe on him equally with the Father.—John xiv. 1. And to be baptized in his name, as well as in the name of the Father.—Matt. xxviii. 19. See also 1 Cor. xvi. 22; Heb. i. 8; Phil. ii. 10.

We may here observe, that when Christ saith that "his Father is greater than he" (John xiv. 28), he does not mean that he is greater with respect to his *nature*, but with respect to his *office* as Mediator; in which respect he is the Father's servant.—Isa. xlii. 1.

That *the Holy Ghost is God*, is evident from the following things:—

1. *Names* peculiar to the Most High God are ascribed to him. He is expressly called *Jehovah*.—Numb. xii. 6. See also 1 Pet. i. 11; 2 Pet. i. 21. He is called *God.*—Acts v. 3, 4. The *Most High God.*—Ps. lxxviii. 56, compared with Heb. iii 7-9.

2. *Attributes* peculiar to the Most High God are ascribed to him. Eternity is ascribed to him.—Gen. i. 1, 2. Omnipresence. —Ps. cxxxix. 7. Omniscience.—1 Cor. ii. 10, 11. Almighty power.—Acts vi. 10, &c.

3. *Works* peculiar to God alone are ascribed to him.—Gen. i. 2; Ps. xxxiii. 6, and civ. 30; Matt. xii. 28; Rom. viii. 11.

4. *Worship* peculiar to God alone is ascribed to him, and required to be paid to him. In his name, as well as in the name of the Father and the Son, are we baptized. Prayer is commanded to be performed to him.—Acts iv. 23, &c., compared with 2 Sam. xxiii. 2, &c. And solemn benedictions are pronounced in his name.—2 Cor. xiii. 14.

Obs. 33.—*The belief of the doctrine of the Trinity is absolutely necessary to eternal salvation.*

Without the knowledge and belief of this doctrine, we can have no real knowledge of the new covenant, in which the Three Persons in the Godhead have such a conspicuous place. This doctrine runs through the whole of religion; so that, if we believe not in it, we can have no saving faith, no saving acquaintance with God.—John xvii. 3, v. 23, and xv. 23.

This doctrine likewise affects the whole of our obedience; and all our comforts, both of a temporal and of a spiritual nature, flow from it. Believers hold communion with God the Father, Son, and Holy Ghost;—with the Father, in contemplating the love which he hath displayed in sending his Son into the world to be a propitiation for their sins, and in admiring the riches of his grace, who thought upon them in their low estate;—with the Son, in what he hath done for them in the various offices which he executes, in every relation in which he stands to them, and in which they appropriate him;—and with the Holy Ghost, in his various gifts and graces, influences and operations, which are all suited to their every case.

INFERENCES.

From this subject we learn,—1. That we must worship the Father, in Christ the Son, by the Holy Spirit; and that, when we pray, we must ask the Father, in the name of the Son, by the Holy Spirit.—Eph. ii. 18, and v. 20. 2. To prize the Word of God, from which alone we can discover the doctrine of the Trinity, and which alone must be the rule of our faith. 3. What ought to be the portion of the soul—a Three-One God, with whom alone is salvation.

CHAPTER II.

CONCERNING GOD'S DOINGS WITH RESPECT TO HIS CREATURES :—UNDER WHICH ARE CONSIDERED THE NATURE AND CHARACTER OF GOD'S DECREES, AND THE EXECUTION OF THEM IN THE WORKS OF CREATION AND PROVIDENCE.

SECT. I.—OF THE NATURE AND CHARACTER OF GOD'S DECREES.

Q. 7.—What are the decrees of God?

The decrees of God are his eternal purpose, according to the counsel of his will, whereby, for his own glory, he hath foreordained whatsoever comes to pass.

ANALYSIS AND PROOFS.

We are here taught,—

1. That God hath formed certain decrees or purposes. Eph. i. 11.—" Being predestinated according to the purpose of him who worketh all things after the counsel of his own will." See also Ps. ii. 7.

2. That God's purposes were formed in his mind from eternity Eph. iii. 11.—" According to the eternal purpose which he purposed in Christ Jesus our Lord."

3. That God's decrees are exclusively the purposes or counsels of his own will. Rom. ix. 18.—" Therefore hath he mercy on

whom he will have mercy, and whom he will he hardeneth. See also Eph. i. 5.

4. That all things, which are agreeable to the purposes or counsels of God, have been predestinated or foreordained by him. Acts iv. 28.—" To do whatsoever thy hand and thy counsel determined before to be done." See also Eph. i. 11.

5. That God hath foreordained all things for his own glory Prov. xvi. 4.—" The Lord hath made all things for himself."

EXPLANATION.

Obs. 34.—*God hath formed certain purposes or decrees.*

By *decree*, when spoken of God, we are to understand, a *purpose*, a *foreordination*, a *will*, and an *appointment*, that such a thing shall take place, or shall not take place.

The decrees of God are exhibited in Scripture under various names. Sometimes they are called *the counsel of the Lord.*—Ps. xxxiii. 11, where they are also called *the thoughts of his heart.* Sometimes they are called *the decrees*, in the abstract.—Ps. ii. 7. Sometimes *the purpose of the Lord.*—Rom. viii. 28. Sometimes his *eternal purpose.*—Eph. iii. 11. Sometimes *the hand of God.*—Acts iv. 28. . Sometimes *the good pleasure of his will.*—Eph. i. 5. Sometimes *the Father's good pleasure.*—Luke xii. 32. And sometimes *predestination.*—Rom. viii. 29, 30.

That there are decrees of God, is evident from the following things:—

1. From the consideration of the above-mentioned passages, compared with the following:—Eph. i. 4; Rom. ix. 22, 23, 33; Heb. v. 17; Exod. xxxiii. 12, 17; Jer. i. 5; Rom. xi. 2; 2 Tim. ii. 19; 1 Pet. i. 2, &c.

2. From the *perfections* of God, such as his omniscience.—Acts xv. 18. This knowledge arises from his having decreed all things; for it is just because he decreed them that they take place.

3. From the *independence* of God, and the *dependence* of all things on some first cause.

4. From *reason*, which informs us, that were God to perform any thing in time, which he did not know and purpose from eternity, he would not be infinitely wise, nor would he be immutable, which is contrary to the very nature of the Deity.—James i. 17.

Although we speak of the divine decrees as various or many, on account of the many objects decreed, yet the decreeing act of God is one simple act; because of the perfect oneness or simplicity of his nature, on account of which he could not but decree all things at once; because all things are naked and open to his omniscient eye,—Heb. iv. 13; and because of his immutability. —Mal. iii. 6.

NATURE AND CHARACTER OF GOD'S DECREES. 49

Obs. 35.—*The decrees of God have various properties.*
1. They are infinitely *wise.*—Rom. xi. 33.
2. They are most *free.*—Eph. i. 11; Rom. ix. 17, 18; Exod. xxxiii. 19.
3. They are most *holy.*—Rom. ix. 14.
4. They are *eternal.*—Acts xv. 18.
5. They are *incomprehensible.*—Rom. xi. 34.
6. They are *perfect.*—Deut. xxxii. 4.
7. They are most *gracious.* To redeem those whom he hath chosen is the design which he hath to accomplish, to the praise of his glorious grace; and they would have been infinitely gracious, had he determined to save only one soul of the numerous race of Adam from sin and all its consequences.
8. They are most *absolute.* They depend on nothing but the will of God.—Isa. xlvi. 10; Dan. iv. 34, 35; Ps. cxxxv. 6.
9. They are *immutable* or *unchangeable,* as God himself is; and this flows from their being absolute, and from God's independence.—Mal. iii. 6; Heb. vi. 17, 18; Ps. xxxiii. 11; Numb. xxiii. 19; 2 Tim. ii. 19.
10. They are *impartial.*—Rom. ix. 21; Matt. xi. 25. Neither *sin* on the part of those who are not elected to life, nor *holiness* on the part of the elect, is the cause of God's passing by the one or choosing the other. The cause of both is the sovereign good pleasure of his will.—Rom. ix. 18, 22, &c.

Obs. 36.—*The decree of God has for its object whatever comes to pass.*

It extends to *all things;* but angels and men are its object in a particular manner.
1. All the actions of the creature, whether good or bad, fall within the decree of God.—Acts ii. 23, and iv. 27; Gen. xlv 8.
2. Those things which appear to us *casual* or *accidental,* fall under the eternal purpose of God.—Matt. x. 29; Prov. xvi. 33; 1 Kings xxii. 34.
3. All things concerning us,—our situation in the world, whether prosperous or adverse,—our calling in the world, &c.,—fall within the eternal purpose of God.—1 Thess. iii. 3, &c.
4. The time, the place, and the manner of every man's death, with every concurring and concomitant circumstance, are the object of God's decree.—Job vii. 1; Gen. xvi. 12, and xxv. 23; Judges xiii.; 2 Sam. vii. 12; 1 Kings xiii. 2; Isa. xlv. 1, &c.; Isa. vii. 14; Mic. v. 2; Mal. iii. 1, &c.; Gen. xix. 13; 2 Sam. vii. 14; 1 Kings xiv. 12, and xxii. 28, and xxi. 22; Dan. v. 25, 26, &c.
5. The everlasting state of angels and of men is fixed by God —1 Tim. v. 21; 2 Pet. ii. 4; Jude 6. See also Rom. ix. 21.

&c., and viii. 29, &c.; Eph. i. 4; John xv. 19; Rev. xxi. 27; Matt. vii. 23; Rev. xvii. 8; Jude 4; 2 Tim. ii. 19, &c.

Obs. 37.—*God hath decreed all things for his own glory.*

The *end* of God's decree is his own *glory*, which is twofold, either the glory of his grace and mercy, or the glory of his justice and awful severity.—Eph. i. 6, 12; Prov. xvi. 4; Rom. xi. 36; Rev. iv. 11; Rom. ix. 15-23.

Obs. 38.—*The doctrine of the decrees of God is calculated for the good both of the righteous and the wicked.*

1. It excites the righteous to self-examination, and to follow on to know the Lord. It has no tendency to make them careless in using the means of salvation; because God hath chosen them to salvation " through sanctification of the Spirit, and belief of the truth."—2 Thess. ii. 13.

2. It is calculated to lead the wicked to consider their ways, to break off their sins by repentance, and to give God no rest until Christ be formed in their souls the hope of glory.

Obs. 39.—*The decrees of God are not the rule of our conduct.*

They are the rule by which God himself acts. " Secret things belong to the Lord our God."—Deut. xxix. 29. Only " those things which are revealed belong to us." We ought, therefore, no more to regard the decree in the matter of believing to the salvation of our souls, than in eating and drinking, and all the other common actions of life. It may be here observed, that we act in this world as *freely* as if there were *no decree;* and as *infallibly* as if there were *no liberty.*

INFERENCES.

From this subject we learn,—1. That nothing whatever comes to pass without the knowledge of God; that nothing takes place by accident or by chance; so that to speak thus is not scriptural. 2. The necessity of patience and resignation to our lot in this world, which is appointed by God. 3. The sovereignty of God. 4. That we must trace every part of our salvation to the eternal purpose of God. 5. The duty of promoting the glory of God, which is his own end in all his ways. 6. The unchangeableness of the love of God. 7. To what we are to refer every event. 8. That all things work together for the believer's good, and tend to bring about the designs of heaven respecting him. 9. To be diligent in the use of every appointed means of salvation. See Phil. ii. 12, 13; 2 Pet. i. 10

SECT. II.—OF THE EXECUTION OF GOD'S DECREES IN THE WORKS OF CREATION AND PROVIDENCE:—UNDER WHICH ARE CONSIDERED THE CREATION OF THE WORLD AND OF MAN, AND GOD'S GENERAL AND SPECIAL PROVIDENCE.

Execution of God's Decrees.

Q. 8.—*How doth God execute his Decrees?*

God executeth his decrees in the works of creation and providence.

ANALYSIS AND PROOFS.

We are here taught,—
1. That God executes his decrees in the work of creation. Rev. iv. 11.—" Thou hast created all things; and for thy pleasure they are and were created."
2. That God executes his decrees in the works of providence. Dan. iv. 35.—" He doeth according to his will in the army of heaven, and among the inhabitants of the earth." See also Ps. ciii. 19.

EXPLANATION.

Obs. 40.—*God executeth his decrees in the works of creation and providence.*

God executes his decrees when he brings them to pass: or when he gives an actual being in time to what he purposed from eternity.—Isa. xlvi. 10.

1. God executed his decrees in the work of creation, in which he made all things according as he eternally purposed to make them.

2. God executes his decrees in the works of providence, in which he preserves and governs all things according to his eternal purpose and counsel.

The difference between God's execution of the work of creation and that of providence, is this:—He executed the work of creation entirely without means; whereas he executes the work of providence generally in the use of them. But whatever use God may make of second causes in executing his purposes, they are all but instruments in his hand to bring about his glorious designs. —Acts iv. 27, 28.

INFERENCES.

From this subject we learn,—1. That every thing which God hath made in the world, and every thing which has taken place, and shall take place in his providence, is the result of his eternal purpose. 2. That all his promises shall be fully accomplished, and not one of them fail.—Mark xiii. 31.

Creation of the World.

Q. 9.—What is the work of Creation?

The work of creation is God's making all things of nothing, by the word of his power, in the space of six days, and all very good.

ANALYSIS AND PROOFS.

We are here taught,—

1. That God created all things. Gen. i. 1.—" In the beginning God created the heavens and the earth." See also John i. 3.

2. That God made all things of nothing. Heb. xi. 3.—" Things which are seen were not made of things which do appear."

3. That God made all things by the word of his power. Heb. xi. 3.—" The worlds were framed by the word of God." See also Ps. xxxiii. 6.

4. That God made all things in the space of six days. Exod. xx. 11.—" In six days the Lord made heaven and earth." See also Gen. i. 31.

5. That God made all things very good. Gen. i. 31.—" God saw every thing that he had made, and behold it was very good."

EXPLANATION.

Obs. 41.—God created all things, or he made all things of nothing.

By *creation* we are to understand a production of something out of nothing; or a giving of being or existence to that which had no being or existence; or a forming of pre-existent matter (which is the work of almighty power), and then a forming of this matter into the various things which we now behold.—Heb. xi. 3.

God, the first cause of all things, created *the world* and *all things whatever*, except himself, who is uncreated.—Gen. i. 1; Prov. iii. 19; Job xxvi. 7; Col. i. 16; Neh. ix. 6; Ps. lxxxix. 11; Isa. xxxiv. 1; Ps. xxxiii. 6; Heb. iii. 4.

The world cannot be *eternal*, as some suppose; for then it would be necessarily existent, and not liable to any possible change. But experience and daily observation teach us, that the world is undergoing many alterations; and we know assuredly that it has already undergone many; which shows that it is not eternal.

Neither angels nor men could have created the world; nor could it have formed itself. For, 1. Angels and men were created themselves; and creation being a work of almighty power, no creature can give being to another. 2. The world is a creature; and, consequently, had the world formed itself, it would have been both creature and creator, which is a gross absurdity.

Although God created all things, yet he did not create *sin*. He permitted it to take place for wise ends, but it cannot be said that he produced sin as such. God made angels and men upright, but they made themselves devils and sinners.

That all things were made *of nothing* is evident, because they are said to have been made *in the beginning*,—that is, when there was nothing but God the Creator, and when there was no measure of time by any thing.—Gen. i. 1.

Obs. 42.—*God created all things by the word of his power*

God brought all things out of nothing *by his powerful word*, he only spake, and it was done; he commanded, and all things stood fast. This may also signify the Personal Word; for it is said in John i. 3, that "all things were made by him; and without him was not any thing made that was made." See John i. 1–3.

Obs. 43.—*God made all things in the space of six days.*

God, who is almighty, could have created all things in a moment of time; but he spent six days in the work, in order that we might the better apprehend the order of the creation, and because he saw it more for his own glory and the good of mankind to set them an example of working six days, and resting on the seventh.

1. On the *first* day, God created the highest or the third heavens; the angels, who are called the hosts of heaven and sons of God,—Job xxxviii. 7; the chaos of earth, and water, and light. He also divided light from darkness; calling the former *day*, and the latter *night*.—Gen. i. 1–5.

2. On the *second* day, God created the firmament, which seems to include both the starry and aërial heavens. He also divided the waters above the firmament of air from those under it.—Gen. i. 6–8.

3. On the *third* day, God collected the waters, which were mingled with the earth, into one place, and called them *seas;* and the dry land which then appeared he called *earth*. He also caused the earth to bring forth all kinds of trees, plants, and herbs, before there was any sun or rain.—Gen. i. 9–13.

4. On the *fourth* day, God created the sun, moon, and stars; placed them in the heavens; and appointed them to rule the day and the night, and to be for signs and for seasons, and for days and for years.—Gen. i. 14–19.

5. On the *fifth* day, God made of the waters all kinds of great and small fishes, and every living creature that moveth in the waters. He also made of the waters all kinds of winged fowls which fly in the open heavens.—Gen. i. 20–23.

6. On the *sixth* day, God made of the earth all kinds of beasts, and cattle, and creeping things. And last of all, he made man, —his body of the dust of the ground, and his soul a spirit immediately breathed into him by himself.—Gen. i. 24–30.

Obs. 44.—*God created all things very good.*

It is said that God created all things *very good*, because, upon a survey of his works, he himself declared them to be so.—Gen. i. 31. This goodness, visible in the creatures, consisted in the perfection of their nature. Every thing perfectly answered the end for which it was created. All the evil which hath since come into the world, is either sin itself, which is the work of the devil and man, or the fruit and consequence of sin.

Obs. 45.—*God created all things for his own glory.*

He made all things, that he might manifest,—
1. The glory of his *power*, in effecting so great a work by a mere word.—Ps. xxxiii. 6; Rev. iv. 11.
2. The glory of his *wisdom*, in the order and variety of the creatures.—Ps. civ. 24.
3. The glory of his *goodness*, especially towards man, for whom he first provided all things necessary, before he called him into existence.

INFERENCES.

From this subject we learn,—1. How glorious that God is whom we profess to worship. 2. That God has sole dominion over us, and that therefore he is entitled to our obedience. 3. That it is our duty to advance the glory of God. 4. That we ought to be thankful for every enjoyment. 5. That seeing all have one Creator, all ought to live as the children of one God. 6. That we ought to meditate on the works of God, and from them to carry our views to God himself, and to Jesus Christ, who hath accomplished the work of redemption, the chief of all the ways of God.

Creation of Man.

Q. 10.—How did God create Man?

God created man male and female, after his own image, in knowledge, righteousness, and holiness, with dominion over the creatures.

ANALYSIS AND PROOFS.

We are here taught,—
1. That God created man male and female. Gen. i. 27.—" God created man; male and female created he them."
2. That man was created in the image of God. Gen. j. 27.—" God created man in his own image; in the image of God created he him."
3. That the image of God consists in knowledge, righteousness, and holiness. Col. iii. 10.—" Put on the new man, which is renewed in knowledge after the image of him that created him." Eph. iv. 24.—" Put on the new man, which, after God, is created in righteousness and true holiness." See also Eccl. vii. 29.

4. That God created man with dominion over the creatures. Gen. i. 28.—"God said unto them, Have dominion over the fish of the sea, and over the fowl of the air, and over every living thing that moveth upon the earth."

EXPLANATION

Obs. 46.—*God created man male and female.*

At first God created one man and one woman,—*man* out of the dust of the ground, and *woman* out of a rib taken from man's side.—Gen. i. 27, and ii. 7, 21, 22.

The import of their names, *Adam* and *Eve*, is this:—*Adam* signifies *earth;* and man was so called, because he was formed of the dust of the earth: and *Eve* signifies *life;* so called, because she was to be the mother of all living,—that is, of all that have been, are, or shall be in the world.

Man consists of two parts—a *body* and a *soul.*

The *soul* was not, like the body, formed from the earth, but was a spiritual substance breathed into him by God,—Gen. ii. 7; and hence God is called *the Father of spirits,* and *the God of the spirits of all flesh.*—Heb. xii. 9; Numb. xvi. 22, and xxvii. 16.

The soul of man differs from his body in every respect, both as to its *nature* and *duration.* The body is *visible,* but the soul is *invisible;* the body is *mortal,* but the soul is *immortal.*

Obs. 47.—*Man was created after the image of God, which consists in knowledge, righteousness, and holiness.*

By the *image of God* we are to understand the similitude or likeness of God.—Gen. i. 26. But this similitude or likeness does not consist in any outward visible resemblance (for God is a spirit, and cannot be seen), but in the inward resemblance of his soul to God, in knowledge, righteousness, and holiness.—Col. iii. 10; Eph. iv. 24.

This image of God, in knowledge, righteousness, and holiness, includes the universal and perfect rectitude of the whole soul:—

1. *Knowledge* in the understanding.—Adam knew much more of the nature and perfections of God, and of his own duty to him, than it is possible for fallen man now to know.

2. *Righteousness* in the will.—In his primitive state, man had a disposition to every thing which was right. There was nothing in him but perfection in its utmost extent.

3. *Holiness* in the affections.—At first man's affections were holy and pure; they were placed upon the most holy, high, and noble objects; his desires were chiefly after God, and his delight was chiefly in him. He was capable of the immediate enjoyment of God. There was nothing in him which offended God; nothing by which his glory was dishonoured.

Obs. 48.—*Man was created with dominion over the creatures*

Man at his creation had dominion, not only over himself and his own affections, but also over the inferior creatures. Before the fall, all the creatures of this world were subject to man; but since that, either they have become a terror to him, or he to them.

INFERENCES.

From this subject we learn,—1. That we should be humble and lowly, seeing we had our beginning in earth, and to earth we must return. 2. The change which sin hath produced upon the whole man. 3. That we should love God, seeing we were at first made after his image; and that we should love one another, seeing we are the children of the same common parents. 4. The necessity of being created anew in Christ Jesus; and of conformity to him who is the "image of the invisible God."

Nature and Character of God's General Providence.

Q. 11.—What are God's works of Providence?

God's works of providence are his most holy, wise, and powerful, preserving and governing all his creatures, and all their actions.

ANALYSIS AND PROOFS.

We are here taught,—

1. That God preserves all his creatures. Ps. cxlv. 15.—"The eyes of all wait upon thee, and thou givest them their meat in due season." See also Heb. i. 3.

2. That God directs and governs all his creatures, and all their actions. Ps. ciii. 19.—"His kingdom ruleth over all." Prov. xvi. 9.—"A man's heart deviseth his way, but the Lord directeth his steps."

3. That God's works of providence are most holy. Ps. cxlv. 17.—"The Lord is righteous in all his ways, and holy in all his works."

4. That God's works of providence are most wise. Isa. xxviii. 29.—"The Lord of hosts, who is wonderful in counsel, and excellent in working."

5. That God's works of providence are most powerful. Ps. lxvi. 7.—"He ruleth by his power for ever." Dan. iv. 35.—"None can stay his hand."

EXPLANATION.

Obs. 49.—*There is a Providence.*

By *Providence*, we are to understand that almighty power, by which, in holiness and wisdom, for his own praise and glory, God preserves, or upholds and governs, the heavens and the earth, and all things in them, from the least to the greatest.

That there is a Providence, which superintends all things may be proved from the following things:—

1. From *reason;* which informs us, that, if all things were left to themselves, they would fail of their intended end.
2. From *conscience;* which, by accusing or excusing, stands forth as a notable testimony of Providence.
3. From *Scripture;* in almost every page of which we have proofs of this. See Col. i. 17; Neh. ix. 6; Heb. i. 3; Ps. cxix. 91; Gen. viii. 21, 22; Acts xvii. 28; Ps. cxxxvi. 25; Job xii. 10; Matt. x. 29, 30; Acts xiv. 17, &c.
4. The same arguments that prove the existence of God, prove that there is a Providence; for the one cannot exist without the other.

Obs. 50.—*The agency of God in providence consists in preserving and governing his creatures and their actions.*
1. In *preserving* his creatures. This he does, both by continuing or upholding them in being, and by providing things necessary for their preservation.—Ps. cxix. 89–91, and cxlv. 15, 16. See also Heb. i. 3; Col. i. 17.
2. In *governing* his creatures and their actions. This he does when he rules over them, and disposes and directs them to the end for which he designed them.—Ps. lxvi. 7; Prov. xvi. 9. See also Acts xvii. 28; Ps. lix. 13; Job xxxiv. 13, and xxxvi. 22, 23: Eph. i. 11; Job xxxiii. 13.

Obs. 51.—*The objects of God's providence are, all his creature and all their actions.*
1. It extends to *all the creatures*, rational and irrational, animate and inanimate, great and small.—Heb. i. 3; Ps. ciii. 19; Matt. x. 29, 31, and vi. 26, 28, 30.
2. It extends to *all their actions:*—All natural actions.—Acts xvii. 28. All casual actions.—Exod. xxi. 12, 13. All morally good actions.—John xv. 5. All morally evil actions or sins. God *permits* sinful actions. But it must be remembered, that God's permission of sin is not a bare permission, as if he could not prevent the sin from taking place, or as if he regarded it not: but that it is connected with his government of the world, and with the ends which he proposes to himself, and which issue in his own glory. An action may be good, which is thus under the providence of God; while, at the same time, it may be a very sinful action, as it proceeds from man; such was the selling of Joseph into Egypt, and such was the crucifixion of the Lord of glory.—See Gen. i. 15-20; Acts ii. 23, 28; Rom. viii. 32.

Obs. 52.—*God's providence is most holy, wise, and powerful.* The *properties* of God's providence are the following:—
1. It is *most holy.*—Ps. cxlv. 17. Infinite holiness and purity are visible in all his administrations. This appears in bringing glory to his mercy and justice out of sin; in making the worst of sinners become the greatest saints,—1 Tim. i. 12, 13; and in executing judgments on sinners, even in this world.—Ps. ix. 16.

2. It is *most wise*. God makes all things subservient to the ends for which he designed them.—Rom. viii. 28: Ps. civ. 24; Isa. xxviii. 29.

3. It is *most powerful*. None can resist the will of God.— Dan. iv. 35; Ps. cxxxv. 6, and lxvi. 7, and lxii. 11.

Obs. 53.—*The providence of God is commonly distinguished into ordinary and extraordinary, common and special.*

1. God's *ordinary* providence is, his observing the order of things appointed by him from the beginning.—Hos. ii. 21, 22.

2. His *extraordinary* providence is, his going beyond or acting contrary to the natural order of things; and such events are called miraculous.

3. His *common* or *general* providence is, that care which he exercises over all the creatures which he hath made, without exception.—Neh. ix. 6; Acts xvii. 28. This is called God's natural government.

4. His *special* providence, or his moral government, is that care which he exercises over the rational creation alone; and this, again, may be limited to that particular care which he exercises over his own people in this world.

INFERENCES.

From this subject we learn,—1. That seeing there is an over ruling Providence, all things shall work together for the good of the people of God. 2. That we ought to submit to the providence of God. 3. That we ought not to account it strange although the wicked flourish, and the righteous be persecuted. 4. That they are a happy people whose God is the Lord. 5. The duty of observing the providences of God. See Ps. cvii. 43.

SECT. III.—OF THE SPECIAL PROVIDENCE OF GOD TOWARDS MAN IN HIS CREATION AND FALL:—UNDER WHICH ARE CONSIDERED, THE COVENANT OF WORKS, THE FALL OF MAN, THE EXTENT OF THE FALL, AND ITS CONSEQUENCES.

Covenant of Works—Its Parties and Terms.

Q. 12.—What special act of providence did God exercise toward Man in the estate wherein he was created?

When God had created man, he entered into a covenant of life with him, upon condition of perfect obedience; forbidding him to eat of the tree of the knowledge of good and evil, upon the pain of death.

ANALYSIS AND PROOFS

We are here taught -

1. That God entered into a covenant with Adam. Hos. vi. 7 (margin).—" They, like Adam, have transgressed the covenant."
2. That it was a covenant of life. Rom. vii. 10.—" The commandment was ordained to life."
3. That the condition of this covenant was perfect obedience. Rom. x. 5.—" The man who doeth those things shall live by them." See also Gen. iii. 3.
4. That man was forbidden to eat of the tree of the knowledge of good and evil. Gen. ii. 17.—" But of the tree of the knowledge of good and evil, thou shalt not eat of it."
5. That the penalty of this covenant was death. Gen. ii. 17. —" In the day that thou eatest thereof thou shalt surely die."

EXPLANATION.

Obs. 54.—*A covenant of works was made with Adam.*

The word *covenant* denotes any thing *fixed* or *established*. See Jer. xxxiii. 25, where we read of the Lord's " covenant with day and night." But it has generally a reference to an *agreement* made and entered into between parties.

That a covenant of works was really made with Adam, as the representative of mankind, while he was in a state of innocence, or when he was created, will be evident from the following things:—

1. The transaction into which God entered with man contains every thing necessary and requisite in a covenant; such as parties, a condition, a promise, and a penalty.

2. It is expressly called a covenant.—Gal. iv. 24; Hos. vi. 7, margin.

3. It had certain signs and seals appended, which gave force to it, and which confirmed it as a covenant. These were, the tree of the knowledge of good and evil, and the tree of life.

4. In Scripture we read of a *twofold law*, the one opposed to the other; namely, the law of works and the law of faith. See Rom. iii. 27, where, by the *law of faith*, we must understand the *covenant of grace;* and by the *law of works*, the *covenant of works;* for what is said of the one is also said of the other. But,

5. Nothing proves more effectually that a real and proper covenant was made with Adam, than the *imputation of his first sin* to all his natural posterity. See Rom. v. 12, 17, 18.

Obs. 55.—*The parties of the covenant of works were, God and man.*

1. On the one side was God, the Father, Son, and Holy Ghost, man's Creator and Sovereign Lord, who is the great Lawgiver, and the Author of all good to his creatures.

2. On the other side was man, God's creature,—Adam, representing all mankind, and covenanting with God, not only for himself, but also for all his posterity, as the natural father of all and the appointed federal head.

In this covenant there was no Mediator; nor was there need of one; for man was yet the friend of God; and his service, while he continued in innocence, was acceptable to him, being fully conformable to his law.

Obs. 56.—*The condition of the covenant of works was perfect obedience.*

By the *condition* of this covenant, we are to understand that which God required of Adam, in order that he might have a right, both for himself and for all his posterity, to eternal life, which was the reward promised.

The *obedience* required, was a regard to the whole law of God—that law which was written on man's heart at his creation: and also to the positive precept that he gave him, which was, "Not to eat of the tree of the knowledge of good and evil;" and all this from a due regard to the Divine authority. This tree was called the tree of the knowledge of good and evil, because, on his eating of it, Adam knew by experience what good he had lost, and what evil he had brought upon himself and his posterity.

With respect to the *nature* of this obedience, it was necessary that it should be,—

1. Perfect in respect of its *principle.* It was to proceed from love to God, who requires not only external, but internal obedience, or the obedience of the heart.

2. Perfect in *parts.* It was to extend to all the commands of God, with respect to thoughts, words, and actions.

3. Perfect in *degrees.* Every act of obedience was to be perfect in degree, wanting nothing of that perfection which the law required. He was to love the Lord his God with all his heart, with all his soul, with all his strength, and with all his mind.

4. Perfect in *duration,*—without interruption, while God should continue him in the state of trial.—Gal. iii. 10.

This was the condition of the covenant of works. On no other terms could Adam have attained to eternal happiness by it, or be justified in respect of his state before God. Hence it appears, that sincere obedience could not have been accepted, and that there was no place for repentance under this covenant. The threatening was, "In the day that thou eatest thereof thou shalt surely die." Such a positive denunciation cut off all hope, and rendered repentance unavailable.

Obs. 57.—*The reward promised in the covenant of works was life.*

The words, "In the day that thou eatest thereof thou shalt surely die," evidently imply, that life should have been preserved, if innocence had not been lost.

The reward promised was life in its fullest extent, both here and hereafter; and hence this covenant is called the *covenant of life*. The life promised was,—

1. *Natural life*, which consists in the union of the soul and body.
2. *Spiritual life*, which consists in the union of the soul with God, the supreme good.
3. *Eternal life*, which consists in the perfect, immutable, and eternal happiness of both soul and body in heaven for ever.

Obs. 58.—*The penalty of the covenant of works, or the threatening denounced in case of disobedience, was death.*

"In the day that thou eatest thereof, that is, of the tree of the knowledge of good and evil, thou shalt *surely die;* or, *dying thou shalt die.*" This includes,—

1. *Natural death*, or the death of the body; to which man became liable the moment he sinned.—See Rom. vi. 23.
2. *Spiritual death;* which consists in the separation of the soul from God.
3. *Eternal death;* or the separation of both soul and body from God for ever, in that place which is prepared for all the workers of iniquity. This is also called the *second death;* and it includes in it the perfect and complete loss of every thing comfortable in respect of this life, as well as of that which is to come.

The penalty of the violated law of works is not properly an act, a mere act, of the *will* of God,—it flows from his perfections; for if we consider the nature of God, we shall find that it is absolutely necessary that there should be such a strict and awful penalty.

INFERENCES.

From this subject we learn,—1. The love of God in condescending to enter into covenant with his own creature. 2. How exalted man was in his primeval glory, seeing he was capable of being a party in a covenant with God himself; and seeing God, as it were, made him his equal! 3. What man is in his fallen state. 4. The deep concern which we all have in this covenant: Adam's sin is our sin. 5. What it is that God will accept, —namely, the same obedience that was required of Adam, either in our own persons, or in the person of a surety. 6. The absolute necessity of a Mediator, seeing this covenant which was made with Adam is now broken, and we ruined by it. 7. The danger of disobedience; and that God is a consuming fire to the sinner. 8. That none can be delivered from the curse of this covenant, but by Jesus Christ, who hath fulfilled its condition, who hath endured its penalty in all its extent, and who is now set forth a complete atonement for sin. 9. The necessity of self-examination, whether we are delivered from the curse of the law, or whether we are still under the law as a covenant of works, and under the power of sin —Gal. iii. 10.

Man's Disobedience and Fall by Sin.

Q. 13.—Did our first Parents continue in the estate wherein they were created?

Our first parents, being left to the freedom of their own will, fell from the estate wherein they were created, by sinning against God.

ANALYSIS AND PROOFS.

We are here taught,—

1. That our first parents were left to the freedom of their own will. Gen. iii. 6.—"When the woman saw that the tree was good for food, and that it was pleasant to the eyes, she took of the fruit thereof, and did eat; and gave also unto her husband with her, and he did eat." See also Gen. iii. 13.

2. That they fell from the estate in which they were created, by sinning against God. Rom. v. 12.—"By one man sin entered into the world, and death by sin." See also Gen. iii. 8, and Eccl. vii. 29.

EXPLANATION.

Obs. 59.—*Our first parents were left to the freedom of their own will.*

By *freedom of will*, we are to understand a liberty in the will, whereby, without any compulsion or external violence, it either chooses or rejects what is set before it. There are three ways in which the will may be said to be free:—

1. It may be said to be free only to good, when it is not compelled or forced, but freely chooses only what is good. Thus, the will of God (to speak after the manner of men), and the will of the holy angels and of glorified saints, are free only to good.

2. It may be said to be free only to evil, when it is not constrained, but freely chooses what is evil or sinful. Thus, the will of the devil and of unregenerate men is free only to sin.

3. It may be said to be free both to good and evil, when it chooses sometimes what is good and sometimes what is evil. Such is the will of regenerate persons in this world. They freely choose good, through a principle of grace implanted in them by the Spirit of God; but sometimes, through the remainder of corruption, their will is inclined to what is sinful.

The *freedom of will* which man had at his first creation, was a freedom both to good and evil. The natural inclination of his will was only to what is good; but, being created mutable, it might, through temptation or some external circumstance, be altered and become inclined to evil. It is the prerogative of God alone to say, "I am Jehovah; I change not."—Mal. iii. 6.

The expression, "Being *left* to the freedom of their own will," does not imply that God withdrew any of the power which he at first conferred upon them; for the gifts and calling of God are without repentance,—*i. e.*, what he bestows he does not recall.— Rom. xi. 29; James i. 13. But it evidently implies, that he did not bestow any more strength upon our first parents than what he conferred on them at their creation. It must ever be remembered, that God is not bound, in any measure, to bestow on any of his creatures what he does not see to be for his own glory, however useful and profitable it may be to them.

Obs. 60.—*Our first parents fell from the estate in which they were created, by sinning against God.*

This was the consequence of being "left to the freedom of their own will." Through the temptation of the devil, through desire of gratifying their appetite, through desire of being made wise and like God, and through hope of escaping the threatened punishment, they ventured to eat of the forbidden tree, against the express command of God.—Gen. iii. 4–6.

That our first parents fell from the estate of innocence in which they were created, will be evident,—

1. If we consider the circumstances as they are given by the sacred historian in the third chapter of Genesis.

2. If we reflect on the gracious promise of a Redeemer which God made to them, we cannot express a doubt respecting their fall from their original state. But,

3. Nothing whatever so fully proves this truth, as what we daily behold in the world around us,—viz., the consequences of sin; such as alienation from God in every respect; and death, which every where bespeaks itself to be "the wages of sin."— Rom. vi. 23.

INFERENCES.

From this subject we learn,—1. The weakness of man when left to himself. If Adam did not continue in innocence when he had sufficient strength imparted to him, how little has man now to glory of, in respect of his power and ability to obey! 2. The necessity of watchfulness in every state in which we can be placed in this world.—1 Cor. x. 12. 3. The necessity of an almighty Deliverer, who can raise us from the ruins of the fall, and restore us to our forfeited privileges, and honour, and happiness.

Nature of Sin in General.

Q. 14.—What is Sin?

Sin is any want of conformity unto, or transgression of, the law of God.

ANALYSIS AND PROOFS.

We are here taught,—

1. That any want of conformity to the law of God is sin.

Gal. iii. 10.—" Cursed is every one that continueth not in all things which are written in the book of the law to do them."
2. That any transgression of the law of God is sin. 1 John iii. 4.—" Sin is the transgression of the law."

EXPLANATION.

Obs. 61.—*Any want of conformity to the law of God is sin.*

By the *law of God* is to be understood the commandments which God, the great Creator and Supreme King and Lawgiver, hath laid upon all men, who are his creatures and subjects, as the rule of their obedience.

This law is to be found written in some measure, though darkly on the hearts of all men,—Rom. ii. 15; but it is most plainly and fully written in the Word of God, or the Scriptures of the Old and New Testaments.

In Scripture there is mention made of three laws:—1. The *judicial* law, which chiefly concerned the Jewish nation, and is not in all respects binding on other nations. 2. The *ceremonial* law, which was binding on none but the Jews, and that only for a time,—namely, until the coming of Christ, by whom it was fulfilled and abrogated. And, 3. The *moral* law, which is perpetually binding on all mankind till the end of the world. And it is this law which is chiefly referred to in this place.

By *want of conformity* to the law, we are to understand an unsuitableness to the law, or a disagreement with it in any respect, or a swerving from it in its strictness, spirituality, and extent.

Want of conformity to the law includes,—
1. Original sin, and the natural enmity of the heart to the law of God,—Rom. viii. 7, which is want of conformity of heart.
2. All sins of omission, which are a want of conformity of life to God's law.

Obs. 62.—*Every transgression of the law of God is sin.*

The word *transgression* signifies a going beyond the bounds or limits assigned to one.

To *transgress the law of God* is to go beyond, or break the bounds or limits which he hath assigned to all our actions; or it is to do any thing inconsistent with, or contrary to, the law, either in thought, word, or deed; which is to sin against God.

The *evil* of sin chiefly consists in the dishonour which it does to God, in its contrariety to his nature and laws. And it may be discovered,—1. From the dishonour which it does to the glorious attributes of Deity. 2. From what God hath done, in order that it may be washed away. 3. From the awful effects of sin, which, if persevered in and unpardoned, is accompanied with everlasting misery.

INFERENCES.

From this subject we learn,—1. That, in order to see what we are, we must examine ourselves by the law of God. 2. That the law of God is exceeding broad, requiring obedience from all, either in their own person, or in the person of a surety. 3. That we ought to hate sin supremely, as the source of every woe and the spring of every sorrow. 4. That there is need of a Saviour to deliver us from sin, which is the worst of evils; and that we ought to give ourselves no rest, until we are washed, and justified, and sanctified in the name of the Lord Jesus, and by the Spirit of God.

Nature of Adam's Sin in Particular.

Q. 15.—What was the Sin whereby our first Parents fell from the estate wherein they were created?

The sin whereby our first parents fell from the estate wherein they were created, was their eating the forbidden fruit.

ANALYSIS AND PROOFS.

We are here taught,—
1. That the first and particular sin of Adam was the eating of the forbidden fruit. Gen. iii. 6.—" She took of the fruit thereof, and did eat; and gave also unto her husband with her, and he did eat."
2. That the eating of the forbidden fruit was the cause of Adam's fall. Rom. v. 17.—" By one man's offence, death reigned by one."

EXPLANATION.

Obs. 63.—*Man has fallen from his original state.*

The state in which man was placed at the beginning, was such, that nothing whatever could have been added to it, to render it more perfect or more happy.

That man has fallen from his original state, will be evident from the following things:—
1. If we look to man himself, sufficient proof presents itself; for sin every where marks his steps, and every thing within him shows that *now* he is not what he once was.
2. If we look to God, the same truth recurs; for he who was once the friend of man, is now the enemy of those who will not have him as their all.
3. If we look around us in the world, we shall behold evidences of our fall; for what is all the affliction, and sorrow, and death which we behold, and to which we are all subjected, but the offspring of sin?
4. If we look to the world to come we shall also find a proof of our apostasy from God; for, had there been no transgressor, there would have been neither punishment nor a place of everlasting woe.

Obs. 64.—*The first and particular sin which was the cause of Adam's fall, was the eating of the forbidden fruit.*

The command which God gave to Adam, to try his obedience, was a positive command not to eat of a certain tree, which was in itself a thing indifferent, in order that he might see that his obedience was to turn upon the strict will of God, which was the best test of his obedience.

The fruit of which our first parents ate, was called the forbidden fruit, not because there was any evil in it as fruit, for this was impossible, all things having been made very good ; but merely because God commanded Adam not to eat of it, for the trial of his obedience.

The eating of the forbidden fruit was not the *first sin* that was committed by man in our world, for before our first parents actually took of the forbidden tree, they were guilty of the sin of *unbelief*, which is the root of all other sins ; for they believed the devil, who said, " Ye shall not surely die," rather than God, who assured them that they should " surely die," if they should but touch it.—Gen. iii. 3, 4. But,

The *eating of the forbidden fruit* was the *first sin* that was *finished*, and that which brought death into the world with all our woe.

Obs. 65.—*The occasion of the sin of our first parents, was the temptation of Satan.*

Satan, or the devil, who is called the serpent, on account of his subtilty, pretended to have a much greater regard for their happiness and comfort than even God himself had ; and, accordingly, he endeavoured to convince them, that however much love God pretended towards them, he wished to contract their comforts in the garden. And in this he too well succeeded.— Gen. iii. 4, 5.

In this temptation the *subtilty* of Satan appeared,—

1. In addressing himself to Eve, who was the weaker vessel, when she was at a distance from her husband.

2. In presenting himself before her with various untruths.

3. In attempting to destroy man so soon after his creation.

Obs. 66.—*The sin of our first parents involves a violation of the whole law.*

Although there are many of the commandments of the moral law which our first parents in a state of innocence could not have openly violated ; yet, by considering circumstances, we shall find that, in some respects, their sin involves a violation of all.

1. They made themselves new gods.

2. They served the Lord according to the counsel of their own heart, and were to give him such worship as seemed good to themselves.

3. They profaned the attributes of their Creator, and despised the ordinance of their God.

4. They rendered themselves incapable of worshipping him on the seventh day, when he rested from all his works.

5. They honoured not their Father who is in heaven, but forgot him who was their benefactor, and were wanting in duty to one another.

6. They murdered themselves and all their posterity.

7. They had no way to cover their nakedness, but by sewing fig leaves together.

8. They were guilty of theft, for they took what did not belong to them.

9. They testified falsely against the Lord, and gave more credit to a lie, than to the truth of God.

10. They murmured at their lot, and were not content with their situation; for nothing would satisfy them until they had laid hold on that which God had reserved for himself.

And, saith the Apostle James, " He that offendeth in one point, is guilty of all."

Obs. 67.—*The sin of our first parents was highly aggravated in the sight of God.*

We shall find this to be the case, if we consider,—

1. The *person guilty:* man in innocence, who was fully able to continue in that state.

2. The *number* involved in the transgression: Adam sinned against God to his own run, and that of all his natural posterity.

3. The *time* when it was committed: which was soon after his introduction into paradise.

4. The *place* where the sin was committed: viz., paradise, which was peculiarly dear to God, and which he had prepared for the habitation of his innocent creature.

5. The *object* of the temptation: which was apparently a matter of little moment; the fruit of a tree, which ought certainly to have had no influence upon him to commit such a sin, seeing he had abundance of every other kind of fruit, and of every thing necessary to his comfort and happiness.

INFERENCES.

From this subject we learn,—1. How weak a creature man is, even in his best state. 2. That, if left to ourselves, we would, like our first parents, immediately choose death. 3. The necessity of watchfulness and prayer. 4. How inexcusable all are who have sinned against God; and how insufficient every plea will be, when God riseth up in judgment. 5. That no sin is small in the sight of God. 6. How vigilant and active Satan is to destroy the soul. 7. The necessity of self-denial. 8. The necessity of Jesus Christ as a Saviour from all sin,—from the sin of our nature, as well as from all actual transgressions.

Adam's Sin in Particular.—1. *Extent of the Fall.*

Q. 16.—Did all Mankind fall in Adam's first transgression?

The covenant being made with Adam, not only for himself, but for his posterity, all mankind, descending from him by ordinary generation, sinned in him, and fell with him, in his first transgression.

ANALYSIS AND PROOFS.

We are here taught,—
1. That the covenant of works made with Adam was for himself and his posterity. Rom. v. 14.—" Nevertheless, death reigned from Adam to Moses, even over them that had not sinned after the similitude of Adam's transgression, who is the figure of him that was to come."
2. That all mankind, descending from Adam by ordinary generation, sinned in him and fell with him. Rom. v. 12.—" By one man sin entered into the world, and death by sin ; and so death passed upon all men, for that all have sinned." 1 Cor. xv. 22.—" In Adam all die."
3. That it was in Adam's first transgression that we sinned and fell. Rom. v. 18.—" By the offence of one (or, by one offence), judgment came upon all men to condemnation."

EXPLANATION.

Obs. 68.—*The covenant made with Adam, was not only for himself, but also for his posterity.*

That Adam was the federal head and representative of all mankind will be evident, when we consider what is said in the Scriptures of truth. Had he been placed only as a private person, having no connection whatever with his posterity, Revelation would not have been what it is. We should not have been there informed, that "by the disobedience of one, many were made sinners,"—Rom. v. 19; that "in Adam all die,"—1 Cor. xv. 22; that "by one man sin entered into the world, and death by sin, and that death passed upon all men, seeing that all have sinned,"—Rom. v. 12. We should not have been informed that we were conceived in sin and brought forth in iniquity,— Ps. li. 5; that, " by the offence of one man, judgment came upon all men to condemnation,"—Rom. v. 18; that " there is none righteous ;" that "all have gone out of the way ;" that " there is none that understandeth ;" that " there is none that seeketh after God."—Rom. iii. 10, &c.

But what sets this in a still clearer light, is the apostle's comparison of Adam and Christ, in 1 Cor xv., where they are opposed to one another, not as private. but as public persons and representatives, and where the apostle speaks of them as if there were none else. See verse 47.

Obs. 69.—*All mankind, descending from Adam by ordinary generation, sinned in him, and fell with him.*

As Adam was the federal head and representative of all mankind; so, when he sinned and fell, *they sinned and fell with him.* This is evident from the passages of Scripture quoted above. That they did not sin and fall with him as he was the *natural root* of mankind, is evident; for had this been the case, it might also be said, that all sin, because their immediate parents have sinned.

That Adam's sin is imputed to his posterity, and that they are included in the covenant, is likewise evident from the *death of infants.* They die, not because they are sinners by imitation (as some affirm), for they cannot imitate any one, but because they *sinned and fell with Adam,* being included in the covenant made with him.

It is here said, that those alone sinned in Adam, who *descend from him by ordinary generation,* to exclude the Lord Jesus Christ, who was descended from Adam, but *not by ordinary generation.*—Gen. iii. 15; Matt. i. And hence it is said, that he was "separated from sinners."—Heb. vii. 26. Jesus Christ could not be represented by Adam, because he himself was to be a representative.—1 Cor. xv.

Obs. 70.—*All mankind sinned in Adam, and fell with him, only in his first transgression.*

The first transgression of Adam was the violation of the covenant that God made with him, by eating the forbidden fruit.

The sins which Adam committed after his first transgression. are not reckoned to his posterity; because, when the covenant was violated, he ceased to be a public person or representative. He could not continue in this capacity any longer, than either until the condition required was fulfilled, or until he had forfeited the promise made to him.

INFERENCES.

From this subject we learn,—1. What sin is, and what it has done; and that its nature must be exceeding sinful, seeing it hath extended over all. 2. That the fall of man is a lesson to all to beware of pride, and of thinking too highly of themselves. 3. The necessity of repairing to the second Adam, who alone can repair the shattered state of things as the first Adam left them. 4. That it is the duty of parents to their children, to consult their present and future welfare.

2.—*Consequences of the Fall.*

Q. 17.—Into what estate did the Fall bring Mankind?

The fall brought mankind into an estate of sin and misery.

ANALYSIS AND PROOFS.

We are here taught,—
1. That the fall of Adam brought mankind into a state of sin. Rom. v. 19.—" By one man's disobedience many were made sinners."
2. That the fall of Adam brought mankind into a state of misery. Rom. v. 17.—" By one man's offence death reigned by one." See also Gal. iii. 10.

EXPLANATION.

Obs. 71.—*Man's fallen state is a state of sin and misery.*

1. It is a *state of sin*, because man is now under the guilt of sin, and sin hath dominion over him.—Rom. iii. 19, and vi. 14.
2. It is a *state of misery*, because, according to the penalty of the law, death and the curse involve him in all manner of misery. —Rom. v. 12.

Sin and misery are inseparably connected. If there were no sin, there could be no misery; for sin is the procuring cause of all misery.

Man's state of sin and misery is expressed in Scripture by a state of darkness,—Eph. v. 8; a state of distance,—Eph. ii. 13; a state of condemnation and wrath,—John iii. 18, 36; a state of bondage or captivity,—Isa. xlix. 24; and a state of death both legal and spiritual,—Eph. ii. 1.

Out of this state of sin and misery no man can deliver himself; Jesus Christ alone can do it; for he alone could satisfy the demands of that law which man has violated.

INFERENCES.

From this subject we learn,—1. That seeing the whole world is guilty before God, every mouth must have been for ever stopped, although he had left all mankind to perish eternally with the fallen angels.—Rom. iii. 19. 2. To admire the infinite love of God in sending his beloved Son to save us from sin, as the only way of being saved from misery.—Heb. ii. 14, 16.

3.—*Sinfulness of Man's State by the Fall.*

Q. 18.—Wherein consists the Sinfulness of that estate whereinto Man fell?

The sinfulness of that estate whereinto man fell, consists in the guilt of Adam's first sin, the want of original righteousness, and the corruption of his whole nature which is commonly called original sin ; together with all actual transgressions which proceed from it.

ANALYSIS AND PROOFS.

We are here taught,—
1. That the sinfulness of man's fallen state consists in the guilt of Adam's first sin. Rom. v. 18.—" By the offence of one, judgment came upon all men to condemnation." See also verse 19.
2. That the sinfulness of man's fallen state consists in the want of original righteousness. Rom. iii. 10.—" There is none righteous, no, not one."
3. That the sinfulness of man's fallen state consists in the corruption of our whole nature, or of original sin. Ps. li. 5.— " Behold, I was shapen in iniquity, and in sin did my mother conceive me."
4. That all our actual transgressions, in which the sinfulness of our state also consists, proceed from original sin. Matt. xv. 19, 20.—" Out of the heart proceed evil thoughts, murders, adulteries, fornications, thefts, false witness, blasphemies; these are the things which defile a man."

EXPLANATION.

Obs. 72.—*There is such a thing as original sin.*

Original sin is that sin which we have from our original and birth, and from which all actual transgressions proceed.

That original sin exists, may be proved,—
1. From various passages of Scripture,—Gen. v. 3, where it is said that Adam begat a son *in his own likeness, after his own image.* These words evidently imply, that the son that was born to him, came into the world with the same corrupt image that he himself bore after the fall. Gen. vi. 5,—from which it is evident, that there must be some corrupt fountain from which all wickedness proceeds; otherwise the very imaginations of the heart could not be *only evil, and that continually.* But this is more fully expressed in chap. viii. 21,—" The imagination of man's heart is evil from his youth;" which points out the source of all to be original depravity. See also Job xiv. 4; James iii. 11; Job xv. 14 · John iii. 6; Ps. li. 5.
2. From *circumcision* under the Old Testament, and *baptism* under the New; which may be considered not only as seals of the covenant, but also as designed to express the impurity and pollution of all when they come into the world, and the necessity of being cleansed or regenerated, in order that they may be fitted, as the real children of God by covenant, for the enjoyment of him.
3. From the conduct of children; from the sickness, and pains, and death itself, to which they are subject when they come into the world; and from the diversity of their tempers and disposi

tions, before they can scarcely form an articulate sound, or communicate their wants and necessities.

4. From the exercises of the people of God, who view original sin as the source of all their troubles, and sorrows, and trials in this world.

5. From the consideration, that the wickedness of man cannot be accounted for, if we deny that it flows from this corrupted fountain.

Obs. 73.—*Original sin consists in the guilt of Adam's first sin, the want of original righteousness, and the corruption of the whole nature.*

It consists,—

1. In *the guilt of Adam's first sin.* By this we are to understand, that we are all chargeable with Adam's first sin, which is made ours by imputation. As the righteousness of Christ is imputed to all his spiritual seed, so the sin of Adam is imputed to all his natural posterity.—Rom. v. 19.

2. In *the want of original righteousness.* By this we are to understand the want of that purity of nature, which Adam had when he was created, and which consisted in the full and perfect conformity of all the powers of his soul to the spotless nature of God, and to that holy law which was written on his heart.—Eccl. vii. 29.

3. In *the corruption of the whole nature.* By this we are to understand the universal corruption and depravation both of the body and of the soul; in the members of the one, and in the powers and faculties of the other.—Isa. i. 5, 6.

At the creation of the soul, God does not *infuse* sin into it. As a righteous Judge and a God of justice, he only withholds that original righteousness which Adam possessed in the beginning, and we in him, and which he is under no obligation to bestow. Adam having cast it off at first, God now denies it, as a punishment of sin, and as an act of justice.

Obs. 74.—*Original sin, as to its nature, is universal, discovers itself where least expected, is a great hindrance in the way of holiness, is the spring of all actual sins, and exposes to the wrath of God.*

1. It is *universal.* Not only is every man depraved, but every part of every man,—all the members of the body, and all the powers and faculties of the soul,—the understanding, the will, the affections, &c.—See Rom. iii. 10, 12, 23; Isa. i. 5, 6; Jer. iv. 22; 1 Cor. ii. 14; Rom. viii. 7; Hos. xi. 7; John v. 40; Tit. i. 15; Ps. cxvi. 13, 21.

2. It *discovers itself where least expected.* It not only breaks forth in the greatest sinners, but also in the most eminent saints, in a way altogether unexpected and sudden.—Jer. xvii. 9; Matt.

xxvi. 69-75; 2 Sam. xi.; Jonah i.; Gen. ix. 21, &c.; 2 Kings viii. 12.

3. It is *a great hindrance in the way of holiness*. It prevents the soul from running in the way of God's commandments; it easily besets us; and it constitutes a remarkable hindrance in spiritual communion with God.—Rom. vii. 19, &c.

4. It is *the spring or source of all actual transgressions*. All the wickedness that is in the world proceeds from this fountain; for if there were no original sin, there would be no actual. See Matt. xv. 18, &c.

5. It *exposes to the wrath of God*. All are by nature the children of wrath.—Eph. ii. 3.

INFERENCES.

From this subject we learn,—1. The source and spring of all sin, and of every trouble to which we can be exposed, both in this world and in the world to come. 2. That parents and children are on the same footing with respect to original depravity. 3. The necessity of being taken out of a natural state, and of being ingrafted into Christ, the second Adam. 4. The absolute necessity of regeneration, and of the Spirit of Christ, who can make all things new.—John iii. 3, 5.

4.—*Misery of Man's State by the Fall.*

Q. 19.—What is the misery of that estate whereinto Man fell?

All mankind by their fall lost communion with God, are under his wrath and curse, and so made liable to all the miseries of this life, to death itself, and to the pains of hell for ever.

ANALYSIS AND PROOFS.

We are here taught,—

1. That all men have, by the fall, lost communion with God. Gen. iii. 8.—" Adam and his wife hid themselves from the presence of the Lord God among the trees of the garden." Ver. 24. —" So he drove out the man." See also Isa. lix. 2, and Rom. viii. 7.

2. That all men by nature are under the wrath and curse of God. Eph. ii. 3.—" And were by nature the children of wrath." Gal. iii. 10.—" Cursed is every one that continueth not in all things which are written in the book of the law to do them."

3. That all men are, by the fall, made liable to all the miseries of this life. Job v. 7.—" Man is born unto trouble as the sparks fly upward." See also Gen. iii. 17.

4. That all men are, by the fall, made liable to death. Rom vi. 23.—" The wages of sin is death."

5. That all men are, by the fall, made liable to the pains of hell. Ps. xi. 17.—" The wicked shall be turned into hell, and all the nations that forget God."

6. That the pains of hell are eternal. Matt. xxv. 46.—" These shall go away into everlasting punishment." See also Isa. xxxiii. 14; Mark ix. 43, 44; and 2 Thess. i. 9.

EXPLANATION.

Obs. 75.—*Man, by the fall, has lost communion with God.*

The *communion* which man enjoyed in innocence, consisted in the uninterrupted enjoyment of the gracious presence and favour of God, together with the most intimate familiarity with him in the garden of Eden.

That man has *lost* this communion, is evident from his being represented as " without God in the world," and as " alienated from the life of God."—Eph. ii. 12, and iv. 18. See Gen. iii. 8, 23, 24.

By losing this communion, man has sustained the greatest loss; because God is the chief good, and man's chief happiness consists in communion with him.

Obs. 76.—*Man is under the wrath and curse of God.*

1. Man is under the *wrath* of God. To be under the wrath of God, is to lie under his anger in the dreadful effects of it, whether they are visible to us, or whether they are concealed from us. —John iii. 36; Eph. ii. 3; Ps. xi. 5.

2. Man is under the *curse* of God. To be under the curse of God, is to be under the curse of his righteous law, which denounces all possible evil against the sinner.—Gal. iii. 10; Ps. xc. 11; Deut. xxviii. 15, &c.; Ps. vii. 11; Rom. i. 18; John iii. 18, 36.

Obs. 77.—*In this world man is liable to all kinds of misery and to death.*

1. Man is subject to all the *miseries of this life*, which concern the *body*. Such are these: public judgments and calamities of every kind; the troubles, afflictions, and diseases to which the human frame is exposed; the losses, crosses, and disappointments, and acts of injustice, to which men are continually liable; and all the poverty, and straits, and difficulties, and wants, which fall to the lot of many in the present state of existence.

2. Man is subject to all the *miseries of this life*, which concern the *soul*. Such are these: blindness of mind,—Eph. iv. 18; a reprobate mind,—Rom. i. 28; strong delusions,—2 Thess. ii. 11; hardness of heart,—Rom. ii. 5; horror of conscience,—Isa. xxxiii. 14; Gen. iv. 13; Matt. xxvii. 4; and vile affections,—Rom. i. 26, &c.

3. Man is subject to *death* itself, or the separation of the soul from the body.—Heb. ix. 27; Rom. vi. 23; Ezek. xviii. 4.

It may be here remarked, that with respect to the outward conduct of Providence, all the external miseries above mentioned equally befall the righteous and the wicked: but they are sent for very different purposes. To the righteous they are only fatherly chastisements, and work together for their good; whereas, to the wicked they come in a way of vindictive wrath, and are the forerunners of eternal sorrow, unless they repent. To the former they are sanctified, and made the means of further holiness; to the latter they are the commencement of wrath on account of their sins, to be revealed in due time.

Obs. 78.—*In the world to come, man is liable to the pains of hell.*

By the *pains of hell* we are to understand the punishment of the wicked, which consists,—

1. In the punishment of *loss:* the loss of God, who alone is and can be the chief good of the soul; the loss of Christ, whose presence is better than life; the loss of the communion of angels and saints; the loss of the soul; and the loss of every possibility of escape.

2. In the punishment of *sense:* which is expressed in Scripture by " being shut up in darkness;" " a lake that burneth with fire and brimstone, which is the second death;" " the worm that dieth not, and the fire that shall never be quenched;" " destruction from the presence of the Lord, and from the glory of his power," &c.

Obs. 79.—*The pains of hell are eternal, or for ever.*

That the punishment of the wicked shall be eternal, is evident from Scripture, which assures us, that the wicked shall be cast into *everlasting* fire—shall go into *everlasting* punishment—shall be punished with *everlasting* destruction—shall be tormented day and night *for ever and ever.* These expressions leave no room for doubt respecting this matter.

The *eternity* of punishment is not essential to the threatening or penal sanction of the law; for had this been the case, there never could have been a satisfaction for sin. But it arises from the *nature of the creature*, which being finite, can never yield a satisfaction of infinite value. So that the punishment of the wicked must be everlasting, as well as the blessedness of the saints, which is so on account of the infinitely valuable satisfaction of Christ in their stead.

INFERENCES.

From this subject we learn,—1. What an evil, what a bitter, and what a hateful thing sin is, which is accompanied with such consequences, and which brings with it such a train of misery, if not washed away in the blood of Christ. 2. That however sweet the pleasures of sin may now appear, it shall prove bitterness in the end. 3. The necessity of fleeing to the man Christ Jesus from the avenger of blood; of repairing to the horns of the altar, that sin may not be our ruin. 4. The value of the gospel, and the value of the soul; and the inconceivable misery of all that are in a state of nature.

SECT. IV.—OF THE SPECIAL PROVIDENCE OF GOD TOWARDS MAN IN REDEMPTION:—UNDER WHICH ARE CONSIDERED THE PLAN OF REDEMPTION, THE APPLICATION OF REDEMPTION, AND THE BENEFITS OF REDEMPTION.

Division 1.—Plan of Redemption.

Q. 20.—Did God leave all Mankind to perish in the estate of sin and misery?

God having out of his mere good pleasure, from all eternity, elected some to everlasting life, did enter into a covenant of grace, to deliver them out of the estate of sin and misery, and to bring them into a state of salvation by a Redeemer.

ANALYSIS AND PROOFS.

We are here taught,—

1. That God hath ordained or elected some men to everlasting life. Acts xiii. 48.—" As many as were ordained to eternal life believed." See also 2 Thess. ii. 13.

2. That God's purpose of election was from eternity. Eph. i. 4.—" He hath chosen us in him before the foundation of the world."

3. That the election of God is the result of his own good pleasure. Eph. i. 5.—" Having predestinated us unto the adoption of children by Jesus Christ to himself, according to the good pleasure of his will."

4. That God entered into a covenant of grace with Christ for the elect. Ps. lxxxix. 3.—" I have made a covenant with my chosen."

5. That the design of this covenant was to deliver the elect from their original state of sin and misery, and to bring them into a state of complete salvation by a Redeemer. Rom. viii. 1.—" There is now no condemnation to them who are in Christ Jesus, who walk not after the flesh, but after the Spirit." Rom. v. 18.—" By the righteousness of one, the free gift came upon all men unto justification of life." See also Matt. i. 21; 1 Thess. i. 10; Tit. iii. 5; and Prov. xxiii. 2.

EXPLANATION.

Obs. 80.—God has elected or ordained some men to eternal life

By *election* we are to understand God's purpose of love and grace towards some sinners of mankind, when he might have left all, without exception, to perish in their sins. Acts xiii. 48; Matt. xx. 16; Luke xii. 32.

That to which the elect are chosen, is *everlasting life*. They are also chosen to the means which lead to this end; for the means and the end are so intimately connected, that they cannot be separated.—Acts xiii. 48; 2 Thess. ii. 13.

At present, the *elect* and *believers* are not of the same extent; but they shall be of the same extent; for all that are elected to everlasting life, shall in due time be brought out of their state of sin and misery, into a state of complete salvation.

Obs. 81.—*God's purpose of election was from eternity.*

The purpose of God concerning the elect took its rise from *eternity.* It never had a beginning; for he loved them from everlasting. Jer. xxxi. 3; Eph. i. 4; 2 Thess. ii. 13. To say that God makes no choice until the day of believing, is as much as to say that he did not know from eternity who should believe, and what should take place in time. And to deny his omniscience and foreknowledge, is to deny his being.

Obs. 82.—*God's purpose of election was the result of his own good pleasure.*

1. God's decree of election was not to save such as should *believe* and *persevere* in a state of holiness. Were this the case, it would render this act of God a thing altogether uncertain; because, if it depended on this circumstance, it would be uncertain whether any should believe, and consequently uncertain whether any should be saved.

2. God did not choose men to eternal life because he *foresaw* their faith and holiness. Scripture never attributes election to faith and holiness foreseen, or afterwards visible in the saints. On the contrary, these are always exhibited as the *fruits* and *effects* of election, and therefore they can never be viewed as the *cause* of it; for the same thing can never, at one and the same time, be both cause and effect. See Eph. i. 4, 5.

3. *Jesus Christ* is not the *cause* of election. If God in love sent his Son into the world, to redeem those whom he had given to him, it cannot for a moment be supposed that he was the cause of electing love. See John iii. 16.

4. The only reason, then, that can be given, and that to which the scriptures everywhere attribute election, is *the mere good pleasure of God.* Eph. i. 5.—" Having predestinated us to the adoption of children by Jesus Christ unto himself, *according to the good pleasure of his will*, to the praise of the glory of his grace, wherein he hath made us accepted in the Beloved." See also Matt. xi. 26; Rom. ix. 16, &c.; Mal. i. 2. 3.

Obs. 83.—*God entered into a covenant of grace with Christ for the elect.*

The misery into which all mankind had plunged themselves by sin, was the *occasion* of the covenant of grace; but the *cause* of it was the amazing love, and condescension, and sovereign grace of God.

In Scripture this covenant is denominated by various names:—

1. It is generally called *the covenant of grace;* because the love and grace of God were the cause of it.

2. It is called *the second covenant;* because, although it was first made, it was last executed.—Heb. viii. 7.

3. It is called *a better covenant,* namely, than the covenant of works; because it is established on better promises.—Heb. viii. 6.

4. It is called *the new covenant;* because it was last intimated, and because it shall continue sure in all its parts to the end of the world.—Heb. viii. 8.

5. It is called *a covenant of peace;* because by it a reconciliation is made between God and man.—Ezek. xxxvii. 26; Isa. liv. 10.

That the covenant of grace was made with Christ, as the representative of the elect, or as the second Adam, will be evident from the following things:—

1. From various passages of Scripture; Ps. lxxxix. 3, &c., where reference is made to the covenant of royalty which was made with David, as representing his seed; but not to the covenant made with him alone. See ver. 19–36, where we have God plainly covenanting with Christ; for these verses are expressed in language too strong to have their full application to the covenant of royalty made with David, as king of Israel; which, however, without doubt, was typical of that made with Christ. See also Heb. viii. 6, and Gal. iii. 16, 17.

2. From Christ being called the *second Adam.* See 1 Cor. xv. 45, 47, where Adam and Christ are evidently contrasted. Christ cannot be called the *second man* in any other sense than as he is the federal head of his spiritual offspring, as Adam was of his natural posterity.

3. From *Christ* and his *spiritual seed* being called by the *same names.* They are both called Israel.—Isa. xlix. 3, and Rom. ix. 6. They are both called Jacob.—Ps. xxiv. 6; Isa. xli. 14. They are both called Christ.—1 Cor. xii. 12; Gal. iii. 16. See also Eph. iv. 13, and v. 30.

4. From the promises of this covenant being all made with Christ.—Gal. iii. 16, 17; Tit. i. 2; 2 Tim. i. 9.

5. From his being the surety of the covenant.—Heb. vii. 22; 2 Cor v. 21.

6. From all the covenants, which were typical and emblematical of the covenant of grace, being made with parents, as representatives of their posterity —Gen. ix. 9, and xvii. 7; 2 Sam. vii 11, &c.

It was necessary that this covenant should be made with Christ, as the representative of his people, for the following reasons:—

1. That the love of God might appear to have been from of old, even from everlasting; and that the covenant might be called an everlasting covenant.

2. Because, if this covenant had not been made with Christ, who is a Divine person, as a representive, it could not have been called a covenant of grace and a covenant of life; nay, it could not have been made at all.

3. That it might be a covenant of rich and absolutely free grace.—Eph. ii. 7. In respect of Christ himself, indeed, it was a pure covenant of works,—that is, a condition was to be performed by him, that life might be obtained for those whom he represented; but to sinners it is a covenant of rich and superabundant grace.—Rom. iv. 4, 5.

4. That there might be a similarity between the way in which sin and death entered into the world, and the way in which righteousness and life should be communicated. Sin and death entered by one man, and therefore righteousness and life must also enter by one man.

5. That the promises of the covenant might be sure to all the elect. See Ps. lxxxix. 2, 19, 22, &c.

Obs. 84.—*The parties of the covenant of grace are, Jehovah and Jesus Christ, and in him elect sinners of mankind.*

1. The party in this covenant on heaven's side is *Jehovah*, essentially considered, as Father, Son, and Holy Ghost,—who must be viewed in this covenant as an *offended Judge*, because of the sin of man; as a *God of love*, designing to display the exceeding riches of his grace and love in the redemption of a lost elect world; and as an infinitely *just and holy God*, who cannot save the sinner, but in a way of magnifying his law, of satisfying his justice, and of vindicating his holiness.

2. The party-contractor on man's side is the *Lord Jesus Christ, the Son of God;* who must be viewed in this covenant as full of compassion, and as a representative, and a living and quickening head to all his spiritual seed. As connected with this covenant, he must also be viewed by us, as bone of our bone; as nearly allied to us, having assumed our nature, that he might die and overcome death, and restore us to our former privileges and blessings in the same nature that sinned; and as a sacrificing priest, who offered up himself once for all, a sweet-smelling savour to God, without spot or blemish.—Heb. ix. 14, 15.

3. The party whom Christ represented—for whom he contracted—for whom he stood bound—and for whom he undertook (all these being terms of the same import and extent), are *sinners of mankind;* who, as connected with this covenant, must

be considered as lost and undone in themselves, by the violation of the first covenant in Adam, who represented all mankind; as altogether unable to recover themselves from their lost state, or to pay to God a ransom for their souls, to glorify his injured perfections, or to retrieve the honour of his law; as distinguished from the rest of the world by the sovereign purpose and grace of God; and as objects of the redeeming love of the Eternal Trinity.

That Christ did not represent *all mankind* in this covenant, is evident from his laying hold of the seed of *Abraham* alone, which are only a part of the seed of *Adam*, the parent of all mankind. See Heb. ii. 16.

Although the first Adam represented the *whole human race*, yet it is no disparagement to the federal representation of Christ, the second Adam, that he represented only *some of mankind;* because it is unspeakably more for Christ to undertake for *one sinner*, than it was for Adam in the beginning to undertake for a *whole righteous world.* See Rom. ix. 21.

Obs. 85.—*The condition of the covenant of grace was the righteousness of the Lord Jesus Christ.*

Nothing whatever but the finished *righteousness of Jesus Christ*, by which he hath satisfied all the demands of the broken law, can be properly and strictly called the *condition* of the covenant of grace. The righteousness of Christ, which was the condition of this covenant, consisted in these things :—holiness of nature,—Heb. vii. 26; righteousness of life,—Isa. liii. 9; John viii. 46; Luke xxiii. 4; John xviii. 38, and xix. 4, 6; and full satisfaction to the penalty of the broken law incurred by the sin of man.

That the righteousness of Jesus Christ alone is the proper condition of the covenant of grace, will be evident from the following considerations :—

1. Christ undertook to discharge, not a *part* only, but the *whole* of the debt of a guilty chosen world; which shows that he left nothing whatever to be performed by them as any part of the condition on which eternal life is to be obtained.

2. Nothing whatever but the fulfilment of the same condition, by the non-fulfilment of which the covenant of works was broken, can be the condition of this covenant,—that is, perfect obedience, which none but Christ could yield.

3. In Scripture we find, that Christ's righteousness satisfies every demand of law and justice; consequently nothing remains to be done by any other besides him, as the condition of this covenant. See Eph. v. 2; Tit. ii. 14.

4. The Scriptures fully show, that believers found their hopes of eternal life upon the righteousness of Christ, and not upon any other thing whatever.—Eph. i. 7; Phil. iii. 8, 9.

5. That which cannot answer the demands of the violated cove-

nant, cannot be called a condition, in the strict and proper sense of the word; but faith, repentance, love, and new obedience, though absolutely necessary on our part, cannot do this; therefore they can by no means be called proper conditions of the covenant of grace. So far from this, they are promises on the part of God himself to those interested in the covenant.—Phil. i. 29; Acts v. 31.

6. This covenant excludes boasting; but this could not be the case, if faith, and repentance, and holiness were the conditions of it.—Rom. iii. 27; Tit. iii. 5.

But although *faith* cannot be properly called the condition of the covenant, yet it is the *means* by which a sinner is put in possession of the blessings of this covenant. It is by this that he becomes one with Christ, by whom he is represented. And by this union all things become the believer's, and all the promises of the covenant become sure to all the seed.

Obs. 86.—*In the covenant of grace, certain promises were made to Christ, and to the elect in him.*

1. Those which immediately respect Christ, were, the promise of assistance in the work to which he was called; the promise of the acceptance of it, connected with his resurrection from the dead; and the promise of a glorious reward.—Isa. xlii. 1, 6, lii. 13, and liii. 11, 12.

2. Those which are made to the elect, and which flow from what Christ hath done, are many and precious. They pertain to life and godliness, to grace here and glory hereafter; and they include every thing necessary for them in this world, and in that which is to come.—Tit. i. 2; 1 John ii. 25.

Obs. 87.—*The administration of the covenant of grace was committed to Jesus Christ.*

By the *administration* of the covenant, we are to understand the management of it, in order that it may become effectual for the end for which it was made.

It is necessary that there should be an administration of this covenant, because there is much to be done in order that the elect may be brought to glory.

This administration is devolved on *Christ*, as a reward of his arduous undertaking, that all the ransomed of the Lord may rest on him for their salvation, and for every mean of salvation.

The *objects* of this administration are sinners of mankind indefinitely. or any of the family of Adam without exception.—See John iii. 14, 15; Luke ii. 10; Matt. xxviii. 18, 19; Prov. viii. 4. Although Christ effectually saves none but the chosen of God, who were given to him; yet by his office, he is the Saviour of the world, suited for every sinner; and all are warranted by God to apply to him for salvation. Hence he is called "the Saviour of all men, especially of those that believe;" and his salvation is called the *common salvation.*—Jude 3. The offer of his salvation is unlimited wherever it is preached.—Mark xvi. 15, 16.

The *foundation* of the unlimited administration of the covenant, in the offer of Christ in the gospel, is the *sufficiency* of his blood for the *salvation of all.* See John i. 29. Christ hath fulfilled the condition of the covenant in all its extent; and his atonement, being infinitely valuable in itself, is considered, as such, a sufficient ransom for all.

Obs. 88.—*The design of the covenant of grace was to deliver the elect out of their state of sin and misery, and to bring them into a state of salvation.*

The great *end* which Christ has in view in the administration of the covenant is, that elect sinners may be *brought out of a state of sin and misery, into a state of salvation;* and this he does by bringing them personally and savingly within the bond of the covenant.

When Christ administers the covenant to the elect, who alone are the objects of its peculiar administration, he bestows upon them *all things,* which he is empowered to bestow, by way of a *testament,*—every thing necessary for their recovery and everlasting happiness.—Luke xxii. 29. And the *means* by which a sinner is put in possession of all these blessings, is *faith,* which is likewise his gift.

INFERENCES.

From this subject we learn,—1. How mysterious the ways of God are to the children of men. 2. The duty of submission to the ways of God. 3. To beware of curiously searching into the hidden things of God; but to seek after scriptural views of him. 4. The sovereignty of the grace of God. 5. The necessity of self-examination, whether or not we are interested in the electing love of God. 6. The necessity of making our calling and election sure; seeing the decree of God is not our rule, and we are to act as if there were no decree. 7. The amazing love of the Eternal Trinity to a self-destroying world. 8. That if salvation could have been obtained in any other way than by a covenant of grace, so much would not have been done for the salvation of the sinner. 9. That this covenant is every way suitable to the case of sinners. 10. How worthy Jesus is of our highest love and esteem, who thus stood in the breach, that wrath might be averted. 11. That Christ is freely offered in the gospel to all men, whatever their character may be. 12. That all are called to examine themselves, what part they have in this well-ordered covenant; whether they are yet brought within the bond of it, or whether they are still far from righteousness. 13. That it is the duty of all to believe that Jesus Christ is the Saviour of the world, and their Saviour in particular, by the appointment of the Father, and by the offer of Christ himself. 14. That if we are not savingly interested in this covenant, we can have no hope beyond the grave; this being the only remedy for the sinner, and the Scriptures having concluded all under sin. 15. That holiness is necessary, as the only way by which we can evidence our interest in the covenant of grace. 16. That, in every time of need, we ought to go to Christ himself for every thing of which we stand in need; seeing he is the administrator of the covenant, to whom all things are committed. 17. That all things shall work together for the good of those who are interested in the covenant. 18. The happiness of the believer, and the misery of the unbeliever. who is in a state of distance from the covenant of grace.

The Person and Character of the Redeemer.

Q. 21.—*Who is the Redeemer of God's Elect?*

The only Redeemer of God's elect is the Lord Jesus Christ, who, being the eternal Son of God, became man, and so was, and continueth to be, God and man, in two distinct natures, and one person for ever.

ANALYSIS AND PROOFS.

We are here taught,—

1. That the Lord Jesus Christ is the Redeemer of God's elect Gal. iv. 4, 5.—" God sent forth his Son, made of a woman, made under the law, to redeem them that were under the law." See also 1 Tim. ii. 5.

2. That Jesus Christ is the only Redeemer of man. Acts iv. 12.—" Neither is there salvation in any other."

3. That Jesus Christ is the eternal Son of God. Mark xvi. 16. —" Thou art the Christ, the Son of the living God." See also Heb. i. 8.

4. That Jesus Christ became man. John i. 14.—" The Word was made flesh." See also Heb. ii. 16.

5. That Jesus Christ is both God and man. 1 Tim. iii. 16.— " And, without controversy, great is the mystery of godliness: God was manifest in the flesh." See also Rom. ix. 5.

6. That Jesus Christ possesses the natures of God and man in one person. Col. ii. 9.—" For in him dwelleth all the fulness of the Godhead bodily."

7. That Jesus Christ will continue to be both God and man for ever. Heb. vii. 24.—" But this man, because he continueth ever, hath an unchangeable priesthood."

EXPLANATION.

Obs. 89.—*The Lord Jesus Christ is the only Redeemer of God's elect.*

It may be here remarked, that he is called *Lord*, because, as

God, he is the Most High over all the earth; and, as Mediator all power in heaven and on earth is committed to him,—Matt. xxviii. 17; that he is called *Jesus*, because he saves his people from their sins,—Matt. i. 21; Luke i. 31; Acts iv. 12; and that he is called *Christ*, because he is the *Anointed* of the Lord. *Christ* in the Greek, and *Messiah* in the Hebrew language, signify the same thing, namely, *Anointed*,—which implies his designation unto, and his being fully qualified for, his mediatorial office.—Ps. xlv. 7; Isa. lxi. 1; Prov. viii. 23; Ps. ii. 7, 8.

Jesus Christ is the *Redeemer* of God's elect. This name has evidently a reference to the *redeemed*. Hence it evidently implies bondage or captivity to sin, Satan, and the world, and to death and hell, because of the breach of the first covenant. And hence also we are called lawful captives.—Isa. xlix. 24. To *redeem*, signifies to *buy back* what is in bondage or captivity; in which all mankind, without exception, are by nature.—Eph. ii. 1, &c. In order that Jesus Christ might redeem lost sinners, or deliver and rescue them, by power and conquest, out of the hands of Satan, and of every enemy, it was necessary that he should give a sufficient ransom to the offended justice of God. And this ransom he gave, when he offered up *himself* a sacrifice for sin; than which nothing more could be demanded, in order that the lawful captives might be set free, and made as though they had not been cast off.—1 Tim. ii. 5, 6; 1 Pet. i. 18.

Jesus Christ is said to be the *only* Redeemer, because none but he was capable of the arduous work of redemption,—Isa. lxiii. 5; none but he was set apart for it by God; none but he was sealed by the Father; none but he received a commission from him to lay down his life for his sheep; none but he is revealed as our Redeemer; and none but he was, in every respect, fitted and qualified for the work.

Obs. 90.—*Jesus Christ is the eternal Son of God.*

He is not so called because of his *office*, as some suppose; for, properly speaking, his office could never procure him the appellation of *the eternal and only begotten Son of God;* but he is the eternal Son of God *by nature.* The eternal Sonship of Christ is as natural and necessary, as it is natural and necessary for the first person to be called the *Father.* That it is clearly distinguished from his office, is evident from John vii. 29,—" I know him; for I am from him, and he hath sent me:" where his being *from* the Father, with respect to his eternal generation, is clearly distinguished from his being sent *by* him, with respect to his office. The nature, however, of the eternal generation of the Son is altogether beyond our knowledge and comprehension; for, saith the prophet, " Who shall declare his generation?"— Isa. liii. 8. This passage may be applied, not only to the number of his seed, but also to his eternal generation.

Obs. 91.—*Jesus Christ became man.*

In order that Jesus Christ might be our Redeemer, it was necessary that he should become *man;* or, that he should be bone of our bone, and flesh of our flesh.—John i. 14; Gal. iv. 4. We are not to suppose, however, that when he became man he ceased to be *God:* he became *Immanuel*—God with us, God in our nature.

It was necessary that Christ should be both God and man in one person; because, if he had not been so, he could not have been a Redeemer at all.

1. If he had not been *God,* he could not have endured that load of wrath which sin deserved; nor could his sufferings, which were but for a time, have been a sufficient satisfaction for sin.

2. If he had not been *man,* he could not have died; he could not have died in that very nature which sinned, which was absolutely necessary, seeing the law saith, "The soul that sinneth it shall die;" he could not have had a fellow-feeling of our infirmities, and we should have had no intercessor in our nature at the Father's right hand.

Obs. 92.—*Jesus Christ is God and man in two distinct natures and one person.*

It is said that Jesus Christ is God and man *in two distinct natures,* to show, that the *divine nature* is not, by its union to the human nature, rendered *finite,* and that it does not lose its divine attributes, or those which belong to God; and to show likewise, that the *human nature* does not, by its union to the divine, possess divine perfections; although, even as he is man, he is inconceivably superior to a mere man.

It is said that Jesus Christ is God and man *in one person,* to show, that, although the two natures are distinct, and possess their respective and essential properties, they are not divided in him; or, in other words, that he has not two persons. That the two natures are united in one person, is evident from Isa. ix. 6. —" Unto us *a child is born;* and his name shall be called *the Mighty God.*"

It was necessary that the Redeemer of God's elect, or the Mediator, should be both God and man in one person, for the following reasons:—

1. That the proper works of each nature might be accepted by God for us, and relied on by us as the works of the whole person, God-man.

2. That he might be a proper Mediator between God and man; that he might be nearly allied to God, and likewise our near kinsman.—Acts xx. 28; 1 John i. 7.

3. That the interests of both parties—an offended God, and offending man—might be attended to; and that every thing necessary for a reconciliation might be effected.

4. That he might apply to us the purchased redemption.

5. That, in a word, in whatever relation he stands to us, his manhood might render it pleasant and delightful, inasmuch as he hath a fellow-feeling of our infirmities; and that his Godhead might render it efficacious, in respect of the blessings which each relation exhibits.

Obs. 93.—*Jesus Christ will continue to be God and man in one person for ever.*

The union of the two natures of Christ is indissoluble and everlasting; for, if he continue for ever as Mediator, which we are assured he will do, as an eternal bond of union between God and man, his manhood must also be retained *for ever.* See Heb. vii. 25; Luke i. 32, &c.; Phil. iii. 21, and ii. 9, &c.

It may here be remarked, that the union which subsists between Christ and believers, which is very close, and the union of his two natures, differ in the following respect:—The two natures of Christ are but one person; whereas believers, although they are said to be in Christ and Christ in them, are never said to be one person with him.

INFERENCES.

From this subject we learn,—1. The greatness of the love of God to perishing sinners; seeing none but God in our nature could accomplish their redemption. 2. The value of the soul, which could not be redeemed but at the expense of the blood of God's eternal Son. 3. The comfort which arises to the soul from the indissoluble union of the two natures of Christ in one person. If this is everlasting, the union of believers with Christ is also everlasting. See John xiv. 19. 4. That all who are far from Christ shall perish for ever, if they leave this world without an interest in him. 5. How dignified man is! How dignified the believer is! inasmuch as his Redeemer assumed his nature, that he might die in his stead.—Heb. ii. 16. 6. The necessity of faith in Christ, seeing he is now exalted; it is by faith alone that we can behold him.—Mark xvi. 16.

The Redeemer's Assumption of Human Nature.

Q. 22.—How did Christ, being the Son of God, become Man?

Christ, the Son of God, became man, by taking to himself a true body and a reasonable soul; being conceived by the power of the Holy Ghost, in the womb of the Virgin Mary, and born of her, yet without sin.

ANALYSIS AND PROOFS.

We are here taught,—

1. That Jesus Christ, the Son of God, became man, by taking

to himself a true body and a reasonable soul. Heb. ii. 14.—
"Forasmuch, then, as the children are partakers of flesh and
blood, he also himself likewise took part of the same." Matt.
xxvi. 33.—" My soul is exceeding sorrowful, even unto death."
2. That Jesus Christ, as man, was conceived by the power of
the Holy Ghost. Luke i. 35.—" The Holy Ghost shall come
upon thee, and the power of the Highest shall overshadow thee."
3. That Jesus Christ was born of the Virgin Mary. Luke i.
31.—" Thou shalt bring forth a Son." Chap. ii. 7.—" And she
brought forth her first-born Son."
4. That Christ was born, and continued to be, without sin.
Heb. iv. 15.—" He was in all points tempted like as we are, yet
without sin." See also Heb. vii. 26.

EXPLANATION.

Obs. 94.—*Jesus Christ became man by taking to himself a true body and a reasonable soul.*

1. It is said that Christ had a *true body*, to show that he had real flesh and bones, as we have ; and that it was not the shape only and appearance of a human body, as some have fantastically supposed. That Christ had a true body, is evident from Scripture, and from his performing the various functions of life. —Luke iv. 39.

2. It is evident from Scripture that Christ had a *reasonable soul*. See Matt. xxvi. 38, and Luke xxiii. 46. If he had not had a reasonable soul, as well as a true body, he would have wanted the principal part of the human nature.

3. It is said that Christ *took to himself* a true body and a reasonable soul, to show that he existed before he assumed the human nature, and likewise that this was a voluntary act. Having voluntarily undertaken the sinner's cause, he rejoiced in the prospect of becoming man, and of working out our redemption. See Gal. iv. 4 ; John vi. 62, and viii. 58 ; Prov. viii. 29, &c. ; Micah v. 2 ; Heb. x. 7, 9.

It may here be remarked, that Jesus Christ did not assume the person of a man. He assumed the human nature, but not a human person. His human nature never subsisted by itself,— that is, it never had an existence separated or distinct from the person of the Son of God.

Obs. 95.—*Jesus Christ, as man, was conceived by the power of the Holy Ghost.*

The soul and body of Christ were formed in a preternatural and miraculous manner, *by the power of the Holy Ghost.*

1. By his almighty power he formed a part of the substance of Mary into his human body ; for, had not this been the case, Christ could not have been bone of our bone, and flesh of our flesh ; nor could he have been called the seed of Abraham, and

of the family of David; nor could he have been said to spring from the tribe of Judah.

2. By the same divine power he created the soul of Christ immediately out of nothing, and formed it in the closest union with his human body.

In this wonderful work, each of the Three Persons in the Godhead had a peculiar part to act:—

1. The *Father* prepared a body for Christ; or, which is the same thing, a human nature.—Heb. x. 5.

2. The *Holy Ghost* formed it, by his overshadowing power, out of the substance of the Virgin.

3. The *Son* of God assumed the human nature thus prepared and formed into personal union with himself.—Heb. ii. 14, &c.

Obs. 96.—*Jesus Christ was born of the Virgin Mary.*

With respect to his human nature, Christ was born of the *Virgin Mary*, who was of the seed of Abraham, and of the family of David, which was at that time in a very low condition. See his double genealogy in Matt. i. and Luke iii. See also Isa. xi. 1, liii. 2, and vii. 14, compared with Matt. i. 18, &c.

It was necessary that Christ should be born of a *Virgin*, for the following reasons:—That the human nature of Christ might be found in its primitive purity; that it might be presented to God as spotless as it was when man was first created; and that it might be free from original sin, which is conveyed to all the posterity of Adam by natural generation.

Obs. 97.—*Jesus Christ was born without sin.*

As the birth of Christ was extraordinary, and as he was not a son of Adam by natural generation, he was in every respect free from every stain of depravity, which is inseparable from man when he comes into the world.

It was absolutely necessary that Christ should be born without sin; because the human nature was united to the person of the Son by an indissoluble union; and also because it was to be a sacrifice for sin, which it could not have been, had it not been without spot and blemish.

INFERENCES.

From this subject we learn,—1. The great love of God and of Christ in the work of redemption, the love of God in giving his Son, and the condescension of Christ in becoming man. 2. The only way by which we can be delivered from sin, both original and actual. 3. How suitable a Saviour Christ is, who has a fellow-feeling of our infirmities,—being bone of our bone and flesh of our flesh. 4. The great encouragement that sinners have to claim Christ as their own; seeing he is clothed in human nature.

The Offices of the Redeemer.

Q. 23.—What Offices doth Christ execute as our Redeemer?

Christ, as our Redeemer, executeth the offices of a prophet, of a priest, and of a king, both in his estate of humiliation and exaltation.

ANALYSIS AND PROOFS.

We are here taught,—
1. That Jesus Christ, as our Redeemer, executeth the office of a prophet. Acts iii. 22.—" A prophet shall the Lord your God raise up unto you." See also John vi. 14.
2. That Jesus Christ executeth the office of a priest. Heb. v. 10.—" Thou art a priest for ever after the order of Melchizedec."—Ps. cx. 4.
3. That Jesus Christ executeth the office of a king. Ps. ii. 6. —" I have set my King upon my holy hill of Zion." See also Matt. xxi. 5.
4. That these offices belong both to his state of humiliation and to his state of exaltation.

EXPLANATION.

Obs. 98.—*Jesus Christ is the prophet, the priest, and the king of his people.*

As Christ really acted the part of a Mediator between God and man, so also doth he really execute every part of the threefold office of prophet, priest, and king. These offices the Scriptures expressly ascribe to him.
1. That he is a *prophet*, is evident from that ever-memorable prophecy of Moses, recorded in Deut. xviii. 15–19. Compare this with Acts iii. 22, &c. See also Heb. xii. 25.
2. That he is a *priest*, is evident from Ps. cx. 4, and many passages in the Epistle to the Hebrews.
3. That he is a *king*, is evident from Ps. ii. 6, and from other passages, where every thing necessary in this respect is represented as belonging to him. He hath a kingdom; a willing people as his subjects; a rod of iron, and a rod of peace; laws by which his kingdom is ruled; and a reward which he confers upon his people, and a punishment which he inflicts upon the disobedient.

Christ did not take the honour of these offices to himself; but he was called or appointed to them in the same manner that Aaron was,— Heb. v. 4, &c.; Isa. lxi. 1.

Each of these offices has respect to the covenant of grace. His *priestly* office belongs to the condition of the covenant, or that part of it which respects his sacrifice: and his *prophetical* and *kingly* offices, together with the *intercessory* part of his priestly office, belong to the administration or management of the covenant.

Each of them has also a relation to our misery. His *prophetical* office respects our ignorance and blindness of mind; his *priestly* office respects our guilt and danger; and his *kingly* office respects our pollution by sin, and our deliverance from it.

Christ executes all these offices in reference to his people. This is evident from 1 Cor. i. 30.—" But of him are ye in Christ Jesus, who of God is made unto us wisdom, and righteousness, and sanctification, and redemption." As a *prophet*, he is made of God to us *wisdom*; as a *priest*, he is made of God to us *righteousness*; and as a *king*, he is made of God to us *sanctification*; and when he executes in regard to us *all* these offices, he is made of God to us *redemption*.

The *order* in which Christ executes these offices in reference to his people, is the following:—his *prophetical* office must go before his *priestly* office, and his *priestly* office before his *kingly* office. He must first enlighten the mind, before he apply his righteousness to the soul; and before the soul can be made willing, his righteousness must be bestowed. See Job xxxiii. 23, &c. But with respect to the *natural order* of these offices, the *priestly* office stands first; and this order we have in the 22d Psalm. He is there said first to have purchased salvation; then he is said to declare it; and, lastly, he is said to possess a kingdom, and to govern his subjects. See Ps. xxii. 1–21, 22–26, and 27–31.

That it was necessary that Christ should sustain and execute the threefold office of prophet, priest, and king, will be evident when we consider the following things:—

1. The threefold misery of man by nature: ignorance, guilt, and bondage.

2. The nature of salvation. Christ is necessary as a prophet, to reveal the way of salvation, and to make offer of it in the everlasting gospel; as a priest, to purchase salvation; and as a king, to confer and apply, by his Spirit, the redemption which he hath purchased.—Heb. ii. 3, and ix. 12; Ps. cx. 2, 3.

3. Our situation in this world. The people of God stand in need of many things; but when they look up to Christ, and contemplate that fulness which is in him, and which in his threefold office he bestows upon them, it cannot fail to encourage and to support them in every time of need.

It may be here observed, that under the Old Testament dispensation, there were several types of Christ in his threefold office. These were, Moses, Samuel, Elijah, Elisha, Daniel, &c., who typified him as a prophet; Melchizedec before the law, and Aaron and his sons during the Jewish dispensation, who typified him as a priest; and David and his posterity, who typified him as a king. None of these, however, were anointed to all these offices, to act in them in a stated manner. Melchizedec was a king and a priest, but not a prophet; David was a king and a prophet, but not a priest; and Moses and Samuel were prophets and civil rulers, but they never acted as stated priests; they only performed this office on particular occasions.—Ps. xcix. 6.

Obs. 99.—*Jesus Christ executed his offices of prophet, priest, and king, in his state of humiliation; and he now executes them in his state of exaltation.*

Although Jesus Christ was not unknown, in his various offices and relations to his people, under the Old Testament dispensation, yet he did not execute them particularly and fully, until he assumed our nature. Since his incarnation, he has executed them, or does execute them, both in his state of *humiliation* and *exaltation.*

1. In his state of *humiliation* he executed his prophetical office, by teaching the people at all times, as one having authority; his priestly office, by offering up himself a sacrifice for sin; and his kingly office, by delivering the people from many enemies; but his glory in this capacity was much obscured in his state of humiliation. See John iii. 2; Matt. ii. 2, and xxi. 5; John xii. 15. He did not, however, execute these offices in all their extent, in his state of humiliation, until he was solemnly invested with them at baptism.

2. In his state of *exaltation* he now executes the office of a prophet, by revealing the way of salvation by his Word and Spirit; of a priest by interceding with God for his people; and of a king, by subduing his people to himself, and by conquering all his and their spiritual enemies.—Heb. vii. 25.

Obs. 100.—*Jesus Christ must be received by faith in all his offices.*

The offices of Christ cannot be separated if he maketh himself savingly known to the soul. He will not manifest himself to any as their prophet, and not as their priest and king; nor will he give himself for any, and not make them wise unto eternal salvation.

For *justification* before God, the faith of the believer rests particularly on the *priestly* office of Jesus Christ. " Christ is the end of the law for righteousness to every one that believeth."— Rom. x. 4.

INFERENCES.

From this subject we learn,—1. The suitableness of Christ as a Mediator to his people. 2. The safety of all who put their trust in him. 3. The great encouragement which all have to claim a relation to Christ, seeing all his offices have a relation to us. 4. Our character, and how helpless all must be without him. 5. The necessity of Christ as a whole Redeemer; of taking him in all his offices, seeing they cannot be separated.

Offices of the Redeemer.—1. *Prophetical Office.*

Q. 24.—How doth Christ execute the Office of a Prophet?

Christ executeth the office of a prophet, in revealing to us, by his Word and Spirit, the will of God for our salvation.

ANALYSIS AND PROOFS.

We are here taught,—

1. That Christ, as a prophet, reveals to us the will of God. John xv. 15.—" All things that I have heard of my Father I have made known to you." See also John i. 18.

2. That Christ reveals the will of God by his Word and Spirit. Hos. viii. 12.—" I have written the great things of my law." 2 Cor. v. 19.—" God hath committed to us the word of reconciliation." John xiv. 26.—" The Comforter, who is the Holy Ghost, whom the Father will send in my name, shall teach you all things."

3. That the purpose for which Christ reveals to men the will of God, is their eternal salvation. John xx. 31.—" These are written, that ye might believe that Jesus is the Christ, the Son of God; and that believing ye might have life through his name."

EXPLANATION.

Obs. 101.—*Jesus Christ, as a prophet, reveals to men the will of God.*

A *prophet* is one who not only foretells future events, but also teaches the will of God.

Christ is called a *prophet*, not only because he foretold many things when he was in this world, which have since received their full accomplishment; but also because he makes known to sinners the will of God for their salvation. Hence, in connection with this office, he is called an *apostle*,—Heb. iii. 1, because he is the great ambassador of heaven, sent to declare the will of God to men; the *messenger of the covenant*,—Mal. iii. 1, because he has fully made known the whole will of God concerning the everlasting covenant for salvation; the *faithful and true witness*,—Isa. lv. 4, and Rev. iii. 14, because he cannot err in the discovery of the will of God; and an *interpreter*,—Job xxxiii. 23, because we cannot understand the great things of God, unless he reveal them to us.

By *the will of God*, which Christ reveals, we are to understand all that is necessary to be known, to be believed, and to be done, in order to the salvation, and comfort, and edification of the sons of men.

Obs. 102.—*Jesus Christ maketh this revelation of the will of God by his Word and Spirit.*

1. He reveals the will of God to his people by his *Word.* From the beginning of the world to his incarnation, he manifested himself by voices, by visions, by dreams, and by appearances of various kinds, which were all suited to the state in which his Church then was upon earth; but now, the Volume of Inspiration being completed, he reveals himself by the preaching of the Word, which has continued since his incarnation, and will continue till the end of the world, the only way by which his will is made known for our salvation.

2. He reveals the will of God to his people by his *Spirit.* Without this, the Word, although sharper than any two-edged sword, will not profit. It is only *through God* that the word is mighty to the pulling down of strongholds, and of every thing which exalts itself against the knowledge of God.—2 Cor. x. 4, 5; Luke xxiv. 45; I Cor. ii. 14; John xvi. 13, &c.

Obs. 103.—*Jesus Christ reveals the will of God for his people's salvation.*

The great end and design which Christ, as a prophet, hath in view, in revealing to his people the will of God, is, that they may be made *wise* unto *eternal salvation.*—See John xx. 31.

INFERENCES.

From this subject we learn,—1. The necessity of the Word of God. 2. The necessity of the Spirit to enable us to understand it. 3. The necessity of waiting upon the means of instruction which Christ has appointed in his Church. 4. That none need be ignorant, who have the offer of Christ to lead them into all truth. 5. The necessity of improving our privileges aright. See Luke xii. 78. 6. The necessity of examining ourselves concerning our knowledge.

2.—*Priestly Office.*

Q. 25.—𝔇𝔬𝔴 𝔡𝔬𝔱𝔥 𝔈𝔥𝔯𝔦𝔰𝔱 𝔢𝔵𝔢𝔠𝔲𝔱𝔢 𝔱𝔥𝔢 𝔒𝔣𝔣𝔦𝔠𝔢 𝔬𝔣 𝔞 𝔓𝔯𝔦𝔢𝔰𝔱?

Christ executeth the office of a priest, in his once offering up of himself a sacrifice to satisfy divine justice, and reconcile us to God, and in making continual intercession for us.

ANALYSIS AND PROOFS.

We are here taught,—

1. That Christ, as our priest, offered himself in sacrifice to God. Heb. ix. 26.—" In the end of the world hath he appeared to put away sin by the sacrifice of himself."

2. That Christ, as our priest, offered himself in sacrifice but once. Heb. ix. 28.—" Christ was once offered to bear the sins of many." See also Heb. vii. 27.

3. That Christ offered himself to satisfy divine justice for our

sins. 1 John ii. 2.—" He is the propitiation for our sins." See also Eph. v. 2.

4. That Christ offered up himself to reconcile us to God. Heb. ii. 17.—" It behoved him to be made like unto his brethren, that he might be a merciful and faithful high priest in things pertaining to God, to make reconciliation for the sins of the people." See also Eph. ii. 16.

5. That Christ, as our priest, maketh continual intercession for us. Heb. vii. 25.—" He ever liveth to make intercession for them."

EXPLANATION.

Obs. 104.—*Jesus Christ is a priest, and the only priest that can take away sin in the sight of God.*

A *priest* is one who, as a public person, deals with God in the name and in the behalf of the guilty, and who reconciles them to God by a sacrifice, which he offers up to him, and which must be sufficient to take away sin.

In the purpose of God, Jesus Christ was set up from everlasting as the *high priest* of his people, and also as a sacrifice for sin; but he did not actually enter upon his priestly office in his own person, until he became incarnate, and was fitted for offering up a sacrifice efficacious for the taking away of sin.

Under the Old Testament dispensation, there were many types of Christ in his priestly office. Every priest under the law was a type of him; and before the proper constitution of the Jewish Church, Melchizedec was a remarkable type of him in the eternity of his priesthood.—Heb. x. 11, &c., vi. 20, and vii. 17.

That Christ is really a *priest*, and the *only* priest, that can take away sin in the sight of God, will be evident, if we consider those things in which Christ excels the Aaronical priesthood:—

1. Christ excels the priests of the order of Aaron in his *person*. They were mere men; but he is the Son of God, and the true God, and eternal life. They were sinners, descending from Adam by ordinary generation; but he is the holy and immaculate Lamb of God. They, being sinful men, needed to offer for their own sins, before they could typically offer sacrifice for the sins of the people; but Christ needed not to offer for himself, before he made atonement for others, seeing he had no sin for which to make atonement. They, being mortal, succeeded one another; but Christ continueth a priest for ever, for he is a priest after the order of Melchizedec.—Heb. vii. 3, 23, 24, 27.

2. The *manner* in which Christ was *invested* with this office is preferable to that of the order of Aaron. " For those priests were made without an oath; but this with an *oath* by him that said unto him, The Lord *sware*, and will not repent. Thou art a

priest for ever, after the order of Melchizedec."—Heb. vii. 21, and ver. 15–17.

3. Christ excelled the priesthood of the Levitical order in the *perfection* and *efficacy* of his offering.—Heb. x. 4, ix. 14, and x. 11, 12.

4. The priesthood of Christ excels the Levitical priesthood in this, that the sacrifice which he offered up was *one only;* whereas the priests of old were commanded to offer up numerous sacrifices, and on almost every occasion.—Heb. ix. 25, &c., and x. 1–14.

5. Another circumstance which shows the superiority of the priesthood of Christ above that of Levi, is that mentioned in Heb. ix. 24.—" For Christ is not entered into the holy places made with hands, which are the figures of the true; but into heaven itself, now to appear in the presence of God for us." Hence, as much superior as heaven, the temple of God, is to the Jewish temple; so much is Christ, the priest of the one, superior to the priests of the other.

6. The Jewish high priests, with their temple and sacrifices, were only types of *him* that was to come, and who was to put away sin by the sacrifice of himself.—Heb. x. 1.

Obs. 105.—*Jesus Christ offered himself in sacrifice to God.*

The *sacrifice* which Christ offered, and which God appointed and prepared, was *himself*—his own human nature—a true body and a reasonable soul.—Heb. x. 5, and ix. 26; 1 Pet. ii. 24; Isa. liii. 10.

The *altar* on which the sacrifice of Christ was offered, and by which it was sanctified, in order that it might answer the high demands of justice and of a violated law, was the *divine nature*. And it was this that gave an infinite value and efficacy to the gift, because of the inseparable union of the two natures. Hence the blood of Christ is called the *blood of God;* and he himself is called the *Lord of Glory*, even when upon the cross.

The *priest* on this occasion was the person of Christ, as Godman; for as he was both the sacrifice and the altar, none but he himself could have officiated as priest.—Heb. v. 5. See also Heb. iii. 1, and vii. 26.

He to whom Christ offered himself was *God.*—Heb. ix. 14. This was necessary, because the party offended was God; and it is his holy law and justice whose demands must be fully satisfied.

Jesus Christ was a sacrifice, not only while he hung upon the cross. He was designed to be a sacrifice from eternity; and when he became incarnate, he was laid upon the altar, and continued upon it during the whole of his humiliation-state; and his offering was completed when he was actually crucified, and while he lay in the grave.

Obs. 106.—*Jesus Christ offered himself in sacrifice but "once."*

The Jewish sacrifices being imperfect, were many,—that is there were numerous sacrifices offered up on many occasions, but the sacrifice of Christ being perfect in every respect, was offered up only *once.*—Heb. ix. 28, and x. 14.—Besides, *once dying* was the penalty of the law; and, consequently, *once suffering unto death* was the complete payment of the penalty; and this on account of the infinite dignity of the sufferer.

Obs. 107.—*Jesus Christ offered up himself in sacrifice only for the elect.*

Although in respect of intrinsic worth, and as the obedience and death of a divine person raised up by God, the satisfaction of Christ is sufficient for the ransom of the whole human race, and although that ransom is suited to the necessities of all, he having died in human nature,—yet having become surety only for the elect, he died for them alone; for certainly he would not become the surety of any, and, at the same time, leave them in a state of sin, or not redeem them.

That Christ died for the elect alone, and not for all mankind, may be proved from the following things:—

1. From the *names* by which they are exhibited in Scripture. They are called *those whom the Father gave unto Christ,*—John xvii. 6; *God's elect,*—Rom. viii. 33; the *Church of God,* and the *body of Christ,*—Acts xx. 28, Eph. v. 23; *Christ's sheep,*—John x. 15, 16, 27, &c.; *Christ's friends,*—John xv. 13; *Christ's children,*—John xvii. 2, 9.

2. From the *satisfaction* and *intercession* of Christ being exactly of the *same extent;* the one including no more than the other. But he himself expressly affirms, that he intercedes not for the whole world of mankind, but only for the elect, or those who were given him; and common sense cannot allow, that he would lay down his life for any one for whom he would not intercede.

3. If Christ died for all men, the following consequences must ensue :—That he hath shed his blood in vain, if all are not saved; and that thus he has lost his end in the redemption of sinners : That he is wanting in power to put his scheme of salvation into execution, in opposition to the corrupt inclinations of men; and hence, that man is stronger than God : That the blood of Christ was shed for many millions of the race of Adam, who, at the very moment in which he was offering himself a sacrifice for sin, were in hell, and beyond all hope of pardoning mercy from God : That he died for those to whom he forbade his gospel to be preached, and whom he forbade his apostles to call to faith and repentance; and who are thus kept without hope of redemption.—Matt. x. 5; Acts iv. 12: and, That he is but a very imperfect Saviour, whose sacrifice is not meritorious to take away sin. To affirm these things, would be blasphemous and absurd in the highest degree

Obs. 108.—*Jesus Christ offered himself to satisfy divine justice for the sins of his people.*

This is one of the ends which Christ had in view in offering himself a sacrifice,—viz., *to satisfy divine justice.*

That Christ *truly* and *properly satisfied* the law and justice of God for the sins of his people, may be proved from the following things :—

1. From his being represented in Scripture as a surety charged in law with his people's sins, and bearing them in the sight of God, and also the punishment of them from God,—Heb. vii. 22; Isa. liii. 5, 10; and as redeeming his people by the price or ransom of his obedience and sufferings.—Gal. iii. 13.

2. From the effects ascribed to the obedience and death of Christ,—namely, the purchasing of men, and the purging away of sin.—Acts xx. 28; Heb. i. 3.

3. From his not giving up his spirit, until he could say that the work and labour of love, which his Father had given him to do, was *finished.*—John xvii. 4, and xix. 30.

4. From his resurrection from the dead, and his ascension into heaven; which plainly evince, that he fully discharged the debt which he undertook, and that the Father was well pleased for his righteousness' sake.

The *efficacy* of Christ's sacrifice, and its entire *acceptableness* in the sight of God, flow from these things,—the choice of God himself, the dignity and holiness of his person, the completeness of his satisfaction, and its agreeableness in every respect to the mind and will of him who sent him.

Obs. 109.—*Jesus Christ offered himself a sacrifice to reconcile sinners to God.*

This is the other end which Christ had in view in offering himself in sacrifice,—viz., *to reconcile sinners to God.*

By *reconciliation* we are to understand, a bringing together of those who were formerly in a state of enmity.

Between an offended God and offending man, a reconciliation can be effected by *Jesus Christ* alone.—Eph. ii. 15, &c.; Rom. v. 10; Col. i. 21. This will be evident, if we consider the following things :—That none could have performed this, but Christ himself, who was in all things fitted for this great work; that none was appointed to it but himself; and that none but he was accepted by God.—Isa. xi. 2, &c.; Acts iv. 12.

Obs. 110.—*Jesus Christ, as a priest, maketh continual intercession for his people.*

This is the second part of Christ's priestly office,—viz., *his continual intercession in heaven.*

The two parts of Christ's priestly office,—viz., his satisfaction and intercession,—are so intimately connected, that they cannot be separated. His satisfaction on earth is as extensive as his intercession in heaven, and his intercession is as extensive as his sacrifice.

The Godhead of the Son is not inconsistent with his intercession. If it were, it would be as inconsistent with the other part of his priestly office, namely, the offering of himself a sacrifice for sin. It must ever be remembered, that it is in his human nature that he is said to appear in the presence of God for us; and in his complete person will he continue to make intercession for us.

They for whom Christ intercedes, are his people; and his prayer on their behalf is, that their happiness may be completed. Christ also interceded for his people while he was on earth; and we must believe, that even then he was a prevalent high priest with God.—Heb. v. 7. In the 17th chapter of the Gospel by John, we have a full account of this part of his office, which he performed while on earth; and we may conceive the same to be his language now when he is exalted at his Father's right hand.

We may consider Christ's intercession in heaven as consisting in the following things:—

1. In presenting himself before God in human nature, and in the merit of his sacrifice, as the ground of bestowing on his people all necessary blessings, according to the tenor of the covenant of grace.—Heb. ix. 24.

2. In making known to his Father *his will*, that the blessings of his purchase may be applied to his people according to their need, and according to the new covenant.—John xvii. 24; Luke xxii. 31, 32.

3. In answering all the accusations preferred against his people by Satan, by the law, by the world, and by conscience; refuting every ground of accusation which is false, and pleading forgiveness for every thing that is justly preferred against them, on the ground of his complete atonement. See Zech. iii. 1, 2; Rom. viii. 33, 34.

4. In presenting to God all the worship and service of his people, which is performed in faith, and rendering it acceptable through his own righteousness. This is beautifully represented in Rev. viii. 3, 4. See also 1 Pet. ii. 5; Lev. xvi. 12, &c.

Christ's intercession in heaven is absolutely necessary; which will appear from the following things:—

1. From a consideration of the *accusations of Satan.*—Rev. xii. 10; Zech. iii. 1.

2. From a consideration of the numerous *sins* and *wants* of the saints.—1 John ii. 12; Heb. iv. 16.

3. From the saints' unworthiness in themselves in the sight of God, and their unfitness for glory.—Heb. ix. 24; Eph. ii. 18.

Jesus Christ is a *prevalent* and an *everlasting* intercessor.

1. He is always a *prevalent intercessor.* This may be inferred from the dignity of his person; the merit of his sacrifice: the

wisdom of his requests, which are always suited to the circumstances of his people, and to their happiness in time and through eternity; and the fervour of them.

2. He is an *everlasting intercessor.*—Heb. vii. 25. The communion and fellowship of the saints in heaven will be maintained for ever in and through him, in such a way as is consistent with their state of purity and perfection there. See Rev. vii. 17.

The *intercession of Christ,* and the *intercession of the Spirit,* mentioned in Rom. viii. 26, differ in the following respect:— Christ intercedes *without us,* by presenting to God the value of his sacrifice; but the Spirit intercedes *within us,* by groanings which cannot be uttered,—viz., by enabling us to plead and wrestle with God at the throne of grace, teaching us what we should pray for as we ought, and in what manner we should pray. so as to be accepted.

INFERENCES.

From this subject we learn the following things :—From the first part of Christ's priestly office, namely, his satisfaction for sin, we learn,—1. The great and only ground of all our hopes— the real satisfaction of Christ for sin in the room of sinners. 2. The superiority of our privileges above the privileges of those who were under the law. 3. The necessity of an interest in Christ's sacrifice, and of faith in him as the great atonement. 4. The danger of rejecting Christ in the capacity of a priest, and the great comfort of an interest in him. 5. That there is such an evil in sin, that man himself cannot take it away. 6. That if a sacrifice had not been provided, the sinner must have died in his sins. 7. That the love of God is unbounded in giving his Son to die for sinners. 8. The greatness of our mercies, who have heard of the way of saving sinners by the sacrifice of Christ. 9. What a hateful thing sin is, and how contrary to the nature and Word of God. 10. The great ground of joy which arises to all, from the Father's being well pleased in Christ.

From the second part of Christ's priestly office, namely, his intercession, we learn,—1. The happiness of those who are in covenant with God. 2. That all things are secured which can render the believer happy in time and through eternity. 3. The love of Christ in acting the part of an intercessor in heaven for us. 4. The believer's certainty of immortality. While Christ is his advocate, who can condemn? 5. The duty of all to apply to him as such. 6. That there is, and can be, no other intercessor within the vail, but Jesus Christ our great high priest.—[1] Tim. ii. 5. 7. The greatness of the love of God in appointing for sinners such an advocate in his presence. 8. That believers need not fear that their cause shall finally miscarry in the hands of this great advocate. 9. That the intercession of Christ is one special ground of the saints' perseverance in a state of grace.—John x

28, 29. 10. That every part of the work of redemption is wonderful, and completely manifests the glory of God. 11. That, if we would have one to plead our cause in heaven, we must apply to Jesus, whom his Father hath appointed to appear in his presence for us. See Heb. xii. 25.

3.—*Kingly Office.*

Q. 26.—How doth Christ execute the Office of a King?

Christ executeth the office of a king in subduing us to himself, in ruling and defending us, and in restraining and conquering all his and our enemies.

ANALYSIS AND PROOFS.

We are here taught,—

1. That Christ, as a king, subdues his people to himself. Ps. cx. 3.—" Thy people shall be willing in the day of thy power."

2. That Christ, as a king, rules his people. Isa. xxxiii. 22.—" The Lord is our judge, the Lord is our lawgiver, the Lord is our king; he will save us."

3. That Christ, as a king, defends his people. Ps. lxxxix. 18. —" The Lord is our defence; and the Holy One of Israel is our king." See also Zech. ii. 5.

4. That Christ, as a king, restrains all his and his people's enemies. Ps. lxxvi. 10.—" Surely the wrath of man shall praise thee; the remainder of wrath shalt thou restrain."

5. That Christ, as a king, conquers and destroys all his own and his people's enemies. 1 Cor. xv. 25.—" He must reign, till he hath put all enemies under his feet."

EXPLANATION.

Obs. 111.—*Jesus Christ is a king.*

That Christ is a *king*, may be proved from the following things:—

1. Titles of *lordship* and *dominion* are ascribed to him. Ps. ii., cx., and lxxii., have an evident reference to him in this capacity, however much they may be applicable to his types of old. See also Isa. xxxii. 1, &c.; Jer. xxiii. 5, &c., where we find him in prophecy marked by titles of dominion.

2. Many *princely* titles are ascribed to him, which can be ascribed to none else. In Acts ii. 36, we find him made *king*. He is denominated *the Prince of life.*—Acts iii. 15. *King of kings* and *Lord of lords.*—1 Tim. vi. 15; Rev. xvii. 14, and xix. 16. Ruler, Judge, Commander, Leader, the Captain of the Lord's host.—Josh. v. 15. And many other names are applied to him, which plainly mark him as designed for royalty, and for the exercise of universal power, as Mediator. See Zech ix. 9; Luke i. 32, &c.

3. All the ensigns of royal power are attributed to him. He is anointed as king.—Ps. xlv. 7. His royalty commenced in Heaven's eternal purpose; and it was made known by angels at his birth.—Luke ii. 11. This was acknowledged by Jesus himself at his death.—John xviii. 36. See also Matt. xxviii. 18; Eph. iv. 8; Phil. ii. 9–11. He is crowned by his Church and by his Father.—Song iii. 11; Heb. ii. 9. A royal throne is ascribed to him, even at the right hand of God.—Ps. cx. 1; Heb. i. 13. A royal sceptre belongs to him.—Ps. ii. 9, and xlv. 6. The laws which he enacts are the laws of a king.—Isa. ii. 3. His servants are the servants or ambassadors of the King of kings.—2 Cor. v. 20. He has a royal retinue, royal revenues, and royal magazines of spiritual armour.—Jude 14; Ps. xlv. 11, &c.; Eph. vi. 10, &c. His power to judge and to acquit or condemn, is the power of the King of kings.—John v. 22. And the subjects of this king are an innumerable multitude out of every nation, and kindred, and tongue, and people.

Before Christ appeared in this world, he was prefigured in his *kingly* office by Melchisedec,—Heb. vii. 1, &c.; by Joshua, the conqueror of Canaan; by David and Solomon; and by all the kings of Israel and Judah.

Obs. 112.—*Jesus Christ has two kingdoms; an essential kingdom, and a mediatorial kingdom.*

1. As God supreme, God equal with the Father and the Holy Ghost, he has an *essential kingdom*. His supremacy and dominion over all things are equal to theirs. He not only in a peculiar manner possesses his mediatorial kingdom, but he is also the governor among the nations.—Matt. xxviii. 18. They all fulfil his pleasure; and great things have they been made to do for the Church in this world. For the sake of his Church, Christ has turned a fruitful field into barrenness; he has destroyed cities and those that dwelt in them; he has caused the sun and moon to stand still in their courses; he has altered the course of nature; he has dried up the sea; and he has made the inanimate creation to fight in her behalf.

2. As God-man, Mediator, and Redeemer, he has a *mediatorial kingdom* which was given him by his Father as a reward for what he hath done for his people. This kingdom in a special manner respects his Church, and is constituted with the design of bringing her real members upon earth to the full enjoyment of the Lord, and of the presence of Zion's King.

Obs. 113.—*Christ's mediatorial kingdom is a very extensive, a spiritual, and an everlasting kingdom.*

1. It is a *very extensive kingdom*. See Matt. xxviii. 18; John xvii. 2; Ps. ii. 8. It extends to persons of all ages, ranks, and nations. Many shall be found in it at last, gathered out of every nation, and people, and language, under heaven; and all

shall be fully satisfied with the riches of this kingdom, which consist of glory, and honour, and immortality.

2. It is a *spiritual kingdom.*—John xviii. 36. "My kingdom," saith Christ, "is not of this world." Hence it is called "the kingdom of heaven," to mark its spirituality; and "the kingdom of God," to show that its original, and tendency, and privileges, and consummation, are all of a spiritual and heavenly nature. Christ, its king, is not a worldly ruler.—Matt. xx. 28; Zech. ix. 9. His throne is not an earthly throne; his throne of glory is in the heavens; his throne of grace is in the Church; and his throne of judgment is to be erected in the aerial heavens at his second coming, when earthly kingdoms shall be no more. His sceptre is a spiritual sceptre.—Ps. cx. 2. His laws are spiritual.—Rom. vii. 12, &c.; Heb. iv. 12. His worship and homage are spiritual.—John iv. 24; Rom. xii. 1; 1 Pet. ii. 8, &c.; Phil. iii. 3. His subjects are spiritual.—Eph. iv. 23; John i. 13; Eph. ii. 10. His ambassadors are spiritual, and sent upon a spiritual embassy.—2 Cor. v. 20. His armour is spiritual.—Eph. vi. 10, &c.; 2 Cor. x. 4. His rewards and punishments are of a spiritual nature.—2 Thess. i. 4, &c. And the designs which he has in erecting such a kingdom are also spiritual.—1 John iii. 8; Acts xxvi. 18.

3. It is an *everlasting kingdom.* As Mediator, he was set up from eternity, ere ever the earth was; and of his dominion there shall be no end. Micah v. 2; Dan. vii. 14; Ps. xlv. 6; Rev. iii. 21.

The mediatorial kingdom of Christ may be distinguished into his *kingdom of grace* in this world, which is his Church that he hath purchased with his own blood; and his *kingdom of glory* in the world to come, which is the Church invisible and of the first-born, whose names are written in heaven. But these are not so much distinct kingdoms, as different states of the same kingdom.

Obs. 114.—*The acts of Christ as a king are these:—His subduing his people to himself, his ruling and defending them, and his restraining and conquering all his own enemies, and those of his people.*

The acts of Christ, the king of Zion, in the administration of his kingdom, are *five;* some of which immediately respect his own subjects, and some his and their enemies; but they all become subservient to the present and eternal good of all those who will have him to reign over them.

1. Christ *subdues* his people *to himself.* Such is their natural aversion and obstinacy to him as king of Zion, that nothing less than almighty power can destroy the enmity of their hearts against him, and make them a willing people to himself.—Rom. viii. 7; 2 Cor. x. 4, 5; Ps. cx. 2, 3.

2. Christ *rules* his people. This he does by giving them laws and ordinances, and by correcting them.—Ps. cxlvii. 19 ; Mic. v. 2 ; Rev. iii. 19 ; Ps. lxxxix. 30, &c.

3. Christ *defends* his people from all their enemies. These are many and powerful ; such as sin, the devil, the world, death and the grave, and the remains of corruption, &c. See Matt. xvi. 18 ; Zech. ii. 5 ; Rom. xvi. 20, and vi. 14 ; John xvi. 33 ; Hos. xiii. 14 ; 1 Cor. xv. 57.

4. Christ *restrains* his own *enemies* and those of his people. This he does by thwarting their designs against his people; by making them see that they shall not prevail ; by convincing them that, however strong they are, he is stronger and more powerful ; that their schemes are well known to him ; and that they can devise nothing that shall prove effectual ; and by making them ashamed of their own attempts. See Numb. xxiii. 10 ; Exod. xiv. 26, &c. ; Ps. lxxvi. 10.

5. Christ *conquers* all his own and his people's *enemies*. This he does in the present world, when he takes away their power in part,—Zech. ii. 5; 1 Cor. xv. 55 ; and this he will do at the last day, when he will destroy all his own and his people's enemies from the presence of the Lord, and from the glory of his power. —1 Cor. xv. 25 ; Rev. xx. 14. This will be the most signal display of the glorious conquests of Zion's king ; and the trophies of his victory will be the subject of the song of the redeemed for ever.

INFERENCES.

From this subject we learn,—1. The safety of the Lord's people in a day of trouble, and in the midst of their enemies. 2. That Christ's willing subjects may rejoice in the inheritance which he hath promised. 3. The duty of all to submit to this king, and the danger of disobedience.—Ps. ii. 12. 4. That Christ's kingdom is spiritual, and perfectly distinct from the kingdoms of the world. 5. The comfort which arises from the consideration that the kingdom of Christ is an extensive kingdom. All are called to receive and obey him as their king. 6. The happiness of this kingdom ; it shall endure for ever. 7. The necessity of obeying Christ, and of being spiritual as he is. 8. The danger of rejecting him from reigning over us. 9. The great comfort which arises from the wisdom of Christ in the administration of his kingdom. 10. The certainty of his having a Church on earth in all ages. 11. The happiness of being ruled by Christ. 12. The certainty of happiness in being under his protection. 13. The certain conquest which the believer shall obtain over all enemies. 14. The honour of following the Lamb whithersoever he goeth, although it be through great tribulation. 15. That they who fight against Christ, and persist in their enmity against him shall be destroyed, and that without remedy.

DIV. 2. — THE STATES IN WHICH THE REDEEMER EXECUTED HIS THREEFOLD OFFICE.

Of Christ's State of Humiliation.

Q. 27.—*Wherein did Christ's Humiliation consist?*

Christ's humiliation consisted in his being born, and that in a low condition; made under the law, undergoing the miseries of this life, the wrath of God, and the cursed death of the cross; in being buried, and continuing under the power of death for a time.

ANALYSIS AND PROOFS.

We are here taught,—

1. That Christ, in becoming man, humbled himself by being born, and that in a low condition. Luke i. 35.—" That holy thing which shall be born of thee shall be called the Son of God." Luke ii. 7.—" And she brought forth her first-born son, and wrapped him in swaddling-clothes, and laid him in a manger." See Phil. ii. 6, 7.

2. That Christ humbled himself by submitting to be made under the law. Gal. iv. 4.—" God sent forth his Son, made of a woman, made under the law."

3. That Christ humbled himself by enduring the miseries of this life. Isa. liii. 3.—" He is despised and rejected of men; a man of sorrows and acquainted with grief."

4. That Christ humbled himself by enduring the wrath of God in our stead. Matt. xxvii. 46.—" Jesus cried with a loud voice, saying, My God, my God, why hast thou forsaken me?" See also Luke xxii. 44.

5. That Christ humbled himself by submitting to the cursed death of the cross. Phil. ii. 8.—" He humbled himself, and became obedient unto death, even the death of the cross."

6. That Christ humbled himself by submitting to be buried, and by remaining in the grave for a time. 1 Cor. xv. 4.—" He was buried, and rose again the third day." See also Matt. xii. 40.

EXPLANATION.

Obs. 115.—*Jesus Christ humbled himself.*

By the *humiliation* of Christ, we are in general to understand his condescending to leave the bosom of his Father, and his being made for a season a little lower than the angels, for the suffering of death.—Phil. ii. 8.

Christ's merely possessing manhood was no part of his humiliation. This, indeed, showed infinite condescension in him who is the Creator of man; but, properly speaking, it was no part of his humiliation; for he still retains his manhood in a glorified state, and will for ever retain it.

The *cause* of Christ's humiliation was, the unmerited *love* of God the Father, and his own *love* to self-destroying sinners. See 1 John iv. 9, 10.

The steps of Christ's humiliation were these:—His being born, and that in a low condition; his being made under the law; his undergoing all the miseries of this life; his enduring the wrath of God; his submitting to the cursed death of the cross; and his being buried, and continuing under the power of death for a time.

Obs. 116.—*Jesus Christ humbled himself by being born, and that in a low condition.*

It was great condescension in the Lord Jesus Christ to be *born* at all; but it was still greater condescension in him to be born *in a low condition*. He was, indeed, of the race and lineage of David, whose family was the most illustrious in the world; but he was born of a virgin of that family, who was then in very low circumstances; he was born in Bethlehem, an obscure village; he was born in a stable, and laid in a manger. See Luke i. and ii.

Obs. 117.—*Jesus Christ humbled himself by being made under the law.*

Although Christ may be said to have been made under the ceremonial and political laws of the Jews, inasmuch as he obeyed them (Luke ii. 21, &c.), yet, properly speaking, it was not any of these laws, but the *moral law* under which he was made, as our Surety. Nor was it under this law as a *rule of life*, but as a *covenant*, demanding perfect obedience as a condition of life, and full satisfaction on account of the violation of the law.—Gal. iv. 4, 5. Now, Christ's humiliation in being made under the law, appears in this, that he who was the Lawgiver, Lord, and Judge of heaven and earth, condescended to become subject to his own law, and for this very purpose, that he might deliver from its curse his people who transgressed it, and fulfil it in their stead.

Obs. 118.—*Jesus Christ humbled himself by undergoing all the miseries of this life.*

He was not only subject to the sinless infirmities of humanity, such as hunger, thirst, weariness, and grief, &c.; but he voluntarily submitted to all the sorrows and afflictions to which his people can be exposed in the present state of existence.—Heb. ii. 14, 18, iv. 15, and v. 2; Matt. viii. 20; Heb. xii. 3, &c.

Obs. 119.—*Jesus Christ humbled himself by enduring the wrath of God.*

The wrath of God and the hiding of his countenance were the greatest miseries that Christ underwent in this world. When in the garden of Gethsemane, the anticipation of this wrath made his soul exceeding sorrowful even unto death; at which time his sweat was like great drops of blood falling to the ground; and the pressure of this wrath upon him made him exclaim, in the agony of his soul, " My God, my God, why hast thou forsaken me?" And nothing but almighty power could inflict or sustain the stroke!

Obs. 120.—*Jesus Christ humbled himself by submitting to the cursed death of the cross.*

The *death of the cross* was a most painful and excruciating death, a lingering death, and a shameful and ignominious death. It was called a *cursed death*, because God had said, " Cursed is every one that hangeth on a tree."—Gal. iii. 13. Jesus, however, endured the cross, despising the shame. The exquisite agony of his sufferings is pointed out to us in various ways. See Ps. xxii. throughout.

Obs. 121.—*Jesus Christ humbled himself by being buried, and by continuing under the power of death for a time.*

Christ was *buried*, and remained in the grave *for three days and three nights*, to show that he was really dead; seeing it is on his death that the hopes and happiness of his people depend. inasmuch as by it transgression was finished, an end put to sin, reconciliation made for iniquity, and an everlasting righteousness introduced. He was buried also, that he might overcome death in its darkest and strongest hold, even in the gloomy recesses of the tomb; and to sanctify the grave to all his friends and followers, that it may be to them a place of repose, where their bodies may rest until the resurrection.

INFERENCES.

From this subject we learn,—1. The amazing grace and condescension of Christ in becoming man to die for sinners. 2. That through much tribulation we must enter into the kingdom of God. —John xvi. 33; 2 Tim. iii. 12. 3. That the law is now magnified; that the justice of God is satisfied; and that he is now pacified towards us, notwithstanding all that we have done. 4. That Christ hath redeemed us from the curse of the law, by being made a curse for us. 5. The misery of all those who are without an interest in Christ, and who have in their own persons to answer to God for the debt which they have contracted, both with respect to obedience and suffering. 6. The happiness of believers. who have Christ as their surety, who has discharged all their debt, and who has freely forgiven all. 7. That Christ's descent into the gloomy mansions of the dead hath, as it were, perfumed this dreary abode; so that the saint may view it no longer loathsome, but as a place of sweet repose, until the sound of the archangel and of the trump of God.

Of Christ's State of Exaltation.

Q. 28.—Wherein consisteth Christ's Exaltation? Christ's exaltation consisteth in his rising again from the dead on the third day, in ascending up into heaven, in sitting at the right hand of God the Father and in coming to judge the world at the last day.

ANALYSIS AND PROOFS.

We are here taught,—
1. That Christ was exalted by rising from the dead on the third day. 1 Cor. xv. 4.—" He rose again the third day according to the Scriptures."
2. That Christ was exalted by ascending up into heaven. Luke xxiv. 51.—" While he blessed them, he was parted from them, and carried up into heaven." See also Mark xvi. 19.
3. That Christ is now exalted by his sitting at the right hand of God. Eph. i. 20.—" He set him at his own right hand in the heavenly places." See also Col. iii. 1.
4. That Christ will be exalted by his coming to judge the world at the last day. Acts xvii. 31.—" He hath appointed a day, in which he will judge the world in righteousness, by that man whom he hath ordained; whereof he hath given assurance unto all men, in that he hath raised him from the dead."

EXPLANATION.

Obs. 122.—*Jesus Christ was exalted in consequence of his humiliation.*

Christ took upon himself the form of a servant, and became obedient unto death, even the death of the cross, not that he might be kept in this humble condition, but that he might be raised up again, and exalted to the most inconceivable glory. Phil. ii. 8, 9.—" He humbled himself, and became obedient unto death, even the death of the cross. *Wherefore* God also hath highly exalted him, and given him a name above every name."

Christ's exaltation respects his manhood or his *human nature* alone; for, as God, he cannot be exalted. Nor can any addition be made to his glory, as he is God; for as such, he was, is, and shall continue to be the same, without any variableness or shadow of turning.

The steps of Christ's exaltation are these :—His resurrection from the dead on the third day; his ascension into heaven; his session at the right hand of God the Father; and his coming to judge the world at the last day. From each of these much may be learned, connected with the salvation of sinners and the glory of Christ himself.

Obs. 123.—*Jesus Christ was exalted by his resurrection from the dead on the third day.*

This is a special article of the faith of believers; and on this in a great measure, rests the Gospel Church.

It may here be remarked, that the divine and human natures of Christ were not separated at death, for they are inseparable. By death, his soul and body were actually separated (see Luke xxiii. 46); but all the time that he lay in the grave, his two natures were most closely united; and when he rose from the dead, he only resumed that life which he had voluntarily laid down for his people.

The resurrection of Christ is abundantly evident from Scripture.

1. It was foretold in ancient prophecy. See Ps. xvi. 10; Job xix. 25, &c.

2. It was typified in various ways. Joseph's deliverance from prison may be considered as typical of Christ's resurrection from the grave, which is called a "taking from prison."—Isa. liii. 8. Abraham's receiving Isaac from the dead in a figure, may also be typical of Christ's resurrection. And Jonah's coming out of the whale's belly is an eminent type of this truth.

3. We have the most direct proofs that it actually took place, and that the very same Jesus who had been crucified, arose from the dead. See Matt. xxviii., Mark xvi., Luke xxiv., John xx.

4. Christ himself, after his resurrection, appeared to many at different times, and by many infallible proofs; and in 1 Cor. xv., we are told that he appeared to five hundred at once.

5. We have strong proof of this truth in the conduct of Christ's disciples after his resurrection; for nothing could prevent them from publishing what they had seen, and what they had full authority to make known.

6. If the descent of the Holy Spirit on the day of Pentecost, according to Christ's promise, be considered as a proof of his ascension, it must also be deemed a proof of his resurrection.

In the resurrection of Christ, all the divine persons in the Godhead concurred. See Acts ii. 24; John ii. 19, &c.; 1 Pet. iii. 18.

It was the same body that was laid in Joseph's tomb, which arose again with all the properties which it formerly possessed. See Luke xxiv. 39.

The time of Christ's resurrection was *the third day* after his burial; and it was very early in the morning of that day, to show, perhaps, that he is "the bright and morning star," "the day-spring from on high," and "the sun of righteousness," who arises on his people with healing in his rays.

At the resurrection of Christ there was an earthquake: an angel shook the place; and majesty appeared all around. This intimated that all was now done which Christ had engaged to do; and that nothing more was necessary on his part, than to take possession of the joy which was set before him.

Obs. 124.—*Jesus Christ was exalted by his ascension to heaven.*

This is another grand article of the Christian faith. That Christ ascended to heaven is evident from Scripture.

1. It was foretold in prophecy. See Ps. xxiv. 7–10, and xlvii. 5, and lxviii. 18.

2. There were very striking types of it. Enoch was translated to heaven, soul and body, without tasting death; which was, under the patriarchal dispensation, evidently typical of Christ's ascension. Elijah, under the law, was also translated in a glorious manner; which typified the same. And when the priests of old carried the blood and incense into the most holy place, it prefigured the ascension of Christ to his Father's right hand, when he appeared in the most holy place not made with hands, where he presents the infinite value of his atoning blood as a propitiation for sin.

3. We have many evidences that he really ascended. See Luke xxiv. 50, 51; Acts i. 9–11, and vii. 55, and ix. 3–5; Rev. i. 10–18. See also John xvi. 7.

It was necessary that Christ should ascend, for the following reasons:—

1. That he might send the Holy Spirit to his disciples, to lead them into all truth, and to bring all things to their remembrance.

2. That he might carry on the work of redemption, in making continual intercession for his people.

3. That he might, in his people's name, take possession of the blessings which he had obtained for them.

After his resurrection, Christ remained on earth forty days, in order that he might give his disciples every possible proof of his resurrection, and that he might instruct them in things pertaining to the kingdom of God. And at the end of the forty days he ascended from Mount Olivet,—the place where he began his sufferings, where he was sore amazed, and where his soul was exceeding sorrowful; thus testifying to his disciples, that his sufferings were now ended, and that the same place may be to a gracious soul both the scene of sorrow and the scene of joy.

Christ was not unmindful of his disciples at his ascension, for he was parted from them while he was blessing them; and thus he was engaged in the work of redemption until his last moments upon earth.

Christ's attendants on this occasion were myriads of angels, who conducted the Lord of Glory to heaven with solemn shouts of praise. See Ps. xxiv. 7–10.

Obs. 125.—*Jesus Christ is now exalted by sitting down at the right hand of God the Father.*

The expression, *the right hand of God*, is not to be understood literally, but figuratively; for God, being a Spirit, has no bodily parts. It denotes the highest honour, power, and authority; to which Christ is now exalted, in consequence of his having humbled himself.—Phil. ii. 8, 9.

Christ's *sitting* at the right hand of God implies a state of rest, and continuance in that state. The days of sorrow which he had on earth shall never return. His crown shall flourish on his head, and his kingdom shall stand firm and be established.

When it is said that Christ *sitteth at the right hand of God*, it denotes,—

1. The accomplishment of the work of redemption; for until this was finished, he was not to return to that glory which he had with the Father before the world began.—Heb. iv. 10.

2. The great delight and satisfaction which the Father hath in Christ, on account of the glorious work which he had finished.—Ps. cx. 1.

3. The inconceivable glory and honour to which he, as God-man, is now exalted in heaven.—Heb. i. 13.

4. His being invested with sovereign dominion and supreme authority and power.—Phil. ii. 9, 10; Heb. ii. 7, 8.

The *ends* for which our Redeemer is set down on the right hand of God are these:—

1. That, as a powerful king, he may protect and defend his Church and people against all their enemies, both temporal and spiritual.—Isa. xxxii. 1, 2; Deut. xxxiii. 26, 27.

2. That he may subdue all the enemies of his kingdom and people; such as the devil, the world, and the flesh, and sin, and hell.—Ps. cx.; Acts ii. 36; Heb. x. 12, 13; 1 Cor. xv. 25.

3. That he may bestow on all his faithful subjects all those gifts which he hath purchased, and which are the necessary means of their salvation.—Acts v. 31.

4. That he may act the part of a powerful intercessor in their behalf.—Rom. viii. 34.

5. That all his friends and followers may, with himself, be advanced to the glorious state of heaven.—Eph. i. 4–6; Rev. iii. 21.

Obs. 126.—*Jesus Christ will be exalted by his coming to judge the world at the last day.*

This will be a more public and a more solemn manifestation of his glory with respect to us, than any of the other parts of his exaltation; and it will strike the world of mankind with greater solemnity, inasmuch as all, without exception, shall witness it, and inasmuch as all shall be interested in it.

That there will be a *day of judgment*, is evident from the following things:—

1. It is evident from Scripture that there will be such a day. See Job xxi. 30; Ps. xcvi. 13, and xcviii. 9; Prov. xxiv. 12; Eccl. xi. 9, and xii. 14; Matt. xii. 36, xiii. 40–43, 49, 50, xvi. 27, xxv. 31–46, and xxvi. 64; Acts xvii. 31, and xxiv. 25; Rom. ii. 3, 5–11, 16; 2 Cor. v. 10, 11; 1 Thess. iv. 16, 17; Heb. vi. 1, 2, ix. 27, 28, and x. 27, 31; 1 Pet. iv. 5, 7. 17, 18; 2 Pet. ii. 4. 9· Jude 6, 14, 15; Rev. i. 7, and xx. 11, 12, 15.

2. The providences of God require such a day, that they may appear to have been equal and just in the view of those who deemed them unequal and unjust; and that the ways of God to man may be fully justified.

3. Jesus Christ requires such a day, for the glory of his name and of his government.

4. The righteous require such a day, that it may appear to all, that although they were deemed the offscouring of all things, they were beloved by God.

5. The wicked require such a day, that they may receive according to their wickedness, and that vengeance may be inflicted upon them to the uttermost; and likewise, that they may be convinced that there is a reality in those things which they despised and ridiculed.

6. There must be such a day, because to judge the world is a part of Christ's exaltation; and likewise, because he must receive from all an account of what they have done in his absence.

With respect to the person of the Judge: the Three-one God, Father, Son, and Holy Ghost, is Judge, in respect of judicial power, authority, and consent; but Christ, as Mediator, is appointed Judge of all, in respect of visible management and execution.—Acts xvii. 31; John v. 22; Acts x. 42.

The *universality* of the judgment is evident from Scripture. Angels and all mankind shall appear before God.—Jude 6; 2 Cor. v. 10; Rev. xx. 12.

Those things respecting which all shall at last be judged, are, in general, all the deeds done in the body. But it may be remarked, that in the presence of an assembled world, the thoughts, the words, and the actions of all mankind, shall be brought into view.—2 Cor. v. 10; Eccl. xii. 14; Jude 15; Matt. xii. 36, 37.

If it be here asked, why *works* shall be produced at last, and what place they shall have in respect of the punishment of the wicked and the reward of the righteous, we answer,—

1. The *good works* of the righteous (mentioned in Matt. xxv.) shall be produced, not as the *ground* or *reason* of their sentence, but only as *evidences* of their union with Christ, and of their right and title to heaven through him. See John xv. 8, 14. The sentence passed on the righteous, is on the ground of *free grace* alone, reigning through the imputed righteousness of Christ, unto everlasting life; and it will be pronounced upon them *according to* their works, as flowing from faith in Christ, or from a renewed and sanctified heart, but not *for* their works, or even *for* faith itself, as if eternal life were merited by them. The righteous are called upon to inherit the kingdom prepared for them; but they do not procure it as servants do their wages.

2. The works of the ungodly, on the other hand, are produced, not only as *evidences* of their state, but as the proper *cause* and *ground* of their condemnation. Good works merit not salvation.

but evil works merit condemnation; for "death is the *wages* of sin; but eternal life is the *gift* of God through Jesus Christ our Lord."—Rom. vi. 23.

On the day of final judgment, a twofold sentence shall be pronounced by Christ the Judge,—one in favour of the righteous, "Come, ye blessed of my Father, inherit the kingdom prepared for you from the foundation of the world;" and the other against the wicked, "Depart from me, ye cursed, into everlasting fire. prepared for the devil and his angels."—Matt. xxv. 34, 41.

INFERENCES.

From this subject we learn,—1. The necessity of setting our affections on things above, where Christ sits at the right hand of God. 2. The necessity of suffering patiently for his sake. 3. That Christ's exaltation is a pledge of the believer's exaltation, and of his being admitted into the presence of God. 4. That God is well pleased with the work of Christ on earth. 5. That believers have no cause to fear any real evil from their enemies; seeing the Lord Christ reigneth in Zion. 6. That the Church of Christ shall prosper in the world. 7. The danger of scoffing at the thoughts of the general judgment. 8. The necessity of meditating on the world to come. 9. The necessity of improving the day of our merciful visitation. 10. That we must all appear before the judgment-seat of Christ. 11. That the last judgment shall glorify the perfections of Jehovah before the world. 12. The happiness of the righteous and the misery of the wicked. 13. The necessity of holiness. 14. That Christ will appear exceedingly glorious in the eyes of all those by whom he has been despised, as well as of those who have believed on him.

DIV. 3.—OF THE APPLICATION OF REDEMPTION.

Of the Agent by whom Redemption is applied.

Q. 29.—How are we made Partakers of the Redemption purchased by Christ?

We are made partakers of the redemption purchased by Christ, by the effectual application of it to us by his Holy Spirit.

ANALYSIS AND PROOFS.

We are here taught,—

1. That redemption has been purchased by Christ for his people. Heb. ix. 12.—"By his own blood he entered once into the holy place, having obtained eternal redemption for us." See also Eph. i. 7.

2. That redemption must be applied to believers. John i. 12. —"As many as received him, to them gave he power to become the sons of God, even to them that believe on his name."

3. That redemption is effectually applied to believers by the Holy Spirit. Tit. iii. 5.—" He saved us by the washing of regeneration, and the renewing of the Holy Ghost." See also Ezek. xxxvi. 27.

EXPLANATION.

Obs. 127.—*Redemption has been purchased by Christ for his people.*

Redemption is deliverance by payment of a price. The redemption purchased by Christ consists of two things: 1. Deliverance from all evil,—from sin, the greatest evil, and from eternal wrath.—Matt. i. 21 ; Rom. vi. 6, 7; 1 Thess. i. 10. 2. Restoration to all good, or the possession of all the happiness and blessings which man forfeited by the fall, which may be all summed up in eternal life, begun in this world and perfected in glory.

The *purchaser* of this redemption was *Jesus Christ,* the Lord from heaven. It was he alone that assumed our nature ; he alone that could redeem our mortgaged inheritance ; and he alone that could bruise the head of the old serpent—the devil, and give him a deadly wound, which could never be healed.

The *ransom* which Christ paid as the price of redemption, was *himself*. In the ransom is included all that he did and suffered for sinners. Although it is true that Christ our Redeemer exerted an almighty power, and delivered the lawful captives, yet it is also true that he paid a ransom for his people,—and this ransom was *himself*, his *life*, his *blood*.—1 Tim. ii. 6 ; Mark x. 45 ; 1 Pet. i. 18.

They who are interested in this ransom, are all that have been or shall be united to Christ by the effectual working of his Holy Spirit ; believers in every age and nation, to whom God hath given and shall give power to become his sons.—John i. 12.

Obs. 128.—*Redemption must be applied to believers.*

To *apply redemption* to sinners, is to interest them in it, to invest them in the possession of it, to make it theirs in all its effects and consequences, and to all the purposes for which it was purchased, both for present peace and comfort, and for future glory.

This application is so *necessary*, that none can have any saving benefit by it until it be applied.—John i. 12. Before this application, the elect are in a state of wrath, their sins are unpardoned, and they have no actual right to the heavenly inheritance. As a remedy cannot recover any one unless it be applied, so men must die eternally, unless the redemption of Christ be applied to them in particular for their recovery from the effects of the fall.

Obs. 129.—*Redemption is effectually applied to believers by the Holy Spirit.*

The *applier* of the redemption purchased by Christ is the *Holy Spirit*. Tit. iii. 5; John vi. 63.—" It is the Spirit that quickeneth." Neither the Father's gift of Christ, nor the Son's dying in our stead, will bring us back to the favour and image of God, if the work of the Spirit be wanting; and it is as impossible for the sinner to apply it to himself, as it is for him to pay to God a ransom for his soul.

This part of the work of the Spirit was typified in a very striking manner, under the law, by the sprinkling of the blood of the sacrifice upon the people. See Exod. xxiv. 8.

In this work, the Spirit is called the *Holy Spirit*, to show, that as he is essentially holy, so all his operations are also holy; and that his work is designed for holy purposes,—viz., the renewing of the whole man, and the rendering of it conformed to the image of God, and meet for the enjoyment of him.

He is here called *Christ's* Holy Spirit, because, although he is also the Spirit of the Father, yet, in applying redemption, he is sent more immediately by Christ. See John xiv. 16, and xvi. 7.

The application is here said to be *effectual*, to show, that there is an application of it which is *not effectual*,—that is, an outward application of it in the ordinances of Christ's appointment, which is not of itself effectual. This is evident from the case of Simon Magus, who was baptized, but to whom the redemption by Christ was not effectually applied; for he was still " in the gall of bitterness and in the bond of iniquity."—Acts viii. 23.

The persons to whom the Spirit applies Christ's redemption, are those, and those alone, for whom it was purchased. The application of redemption is as extensive as the purchase of it, but not more so.—Eph. i. 13.

The *means* which the Spirit makes use of in the application of redemption are, the reading and hearing of the Word; but the preaching of the Word is more generally the effectual means of working upon the heart of the sinner. Hence see 1 Cor. iii. 5.

INFERENCES.

From this subject we learn,—1. The necessity of the redemption purchased by Christ. 2. The happiness of all those who are interested in this redemption; and the misery of all those who have no interest in it. 3. The duty of self-examination, that we may know whether Christ be our Redeemer—whether we are brought out of slavery or bondage into the glorious liberty of the children of God. 4. The necessity of the work of the Spirit on the soul. 5. The happiness of all who have the Spirit of Christ. 6. The danger of all who reject the Holy Spirit of promise, by whom the soul is sealed to the day of redemption.

Of the Means used for the Application of Redemption in Effectual Calling.

Q. 80.—How doth the Spirit apply to us the Redemption purchased by Christ? The Spirit applieth to us the redemption purchased by Christ, by working faith in us, and thereby uniting us to Christ in our effectual calling.

ANALYSIS AND PROOFS.

We are here taught,—
1. That in applying redemption to the people of God, the Spirit worketh faith in them. Eph. ii. 8.—"By grace are ye saved through faith; and that not of yourselves: it is the gift of God."
2. That by faith believers are united to Christ. Eph. iii. 17. —"That Christ may dwell in your hearts by faith."
3. That believers are united to Christ in their effectual calling. 1 Cor. i. 9.—"God is faithful, by whom ye were called unto the fellowship of his Son Jesus Christ, our Lord."

EXPLANATION.

Obs. 130.—*In applying redemption to sinners, the Spirit worketh faith in them.*

When the Spirit applies redemption to those sinners for whom it was purchased by Christ, he works *faith* in them. Hence he is called *the Spirit of faith.*—2 Cor. iv. 13. He alone is the efficient cause of faith in the soul. It requires the same power to work faith in the soul, that was wrought in Christ when he was raised from the dead. See Eph. i. 19, &c.

The way in which the Spirit works faith is this:—He first comes in the Word, and enters into the heart of the elect sinner dead in sin; and when he has thus entered, he quickens it by working faith in it. By this faith the soul apprehends Christ, and actually unites with him. Being quickened and actuated, it acts in believing. Hence there is a twofold reception of Christ. 1. A *passive* reception of him, in which Christ comes by his Spirit into the soul dead in sin, and quickens it, and joins himself to it. 2. An *active* reception of him, when the soul, having faith wrought in it, actually believes and receives Christ, embraces him, and joins itself to him.

Obs. 131.—*By faith the believer is united to Christ.*

That there is such a thing as *union with Jesus Christ*, will be evident from the following things:—
1. From the use of many expressions in Scripture to point it out. Christ is said *to be in believers*, and believers are said *to be in Jesus Christ;* which, as it were, completes the union; for if Christ be in his people, and they in him, then must this be a

truth.—Col. i. 27; 1 Cor. i. 30. Christ is also said to dwell in *his people*, and they are said to *dwell in him.*—John vi. 56. They are also said to *abide* in one another; which denotes a settled rest,—John xv.; and his people are said to be *one spirit* with him, and to *put on* Christ.—1 Cor. vi. 17; Gal. iii. 27.

2. From the use of many similitudes, in order that we may be able to form some idea of its glory. Various unions are exhibited in Scripture to illustrate it; some of which far surpass the union between Christ and believers, and others are far surpassed by it. This union is compared to the *marriage union* between husband and wife; to the union which exists between the *foundation* and *superstructure;* to the union between the *root* of a tree and its *branches;* to the union between the *head* and the *members;* to the union of our *food* with our *body*, and hence Christ is called our *life;* and to the union between the *persons of the Godhead,*—all which shows, that the union between Christ and believers is more than a *relative union*, or a union which takes place in this world in the various circumstances of life.

3. From our union with the first Adam. When he fell from his state of innocence, all his posterity fell with him, because they were federally one with him. In like manner, when Jesus fulfilled all righteousness, it was in the room of his people; so that they must be federally one with him as their head and husband.

With respect to the bond of this union:—1. On the believer's part, it is *faith*, which is wrought in him, not by any power of his own, but by the powerful operation of the Spirit of God. 2. On the part of Christ, it is the word of the Father pledged, that faith shall be wrought in the souls of his people; and the Spirit pledged also, that they may not depart from Christ.

Obs. 132.—*Believers are united to Christ in effectual calling.*

The union between Christ and believers is formed in the day of *effectual calling,*—termed a *calling*, because the work of the Spirit supposes all to be at a distance from God, as they certainly are while in a natural state, or while not united to Christ; and an *effectual* calling, because the work of the Spirit actually unites the soul to Christ.

Obs. 133.—*The union between Christ and believers is a real a mysterious, an intimate, a spiritual, and an eternal union.*

1. The union between Christ and believers is a *real* union. It is much more than a relative union, or such a union as takes place in several relations in life; although it is compared to some of these. See Eph. v. 30; John xiv. 20; 1 John v. 12; Heb. iii. 14.

2. The union between Christ and believers is a *mysterious* union. See Eph. v. 32. and Col. i. 27; where a higher name is given to it. See also 2 Cor. vi. 16; Gal. ii. 20 1 John iv. 16. Gal. iii. 27; John vi. 56.

3. The union between Christ and believers is a most *intimate* union. See John xvii. 21.

4. The union between Christ and believers is a *spiritual* union.—1 Cor. vi. 17; Rom. viii. 9. This is evident from its consequences; for no sooner does it take place, than the soul is engaged in spiritual exercises.

5. The union between Christ and believers is an *indissoluble* or an *eternal* union. See Eph. iv. 13: John x. 28, 29; Rom. viii. 35, &c.; Isa. liv. 10.

INFERENCES.

From this subject we learn,—1. The duty of believers,—viz., to give evidence, by their conduct in the world, that they are in Christ. 2. That sinners ought to seek after such a happy relation while it may be found, and while, in the offer of the gospel, Christ is ready to come in, and to take up his abode in the soul for ever. 3. The absolute necessity of faith in forming this mysterious union. 4. That there is no happiness to be compared with that of being in Christ. 5. That if we are in Christ, God the Father is well pleased with us. 6. That believers have an inexhaustible source of every comfort, to which they may repair in every time of need. 7. That as all believers are joined to the Lord by one spirit, they ought to live together in the bonds of brotherly love. 8. That believers shall not fall finally.

Of the Manner and Order of the Application of Redemption in Effectual Calling.

Q. 31.—𝔚hat is 𝔈ffectual 𝔈alling?

Effectual calling is the work of God's Spirit, whereby, convincing us of our sin and misery, enlightening our minds in the knowledge of Christ, and renewing our wills, he doth persuade and enable us to embrace Jesus Christ, freely offered to us in the gospel.

ANALYSIS AND PROOFS.

We are here taught,—

1. That effectual calling is the work of the Holy Spirit. John xvi. 14.—" He shall receive of mine, and shall show it unto you." See also 2 Tim. i. 9.

2. That in effectual calling the Spirit convinces of sin. John xvi. 8.—" He will reprove (or convince) the world of sin."

3. That in effectual calling the Spirit convinces of misery. Acts xvi. 29, 30.—" He came trembling, and fell down before Paul and Silas,—and said, Sirs, what must I do to be saved?" See also Rom. vii. 10, and Acts ii. 37.

4. That in effectual calling the mind is enlightened in the knowledge of Christ. 1 Pet. ii. 9.—" Who hath called you out

of darkness into his marvellous light." See also Eph. i. 18, and Phil. iii. 8.

5. That in effectual calling the will is renewed. Ezek. xxxvi 26.—" A new heart also will I give you, and a new spirit will I put within you."

6. That in effectual calling we are persuaded to embrace Jesus Christ. John vi. 44.—" No man can come to me, except the Father, who hath sent me, draw him." See also Heb. xi. 13.

7. That in effectual calling we are enabled to embrace Jesus Christ. Phil. ii. 13.—" It is God which worketh in you both to will and to do of his good pleasure." See also Ezek. xxxvi. 27.

8. That Jesus Christ is freely offered to all men in the gospel. Rev. xxii. 17.—" Whosoever will, let him take the water of life freely." See also Isa. lv. 1.

EXPLANATION.

Obs. 134.—*Effectual calling is the work of the Spirit of God.* The call of the gospel is twofold.

1. There is the *external* or *outward* call of the Word; by which we are to understand the free and unlimited offer of Christ in the gospel to all the hearers of it, without money and without price. —Isa. lv. 1. This call, however fervent and importunate it may be, and however much designed for the salvation of those to whom it is directed, is rejected by the greater part of the hearers of the gospel.

2. There is the *internal*, or inward and *effectual* call; by which we are to understand the Holy Spirit's accompanying the external call with power and efficacy on the soul, for its everlasting salvation.—John v. 25.

Should it be here objected, that it is inconsistent to call all to embrace Christ, when they *cannot*, and when they *shall never be enabled* to believe in and embrace him; we answer, that as there is an unlimited offer made of Christ in the gospel to all men, whatever their character and state may be, so it is the duty of ministers of the gospel, who are altogether ignorant of the purposes of God, to invite all who hear them to come to him. It is true, indeed, that none are able of themselves to embrace Christ or believe in him; but it is equally true, and much worse, that they *will not* believe in him. See John v. 40.

The work of the Spirit is termed a *calling*, because all are supposed to be naturally far from God and from righteousness. to be at a distance from him who is the portion of the soul; and because it requires the voice of the Son of God, speaking in the Scriptures, to bring sinners to embrace him as he is offered in the gospel.

Effectual calling is termed a *work*, because it is not perfected or completed at once, but performed by various operations or workings of the Spirit of God on the soul. —Eph. i. 17, &c., Acts ii. 37, 38.

That the work of the Spirit in effectual calling is absolutely *necessary*, is evident from the condition of sinners by nature. If by nature they are dead, they cannot put life into themselves; if they are asleep in their sins, they must be awaked; if they are afar off, they must be brought nigh; if they are stout-hearted, their hearts must be softened; if they are in their sins, they must be convinced of sin; if their understandings are darkened, they must be enlightened; if their wills are perverted, they must be renewed; if they are unwilling to embrace Christ, they must be made willing; if they are unable to do it, they must be enabled.

Obs. 135.—*In effectual calling the Spirit convinces of sin and misery.*

This he does when he gives a clear sight and full persuasion of the guilt of sin, both original and actual; and when he gives a feeling apprehension of the dreadful wrath of God, and the endless miseries of hell, which the sinner has deserved on account of sin, and to which it exposes him. This wounds the conscience, and fills the sinner with anxiety respecting his salvation.—John xvi. 8; Acts ii. 37, and xvi. 27.

The *means* which the Spirit makes use of to convince of sin and misery, is the Word of God, and particularly the *law;* for " by the law is the knowledge of sin."—Rom. iii. 20. When the sinner views the holy commandments of the law, he is convinced of the evil nature of sin; and when he contemplates the threatenings of the law, he sees the guilt of sin and what it deserves.—Rom. vii. 7; Gal. iii. 10.

It may here be remarked, that conviction is not alike in all. But it is absolutely necessary that every sinner be convinced of the sin of his nature, and of the sins of his heart and life, and also of his absolute need of Christ and his salvation. It must, however, be remembered, that this measure of conviction is necessary, not as a *condition* of our welcome to Christ, nor as a *qualification* fitting us to believe in him, but only as a *motive* to excite us to make use of our privilege of free access to him.—Hos. xiv. 1.

Obs. 136.—*In effectual calling the Spirit enlightens the mind in the knowledge of Christ.*

After convincing of sin and misery, the Spirit *enlightens the mind* or the understanding *in the knowledge of Christ*,—that is, the knowledge of his *person ;* of his *offices*, as Mediator between God and man; of his *righteousness*, as surety of the covenant; of the *fulness, sufficiency, efficacy*, and *suitableness* of his atonement; in a word, of his *ability* and *willingness to save* to the uttermost. Hence the author of this divine and saving illumination is called, " the Spirit of wisdom and revelation in the knowledge of Christ."—Eph. i. 17.

The *means* by which the Spirit enlightens the mind in the knowledge of Christ, is the *gospel*, of which Christ is the great subject.—Acts xxvi. 17, 18; Rom. x. 14, 17.

Obs. 137.—*In effectual calling the Spirit renews the will.*

This part of the work of the Spirit consists in the implantation of a new propensity or inclination to good, and a fixed aversion to what is sinful and hateful in the sight of God. Divine illumination and a renewed will accompany each other; for no sooner does the Lord send the rod of his strength out of Zion, than a willing people is made in the day of almighty power.— Ps. cx. 2, 3.

The way in which the Spirit effects this work upon the soul cannot be discovered; for, saith our Lord, "The wind bloweth where it listeth, and thou hearest the sound thereof, but canst not tell whence it cometh and whither it goeth; so is every one that is born of the Spirit."—John iii. 8. But we may rest assured, that the effect is produced in a way consistent with the rational nature. No compulsion—no violence upon the will is used, that it may be renewed; for a *willing* people is made in the day of power, when Jehovah's great strength is sent out of Zion.

Obs. 138.—*In effectual calling, the Spirit persuades and enables us to embrace Jesus Christ freely offered in the gospel.*

This is the happy effect of the work of the Spirit on the understanding and the will.

To *embrace* Jesus Christ, is to clasp him in the arms of our faith as really as Simeon did in his arms, and with as much pleasure and delight,—as the portion of the soul for ever, and the author of every spiritual and saving blessing.

It is in the promises of *the gospel* that faith embraces Christ. There he, with all the benefits of his redemption, necessary both for present comfort and future glory, are offered without money and without price; which surely ought to be an encouragement to sinners to lay hold on and embrace him.—John iii. 16; Isa. xlv. 22; Rev. xxii. 27; John vii. 37.

The gospel offer is tendered to all as sinners of Adam's race: for, were not this the case, the gospel could not properly be called "good news, or glad tidings of great joy, to all men."— Luke ii. 10, 11.

The *faith* of the gospel offer is a *belief* that Jesus Christ, with his righteousness and all his salvation, is offered by himself to sinners, and to each in particular.—Prov. viii. 4; John vii. 37.

There is no qualification required of us to fit us for having a right to the offer of salvation by Christ in the gospel, because none is necessary. All are invited to come just as they are, with all their sins; and although Christ saith, "Come unto me, all ye that *labour* and are *heavy laden*, and I will give you rest;" it only implies that they alone who are in this situation come to him. Others will not accept of him in the offer, not because they have no need of him, but because they know it not, concluding that all is well with them.

But although Christ is freely offered to all in the gospel, yet none have any *natural inclination* to embrace him as therein offered. The Spirit of the Lord must *persuade* the sinner to embrace Christ; and this he does, on the one hand, when he shows him that he is for ever undone, if he do not comply; and, on the other, when he shows him that Christ is able and willing to save him, and also that he will be perfectly happy upon his compliance.

Again, if man has no natural inclination, he surely can have *no ability* or power to believe in Christ to the salvation of the soul. The Spirit is absolutely necessary to *enable* him to embrace Christ.—Eph. i. 19, 20; John vi. 44. The Spirit is called (2 Cor. iv. 13), "the Spirit of faith;" but there would be no need of the Spirit, as a Spirit of faith, if the sinner could believe of himself.—Eph. ii. 8; Phil. i. 29. The whole work of salvation, from its commencement to its consummation, must be considered as the work of God; and this, in order that Christ may have all the glory.

Should it be here asked, if man in his natural state can do nothing good, we answer, that he can do nothing *spiritually good;* but he may both will and do many things *materially good*. He may read and hear the Word; he may pray and meditate on the Scriptures; and he may also reform his outward conduct; but he may do all this without any experience of the almighty power of God upon the soul, causing him to will and to do his good pleasure, in a spiritual and an acceptable manner.

If man of himself could do any thing spiritually good, these things would follow:—1. That the saints would not so often dishonour God, as the best of them too often do. 2. That there would be no necessity for the Spirit of God, if man had a holy will of his own. 3. That the number of those who savingly embrace Christ would be much greater than it is. 4. That the world would not be what it is—full of all manner of wickedness.

Obs. 139.—*As "the sin against the Holy Ghost" is, in a special manner, connected with his work in effectual calling, we shall give a very concise description of it.*

This sin is an open, malicious, and obstinate rejection of the Lord Jesus Christ, and of the way of salvation through him, or of the truth of the gospel;—a malicious blaspheming of the Holy Spirit, by which Christ spoke and acted, notwithstanding a conviction of the reality of these things by the operation of the Holy Spirit; and the whole done wilfully and with the utmost deliberation. Compare together Matt. xii. 31, &c.; Mark iii. 22 &c.; Heb. vi. 4. &c.. and x. 26. &c.

The character of such a forlorn sinner may be thus described in few words:—He is one who is obstinate against God, who obstinately and maliciously rejects the way of salvation through the Lord Jesus Christ and him crucified, who disdains the idea of deriving any hope or benefit from the death of the Son of God, and who blasphemes the Spirit of the Most High in his influences and operations; and all this, after he has been convinced of these truths, and in some measure felt the power of them.

The sin against the Holy Ghost is said to be *unpardonable*, not because there is any want of virtue or efficacy in the blood of Christ, for he is able to save to the uttermost all that come to God through him; but because the very nature of this sin excludes what is necessarily connected with salvation, namely, faith and repentance.—Luke xiii. 3. Without repentance there can be no faith; and without faith there can be no repentance.— Heb. x. 26, 27.

INFERENCES.

From this subject we learn,—1. The happiness of all those who are effectually called by the Holy Spirit. 2. The misery of all who have not the Spirit of God. 3. The vanity of concluding that we can save ourselves. 4. The danger of all who hear the gospel in vain. 5. The necessity of faith and of embracing Christ. 6. The happiness of all that have already embraced him. 7. That we are the persons to whom Christ is offered. 8. That none can persuade themselves to embrace Christ in the gospel offer. 9. The necessity of the Spirit to persuade and enable us to embrace him. 10. The necessity of becoming debtors to the free grace of God in Christ Jesus. 11. The necessity of the work of the Spirit in convincing us of sin and misery. 12. The necessity of considering well the nature of our convictions. 13. The danger of all who stifle the convictions which may have been wrought in them. 14. The necessity of being enlightened by the Spirit of God. 15. The necessity of the renovation of the will, without which there can be no acceptable obedience. 16. The necessity of believing in the Holy Spirit, of accepting him in all his influences and operations, and of continually depending upon him.

DIVISION 3.—OF THE BENEFITS OF REDEMPTION.

Benefits of Redemption in this Life.

Q. 32.—What benefits do they that are effectually called partake of in this life?

They that are effectually called do in this life partake of justification, adoption, and sanctification, and the several benefits which in this life do either accompany or flow from them.

ANALYSIS AND PROOFS.

We are here taught,—

1. That they who are effectually called partake of justification. Rom. viii. 30.—" Whom he called, them he also justified."

2. That they who are effectually called partake of adoption. Rom. viii. 15.—" Ye have received the spirit of adoption, whereby we cry, Abba, Father." See also 2 Cor. vi. 17, 18.

3. That they who are effectually called partake of sanctification. 1 Thess. iv. 7.—" God hath called us unto holiness." See also Heb. x. 10.

4. That they who are effectually called partake of all the benefits which in this life accompany or flow from justification, adoption, and sanctification. 1 Cor. iii. 22.—" All things are yours." See also 2 Pet. i. 3.

EXPLANATION.

Obs. 140.—*In this life, believers partake of justification, adoption, and sanctification, and of those benefits which accompany or flow from them.*

The three grand benefits, of which they who are effectually called partake in this life, are these :—

1. Justification; or deliverance from the condemning sentence of the law.

2. Adoption; or the translation of sinners from the family of Adam into the family of God.

3. Sanctification; or deliverance from the power of sin.

These benefits cannot be separated. Although, on account of our narrow and limited capacities, we are under the necessity of considering them separately; yet we must remember, that, essentially and really, they become the believer's at once ; for, when he is called, he is justified,—that is, brought from under the curse of the broken law to an interest in the righteousness of Christ; he is adopted,—that is, brought from the family of the wicked one into the family of God; and he is sanctified,—that is, made holy in part, or the work of the Spirit is begun in the soul, which shall be perfected at death.

Believers are made partakers of these benefits *in this life*. This is evident from Rom. viii. 30. That sinners must be called in time, cannot be denied; for none can be called without the gospel, which is the means appointed that this effect may be produced.

In this life, believers also partake of those benefits which accompany or flow from justification, adoption, and sanctification. Some of these, besides those afterwards mentioned, are the following:—1. Peace with God.—Rom. v. 1. 2. Freedom of access to God at all times as children to a father. 3. Fatherly correction.—Heb. xii. 6, 7. 4. A title to immortality. 5. A happy death.—Ps. xxiii. 4.

Obs. 141.—*Justification and sanctification differ in various respects.*

They differ—

1. In their *nature.* Justification changes our state before God; sanctification changes our heart and life;—the one, as a judge; the other, as a father and a friend.

2. In their *order.* Justification precedes sanctification, which is the evidence of justification.

3. In their *matter.* The righteousness of Christ is our justifying righteousness; but the grace of God implanted is the matter of our sanctification.

4. In their *properties.* Justification is an act completed at once; sanctification is a work carried on by degrees, and not perfected till death.

5. In their *subject.* Justifying righteousness is *in* Christ, and *upon* us as a robe; sanctification is *from* Christ, and *in* us as a new nature.

6. In their *objects and extent.* Justification respects our persons, and relates particularly to the conscience; sanctification respects the whole man, for the whole man must be renewed.

7. In their *ingredients.* In justification, the love of God and the righteousness of Christ are manifested to us; in sanctification, our love to God, and holiness of life appear, or are evidenced.

8. In their *evidence* or *visibility.* Justification is a hidden act; sanctification is the evidence of our justification, and may appear to all.

9. In their *relation to sin.* Justification removes the guilt of sin; sanctification removes its power and defilement.

10. In their *relation to the law of God.* Justification delivers us from the law as a covenant; sanctification renews the image of God, and makes us conformed to the law as a rule of life.

11. In their *relation to God.* Justification delivers us from his avenging wrath, and brings us into his favour again; sanctification conforms us to his image.

12. In their *relation to the offices of Christ.* Justification is founded immediately on his priesthood and its work; sanctification proceeds immediately from his prophetical and kingly offices.

13. In their *usefulness* to the people of God. Justification frees us from all obnoxiousness to every legal punishment, and entitles us to the happiness of heaven; sanctification delivers us from the bondage and slavery of every lust, and prepares us for the enjoyment of God in heaven.

INFERENCES.

From this subject we learn,—1 How wonderful the wisdom

of God is in the plan of salvation. 2. The necessity of obtaining the favour of God in the benefits mentioned. 3. The danger of not being made partakers of them; in which case God is our enemy, and we can have no hope at death. 4. That, if we have God as our justifier, adopter, and sanctifier, we shall possess all things.—1 Cor. iii. 21–23. 5. The necessity of improving our privileges. 6. That it is by sanctification that we can come to the comfortable evidence that we are justified and adopted. 7. That we all stand in need of the benefits mentioned. 8. The misery of all that are not partakers of them. 9. That complete glorification, which is the sum of every purchased blessing, shall be the believer's portion for ever.

Benefits of Redemption:—1. *Of Justification.*

Q. 33.—*What is Justification?*

Justification is an act of God's free grace, wherein he pardoneth all our sins, and accepteth us as righteous in his sight, only for the righteousness of Christ imputed to us, and received by faith alone.

ANALYSIS AND PROOFS.

We are here taught,—
1. That justification is an act of the free and unmerited grace of God. Rom. iii. 24.—" Being justified freely by his grace."
2. That all our sins are pardoned in justification. Ps. ciii. 3.—" Who forgiveth all thine iniquities."
3. That the perfect righteousness of Christ is imputed to the believer in justification. 2 Cor. v. 21.—" He hath made him to be sin for us, who knew no sin; that we might be made the righteousness of God in him."
4. That the believer is accepted as righteous by God, only by the imputation of Christ's righteousness. Rom. v. 19.—" As by one man's disobedience many were made sinners; so by the obedience of one shall many be made righteous."
5. That the benefit of Christ's imputed righteousness is received by faith alone. Rom. iii. 22.—" The righteousness of God, which is by faith of Jesus Christ, unto all and upon all them that believe." See also Gal. ii. 16.

Obs. 142.—*Justification is an act of the free and unmerited grace of God.*

To *justify* signifies not to *make righteous*, but to *pronounce righteous*. In Rom. vii. 34, justification is opposed to condemnation. Now, *condemnation* does not make a person wicked. but is only the *pronouncing* of a sentence upon him, according to his transgression of the law. In like manner, *justification* does not infuse righteousness into a person, but is only the *pronounc-*

ing or *declaring* of him to be righteous, in consequence of a trial.

The *justifier* of sinners, is God essentially considered—God the Father, Son, and Holy Ghost. With respect to consent and authority, all the three persons concur in the act of justification; but there are parts carried on by them which more immediately belong to each of them. 1. God, essentially considered in the person of the Father, justifies the ungodly who believe in Jesus. It belongs to him in this respect, because it is his to forgive. 2. Our Lord Jesus Christ justifies, inasmuch as all judgment is committed to him; inasmuch as he is exalted to be a Prince and a Saviour, to give repentance and remission of sins; and inasmuch as his righteousness is the alone meritorious cause of our justification, exclusive of all things done either before or after the state of justification. 3. The Holy Ghost justifies, inasmuch as he applies the redemption purchased by Christ.

That which moves God to justify a sinner, is his own *free grace*. Justification is called an *act*, because it is the sentence of a judge, completed at once, and not carried on by degrees; and it is called an *act of God's free grace*, because there is nothing whatever in the sinner to influence him to justify him,—nothing to merit the least favour from him.—Eph. ii. 8, 9. Faith, repentance, and good works, can have no merit in the sight of God in respect of justification; for they are all his gifts; and one free gift cannot be the cause of God's conferring another; and hence we must view this act of God as *entirely free*.

As justification belongs only to the elect, for them alone did Christ represent in the new covenant, so from *eternity* God decreed to justify them in *time*, because from eternity he gave them to Christ to be redeemed from wrath. But they could not have been justified from eternity in any other way than in the *decree;* because none are justified until they are called; and all that are justified are by nature children of wrath even as others.—Rom. viii. 30; Gal. iii. 8.

The promise of actually applying Christ to the elect is in due time accomplished in two ways: either by sending the gospel to them, or by casting their lot, or causing them to come, where it is preached; and this is done at the time promised, and takes place according to the good pleasure of the Lord.

Obs. 143.—*In justification the perfect righteousness of Christ is imputed to the believer.*

By the *righteousness* of Christ we are to understand his *obedience*, which is commonly distinguished into *active* and *passive*. By Christ's *active obedience*, we are to understand, the holiness of his life, and his perfect conformity to the whole law of God, in thought, word, and action, without failing in it either in kind or in degree; and by his *passive obedience*, we are to understand, his submission to the curse of the law, in his satisfaction for sin, and his enduring all that wrath which was due to his people, for their rebellion against God, and the dishonour which was thereby done to him. See Jer. xxiii. 6; 1 Cor. i 30; 2 Cor. v. 21.

This righteousness of Christ is *imputed* to believers in justification,—that is, it is accounted theirs in law; or, on account of it, their persons are accounted righteous in the sight of God, as if they had fulfilled the law themselves, and had not sinned. See Rom. v. 18, and iii. 10, 20; Eph. ii. 9; Gal. ii. 16; Phil. iii. 9.

Obs. 144.—*In justification all the believer's sins are pardoned.*

The *pardon* of sin is a being absolved from *guilt* by the sentence of God, through the imputed righteousness of his Son; and although there is the *power* of sin as well as its guilt, yet, properly speaking, this is removed in regeneration,—the *defilement* of sin is removed in the progress of sanctification, and the *indwelling power* of sin is removed in glorification.

In justification God pardons *all our sins*. Past sins are forgiven, and future sins will not be imputed; so that the pardoned sinner cannot come into condemnation; for if he is once pardoned, then is he in Christ Jesus, and " to them that are in Christ Jesus there is no condemnation."—Rom. viii. 1.

It may here be remarked, that *repentance* is no condition of pardon. Repentance is absolutely necessary; and no sinner can expect pardon without it.—Luke xiii. 3, 5. But it is not a condition of pardon; for if it were so, it would bring in works as the matter or material cause of our justification before God,—which is contrary to Scripture.—Gal. ii. 16; Rom. iii. 20–28.

Obs. 145.—*In justification the believer is accepted by God as righteous, only by the imputation of Christ's righteousness.*

The *acceptance of a sinner as righteous in the sight of God*, must, with respect to order, follow pardon of sin; for until the sentence of the broken law be dissolved by pardon, it is impossible that the person of the sinner can find acceptance with Heaven, or that any blessing of the new covenant can be conferred upon him.

Pardon and *acceptance* are here connected, because all that are pardoned are accounted righteous in the sight of God. In courts among men, when a criminal is forgiven, he may not be declared righteous; at least he may not be received into favour. But not so with God; for all that are declared righteous are accepted in his sight, and received into the closest friendship with him.

By the *acceptance* of a sinner, we are not to understand the acceptance of him *on account of his works*, but the acceptance of his person *through the righteousness of Christ*, imputed to him and received on his part "by faith alone." We must, however, guard against supposing, that it is owing to any thing meritorious in believing that the sinner becomes interested in the righteousness of Christ. This would be quite inconsistent with what is said by the apostle in Rom. iv. 1-6. We would in this case have something whereof to glory. Faith is only the way appointed by God, in which we become connected with the Lord Jesus Christ, and personally interested in his atoning merits.

Obs. 146.—*The benefit of Christ's imputed righteousness is received by faith alone.*

It is *by faith alone* that the sinner receives Christ and his righteousness as the free gift of God; and hence he is said to be *justified by faith.*—Rom. v. 1. See the following passages of Scripture, where several expressions occur which clearly prove that justification is *by faith*, or that Christ's imputed righteousness, by which the sinner is justified, is received by faith.—Rom. iii. 22, 28, and v. 1; Heb. xi. 7; Phil. iii. 9; Gal. ii. 16. But none of them imply that the sinner is justified *on account of faith*. It is not *the receiving* of Christ's righteousness, but *the righteousness itself*, that justifies the sinner; in the same manner as it is not the hand, but what is received by the hand, that nourishes.

But the sinner is also said to be justified by *grace*, by the *blood of Christ*, and by *works*.

1. He is said to be justified *by grace* (Rom. iii. 24), because grace accompanies every step of salvation. It was grace that provided the sacrifice, and that was pleased to accept of the satisfaction of Christ. It is grace that applies this purchase to the sinner. It is grace that pardons and forgives transgression and sin; for it is for his name's sake that the Lord pardoneth iniquity.—Ps. xxv. 11. And it is grace that enables the believer to hold out to the end, and to be faithful unto death.

2. He is said to be justified *by the blood of Christ* (Rom. v. 9), because the shedding of his blood was the last act of his obedience. This, however, does not exclude the other parts of his obedience, both active and passive. See Lev. xvii. 11; Heb. ix. 22.

3. He is said to be justified *by works*, and not by faith only.—James ii. 24. But this must be understood of evidencing the reality of our faith by those works in sanctification which flow from faith. True faith and true holiness will discover themselves by good works, as naturally as good fruit grows on a good tree.

"If any human doing or suffering could have procured salvation, it is self-evident that God would have spared his Son, and that the Son would have spared himself from the work of redemption. Yea, if by any degree of assistance, however great we could have been enabled to save ourselves, it is morally certain, from the whole character of God, and from the whole analogy of his government, that he would have enabled us to do so, instead of sending his Son to do it. But as he sent him in the form of a servant, and in the office of a substitute, it is the very height of absurdity to imagine that salvation can be owing to any cause but his atoning sacrifice."

All these ways, then, entirely agree: they imply no contradiction. Grace is the moving cause; faith is the hand which receives the righteousness of Christ; the blood of Christ justifies, because without shedding of blood there is no remission; and works justify, only as they are evidences of the reality of our faith—as they discover to ourselves and to our brethren that our faith is not dead. Hence all these different ways imply one another; and hence we conclude, that a man is justified by faith alone before God,—that is, by Christ's imputed righteousness received by faith alone.

Obs. 147.—*No obedience of ours can in any measure recommend us to an interest in Jesus Christ.*

"It is the plan of the gospel to save sinners entirely by free grace. There is no medium between salvation by the deeds of the law and salvation by grace. As none can plead perfect obedience, they cannot be saved in the former way. All, then, whatever their former character has been, must come and be saved in the same way—by the free grace of God through Jesus Christ. This shows how much some misunderstand the gospel, who, when they are first awakened to a concern about their souls, are disposed to decline coming immediately to the Saviour; hoping that they may previously become (as they think) somewhat better, and have a better claim to his regard. This sentiment, though often assuming the semblance of much humility, plainly savours of a self-righteous spirit. It is attempting, as it were, to divide the honour of our salvation with the heavenly Saviour,—that is, we wish to be allowed to deal a little in this great work, though we would give him the chief share of the glory. Such a spirit is quite opposed to the plan of salvation revealed in the gospel. There we are required to come as we are, and without delay, to the Lord Jesus. He claims all the glory of the salvation of his people."—Matt. i. 21; Acts ii. 38, and xvi. 30; 1 Tim. i. 15, 16.

Obs. 148.—*To speak of "sincere obedience" as being under the gospel dispensation substituted in the room of "perfect obedience," is altogether improper and absurd.*

The reason of this is,—" Because the perfect obedience required by the law, is strictly and fully paid under the gospel The moral law is, like its Author. holy, just and good. Its de

mands are founded on unchangeable righteousness, and therefore it could not be altered. This appears from the nature of its precepts. Thus, it could never cease to be the duty of man, as a creature of God, supremely to love and obey his Creator, and agreeably to his command to love his neighbour as himself. Had the demands of the law been lowered, it would have argued that it originally required too much; and, consequently, that it was not founded on essential rectitude. But although this may be often a reason for changing human laws, it could never apply to the law of the living God. Salvation is, then, revealed in the gospel, not by altering the standard of law, but by completely fulfilling all its demands. Did it demand the punishment of the transgressor, and a perfect obedience, as necessary to furnish a claim to eternal life? These demands were completely answered by the obedience unto death of the Lord Jesus Christ as the surety of his people. It is not, then, sincere obedience which is under the gospel substituted in the room of perfect obedience; but the *perfect obedience of the Lord Jesus Christ*, in the room of his people, is substituted in the place of that *perfect personal obedience*, which the law would otherwise have required of them."
—Matt. v. 17; Rom. vii. 12, and x. 4; Ps. xix. 7.

" But although believers cannot yield perfect obedience to the law of God, they are nevertheless called to yield sincere obedience. This is undoubtedly the case. This sincere obedience, however, is the effect of gratitude to the Saviour, on account of the free communication of pardoning mercy. Deliverance from sin, too, and being enabled to walk in newness of life, is to be viewed as forming a part of that salvation which the Lord Jesus Christ reveals. But it is not to be considered as at all coming in the room of that perfect obedience which the law originally required."

Obs. 149.—*The doctrine of salvation through the merits of Jesus Christ alone, has no tendency to encourage men to continue in sin.*

Instead of this, " when properly understood and believed, it must have the very opposite effect. This doctrine exhibits the evil as well as the danger of sin, in the most striking manner. No man, therefore, can embrace it without discovering both of these; and wherever this is the case, there must be a strong desire to be delivered from it. Deliverance from the power and the love of sin is accordingly revealed as a part of the salvation of the gospel, as well as freedom from its guilt. Further, this doctrine tends to promote obedience in another way,—viz., by means of love to the Saviour. No man can believe in Jesus as a Saviour, without loving him; and he who loveth him will keep his commandments."—Matt. i. 21; John xiv. 15, and xv. 14; Rom. vi. 1-14. &c. and viii. 2; Tit. ii. 11; Eph. ii. 1-10

· Such is the testimony of Scripture; and we see it fully confirmed by what takes place in the world around us. We almost uniformly see those who are most disposed to place confidence in their own righteousness, discovering a considerable degree of laxness in their conduct; while such as depend solely on the merits of Jesus for justification and salvation, are much more careful to be found walking in newness of life."

Obs. 150.—*This method of acceptance with God, through the righteousness of his Son, redounds more to his honour and glory, than if sinners could have obeyed perfectly in their own persons, or than if they had been doomed to perish for ever in their sins.*

By the obedience and death of his own Son, God must be glorified more than if man had obeyed and suffered; because, in the world to come, the praises of the redeemed shall be full of a God in Christ, and his redemption shall be the burden of their song and the subject of their glorying. But surely the doings of man himself, although they were perfect, do not deserve to be once remembered in the presence of a holy and an all-sufficient God. This shows, that the acceptance of the sinner, through the righteousness of the Redeemer, is entirely consistent with the perfections of Jehovah.

INFERENCES.

From this subject we learn,—1. That the greatest sinners may be justified; that grace may apprehend the chief of sinners. 2. The sovereignty of God. 3. The necessity of justification. 4. The happiness of the justified, and the misery of all that continue enemies to God. 5. That the righteousness of Christ is an invaluable gift, seeing it can cover the sinner in the day of God's fierce anger. 6. That we cannot take this righteousness to ourselves; but being the gift of God, it must be imputed to us. 7. That the gospel is the best news that ever reached the ears of sinners. 8. The necessity of faith in Christ in order to justification. 9. That God ought to have all the glory of redeeming grace. 10. That works ought to have their own place in the system of grace, and not to usurp the place of that righteousness which is pleasing in the sight of God. 11. That we ought to seek after scriptural views of a sinner's justification before God. 12. That there is no way of becoming his friends, but by the justifying act of God. 13. The necessity of the gospel, and of faith in it. 14. The necessity of pardon of sin. 15. That if guilt be not removed, we are still the enemies of God. 16. That if pardon be obtained, sinners may rejoice in hope of glory, for they are at peace with God. 17. That boasting is excluded from the sinner in the matter of justification. 18. The misery of the sinner who despises the riches of divine grace. 19. That if we are justified, we possess all things.

Benefits of Redemption :—2. *Of Adoption.*

Q. 34.—What is Adoption?

Adoption is an act of God's free grace, whereby we are received into the number, and have a right to all the privileges of the sons of God.

ANALYSIS AND PROOFS.

We are here taught,—
1. That adoption is an act of God's free grace. 1 John iii. 1. —" Behold what manner of love the Father hath bestowed upon us, that we should be called the sons of God!"
2. That by adoption we are received into the number of God's children. Eph. i. 5.—" Having predestinated us unto the adoption of children." See also John i. 12.
3. That by adoption we receive a right to all the privileges of God's children. Rom. viii. 27.—" If children, then heirs; heirs of God, and joint heirs with Christ."

EXPLANATION.

Obs. 151.—*Adoption is an act of God's free grace.*

To *adopt*, signifies to take a stranger into a family, and to deal with him as if he were a son and heir.

The *adopter* of sinners is God essentially considered—God the Father, Son, and Holy Ghost. 1. God the *Father* adopts, inasmuch as he predestinates his people to the adoption of children by Jesus Christ, according to the good pleasure of his will, to the praise of his glorious grace.—Eph. i. 5, 6. 2. God the *Son* adopts, inasmuch as by his power he rescues his people from the family of Satan; and thereby gives them a right to become the sons of God. 3. God the *Holy Ghost* adopts, inasmuch as he is sent forth by God into the hearts of the adopted, and teaches them to cry, " Abba, Father."

According to our manner of conception, we must believe that adoption follows justification; for the sentence of condemnation must first be removed, before the sinner, who is exposed to the curse of the law, can be made a son; but with God they both take place at once. Properly speaking, they are both relative changes,—that is, changes of *state*, and not changes of *nature*, although this also accompanies them.

Adoption is called an *act*, because, like justification, it is completed at once, and not carried on by degrees; and as these are acts, no one of the people of God can be justified or adopted in a greater degree than another.

That adoption is an act of God's *free grace*, will be evident from some of the following particulars, in which adoption, as it is an act of God, differs from it as it is a deed among men.

1. Among men, only *one* in general becomes partaker of this privilege in one family. But by God, a whole elect world—every believer in Christ—is made partaker of all the privileges of the sons of God.

2. Among men, the adopter is of the *same nature* with the person adopted; both are sinners, and both are guilty before God. But it is not so with God; he is not to be compared with the highest of the sons of men, who are but the works of his own hands.

3. Among men, there is some kind of *equality* between the adopter and the adopted. But there is and can be no equality between God and the sinner whom he brings to himself.

4. Among men, there is in general something that influences man to show such kindness to any. But with respect to God's adopting of sinners, nothing of this kind appears; for there is nothing in or about them which can influence him to show them the least regard,—no amiable quality to court his regard, for all are filthy, and polluted, and unworthy of his favour, deserving nothing but to be cast off for ever. Hence it is evident, especially from the last particular, that adoption is *an act of God's free grace*.

Obs. 152.—*By adoption sinners are received into the number of the children of God.*

The purpose of God respecting the adoption of sinners reaches back to *eternity*, when their names were enrolled in the Lamb's book of life, as future members of the family of heaven ; but they are not actually admitted into this family until the day of effectual calling—until the moment of their union with Christ by faith, and their regeneration after his image. It must, however, require some time, before they can come to the comfortable evidence of this gracious state.—Eph. i. 5.

Adoption may be distinguished into *general* adoption and *special* adoption.

1. The *general* act is that by which God gathers from the world an indefinite number, erects them into a Church, and bestows on them the external privileges of his children. This is indeed a great blessing ; but many enjoy it who are not truly the children of God. See Rom. ix. 6.

2. The *special* act is that by which a sinner is made a son, to translated from the family of Satan into the kingdom of God's dear Son. This privilege does not belong to any but to those who receive the Lord Jesus Christ by faith. See John i. 12.

We may here notice some of the *effects* of the Spirit of adoption, which is peculiar to believers. They are these :—1. Filial *love to God;* which flows from that view of the excellencies of the Divine character, of which the adopted had formerly no knowledge.—1 John iv. 19. 2. Filial *obedience.* Adoption into the family of God is the greatest obligation to obey him. 3. The *hope* of children ; or the hope of a share in God's love, and in that goodness which he hath laid up for them that trust in him. 4. *Enjoyment* of God, and *communion* with him in his ordinances. 5. *Love to others*, and especially to those who are of the " household of faith." See 1 John v. 1, 2.

Obs. 153.—*By adoption believers receive a right to all the privileges of the sons of God.*

Of these *privileges* the following are a few :—

1. A comfortable portion of the good things of this life, and the blessing of Heaven with them.

2. A new name.—Rev. ii. 17, and iii. 12.

3. The comfort and consolation of the Holy Spirit. See John vii. 38, 39, and xvi. 13.

4. Liberty ; which may be distinguished into gracious liberty, or that which is conferred upon them in this world ; and glorious liberty, or that which they shall enjoy in the world to come.— Heb. ii. 14 ; Rom. vi. 14, 18, and viii. 21.

5. Access to God as a Father through Jesus Christ by one Spirit ; which arises from the firm belief of his faithfulness and love to them, now that every difficulty is removed. See Rom. iv. 21 ; Eph. iii. 12 ; 1 John v. 14, 15.

6. A title to the whole inheritance. Every heir of God shall receive as much as if there were but one; and yet they shall all be glorified, and shall receive as much as it is possible for them to receive.—1 Cor. iii. 22 ; Heb. xi. 7 ; 1 Pet. iii. 7 ; Rom. viii. 17.

7. The care and superintendence of angels.—Heb. i. 14 ; Matt. xviii. 10.

8. Sanctified affliction, or fatherly chastisement or correction. —Heb. xii. 6, 7, &c. ; Ps. xxx. 7, and li. 8, &c.

9. Fatherly protection, and fatherly direction and instruction in all things.

In a word, the believer has the provision of the new covenant in every thing necessary, both for soul and body, for time and eternity—every thing necessary that he may be built up in holiness, and be more and more conformed to the Divine image.

INFERENCES.

From this subject we learn,—1. The happiness of those who are the sons of God. 2. The danger of all that are in a state of alienation from him, or that are the children of the wicked one. 3. That a name to live among the children of God will not profit. 4. That external adoption, or visible Church membership, and the enjoyment of its privileges, will not entitle to the inheritance of children, if not specially adopted by God. 5. The necessity of self-examination, in order that we may discover whether or not we have the Spirit of adoption. 6. The necessity of loving the children of God in every place. 7. That believers have no reason to envy the prosperity of others. 8. That they are as honourable as God can make them. 9. That they need not want any comfort in time of need. 10. The necessity of walking worthy of such privileges. 11. How preferable a state of grace is to a state of nature, and a state of glory to a state of grace. 12. That the sons of God possess all things beyond the grave. 13. That no enemy shall prevail against them. 14. That believers are most precious in the sight of the Lord. 15. That all those who are not the children of God, are the children of the devil.

Benefits of Redemption :—3. Of Sanctification.

Q. 35.—*What is Sanctification?*

Sanctification is the work of God's free grace, whereby we are renewed in the whole man after the image of God, and are enabled more and more to die unto sin and live unto righteousness.

ANALYSIS AND PROOFS.

We are here taught,—

1. That sanctification is a work of God's free and undeserved grace or mercy. Tit. iii. 4, 5.—" But after that the kindness and love of God our Saviour towards man appeared, not by works of righteousness which we have done, but according to his mercy he saved us, by the washing of regeneration, and renewing of the Holy Ghost." See also Exod. xxxi. 13; Phil. ii. 13.

2. That sanctification is a progressive work, or a work carried on by degrees. 2 Cor. iii. 18.—" But we all, with open face, beholding, as in a glass, the glory of the Lord, are changed into the same image, from glory to glory, even as by the Spirit of the Lord." See also 2 Cor. iv. 16.

3. That, in sanctification, there is a renewing of the sinner's mind. Rom. xii. 2.—"And be not conformed to this world; but be ye transformed by the renewing of your mind, that ye may prove what is that good, and acceptable, and perfect will of God." See also Eph. iv. 23.

4. That, in sanctification, the renewal, though gradual, is complete, or extends to the whole man. Ezek. xxxvi. 26.—" A new heart also will I give you, and a new spirit will I put within you ; and I will take away the stony heart out of your flesh, and I will give you a heart of flesh." See also 1 Thess. v. 23.

5. That, in sanctification, the sinner is renewed after the image or likeness of God. Eph. iv. 24.—" And that ye put on the new man, which, after God, is created in righteousness and true holiness." See also Col. iii. 10.

6. That, in the progress of sanctification, the sinner is enabled to die unto sin. Rom. vi. 6.—" Knowing this, that our old man is crucified with him, that the body of sin might be destroyed, that henceforth we should not serve sin."

7. That, in the progress of sanctification, the sinner is enabled to live unto righteousness. Rom. vi. 22.—" But now, being made free from sin, and become servants to God, ye have your fruit unto holiness, and the end everlasting life." See also 1 Pet. ii. 24.

8. That dying to sin, and living to righteousness, is a constant and daily work. 2 Cor. iv. 16.—" For which cause we faint not; but though our outward man perish, yet the inward man is renewed day by day."

EXPLANATION.

Obs. 154.—*Sanctification is a work of God's free grace.*

In Scripture, the word *sanctification* is used in various acceptations. It imports a *setting apart* of persons or things to holy uses,—Isa. xiii. 3; a *purification* from ceremonial defilement, or freedom from gross idolatry, or error, or wickedness,—Heb. ix. 13; 1 Cor. vii. 14; and a *deliverance from the guilt of sin*,—John xvii. 19. But most commonly and most properly it denotes what is expressed above, namely, " A work of God's free grace, whereby we are renewed in the whole man, after the image of God, and are enabled more and more to die unto sin and to live unto righteousness."

Although sanctification is ascribed both to *God the Father*, and to *God the Son*,—Jude 1; Eph. v. 26,—yet it is the peculiar work of *God the Holy Ghost*. See Ezek. xxxvi. 27; Rom. v 5; 1 Cor. vi. 11; Tit. iii. 5, 6; 2 Thess. ii. 13; 1 Pet. i. 2, 22.

Sanctification is called a *work*, because it is progressive or carried on by degrees, and not completed till death. Justification and adoption are *acts* of God's free grace, perfected at once; but sanctification is a *work*, always carrying on while the saint is in this world. This is evident from its being called " a pressing towards the mark for the prize of the high calling of God in Christ Jesus;" " a warfare;" " a running a race;" " a working out salvation with fear and trembling," &c.

Sanctification is called a *work of God's free grace*, because that which moves God to it, is his own free grace and good pleasure.—Phil. ii. 13. All the children of men are by nature wholly polluted with sin, and it is wholly of God's free grace that any of them are sanctified. It may be here remarked, that the meritorious cause, or the price of our sanctification, is the surety-righteousness of Jesus Christ.—1 John iii. 5; 1 Pet. i. 18, 19.

Obs. 155.—*In sanctification the sinner is renewed in the whole man after the image of God.*

The effect of the work of the Spirit of God in sanctification, is the *renewal of the whole man*. This expression is very comprehensive, and shows the necessity of a *universal change* being wrought on the whole man, both *soul* and *body;* for such a one can alone be called a *new creature*. See 1 Thess. v. 23. The soul must be renewed in all its powers, and faculties, and affections,—not that the very substance is changed, but new qualities must appear in the whole soul; and all the members of the body must become instruments of righteousness to work holiness. In a word, the whole man must be devoted to God, and an unreserved surrender made to him; which alone is a reasonable service, and which alone can constitute a living sacrifice, holy and acceptable to him through Jesus Christ.—Rom. xii. 1.

The sinner must be renewed *after the image of God*. This consists in knowledge, righteousness, and holiness, and every other spiritual grace.—1 Cor. xv. 49; Col. iii. 10. But there can be no likeness to God, without studying conformity to his Son Jesus Christ, who is "the image of the invisible God," to whom we must be conformed in his life, and death, and resurrection.

Obs. 156.—*In sanctification the believer is enabled more and more to die unto sin, and to live unto righteousness.*

Here it may be remarked, that the "renewing of the whole man after the image of God," refers to the renovation of the *nature;* and that the "being enabled more and more to die unto sin, and to live unto righteousness," refers to the renovation of the *life*, by which alone it can be discovered that a change has taken place.

The renovation, which respects the life and conduct, consists of two parts:—

1. A *dying unto sin*. This consists in an earnest endeavour, with the assistance of the grace of God, to destroy the root of sin in the soul, by a continual application of the blood of Christ to the conscience; by which the guilt of sin is removed, and the conscience purified from dead works to serve the living God. And together with this, there must be a hatred of all sin, and of every appearance of evil; and an earnest endeavour to improve the death and resurrection of Jesus Christ, and his Word and Spirit; and a looking up to him for grace, that corruption may be more and more weakened.

2. A *living unto righteousness*. This consists in loving and abounding more and more in inward holiness, and in the practice of every good word and work, flowing from the principle of grace implanted in the soul by the Spirit of God.

The *nature* of that *righteousness* or obedience which is required of believers may be thus described:—

1. New obedience must be built on a *gospel foundation:* it must be regulated by the Word of God.

2. New obedience must proceed from *gospel principles*. The mind must be enlightened with the knowledge of Christ; the conscience must be sprinkled from dead works to serve the living God; and the will and affections must be renewed by the Holy Spirit.

3. New obedience must be influenced by *gospel motives*. Such are these:—the redeeming love of God; his authority laid upon us as our God in Christ; the example of Christ, and of God in him, as our Father and Friend; and the hope of eternal life as the free gift of God.

4. New obedience must be performed in a *gospel manner*,— that is, in the exercise of faith in Christ, of love to him, and of humility.—Heb. xi. 6; Luke xvii. 10.

5. New obedience must be directed to a *gospel end*,—that is, that we may be made like God; that we may be a praise and a name to him in the earth; that we may be fitted for the inheritance of the saints in light; and that we may edify others and endeavour to promote their happiness.—Matt. v. 16; 1 Cor. x. 31.

That which *enables* the sinner more and more to die unto sin, and to live unto righteousness, is the *grace of God*, which is strengthened from time to time by the Spirit, and at death springs up unto everlasting life.—Isa. xl. 31; John i. 16.

The *means* which the Spirit of God makes use of for the promotion of holiness of heart and life, are the following:—

1. The reading of the Word, the hearing of the Word read and preached, meditation, prayer, and the sacraments. But in order that these may prove effectual, the blessing of the Spirit must be sought.

2. The example of the saints, so far as they followed the Lord; but above all, the example of Jesus Christ, who "hath left us an example that we should follow his steps."

3. The providences of God; a due improvement of which cannot fail to show the evil, and deformity, and danger of sin, and the beauty of holiness as well-pleasing to the Lord.—Rom. ii. 4.

Death unto sin, and *life unto righteousness*, spring from the virtue that is in the death and resurrection of Christ; by which the members of his mystical body are rendered conformable to him. This appears from Rom. vi. 4–6. See also Phil. iii. 10.

Here it may be remarked, that although holiness is absolutely necessary, it is not necessary that upon it we may build our title to eternal life,—that by it we may render ourselves accepted in the Beloved,—that by it we may be justified in the sight of God,—that it may be the ground of our hopes for eternity; for, were this the case, the finished work of Christ would be of little moment. See 1 Pet. i. 16; 1 Thess. iv. 3; Tit. ii. 14; Rev. x. 27.

INFERENCES.

From this subject we learn,—1. That believers must work while it is called to-day. 2. That they stand in continual need of the grace of the Spirit for subduing remaining corruption. 3. The necessity of prayer for the Spirit of holiness. 4. That man cannot sanctify himself; and that every saved sinner may sing of the freeness of Jehovah's grace. 5. That partial love to God evidences no sincerity of love. 6. That it is the duty of the believer to die more and more unto sin, and not to give over the contest until it be completely destroyed. 7. That unless we bear the image of God, we cannot enjoy him. 8. That the divine life is a hidden, but an active life. 9. That every change is not a change after the image of God. 10. That the sanctified soul is not idle in the work of the Lord. 11. The beauty of holiness, and the deformity of sin. 12. That it is the Spirit that sanctifies. 13. The happiness of the holy, and the misery of the unholy.

4. *Additional Benefits of Redemption.*

Q. 36.—What are the Benefits which in this life do accompany or flow from Justification, Adoption, and Sanctification?

The benefits which in this life do accompany or flow from justification, adoption, and sanctification, are, assurance of God's love, peace of conscience, joy in the Holy Ghost, increase of grace, and perseverance therein to the end.

ANALYSIS AND PROOFS.

We are here taught,—
1. That the believer has the assurance of God's love. Rom. v. 5.—" The love of God is shed abroad in our hearts by the Holy Ghost which is given to us." See also Isa. xxxii. 17 and xii. 1.
2. That the believer enjoys peace of conscience. Rom. v. 1. —" Being justified by faith, we have peace with God, through our Lord Jesus Christ."
3. That the believer possesses joy in the Holy Ghost. 1 Pet. i. 8.—" In whom, though now ye see him not, yet believing, ye rejoice with joy unspeakable and full of glory." See also Rom. xiv. 17.
4. That the believer increases in grace. Prov. iv. 18.—" The path of the just is as the shining light, that shineth more and more unto the perfect day." See also Hos. xiv. 5.
5. That the believer is enabled to persevere in grace. Jer.

xxxii. 40.—" I will put my fear in their hearts, that they shall not depart from me." See also 1 Pet. i. 5.

EXPLANATION.

Obs. 157.—*All those benefits which are said to accompany or flow from justification, adoption, and sanctification, are inseparably connected with them.*

This is evident; for all that are justified, are adopted; and all that are justified and adopted, are sanctified and glorified; according to Rom. viii. 30, &c. They are inseparably connected in the purposes of God, in the promises of God, and in the doctrines of the gospel,—Luke i. 74, &c.; Heb. viii. 10, &c. They are connected in the experience of believers,—1 Cor. vi. 11; in the use of the law of God, not as a covenant, but as the rule of life to believers,—Rom. viii. 1–4; in the offices of Christ,—1 Cor. i. 30; and in the end of the death of Christ,—Tit. ii. 14; and they are connected in the offer of the gospel,—1 Thess. iv. 7.

It may be here remarked, that the first three benefits here mentioned, viz., assurance of God's love, peace of conscience, and joy in the Holy Ghost, flow from a *sight* and *sense* of justification, adoption, and sanctification; and that the last two, viz., increase of grace, and perseverance therein to the end, belong to the *being* of a justified, adopted, and sanctified state.

Obs. 158.—*In this life the believer has the assurance of the love of God.*

Assurance of the love of God may be viewed in two respects:—the *assurance of faith* and the *assurance of sense.* The foundation of the former is the infallible Word of God, who cannot lie; that of the latter is the person's present experience of the communications of Divine love. By the former, we are assured of the truth of God's revealed declaration, particularly in the offer of Christ in the gospel; by the latter, we are assured that the work of God is begun in the soul, and that this work is saving and gracious. By the former, we are assured, on God's own testimony, that he hath given us Christ and his salvation fully and without reserve; by the latter, we are assured that the work of salvation is already begun in the soul.

The *assurance of faith* may be thus briefly defined:—It is not an assurance that I am in a state of grace, but an assurance that God is willing to receive me, if now for the first time I believe in the Lord Jesus Christ. This assurance is absolutely necessary to salvation, being neither more nor less than *faith itself*, or a *belief* that God hath given his Son to be the Saviour of sinners, and that Christ is able and willing to save them. That this is not the assurance here referred to, is evident from this, that it is said to accompany or flow from justification, adoption, and sanctification; whereas the assurance of faith, or faith itself, is absolutely necessary to put us in possession of these great benefits.

The *assurance of sense*, or the sensible assurance of God's love, which is that here referred to, is not absolutely necessary to the happiness of the believer's state; but is peculiarly useful in some things, which are much calculated to promote the glory of God, and the good of the soul; and as it is attainable, we ought to give diligence that it may be obtained. See Isa. i. 10.

That the assurance of sense, or the sensible assurance of God's love, is attainable, is evident from many instances mentioned in Scripture. This favour was obtained by Job, by Jacob, by Moses, by David, by Asaph, by Heman, by Jeremiah, by Daniel, by Habakkuk, by Simeon, by Mary, by Thomas, by Paul, and by many others mentioned in Scripture. See Job xix. 25; Gen. xlviii. 3, and xlix. 18; Exod. xv. 2; Ps. xviii. 1, &c., lxxiii. 23, &c., and lxxxviii. 1; Jer. xxxi. 3; Dan. ix. 19; Hab. iii. 17–19; Luke ii. 25, &c., and i. 47; John xx. 28; Gal. ii. 20, &c.

In order to the attainment of the sensible assurance of our state, and of the truth of our grace, various things are necessary, such as these:—1. Strong faith in the declarations of the gospel, directed to us as sinners.—1 Tim. i. 15.   2. A diligent study of universal holiness in heart and life, which is well-pleasing to God.—Luke i. 6.   3. A due attention to the work of the Spirit on the soul, and a taking heed not to quench the Spirit.—Eph. iv. 30; 1 Thess. v. 19.   4. Much serious self-examination.— 1 Cor. xi. 28.   5. With all these things we must diligently seek the testimony of the Spirit of God, which is necessary, that he may bear witness with our spirits that we are the children of God. See Isa. xxxii. 17; Rom. viii. 16.

It may be here remarked, and it must ever be remembered, that although the *assurance of faith* is *strengthened* or *encouraged* by the inward evidences of grace, yet it is not to be *founded* upon them. The only foundation of the *assurance of faith*, is *the Divine truth of the promises of salvation*. Both these kinds of assurance, however (viz., that of present grace, and that of future glory), are produced by the testimony of the Spirit of adoption, witnessing with our spirits that we are the children of God. Thus, the Word is the foundation, a sense of inherent grace is the encouragement, and the Holy Spirit is the efficient cause, of the assurance of future glory.

The following are a few of the *consequences* of assurance of the love of God:—1. Assurance, if genuine, humbles the believer, and renders him self-denied.—Gal. ii. 19, &c. Whereas, on the contrary, presumption puffeth up with much spiritual pride. –2 Kings x. 15, 16.   2. Assurance begets in the soul a love to the Lord, which encourages in the practice of every commanded duty.—Ps cxix. 32.   Whereas presumption, on the other hand, indulges a vain and dangerous security, and speaks peace to itself, although there is no peace. 3. Assurance meets self-examination with confidence, and avoideth not the search of the Lord.—Ps. xxvi. 1, &c. Whereas presumption hateth the light, lest its wicked deeds should be discovered and reproved.—John iii. 20. 4. Assurance has a powerful effect on sanctification.—2 Cor. vii. 1. 5. Assurance gives one a true view of the world and all its enjoyments. 6. Assurance keeps all things right with the soul, and makes it go on its way with confidence and joy. 7. Having the precious faith of God's elect, assurance studies to preserve this pearl of great price, that no man take it away.

Obs. 159.—*In this world the believer enjoys peace of conscience.*

By *peace of conscience* we are to understand that inward and delightful calm of spirit, which proceeds from the purging of the conscience from guilt before the Lord, and from a sensible and believing view of being in a state of favour with God, and of growing conformity to his image. It is an intimate companion of the sensible assurance of the love of God.

The *value* of this privilege of peace of conscience is very great. When the soul is at peace with God, it can go with boldness and confidence to him as its God,—Heb. iv. 16, and x. 19, &c.; it can view the saints as its companions in the house of its pilgrimage, —Ps. cxix. 63; and it is fully resigned to every dispensation of Providence, because it knows that, whatever may take place, all is and shall be well. This is a state infinitely superior to that of those who are plunged in carnal security and in a false peace, or whose hopes are built on a sandy foundation.

Peace of conscience is *obtained* by the sprinkling of the blood of Jesus on the conscience, and by the renewing of the whole man; and it flows from peace with God.—Rom. xv. 13, and v. 1.

Peace of conscience is *maintained* or *preserved*,—1. By an habitual application of the blood of Jesus to the conscience.—Heb. x. 22. 2. By meditation on the glorious excellencies and relations of Christ, and their suitableness in every time of need; on the excellencies of God, reconciled in him, as our God and Father; and on the administration of the well-ordered covenant. —John xiv. 21; Ps. civ. 34. 3. By habitual communion with God.—Ps. lxiii. 4. By an earnest study of universal holiness, and by watchfulness against every known sin.—Acts xxiv. 16; Ps. cxix. 165; 1 John iii. 3. 5. By frequently renewing our repentance.—Ps. li. 6. By a full resignation of ourselves to the Lord, at all times, as our Father and our all, who ordereth all things well concerning us, and who, in his own time, will accomplish his work upon the soul, and bring it to himself through faith.

Obs. 160.—*In this world the believer possesses joy in the Holy Ghost.*

Joy in the Holy Ghost is a joy arising in the soul on the enjoyment of spiritual mercies; from the love of God being shed abroad in the heart by the Spirit; from a view of Christ as presented in the gospel; from believing in him; and from the hope of enjoying his favour for ever; and it is produced by the inhabitation of the Spirit in the heart.—1 Pet. i. 8. They only possess this joy who are the temples of the Holy Ghost—in whom the Holy Ghost dwells.

The *grounds* of this joy, which render it a reality, whether it be felt or not, are these :—What a God in Christ is to the believer; what the Eternal Three have done for him and wrought in him; what his privileges are in this life; and what the character of his God secureth for him in the life to come.

Several of the *means* used by the Spirit, in order that this joy may arise in the souls of believers, are these :—1. The Word of God read or preached. 2. A participation of the sacraments of Christ's appointment in faith, where every comfort is sealed and ratified with blood.—Acts viii. 39. But the chief mean is, 3. Faith, without which we cannot expect such a favour from the Lord. as to rejoice in the Son of his love, and in our being found in him as our all in all.—Rom. xv. 13; 1 Pet. i. 8.

The *nature* of this joy, which is altogether different from every other kind of joy, from whatever source it may arise, may be learned from the following things :—

1. Joy in the Holy Ghost arises in the soul in consequence of the Scriptures being understood according to the mind of the Spirit of God; and no true spiritual joy can arise but from the Word.

2. Joy in the Holy Ghost is lasting; whereas the joy of the hypocrite is delusory and but for a moment. See the Parable of the Sower, Matt. xiii.

3. Joy in the Holy Ghost takes place in the soul, after it has been convinced of sin and pressed down under a sense of it; whereas the joy of the hypocrite may appear when there is no conviction of sin whatever.—Acts ii. 37, &c.; John xvi. 20; Isa. lxi. 2, and xxxv. 10.

4. Joy in the Holy Ghost makes a man appear exceedingly low in his own eyes, and God all-glorious; whereas false joy puffeth up and renders high in one's own esteem, so that, on account of self-greatness, God is scarcely to be seen.—Gen. xxviii. 15, 17; Exod. iii. 1, &c.; Luke ii. 8, &c.; Job xlii. 5, 6.

5. Joy in the Holy Ghost excites the believer to much diligence in the work of the Lord; whereas false joy makes the hypocrite conclude that he has already done enough in the way of obedience. See Phil. iii. 12.

6. Joy in the Holy Ghost is of an enlivening nature, and keeps the soul joyful; and a holy serenity pervades the whole man, totally different from the joys of the world.

Joy in the Holy Ghost is not alike strong at all *times* in the same believers; nor is it so strong in some as it is in others. It is generally greatest,—1. At the conversion of a soul, if there has been great grief. 2. After a dark night of spiritual desertion and temptation.—Isa. liv. 6, &c., and lvii. 16, &c.; Ps. xvi. 10, &c. 3. During a time of tribulation for the sake of Christ and his gospel.—Acts v. 41, and xvi. 25; 1 Pet. iv. 13, &c. 4. When the Lord appears in a remarkable manner in behalf of his Church.—Exod. xv.; Judg. v.; Rev. xii. 10, xiv. 1, &c., and xix. 1, &c. 5. When any favour is conferred, which was somewhat unexpected.—1 Sam. ii.; Luke i. 47, &c. 6. When the believer is about to go to his Father's house.—Ps. xxiii. 4; Job xix. 25 &c.

Obs. 161.—*In this life the believer increases in grace.*

The doctrine of *increase of grace* is evident from Prov. iv 18, and Eph. iv. 13, where we are informed of a certain measure of holiness, which the saints must accomplish or fill up; or, which is the same thing, a certain " stature of the fulness of Christ," at which they must arrive. See also Ps. lxxxiv. 7; John xv. 2.

The *cause* of this increase of grace, is *union with Christ by faith*, together with the *influences of the Spirit*, which he sends down as rain upon the mown grass, or as showers that water the earth. See the Parable of the Vine and its Branches, John xv.

The *ways* in which the believer grows in grace, are these:—1 He grows *upwards* in love, and affection, and heavenly desires. 2. He grows *downwards* in true humility.—Isa. xxxvii. 31. 3 He grows *inwardly*, by cleaving fast to Christ. And, 4. He grows *outwardly*, by a life of holiness.

The growth of a real Christian, and that of a hypocrite, differ in the following respects:—

1. The believer's growth in grace is quite regular, and such as it ought to be. The graces of the Spirit being inseparably connected, and that in their very nature, when one is implanted in the soul, the seeds of all the others are to be found in it; and when one grows, they all grow. See Phil. iii. 12.

2. The hypocrite, on the other hand, does not grow in a natural way. He increases in some things, while in others he does not. For instance, he may have much knowledge, while he has no holiness—see 2 Tim. iii. 5;—and he may soon leave off his desire after knowledge; for, when he proceeds a certain way, he concludes that he has done well—that now he is perfect—and that all is well with him.

Obs. 162.- *In this life the believer perseveres in a state of grace.*

The doctrine of the *final perseverance* of the saints in a state of grace, is evident from the following things:—

1. From the *immutability* of God's love towards them.—Jer. xxxi. 3; Mal. iii. 6; Rom. viii. 38, 39, and xi. 29.

2. From the *Scriptures* of truth. See, among many other passages, the following:—Isa. liv. 10; Rom. viii. 30, 35; 1 John ii. 19, and v. 18; Isa. lv. 3, and lix. 21; Matt. xxiv. 24, and xvi. 18; John x. 27–30; Rom. v. 1, &c.

3. From the *nature* of the covenant of grace. See Jer. xxxii. 40. What grace would there be in that covenant, if it did not secure from eternal wrath?

4. From the *merit* of Christ's sufferings and death. It cannot be supposed that Christ would have suffered so much, both in soul and body, from men, from devils, and from his Father, if he had not been assured, that the reward promised him should be made good. See Heb. ix. 12, and x. 14; John vi. 39, and xvii. 12.

5. From the *intercession* of Christ. See John xvii. 11, 20, and xiv. 16; Luke xxii. 32; Heb. vii. 25.

6. From the intimate *union* which subsists between Christ and believers. See 1 Cor. xii. 12, &c.; John xiv. 19. Without Christ the head, believers, who are the members of his body, would be dead; and without the members, Christ the head would have no body; and his death would be in vain.

7. From the *prayers* of believers at the throne of grace. Christ was heard when he prayed for Peter, which is an encouragement to believers to pray the same prayer; convinced that in Christ their prayer will be heard and answered.

8. From the *continued influences* of the Holy Spirit. If believers are the temples of the Holy Ghost, it must be inconsistent with his dwelling in them, to say that they may fall away. See 1 Cor. vi. 19; Eph. i. 13, and iv. 30, where his work is expressed by *sealing*. See also Phil. i. 6.

9. From considering this work in those who have been guilty of aggravated sins, after they have been in a state of peace with God. Who can say that Peter, on the denial of his Lord, fell finally from a state of grace? who can say that David, on account of his sin, forfeited for ever the favour of God? or, who can prove that the gracious relation, which formerly subsisted between him and his God, was now finally dissolved? See Ps. li.

But although the children of God cannot fall finally from grace, yet they may, and often do, fall into many and great sins; and by these sins they may be, and often are, subjected, not indeed to the wrath of God as an angry judge, but to the chastisement of God as a father, who is displeased with them. See Ps. lxxxix. 30–34.

It may here be remarked, that this doctrine of the perseverance of the saints does not afford the least encouragement to licentiousness, as some are pleased to affirm. Every real believer, the more he is convinced of the love of God to his soul, and the more he feels the love of God shed abroad in his heart, will be the more zealous to promote the honour of that grace which he experiences. See Rom. vi., where this objection is fully refuted.

INFERENCES.

From this subject we learn,—1. The necessity of placing every part of the scheme of salvation in its due order, that the connection of one part with another may appear, and that the comfort of the believer may not be marred. 2. That we ought to seek after the sensible assurance of the love of God. 3. The necessity of using every spiritual means that it may be obtained. 4. That the wicked cannot have this assurance; seeing it is a benefit flowing from justification and sanctification. 5. The greatness of those comforts which arise from assurance. 6. That they who possess it are much indebted to the Spirit of grace; and that, if they grieve him, he may depart from them. 7. That peace of mind will fit us for every providence. 8. That peace of conscience can be obtained from the Word alone; and that peace obtained in any other way is extremely dangerous. 9. That the unbeliever cannot experience joy in the Holy Ghost. 10. That this joy can support in the midst of the most adverse providences. 11. That we ought to study to obtain it. 12. That the thoughts of the hypocrite and of the world, respecting the portion of the soul for ever, are diametrically opposite to those of the believer. 13. That every source of worldly joy shall soon fail, in the moments of affliction and at death; whereas the source of the believer's joy is inexhaustible. 14. The necessity of having this joy, if we would consult our best interests. 15. That they who have it should study to preserve it; and that all who have it not, should study to possess it. 16. The necessity of using every means that we may grow in grace. 17. That careless sinners are but barren in the Church of God, and in danger of being cut down as cumberers. 18. That believers have no cause to fear that they shall be given over unto death. 19. The danger of those who draw back from following the Lord. 20. That all who are pleased with a mere form of godliness, are unfruitful. 21. The necessity of an interest in the Spirit, that we may grow up before the Lord. 22. That every thing in the everlasting covenant is well-ordered and sure. 23. The security of the believer's blessedness for ever. 24. That the gifts and calling of God are without repentance. 25. That the hypocrite's case is most dangerous; and hence see the necessity of grace. 26. That it is dangerous in the extreme to go on in sin, because the grace of God abounds.

Benefits of Redemption at Death.

Q. 37.—What Benefits do Believers receive from Christ at Death?

The souls of believers are at their death made perfect in holiness, and do immediately pass into glory; and their bodies, being still united to Christ, do rest in their graves till the resurrection.

ANALYSIS AND PROOFS.

We are here taught,—

1. That the souls of believers are at death made perfect in holiness. Heb. xii. 23.—" To the spirits of just men made perfect."

2. That, after death, the souls of believers pass immediately into glory. Luke xxiii. 43.—" Jesus said unto him, Verily, I say unto thee, To-day shalt thou be with me in paradise." See also 2 Cor. v. 8.

3. That the bodies of believers, while in their graves, remain united to Christ. 1 Thess. iv. 14.—" Them also who sleep in Jesus will God bring with him."

4. That the bodies of believers " rest " in their graves. Isa. lvii. 2.—" They shall rest in their beds, each one walking in his uprightness."

5. That the bodies of believers shall be raised from their graves at the last day. 1 Thess. iv. 16.—" The dead in Christ shall rise first." See also Job xix. 26.

EXPLANATION.

Obs. 163.—*At death the souls of believers are made perfect in holiness.*

In the souls of believers at death, perfection appears in the following respects :—They feel themselves at liberty among the spirits of just men made perfect; they are delivered from sin, and from all the enemies with which they were surrounded in this world; they feel no more pain from the commission of sin; they are no longer vexed with the filthy communication of the wicked; they have now arrived at the full stature of perfection in Christ Jesus; they have now reached the summit of holiness and perfection; they are now perfect as God is perfect, and pure as he is pure; in a word, they are now the image of Jehovah, and conformed to Jesus, who is " the image of the invisible God."

Obs. 164.—*After death, the souls of believers immediately pass into glory.*

That the *souls of believers immediately pass into glory* is evident from several passages of Scripture : and it is a most pleasant subject of anticipation to the children of God; see Luke xxiii. 43,—where by *paradise* must be meant *heaven*, or the state of glory; Luke xvi. 22,—where *heaven* is expressed by *Abraham's bosom;* and Rev. xiv. 13,—where it is said, "Blessed are the dead who die in the Lord;" but where would the blessedness be, if the souls of believers sleep until the resurrection? See also Phil. i. 23; 2 Cor. v. 1, &c.; Rev. viii. 3.

The *glory* into which the souls of believers pass immediately after death, is inconceivable; for "eye hath not seen, nor ear heard, neither have entered into the heart of man, the things which God hath prepared for them that love him."—1 Cor. ii. 9. In Scripture, however, it is compared to a *kingdom*, to show the glorious dignity to which the saints are advanced,—Luke xii. 32; Rev. i. 6; to a *house not made with hands*, to denote the unspeakable excellency of the heavenly mansions, above the most stately mansions built by men,—2 Cor. v. 1; to an *incorruptible inheritance*, to intimate that the happiness of the saints will be eternal,—1 Pet. i. 4; and to a *better country*, to show that the things which are seen and temporal, are not to be compared to the things which are unseen and eternal,—Heb. xi. 16; 2 Cor. iv. 18.

Obs. 165.—*The bodies of believers "rest" in their graves, where they are still united to Christ.*

They are said to *rest* in their graves; because their graves are like beds of ease, where their bodies sleep in safety till the morning of the resurrection.—Isa. lvii. 2.

That their bodies remain *united to Christ* is evident; for death cannot dissolve the inseparable union which exists between Christ and believers,—2 Thess. iv. 14; see also John xi. 11, where Christ speaks of Lazarus as his friend after death; and Rom. viii. 11, which passage evidently implies as much as that we must believe, that the Spirit who dwells in the children of God, shall quicken their mortal bodies; which shows, that although in the grave, they are still members of Christ, seeing his Spirit dwells in them.

Obs. 166.—*The bodies of believers shall be raised from their graves at the last day.*

They shall rest in their graves *until the resurrection*, but no longer. Then the gates of death shall be unlocked, and the bars of the grave shall be broken off, and they shall be raised up and united to their souls; after which the whole man shall rest eternally in the love of God, and Christ shall bear the glory.

Obs. 167.—*At death, the state of unbelievers is very different from that of believers.*

To unbelievers the grave is a *prison*, where they are kept in close confinement until the resurrection; and their souls are sent immediately to hell, where they are filled with horror and anguish, and reserved, together with the fallen angels, in chains of darkness until the judgment of the great day.—2 Pet. ii. 4.

INFERENCES.

From this subject we learn,—1. The necessity of growing in conformity to the image of Jesus, which alone can qualify for the enjoyment of God in glory. 2. That the saints have much comfort in affliction. 3. That the believer cannot be deprived of his happiness, when he is prepared for it. 4. The happiness of believers, and the misery of unbelievers, immediately after death. 5. The strength of Christ's love to his people: it is stronger than death, for death cannot destroy it.—Rom. viii. 38, 39. 6. The safety of believers, even after they leave this world, and before they enter upon the full reward promised. 7. That there shall be a resurrection, when the grave shall not be able to retain their precious dust. 8. That nothing should discourage the Lord's people while they are in this world, seeing he will accomplish the good work which he hath begun. 9. That believers have no reason to be afraid at death. 10. That sorrow above measure for the death of departed friends is incompatible with a belief of the resurrection.

Benefits of Redemption at the Resurrection.

Q. 38.—What Benefits do Believers receive from Christ at the Resurrection?

At the resurrection believers being raised up in glory, shall be openly acknowledged and acquitted in the day of judgment, and made perfectly blessed in the full enjoying of God to all eternity.

ANALYSIS AND PROOFS.

We are here taught,—

1. That at the resurrection believers shall be raised up in glory. 1 Cor. xv. 43.—" It is sown in dishonour, it is raised in glory."

2. That believers shall be openly acknowledged by Christ at the day of judgment. Luke xii. 8.—" Whosoever shall confess me before men, him shall the Son of Man also confess before the angels of God." See also Matt. x. 32.

3. That believers shall be acquitted by Christ in the judgment. 1 Pet. i. 7.—" That the trial of your faith being much more precious than of gold that perisheth, though it be tried with fire, might be found unto praise, and honour, and glory, at the appearing of Jesus Christ." See also Matt. xxv. 21.

4. That believers shall be made perfectly blessed in the enjoyment of God. 1 Cor. ii. 9.—" Eye hath not seen, nor ear

heard, neither have entered into the heart of man, the things which God hath prepared for them that love him." See also 1 John iii. 2.

5. That believers shall enjoy God through all eternity. 1 Thess. iv. 17.—" So shall we ever be with the Lord."

EXPLANATION.

Obs. 168.—*At the resurrection believers shall be raised up in glory.*

That there shall be a *resurrection*, is evident from the following passages of Scripture:—Dan. xii. 2.—" And many of them that sleep in the dust of the earth shall awake, some to everlasting life, and some to shame and everlasting contempt." John v. 28, 29.—" Marvel not at this; for the hour is coming, in which all that are in their graves shall hear his voice, and shall come forth, they that have done good unto the resurrection of life, and they that have done evil unto the resurrection of damnation." 1 Cor. xv. 13, 14.—" But if there be no resurrection of the dead, then is Christ not risen. And if Christ be not risen, then is our preaching vain, and your faith is also vain." And again, ver. 16-18.—" For if the dead rise not, then is not Christ raised; and if Christ be not raised, your faith is vain; ye are yet in your sins. Then they also who are fallen asleep in Christ are perished." See also Job xix. 25-27. Seeing, then, that God hath revealed in his Word that he will raise the dead, and seeing also that he is infinite in power, and consequently, can raise them, it cannot be doubted that there will be a general resurrection. We have several evidences of God's power in raising the dead, both in the Old and New Testaments. See 1 Kings xvii. 22; 2 Kings iv. 35, and xiii. 21; Mark v. 41; Acts ix. 40; Luke vii. 12, 15; John xi. 39, 44.

The dead shall be raised with the *same* bodies, see 1 Cor. xv. 42-44, 53, 54; from which it is evident, that with respect to substance, the same bodies shall be raised, although they shall be endued with different qualities; for were not this the case, it would be a creation, and not a resurrection.

At the resurrection, the bodies of believers shall be raised up *in glory.* By this we are to understand, that they shall be raised incorruptible, glorious, powerful, and spiritual.—1 Cor. xv. 42-44. They shall be *incorruptible;* they shall be no more subject to disease or to death. They shall be *glorious;* no defect shall be observable in them, but they shall be full of splendour and brightness for they shall be fashioned like unto Christ's glorious body.—Phil. iii. 21. They shall be *powerful;* they shall not know weariness, for they shall be girded with strength, and in the strength of the Lord shall they go. They shall be *spiritual;* they shall not indeed be changed into *spirits*, but they shall be endued with spiritual qualities; they shall be of a very refined constitution; for they shall hunger no more, neither thirst any more; nor will they ever sleep, but serve God day and night in the heavenly temple. —Rev. vi. 15, 16.

Obs. 169.—*Believers shall be openly acknowledged and acquitted by Christ at the day of judgment.*

1. They shall be *openly acknowledged* or owned by Christ as his. They shall be owned by him, not in the presence of a few, not only before their brethren, but before many witnesses, before an assembled world, before devils, and before God and the holy angels.—Matt. x. 32.

2. They shall be *acquitted* by Christ, the judge of all. They shall be acquitted, not only from every false aspersion cast upon them, but also from the real guilt of all their sins, on account of their interest in Christ and his righteousness. Neither men. nor devils, nor law, nor conscience, shall have any thing to prefer against them, which shall not be fully answered by Jesus.—Rom. viii. 33, 34.

There are several other benefits, of which believers shall partake in the day of judgment, besides those above mentioned. They shall be gathered together from all quarters of the earth by the angels,—Matt. xxiv. 31; they shall be caught up together in the clouds to meet the Lord Jesus, who will descend from heaven with a shout,—1 Thess. iv. 16, 17; they shall be placed at the right hand of Jesus,—Matt. xxv. 33; they shall be invited by Christ to take possession of the glorious inheritance prepared for them,—Matt. xxv. 34; they shall sit with Christ as assessors in judgment on fallen angels and wicked men.—1 Cor. vi. 2, 3.

Obs. 170.—*Believers shall be made perfectly blessed in the full enjoyment of God to all eternity.*

They shall be *made perfectly blessed,* or they shall be completely delivered from all sin and misery, and fully possessed of all happiness. Blessedness consists in freedom from sin and sorrow, from suffering and temptation, and from all evil whatever. But there can be no freedom from these things till death; nor even at death are believers perfectly blessed, for before this can take place, the soul and the body must be united; and when these are united, they shall be fully satisfied. " When Christ, who is their life, shall appear, then shall they also appear with him in glory."—Col. iii. 4.

The highest degree of happiness consists in the *full enjoyment of God,* the chief good.—Ps. lxxiii. 25. This implies that believers shall have the glorious presence of God with them,—Rev. xxi. 3; that they shall have the immediate and beatific vision of his face,—Rev. xxii. 4; 1 Cor. xiii. 12; 1 John iii. 2; that they shall have a full persuasion and sense of God's love to them, and perfect love in their hearts to him which necessarily results from the vision of God in heaven; and that they shall have fulness and exceeding joy.—Ps. xvi. 11; Jude 24.

And this full enjoyment of God by believers shall continue *through all eternity.* It shall be without interruption and without end.—1 Thess. iv. 17.

Obs. 171.—*At the last day, the state of unbelievers shall be very different from that of believers.*

In the day of judgment, the condition of the wicked will be miserable beyond expression. Their bodies shall be raised from the grave by Christ as their offended judge; and shall be endued with strength and immortality, only to render them capable of eternal misery. They shall with horror behold Christ coming in flaming fire, to take vengeance upon them.—Rev. i. 7; 2 Thess. i. 7, 8. They shall be placed before the judgment-seat of Christ, where they shall be judged and sentenced to eternal punishment. —Rev. xx. 11, 12; Matt. xxv. 41. And immediately after this, they shall be driven from the presence of the Lord into hell, where they shall be punished both in soul and body throughout the endless ages of eternity.—Matt. xxv. 46; Rom. ii. 8, 9; Rev. xiv. 11.

INFERENCES.

From this subject we learn,—1. The encouragement which believers have to go on their way rejoicing. 2. That there shall be a great difference between the righteous and the wicked at the resurrection. 3. That believers shall soon obtain the redemption of their bodies. 4. The happiness resulting from confessing Christ before men, and the danger of denying him. 5. That the enemies of believers shall in due time have their reward. 6. That the saints have no cause to fear the consequences of the resurrection. 7. That believers, while in this world, can enjoy no blessedness which is full. 8. That a final separation shall be made between the righteous and the wicked at the day of general judgment.

PART SECOND

THE DUTY WHICH GOD REQUIRES OF MAN.

INTRODUCTION.

Nature of Man's Duty in General

Q. 39.—*What is the duty which God requireth of man?*
The duty which God requireth of man, is obedience to his revealed will.

ANALYSIS AND PROOFS.

We are here taught,—
1. That there are certain duties required by God from men. Deut. x. 12.—" And now, Israel, what doth the Lord thy God require of thee, but to fear the Lord thy God, to walk in his ways, and to love him, and to serve the Lord thy God with all thy heart, and with all thy soul."
2. That the sum of man's duty to God is obedience. 1 Sam. xv. 22.—" Behold, to obey is better than sacrifice, and to hearken than the fat of rams."
3. That the extent of the obedience required by God is a universal obedience. James ii. 10.—" Whosoever shall keep the whole law, and yet offend in one point, he is guilty of all."
4. That the quality of the obedience required from man is a perfect and perpetual obedience. Matt. xxii. 37.—" Thou shalt love the Lord thy God, with all thy heart, and with all thy soul, and with all thy mind."
5. That the only rule of man's obedience is the revealed will of God. Micah vi. 8.—" He hath showed thee, O man, what is good ; and what doth the Lord require of thee, but to do justly, and to love mercy, and to walk humbly with thy God."

EXPLANATION.

Obs. 172.—*The duty which God requires of man is obedience.*

As all mankind are the servants, the children, and the subjects of God (that is, in respect of obedience, although not in a gracious sense), all men are equally bound to obey him.

The *obligations* under which man is to yield that obedience which God requires, are these:—

1. Man is bound to obey God, because he is his creator, preserver, and benefactor.

2. Man is bound to obey God, because he is the supreme sovereign Lord, king, and lawgiver. As he is the one lawgiver of all, and ours in particular, having committed to us his law, we are bound to receive it in the love of it, and to make it appear that we have not received it in vain.

3. Man is bound to obey God, because this is the chief end for which man was made.

4. Man is bound to obey God, because of his glorious excellencies. Surely they must be blinded to the excellencies of the Divine nature, who see nothing in God why he should be loved. And how can love to him be manifested but by obedience?

5. Man is bound to obey God in a special manner, from a sense of his *love* to sinners in *Jesus Christ*. If this love, which passeth all understanding, has no effect in producing an unfeigned obedience, nothing whatever will. This is the peculiar motive by which the friends of Jesus are actuated. See 1 John iv. 19; 2 Cor. v. 14, &c.

Obs. 173.—*The rule of man's obedience is the revealed will of God.*

The will of God is either *secret* or *revealed*.

1. God's *secret will* respects all things that are done and shall be done; and it extends even to sinful actions, which he permits and overrules to his own glory. This is the rule by which God himself acts, and not the rule of man's obedience.—Deut. xxix. 29.

2. God's *revealed will* respects those things which may and ought to be done; and it extends only to those things which are duty, and which in themselves tend to his glory. This is that which is contained in the Scriptures of the Old and New Testaments, and is the only rule of man's obedience.—Micah vi. 8.

Obs. 174.—*The obedience which God requires of man is universal, perpetual, perfect, sincere, inward, and willing obedience.*

1. God requires *universal* obedience. Our obedience must have respect to all God's commandments.—Ps. cxix. 6. They are all stamped with the same Divine authority. See James ii. 10, 11.

2. God requires *perpetual* obedience. We must keep God's law continually.—Ps. cxix. 44. We must be constant and steady in our obedience to the will of God, and never dare to act contrary to it.

3. God requires *perfect* obedience. The law must be obeyed perfectly, either by the sinner himself, or by a surety. But the

former is impossible; and therefore all those who reject Christ, the only surety of sinners, must assuredly perish.

4. God requires *sincere* obedience. Without sincerity, or when the heart is not engaged, there can be no acceptable obedience. Hypocritical obedience may please men, but it cannot please God, who is the searcher of hearts.

5. God requires *inward* obedience as well as outward. His law extends to the thoughts of the *heart*, as well as to the actions of the *life*.

6. God requires *willing* obedience. They who obey the law of God from constraint, and not willingly, are *slaves*, and not *sons*.

INFERENCES.

From this subject we learn,—1. That no excuse can be given why man should not obey God. 2. That man is bound to obey God, in whatever circumstances he may be placed. 3. That man ought to reverence every part of the Word of God, which is calculated to point out his duty in every circumstance. 4. That God requires the obedience of the heart, as well as external obedience. 5. That man is bound by the law of God as long as he lives; and that every part of it ought to be regarded by him. 6. That love ought to be the great motive of our obedience. 7. The necessity of an interest in Christ, who hath magnified the law and made it honourable. 8. That man is not left to act in the matter of obedience according to the dictates of his own mind. 9. That it is the honour of man to serve the Lord. 10. The happiness of the obedient, and the misery of the disobedient. See Isa. iii. 10, 11.

CHAPTER I.

SECT. I.—OF THE MORAL LAW, BINDING ON ALL RATIONAL CREATURES, AS SUMMED UP IN THE TEN COMMANDMENTS, WHICH ARE DIVIDED INTO TWO TABLES ;—THE FIRST COMPREHENDING OUR DUTY TO GOD, AND THE SECOND OUR DUTY TO MAN.

Of the Moral Law.

Q. 40.—What did God at first reveal to Man for the rule of his obedience?

The rule which God at first revealed to man for his obedience, was the moral law.

ANALYSIS AND PROOFS.

We are here taught,—

1. That the first rule of obedience was given to man in the

constitution of his nature. Rom. ii. 15.—" Who show the work of the law written on their hearts."

2. That the first rule of obedience given to man in the constitution of his nature, was the moral law. Gen. i. 27.—" God created man in his own image." See also Eccl. vii. 29.

3. That the moral law is universal and unchangeable. Matt. v. 18.—" Verily, I say unto you, Till heaven and earth pass, one jot or one tittle shall in nowise pass from the law, till all be fulfilled."

EXPLANATION.

Obs. 175.—*The laws of God are distinguished into natural and positive.*

1. The *natural law*, or *law of nature*, is that necessary and unalterable rule of right and wrong, founded in the nature of God; and by which all men, as rational creatures, are indispensably bound.—Rom. ii. 14, 15.

2. *Positive laws* are those laws or institutions which depend upon the sovereign will and pleasure of God; and which he might not have enjoined if he had pleased, without making any change in his nature. Such was the command given to our first parents respecting the forbidden fruit, and such were all the ceremonial precepts enjoined upon the Hebrews under the Old Testament dispensation.

Obs. 176.—*The first rule of obedience given to man in the constitution of his nature, was the moral law.*

It is here supposed that man has always been under a law; for, being a rational creature, capable of knowing and obeying the will of God, and owing obedience to his Creator by virtue of his natural dependence on him, it behoved him to be always under a law.

The *first rule of obedience* which God gave to man, was the moral law.

Although the word *moral* has literally a respect to the *manners* of men, yet, when applied to the law, it signifies that which is *perpetually binding*, in opposition to that which is binding only for a time.

Of the moral law there was no express revelation made to Adam in his state of innocence; for there he needed none, seeing it was interwoven in the constitution of his nature, he having been created after the image of God.—Eccl. vii. 29. When it is said, then, that the moral law was *the rule which God at first revealed to man*, we are to understand by this expression, that the moral law was so distinctly written in his heart and impressed in his nature, that it was equal to an express revelation.

But the moral law is not only to be viewed as the *rule* of our obedience, it must also be viewed as the *reason* of it. We must not only do what the law requires, and avoid what it forbids, but we must do the one, for this very reason, that God commands us to do it; and we must avoid the other, for this very reason, that God commands us to avoid it. See Lev. xviii. 4, 5.

Obs. 177.—*The moral law is a universal, an unchangeable, a perfect, and a spiritual, holy, just, and good law.*

1. The moral law is a *universal* law. It is binding on all men, at all times, and in every situation in which they can be placed.—Rom. ii. 14, 15.

2. The moral law is an *unchangeable* law. With respect to God, indeed, those precepts which do not flow absolutely and immediately from his nature, may, in certain cases, be altered or changed, provided it be done by his own express appointment. But with respect to man, all the precepts of the moral law are of immutable obligation, and none of them can be dispensed with by him, on any condition whatever.—Matt. v. 18.

3. The moral law is a *perfect* law. It comprehends the whole of man's duty to God, to his neighbour, and to himself.

4. The moral law is a *spiritual, holy, just,* and *good* law. It is spiritual, inasmuch as it reaches the thoughts and intents of the heart; holy, inasmuch as its end is to render man holy; just, inasmuch as every part of it is congenial to the eternal rules of equity and justice; and good, inasmuch as it is designed to make man good, and useful to his neighbour and to himself, and to make him honour God.

Obs. 178.—*Righteousness and life cannot be obtained by the moral law.*

The moral law was indeed revealed at first, that by obedience to it man might be justified; but now it is not revealed for that end; for no man can obey it perfectly, so as to obtain justification by it. Since the first transgression of man, the language of Scripture is, " By the deeds of the law there shall no flesh be justified."—Rom. iii. 20. Had it been possible that man could have obtained justification by the law, we should have never heard of the Son of God " appearing in the likeness of sinful flesh, and putting away sin by the sacrifice of himself."

It is said, indeed, that " the man who doeth these things shall live by them ;" but this expression, and others of similar import. are only designed to show how impossible it is to obtain life by the moral law; and to lead us to see the necessity of obtaining it in some other way than by our own obedience.—Gal. iii. 24.

It may here be remarked, that when it is said that believers are " not under the law but under grace" (Rom. vi. 14), we are to understand by this expression, that they are not under the law as a *covenant of works,* as Adam was, to be justified or condemned by it: but that they are under it only as a *rule of life.*

Obs. 179.—*The moral law may be viewed in three forms,— as a law of nature, as a covenant of works, and as a rule of life.*

First, It may be viewed as a *law of nature,* antecedent to, and disengaged from, any covenant transaction between God and man. And here the following things may be observed:—
 1. God imposed it as a creator and an absolute sovereign.
 2. It was written upon man's heart at his creation.—Gen. i. 26; Eccl. vii. 29. If man was made in the Divine image, power to obey the law must have been created with him, otherwise he would not have been perfect when he came from the creating hand of God.
 3. It contained no positive precept, but obliged all its subjects to believe everything which God should reveal, and perform everything which he should command. And hence,
 4. Its subjects not being confirmed in holiness of heart and life, it implied a sanction of infinite punishment to every transgressor, as the due reward of his sin.
 5. The most perfect obedience of innocent man having no proper desert before God, especially of eternal happiness, it implied no promise of any such reward, or that men should ever be confirmed under it as an easy and delightful rule of life. And hence,
 6. It did not admit of God's accepting anything less than perfect obedience. This is evident from Rom. vi. 23,—"Death is the wages of sin." See Ezek. xviii. 4.
 7. All men, as rational creatures, were subject to this law; it having been written on man's heart at his creation.—Rom. ii. 14, 15.

Second, It may be viewed as a *covenant of works;* in which form we ought to be well acquainted with the law; for it is in this form that we see both the misery of those who are under it, and the happiness of those who have been delivered from it. And here the following things may be remarked:—
 1. An absolute God, condescending to friendship, made alliance and familiarity with holy and perfect man; and was the imposer of it. See Gen. ii. 17.
 2. It included not only all the commands of the law of nature, but also some positive institutions. See Gen. ii. 16, &c.
 3. It not only denounced infinite punishment against every transgressor of it, but also promised eternal happiness to the perfect fulfiller of it.
 4. It binds mankind, not only as authoritatively imposed by God their sovereign, but also as accepted by themselves, in their own self-engagement to fulfil it. See Gen. iii. 2, 3; where we find that our first parents agreed to the condition, and acquiesced in the threatening.

5. The original scope and end of it was, that man might obtain eternal life by his own obedience as its condition. See Rom. vii. 10, and x. 5.

6. As it did not admit of God's accepting any obedience, but that which was absolutely perfect and answerable to all its demands; so the acceptance of the fulfiller's person depended on the acceptance of his obedience.

7. In consequence of God's making this law-covenant with Adam, all his natural descendants, while in their natural state, are under it before God. See Eph. ii. 3; Rom. ix. 30, &c.

Third, It may be viewed as the *law of Christ*, or as a *rule of life*. And here the following things may be observed:—

1. It has the whole authority of God, as a creator and sovereign, as well as a redeemer, giving it a binding force. See Matt. v. 48; 1 Pet. i. 18.

2. It proceeds immediately from Jesus Christ, God-man, Mediator; and from God, as our creator and sovereign, as reconciled and dwelling in him. See 1 Cor. ix. 21; Gal. vi. 2; 2 Cor. v. 19, &c.

3. Its precepts are the very same as those of the covenant of works, and demand the same perfection of obedience. See Matt. xxii. 36, &c.; Phil. iv. 8. For if the law of Christ did not demand the same perfection of obedience, it would be changeable in its demands; and, consequently, would cease to be an exact transcript of the Divine nature.

4. The subjects of it being fully and irrevocably instated in the favour of God, and entitled to eternal life in Christ, it has no sanction of judicial rewards and punishments. See John v. 24: Rom. v. 21, and viii. 1, 33, &c.

5. The end which God had in view in giving this law, is different from that which was proposed in giving the law as a covenant of works. The end which he had in view, in giving the law as a covenant of works, was, that life might be obtained by it, and that his favour might be procured as a judge, and also a title to happiness. But the end which he had in view in giving it as a rule of life, was to direct, and to bind, and to excite believers in Christ to improve their full and irrevocable justification, and begun possession of eternal life, in cordial gratitude to him, and also in preparation for complete salvation; so that their obedience, in its highest view, is a part of their happiness here, as well as it will be hereafter. See Luke i. 74. &c.; Rom. vii. 4, &c.; Heb. xii. 28; 1 Pet. ii. 9; Gal. ii. 19.

6. It supposes all its subjects to have already full strength and sufficient motives and encouragement in Christ; and although it required perfect obedience from Christ, yet it admits of God's accepting the imperfect "obedience of faith:" but this is not to be viewed as the ground of the believer's acceptance, or what is called the condition of eternal life; but only as a fruit of his union

with Christ, and an evidence of his being fully accepted in him. See Eph. i. 6; Rom. xii. 1; 1 Cor. xv. 58.

7. All believers, and they alone, are the subjects of this law of Christ; for they who are not in Christ, are still in a natural state, and consequently under the law as a covenant of works. See 1 Cor. ix. 21; Gal. vi. 2.

Obs. 180.—*The moral law is of use—to all men in general, to unregenerate men, and to believers.*

First, The moral law is of use to *all men* in the following respects:—

1. To teach them their duty to God, to their neighbour, and to themselves; and to bind them to it by the infinite authority of God.—Micah vi. 8.

2. To discover to them the holiness, the equity, and the goodness of the nature and works of God.—Rom. vii. 12.

3. To restrain them from sin, and to encourage them to holiness.—Ps. xix. 11; Isa. i. 19; Ezek. xviii.; Deut. iv. and xxx.

4. To convince them of their sinfulness, and their misery on account of sin, and of their utter inability to recover themselves by keeping the commandments.—Rom. v. 20, iii. 19, &c., and vii. 8, &c.

5. To show them their need of Christ, and of his righteousness and grace; and to excite them to apply them to their souls.—Gal. iii. 24.

Second, The moral law is of use to *unregenerate men* in the following respects:—

1. To convince and awaken their consciences.

2. To denounce the wrath of God against their sins, and thus to affect them with a deep sense of it.—Rom. ii. 8, 9.

3. To bridle the rage of their lusts.—1 Tim. i. 9.

4. To drive them, when convinced of their sin and misery, and their inability to recover themselves, to Jesus Christ as their almighty Saviour.—Gal. iii. 24; Rom. x. 4.

5. To fix in their consciences a deep sense of their having those very characters of sinfulness and misery, by which men are particularly invited to receive Jesus Christ and his salvation.—1 Tim. i. 15; Isa. xlvi. 12, lv. 2, &c., and lxv. 1, &c.; Matt. ix. 13, xi. 28, and xviii. 11; Prov. i. 22; Jer. iii. 1, &c.

6. To consign them to redoubled damnation if they reject Jesus Christ. For by the law all are condemned already; and if they still continue in unbelief, they are condemned in this way too; so that they are doubly condemned, and no remedy awaits them.—John iii. 18, 36; Heb. ii. 3, and x. 26, &c.; Matt. xi. 20, &c.

Third, The moral law is of use to *believers* in the following respects:—

1. To show them what Christ, from love to their souls, did

and suffered in their stead.—Gal. iii. 13, and iv. 4, 5; Rom. viii. 3, &c.

2. To show them their inexpressible deficiency in holiness.

3. To instruct them what grateful service they owe to Christ and his Father, and at what perfection of holiness they ought always to aim.—Phil. iii. 8, 9; 1 Tim. i. 5; 2 Cor. vii. 1; 1 Pet. i. 13, &c.; 2 Pet. i. 5, &c.; Matt. v. 48.

4. To attest the truth of their begun sanctification, and to comfort them as Israelites indeed, who walk in the law of the Lord after the inward man of implanted grace.—1 John iii. 14; 2 Cor. i. 12.

Obs. 181.—*Besides the moral law, there are other laws,— namely, the ceremonial and judicial, which God gave to his people of old as the rule of their obedience.*

1. The *ceremonial law* was a system of positive precepts, concerning the external worship of God; chiefly designed to typify Christ *as then to come*, and to lead them to the knowledge of the way of salvation through him.—Heb. x. 1. This law is not obligatory under the New Testament dispensation; for although the Divine truths represented by these ceremonies, which were instituted by God himself, are unchangeably the *same;* yet the observation of the ceremonies themselves was abrogated by the death and satisfaction of Christ, in which they were fully accomplished.—John i. 17. That the ceremonial law was abolished by Christ, is evident from the destruction of the temple of Jerusalem, in which alone it was lawful to offer sacrifices. God would have never permitted this to have taken place, if these ceremonial institutions had been to subsist after the death of Jesus Christ, of whom it was predicted, that he should "cause the sacrifice and the oblation to cease."—Dan. ix. 27. See also Jer. iii. 16.

2. The *judicial law* was that body of laws given by God for the government of the Jews, partly founded in the law of nature, and partly respecting them as they were a nation *distinct* from all others. See Lev. xxv. 13; Exod. xxiii. 11; Numb. xxx. 15; Deut. xvi. 16. As far as this law respects the peculiar constitution of the Hebrew nation, it is entirely abrogated; but, as far as it contains any statute founded in the law of nature common to all nations, it is still obligatory.

INFERENCES.

From this subject we learn,—1. That seeing God is man's Sovereign, man ought to obey him. 2. That no law can bind, or ought to bind the conscience, but the moral law. 3. That man is inexcusable, if he obey not the moral law, which is revealed to him. 4. The danger of trusting in our own obedience for justification and life. 5. The necessity of an interest in *him*, who has obeyed the law in every part, and who alone can deliver from its curse. 6. That we have great reason to humble ourselves under the mighty hand of God; seeing we have sinned times and ways without number. 7. That man is fallen from his first state. 8. That, considering circumstances, the way to life was easy under the first covenant. 9. The misery of sinners in a natural state; seeing they are still under the law as a covenant of works. 10. The happiness of believers in Christ; for they are now delivered from the law as a covenant. 11. That there is only one way to the Father; the way by working being for ever shut up. 12. The advantages and obligations of those who are in Christ. 13. That Christ is the only refuge for sinners. 14. The necessity of faith and repentance. 15. That salvation is wholly by grace; and that Christ is our salvation. 16. That the obedience of believers is an evidence of their election by God.

Of the Summary of the Moral Law.

Q. 41.—Where is the Moral Law summarily comprehended?

The Moral Law is summarily comprehended in the Ten Commandments.

ANALYSIS AND PROOFS.

We are here taught,—

1. That the moral law is fully contained in the Scriptures. 2. Tim. iii. 16, 17.—"All Scripture is given by inspiration of God, and is profitable for doctrine, for reproof, for correction, for instruction in righteousness; that the man of God may be perfect, thoroughly furnished unto all good works."

2. That there are summaries of the moral law. Rom. xiii. 9.—"If there be any other commandment, it is briefly comprehended in this saying, Thou shalt love thy neighbour as thyself."

3. That the sum of the moral law is contained in the Ten Commandments. Deut. x. 4.—"He wrote on the tables, according to the first writing, the Ten Commandments, which the Lord spake unto you in the mount." See also Matt. xix. 17, &c.

EXPLANATION.

Obs. 182.—*The Ten Commandments were written by the finger of God himself on two tables of stone, and delivered by him to the Israelites from Mount Sinai with an audible voice, accompanied with great terror.*

1. They were written immediately by God himself on two tables of stone. This was done twice. The first two tables having been broken by Moses, on occasion of the Israelites' idolatry, God condescended to write on other two tables the same words that he wrote on the former two.—Exod. xxxii. 16,

and xxxiv. 1. These last two tables were hewn by Moses, the typical mediator, and laid up in the ark. This was intended to show, that, although the covenant of works, made with the first Adam, was violated by him, yet it was fulfilled in every respect by Jesus Christ the true Mediator. The Ten Commandments were written on *stone*, to intimate the perpetuity and eternal obligation of the moral law.—Ps. iii. 8.

2. They were delivered by God from Mount Sinai with an audible voice, accompanied with great terror. They were given in a very solemn manner, with dread and awful majesty; and the promulgation of them was accompanied with thunder and lightning; and hence the law is called a *fiery law*. All this showed how vain it was for sinners to expect life by the works of the law; and hence it also pointed out the necessity of a Mediator.

The law was thus given and renewed for the following reasons: —1. To confirm the natural law. 2. To correct the same in those things in which it was corrupted by the fall, and supply its defects. The law of nature is defective; because it cannot discover to man the cause of all his misery, nor the evils that reign in his heart; because natural judgment is perverted, so that it is ready to call good evil, and evil good; because it does not drive men from themselves to the only remedy. 3. To supply what was wanting in the law of nature, or what was defaced by sin. And, 4. To convince men of their inability to yield that obedience which it requires, and thus to lead them to see the necessity of a Mediator to satisfy the law, both with respect to its commands and its penalty.

Obs. 183.—*The moral law, which is fully contained in the Scriptures, is summarily comprehended in the Ten Commandments.*

To be *summarily comprehended*, is to be briefly summed up in a few words, and these words so well chosen, that they comprehend much more than they express. See Rom. xiii. 9.

The Ten Commandments comprehend the moral law, or the whole duty of man—all that he is to believe, and all that he is to practise. There is nothing commanded or forbidden by God, which is not implied in some one or other of the Ten Commandments.

That the Ten Commandments are a summary of the whole Word of God, with respect both to *faith* and *practice*, will be evident, if we consider them as they were promulgated by God from Mount Sinai :—

I. The First Commandment shows that there is no god besides the living and true God; that this God is to be worshipped; and that Divine worship is to be given to none else. It also shows that faith in this God is absolutely necessary; and that we are bound to receive whatever he hath been pleased to reveal: for, if we do not believe what he hath revealed, we do not acknowledge him to be God.

II. The Second Commandment also shows us the object of worship; but it also points out the necessity of giving to God that glory which is due unto his name; which is done by worshipping him as he hath appointed in his Word, by receiving all his ordinances, and by preserving them, as he hath enjoined,—not falsifying them, or mixing them with the foolish inventions of the human mind.

III. The Third Commandment respects the name of God; and points out the use which we ought to make of it, and of the various venerable attributes ascribed to him in Scripture,—that as they are holy, so they ought to be kept holy; and also the right use of all his ordinances, of his Word, and of his works.

IV. The Fourth Commandment shows us that a particular portion of our time is to be devoted to the service of God, namely, that day which he hath called by his own name; and that it ought to be kept holy in all manner of conversation, and spent in the public, and private, and secret duties of religion.

V. The Fifth Commandment shows us the manner in which we are to perform the various duties which are incumbent upon us in the various relations in which we are placed; whether we view ourselves, with respect to others, either as superiors, or inferiors, or equals. To this commandment are referred relative duties of every kind.

VI. The Sixth Commandment not only requires an abstinence from open and avowed murder, but also shows us the necessity of using every means for the preservation of our own life and of the life of our neighbour.

VII. The Seventh Commandment requires every means to be used by us, that the chastity both of ourselves and others may be preserved in heart, speech, and behaviour; and that nothing may be done in this respect which dishonours God, and which warreth against the soul.

VIII. The Eighth Commandment requires honesty in every respect; and the use of every lawful means of procuring and furthering the wealth and outward estate both of ourselves and others.

IX. The Ninth Commandment shows the necessity of maintaining and promoting the truth among men; and of speaking the truth, and nothing but the truth, when lawfully called to do so, especially in bearing witness.

X. The Tenth Commandment shows the necessity of contentment in the various stations in which we may be placed in the providence of God; and of not envying others on account of their prosperity; and it also requires us to have and to maintain a right and charitable disposition towards our neighbour and all that he hath

Obs. 184.—*That the Ten Commandments may be properly understood, that we may know the extent of our duty, and that the law may not be deprived of its due, various rules are necessary to be observed.*

1. The law is perfect, and binds every one to full conformity in the whole man to the righteousness thereof, and to entire obedience for ever; so as to require the utmost perfection of every duty, and to forbid the least degree of every sin.—Ps. xix. 7.

2. The law is spiritual; and so reacheth the understanding, the will, and the affections, and all the other powers of the soul; as well as words, and works, and gestures. See Rom. vii. 14; 1 Tim. i. 5.

3. One and the same thing, in different respects, is required or forbidden in several commandments.

4. Where a duty is commanded, the contrary sin is forbidden; and where a sin is forbidden, the contrary duty is commanded. Where a promise is annexed, the contrary threatening is included; and where a threatening is annexed, the contrary promise is included.

5. What God forbids is at no time to be done; what he commands is always our duty; and yet every particular duty is not to be done at all times.

6. Under one sin or duty, all those of the same kind are forbidden or commanded; together with all the causes, means, occasions, and appearances thereof, and provocations thereunto.

7. What is forbidden or commanded to ourselves, we are bound, according to our places, to endeavour that it may be avoided or performed by others, according to the duty of their places.

8. In what is commanded to others, we are bound, according to our places and callings, to be helpful to them; and to beware of partaking with others in what is forbidden them.

To these rules, which are given in the Larger Catechism, the following one may be added:—

The duties of the *First Table* of the law, or those which we owe to God, are of greater importance than the duties of the *Second Table*, or those which we owe to man. Our love to God can be discovered to be *supreme*, only by preferring him above our chief joy—by loving him above every earthly consideration. Whatever duties, then, we are commanded to perform to our neighbour, those which we owe to God must be preferred; and when his glory is concerned, we must not hesitate a moment what we should do. What regards ourselves must also be omitted, when the glory of God is concerned; for, if we lose our life for his sake, we shall find it; but if we seek to preserve it, when he calls for it, we shall lose it.—Matt. x. 39.

INFERENCES.

From this subject we learn,—1. That we may know our duty

and that we are without excuse, if we honour not the Ten Commandments with an unreserved obedience. 2. That, seeing we have the Scriptures, we ought to seek after the knowledge of our duty more and more, that we may become more and more holy. 3. That, seeing the law is so clearly revealed, the sin of those who trample it under foot is highly aggravated. 4. That the God who gave this law, is full of glorious majesty. 5. That the disobedient shall not escape the curse of the law, if they go on still in their trespasses. 6. That Jesus alone is the hope of the sinner; for he hath magnified the law and made it honourable. 7. That all may deem a Saviour from the curse of the law an unspeakable blessing; for to him they may go, and they shall be saved. 8. The character of the law, and the necessity of obedience, and consequently of Jesus Christ. 9. That the law of God is beautifully harmonious in every part of it. 10. That God is a rewarder of those who love him, as well as a just God to the workers of iniquity. 11. The necessity of shunning every sin whatever. 12. That all ought to take heed, lest they be ensnared by sin, or by the means which lead to the commission of it. 13. That we are in part our brother's keeper, and ought not to suffer sin upon him. 14. That God is the object of our supreme regard, and that we do not glorify him if we do not act accordingly.

Sum of the Ten Commandments.

Q. 42.—What is the Sum of the Ten Commandments?

The sum of the Ten Commandments is, to love the Lord our God with all our heart, with all our soul, with all our strength, and with all our mind; and our neighbour as ourselves.

ANALYSIS AND PROOFS.

We are here taught,—

1. That the whole of man's obedience is comprehended in love. Rom. xiii. 10.—" Love is the fulfilling of the law."

2. That the first great object of our love is the Lord our God. Matt. xxii. 37, 38.—" Thou shalt love the Lord thy God.—This is the first and great commandment."

3. That our love to God must be supreme. Matt. xxii. 37.—" Thou shalt love the Lord thy God with all thy heart, and with all thy soul, and with all thy mind."

4. That ourselves and our neighbour constitute the next object of our love. Matt. xxii. 39.—" The second is like unto it, Thou shalt love thy neighbour as thyself."

EXPLANATION.

Obs. 185.—*The first and principal subject of the Ten Commandments, is love to the Lord our God.*

The *nature* of that love which we owe to God, may be seen from the following things:—

1. Love to God must be *cordial* and *affectionate*. We must love him *with all our heart*, or with all our affections.—Ps. cxix. 10; 1 Tim. i. 5.

2. Love to God must be *ardent* and *vigorous*. We must love him *with all our strength*, or with all the exertion and perseverance of which we are capable. Love may be sincere, although not most intense; and this the gospel may accept, but the law requires perfection in degree.

3. Love to God must be *supreme*. We must love him *with all our soul*, and *with all our mind*, or with all the powers of our mind, and all the inclinations of our will. We must not only love nothing more than God, but we must love nothing so much as God, or equally with him; for this would be to have more gods than one.—Matt. x. 37; Luke xiv. 26; Ps. lxxiii. 25; Isa. xxvi. 8, 9.

4. Love to God must be *purely for himself;* or, in other words, on account of the glorious excellencies of his nature. We are indeed to love him as our benefactor; but we must love him chiefly for his excellencies; such as his truth, holiness, justice, and mercy, &c.—Cant. i. 3.

5. Love to God must be an *intelligent* love, or a love of which we understand the cause. We must have some knowledge of God; for without this we cannot love him; and the more that we know respecting him, the greater cause we shall have to love him, and the more we will love him. See Mark xii. 33; Ps ix. 10.

6. Love to God must be an *active* love. It must appear genuine, by doing all things to his glory; by making an unreserved surrender of the whole man to him, to be for him and not for another; and by presenting the body a living sacrifice to him, which is a reasonable service.—1 John iii. 18.

The best *evidence* of love to God, or of a due regard to the duties of the first table of the law, is love to man, or the performance of the duties of the second table of the law. See 1 John iv. 20, 21; John xiii. 35.

Obs. 186.—*The second subject of the Ten Commandments is love to our neighbour and ourselves.*

By our *neighbour* we are to understand *all mankind*, whether high or low, rich or poor, good or bad, saint or sinner, friend or foe, known or unknown,—*all*, in a word, to whom in any way we may be useful in promoting their happiness here or hereafter.

The *nature* of that love which we owe to our neighbour will be evident from the following things:—

1. We must love *all men* in general with a love of *benevolence;* or, we must wish or desire all good to them: and this

is evidenced by praying for all men, that they may be saved; that not only ourselves, but that all may see the salvation of God.

2. We must love *all men* with a love of *beneficence;* or, we must do them all the good we can, both with respect to their bodies and their souls.—Gal. vi. 10; 1 John iii. 18.

3. We must manifest our love to our neighbour, by esteeming him according to his worth or merit. Whatever gift any one possesses, we are to esteem him on account of it; for "every good and perfect gift cometh down from the Father of lights."

4. We must in a special manner love the *saints*, who are "the household of faith," and "the excellent ones of the earth;" and these ought to be loved with a love of *complacency* and *delight.* See Gal. vi. 10; Ps. xvi. 3.

5. With respect to our *enemies*, we are not to do to them as they do to us. If they hate us, we must love them; if they curse us, we must pray for them; if they do us hurt, we must forgive them; and if they say all manner of evil against us falsely, we must bless and not curse them. See Matt. v. 43, 44.

With respect to the *manner* in which we must love others, it is said, that we are to love our neighbour *as ourselves,*—that is as truly and sincerely as we love ourselves.—Matt. vii. 12.

We may here make a remark respecting the following injunction of the Apostle Paul: "In lowliness of mind, let each esteem another *better* than himself."—Phil. ii. 3. The meaning of this injunction is, that we are not to boast of ourselves on account of any thing which we possess. If we differ from others, it is wholly owing to the grace of God; for it is he who maketh one to differ from another. The more of his grace that there is in the heart, the more unworthy we will deem ourselves; and thus we will be readily disposed to consider others as better than ourselves.

INFERENCES.

From this subject we learn,—1. That love to God is not what men in general suppose it to be. 2. That, upon trial, the obedience of many will be found to be no true evidence of love to God. 3. That the religion of those who are destitute of true love to God, is vain. 4. That God's love to us should excite our unfeigned love to him. 5. That we cannot exceed in our expressions of love to God. 6. That God is entitled to supreme love from man. 7. That this can be evidenced only by keeping his commandments. 8. That love to man holds a high place in the moral law. 9. That hatred to our neighbour is a violation of the second table of the law. 10. That the love of Christ ought to constrain us to love our neighbour. 11. That they are chargeable with hatred to their neighbour, who do not allow their love to flow through all mankind. 12. The danger of loving in word only, and not in deed and in truth. 13. That party-spirit ought to be banished from every society. seeing it cuts the very sinews of love. 14. That we ought not to allow every little circumstance to extinguish the flame of our love to others. 15. That we cannot love God, and hate our neighbour; for, saith the beloved disciple, " He that loveth not his brother whom he hath seen, how can he love God whom he hath not seen?"—1 John iv. 20.

Preface to the Ten Commandments.

Q. 43.—What is the Preface to the Ten Commandments?

The Preface to the Ten Commandments is in these words: " I am the Lord thy God, which have brought thee out of the land of Egypt, out of the house of bondage."
Exod. xx. 2; Deut. v. 6.

Q. 44.—What doth the Preface to the Ten Commandments teach us?

The Preface to the Ten Commandments teacheth us, that because God is the Lord, and our God, and Redeemer, therefore we are bound to keep all his commandments.

ANALYSIS AND PROOFS.

We are here taught,—
That we are bound to keep all God's commandments. Deut. xi. 1.—" Thou shalt keep his commandments alway."
2. That we should keep God's commandments, because he is the Lord. Lev. xix. 37.—" Ye shall observe my statutes, and do them: I am the Lord." See also Ps. xlv. 11.
3. That we should keep God's commandments, because he is our God. Josh. xxiv. 18.—" Therefore will we serve the Lord; for he is our God." See also Lev. xx. 7.
4. That we should keep God's commandments, because he is our Redeemer. 1 Cor. vi. 19, 20.—" Ye are not your own; ye are bought with a price; therefore glorify God in your body, and in your spirit, which are God's."

EXPLANATION.

Obs. 187.—*We should keep the commandments of God, because he is the Lord.*

This reason is expressed in these words:—" I am the Lord;" and it implies, that God is the eternal God—from everlasting to everlasting—without beginning of days or end of life; that he is the immutable God—the same yesterday, to-day, and for ever—unchangeable in his purposes, or in any of his ways; that he is the almighty God, with whom nothing whatever is impossible; that he has his being in and of himself, and is dependent on none; and that he gave being to all things, and preserves them all by the same power by which he called them from nothing into existence.

This reason is full to the purpose; for the least reflection will convince any one, that the excellencies of the Divine nature, the goodness of God in creating man, and his continued goodness in preserving him, call for an unlimited obedience from all.

Obs. 188.—*We should keep the commandments of God, because he is our God.*

This reason is expressed in these words :—" I am thy God;" and it implies, that a Divine Revelation has been committed to us, in which God hath made himself known as a God in covenant; and that, according to the tenor of the covenant of grace, what he is, and what he has as God, is made over to us in his Word; so that we can want no good thing, either in time or through eternity.

This is a powerful motive to obedience; and a more powerful one cannot be conceived. If God makes himself over to sinners of Adam's race in this covenant, as it is revealed in his Word, surely it ought to excite us to a willing obedience, and to walk in all his commandments and ordinances blameless.

But these words, "I am the Lord thy God," not only propose a reason why we should obey God; they also *enable* us to perform all his pleasure; for, if the covenant provides all things necessary for an acceptable obedience, then *strength* for the performance of every duty must be included in the promises of the covenant. And, accordingly, the tenor of the covenant is this (Jer. xxxi. 33) :—" This shall be the covenant that I will make with the house of Israel : After those days, saith the Lord, I will put my law in their inward parts, and write it in their hearts; and I will be their God, and they shall be my people." See also Ezek. xxxvi. 25-27; Jer. xxxii. 40.

It may be here remarked, that obedience to the commandments of God is not the *condition* of the covenant, or of obtaining its privileges; for this would be to dishonour the covenant, as if it were not well ordered in all things and sure. Before God pronounced any of the commandments on Sinai, he said, "I am the Lord thy God;" which evidently shows, that all are commanded first to lay hold of the promise in these words, and then to obey the commandments. Obedience is the evidence of interest in the covenant, and of the sincerity of love to God, who proposes himself as *our God.*

Obs. 189.—*We should keep the commandments of God, because he is our Redeemer.*

This reason is expressed in these words :—" Which have

brought thee out of the land of Egypt, out of the house of bondage;" and it binds believers now, as well as it bound the children of Israel, to that obedience which the Lord requireth. For whether we consider it as referring to them or to ourselves, the argument is most weighty; and there are many considerations included in it, which are very powerful, and highly calculated to remind us of the necessity of giving up ourselves to the Lord.

This argument, in respect of the posterity of Abraham, to whom it was first proposed, will be found peculiarly strong, if we consider the following things:—1. That this deliverance from Egypt reminded the Israelites of the accomplishment of the promise which God had made to them long before they stood in need of the exertion of almighty power. See Gen. xv. 13, 14: Exod. xii. 41. 2. That what God had done for the children of Israel, in delivering them from the Egyptians, was a mercy which they surely had not yet forgotten. 3. That they were utterly unable of themselves to have effected this great deliverance. 4. That it was not a common deliverance, nor accomplished by the use of ordinary means. 5. That it was both a temporal and a spiritual favour done to them. They were delivered from bondage, by which their souls were made bitter within them; and they were delivered from a land of graven images, and were to be constituted the only Church of God upon earth. To them the lively oracles of truth were to be committed. To them promises were made, and were to be fulfilled. They were to be accounted a holy priesthood, a royal nation, a peculiar people. To them the knowledge of the living God was to be revealed; and to them was to be made known the way of salvation; while the rest of the world was sitting in moral darkness and in the region and shadow of spiritual death.

The *motive* by which *we* should be influenced, is, the love of God in sending his Son into this world, to deliver us from the bondage of sin and Satan, of the world and the flesh; of which the deliverance from Egyptian bondage was typical.

The *design* of God in delivering sinners from *spiritual bondage* is the same that it was in delivering the Israelites from *Egyptian bondage*. His design in delivering the Israelites was, that they might serve him; and his design in delivering us from spiritual bondage is, that we may serve him without fear, in holiness and righteousness all our days.

INFERENCES.

From this subject we learn,—1. The necessity of studying the character of God, that we may know him and obey him; for without knowledge there can be no obedience. 2. That obedience is the duty of all; and that gracious motives are proposed to influence to it. 3. That sinners have the greatest encouragement to a life of holiness. 4. That the Lord draweth sinners with the cords of love.—Hos. xi. 4. 5. The danger of not complying with God's commandments. 6. That the slavery of sin is the worst bondage. 7. The necessity of being delivered by Jesus Christ out of the hands of all our spiritual enemies. 8. The necessity of gratitude to Jehovah for the revelation of the gracious scheme of deliverance from every evil. 9. That we ought to view his service as our pleasure in this world, seeing this is the great design of his grace being manifested to any. 10. That the greater the mercy conferred upon us is, the more unfeigned ought our gratitude to be.

SECT. II.—THE DUTIES WHICH WE OWE TO GOD—CONTAINED IN THE FIRST FOUR COMMANDMENTS OF THE LAW.

DIV. 1.—THE FIRST COMMANDMENT.

Q. 45.—Which is the First Commandment?

The First Commandment is, "Thou shalt have no other Gods before me."

Exod. xx. 3; Deut. v. 7.

Duties Required.

Q. 46.—What is Required in the First Commandment?

The First Commandment requireth us to know and acknowledge God to be the only true God and our God; and to worship and glorify him accordingly.

ANALYSIS AND PROOFS.

We are here taught,—

1. That we are required to know God. 1 Chron. xxviii. 9.—"Know thou the God of thy father." See also Job xxii. 21.

2. That we are required to acknowledge God. Prov. iii. 6.—"In all thy ways acknowledge him."

3. That we are required to know and acknowledge God as the only true God. John xvii. 3.—"This is life eternal, that they might know thee, the only true God." 1 Kings viii. 33.—"When Israel shall confess thy name."

4. That we are required to know and acknowledge God as our God. Deut. xxvi. 7.—"Thou hast avouched the Lord this day to be thy God."

5. That we are required to worship and glorify God as the only true God. Matt. iv. 10.—"Thou shalt worship the Lord thy God, and him only shalt thou serve." 1 Chron. xvi. 25, 26.—"Great is the Lord, and greatly to be praised: he also is to be feared above all gods. For all the gods of the people are idols: but the Lord made the heavens."

6. That we are required to worship and glorify God as our God. Ps. xcv. 6, 7.—" O come, let us worship and bow down; let us kneel before the Lord our Maker. For he is our God; and we are the people of his pasture." Ps. cxlv. 1.—" I will extol thee, my God, O King; and I will bless thy name for ever and ever."

EXPLANATION.

Obs. 190.—*The First Commandment requires us to know and acknowledge God.*

To *know God*, is to know that he exists, and that he is such as he hath manifested himself to be in his Word. Heb. xi. 6. It is here that we have the only true account of what he is; of the various relations in which he stands to all men in general, and to his own people in particular; and of the various characters which he sustains, as a present help in every time of need. But this knowledge must be, not a mere speculative knowledge, but a practical and saving knowledge,—such a knowledge as will influence us to do whatever he hath commanded.

To *acknowledge God*, implies a steady belief in the existence of God—of that God who hath revealed himself in his Word; a firm belief that all the perfections, and titles, and attributes, which are ascribed to God in his Word, belong to him and to none else; and also a confessing him in secret and before the world,—Rom. x. 10; and a maintaining of his perfections in opposition to what may be said against them.

Obs. 191.—*The First Commandment requires us to know and acknowledge God as the only true God.*

To know and acknowledge God as *the only true God*, is to believe and profess that he alone is possessed of infinite perfection; and that the perfections of his nature are eminently displayed and manifested in the Lord Jesus Christ.—Hos. xiii. 4.

Obs. 192.—*The First Commandment requires us to know and acknowledge God as our God.*

To know and acknowledge God as *our God*, is to profess our relation to him as his people, on the faith of the grant that he makes of himself to us in the Word.—Deut. xxvi. 17, 18; Ps. xlviii. 14. But this cannot be done without faith in him, and in his Son Jesus Christ, through whom alone any can come to God.—John xiv. 6, 9; 1 John iii. 23.

That which is connected with this acknowledgment of God, and in a great measure shows an unfeigned faith in this one God as our God, is an acknowledgment of God in all our ways, and an acknowledgment of him in all his ways to us. We must acknowledge him in all his providences towards us, in all his promises and their accomplishment, and in all his threatenings and judgments.

Obs. 193.—*The First Commandment requires us to worship and glorify God as the only true God and as our God.*

To *worship God*, is to make him the supreme object of our esteem and delight, both in public, private, and secret.—Ps. lxxi. 19, lxxiii. 25,.cxlii. 5, and cxi. 1.

To *glorify God*, is to ascribe to him all possible glory and perfection; and to endeavour, in all our actions, to promote his honour and glory.—Exod. xv. 11 ; 1 Cor. x. 31.

To worship and glorify God *accordingly*, imports, that as we must know and acknowledge God to be the only true God and our God, so we are bound, in every part of our obedience, to act towards him as those who stand in such a near relation to him. —Ps. xlv. 11; 1 Cor. vi. 20. We cannot, however, yield any acceptable obedience, unless we acknowledge him to be our God in Christ; for the belief of the promise is the foundation of all acceptable worship and obedience. All true obedience is the obedience of faith; and without faith it is impossible to please God.—Rom. vi. 26; Heb. xi. 6.

There are two ways in which God must be worshipped and glorified:—in our hearts and in our lives.—John iv. 24; Matt. v. 16.

1. To worship and glorify God in our *lives*, or *externally*, is to have a respect to all his instituted ordinances; to avoid all manner of sin, and to shun every appearance of evil; to provoke to love and to good works; to stir up others to serve the Lord; and, in a word, to frame our lives according to the Scriptures.

2. To worship and glorify God in our *hearts*, or *internally*, is to think and meditate upon him,—Mal. iii. 16; Ps. lxiii. 6; to remember him,—Eccl. xii. 1; to honour and adore him,—Mal. i. 6; Isa. xlv. 23; to love and esteem him highly,—Deut. vi. 5; Ps. lxxi. 19; to desire and choose him as our God,—Ps. lxxiii. 25; Josh. xxiv. 15; to trust, and believe, and hope in him,— Isa. xxvi. 4; Exod. xiv. 31; Ps. cxxx. 7; to fear him,—Isa. viii. 13; to delight and rejoice in him,—Ps. xxxvii. 4, and xxxii. 11; to call upon him, and to give all praise and thanks unto him,— Phil. iv. 4; to be zealous for him,—Rom. xii. 11; to yield all obedience and submission to him with the whole man,—Jer. vii. 23; James iv. 7; to be careful in all things to please him, and sorrowful when in any thing he is offended,—1 John iii. 22; Jer. xxxi. 18; and to walk humbly with him,—Micah vi. 8.

INFERENCES.

From this subject we learn,—1. The necessity of searching the Scriptures. 2. The necessity of examining the nature of the knowledge which we have of God; whether our intentions of cleaving to the Lord as our God are sincere, and whether we are careful to evidence our sincerity by keeping his commandments. 3. That we have the greatest possible encouragement to serve the

Lord. 4. That the most comfortable situation of the soul is, when it can call God its God. 5. That the best evidence of this is, to worship and glorify him as such. 6. Wherein much personal godliness consists. 7. Wherein much of that internal worship consists which belongeth unto God. 8. That the law of the Lord is infinitely holy, and exceeding broad. 9. That none can obey it, so as to obtain life by it.

Sins Forbidden.

Q. 47.—*What is forbidden in the First Commandment?*
The First Commandment forbiddeth the denying, or not worshipping and glorifying the true God, as God, and our God; and the giving of that worship and glory to any other which is due to him alone.

ANALYSIS AND PROOFS.

We are here taught,—
1. That we are forbidden to deny God. Ps. xiv. 1.—" The fool hath said in his heart, There is no God."
2. That we are forbidden to refuse or neglect to worship and glorify God. Isa. xliii. 22.—" Thou hast not called upon me, O Jacob; thou hast been weary of me, O Israel." Dan. v. 23.— " The God in whose hand thy breath is, and whose are all thy ways, hast thou not glorified."
3. That we are forbidden to worship God improperly, as if he were not the only true God. Matt. xv. 8.—" This people draweth nigh to me with their mouth, and honoureth me with their lips; but their heart is far from me."
4. That we are forbidden to worship God, as if he were not our God. Ezek. xliv. 9.—" Thus saith the Lord God, No stranger uncircumcised in heart, or uncircumcised in flesh, shall enter into my sanctuary."
5. That we are forbidden to give that worship and glory to any other which is due to God alone. Rom. i. 25.—" Who changed the truth of God into a lie, and worshipped and served the creature more than the Creator, who is blessed for ever. Amen." Ps. xcvii. 7.—" Confounded be all they that serve graven images, that boast themselves of idols: worship him, all ye gods."

EXPLANATION.

Obs. 194.—*The First Commandment forbiddeth the denying of the true God; or atheism.*

Atheism is distinguished into *speculative* and *practical*.
1. *Speculative atheism* is a full persuasion in the heart that there is no God, and an open profession of it with the mouth; or it is a rejection of those essential truths which clearly prove the existence of God The denial of a revelation from heaven.

or that the Bible is such a revelation, is likewise called atheism or deism, which is the acknowledgment only of the God of nature and providence. But, according to the Scriptures, they who reject the Bible, in which is revealed the way of salvation through Jesus Christ, are also guilty of denying the Father. See 1 John ii. 23.

2. *Practical atheism* is to confess that there is a God, and, at the same time, to deny him by works, or to live as if there were no God. See Ps. x. 4, 11; Tit. i. 16.

They are guilty of *practical atheism*, who do not worship and glorify the true God, as God, and their God,—who have an opportunity of knowing the true God, but remain ignorant of him, —who forget God, and do not ask counsel of him, but walk according to the light of their own eyes,—who do not worship God according to his Word, but live in the habitual neglect of those duties which he hath enjoined,—who do not glorify God according to his Word, but set themselves up as their own rule and propose themselves as their own end, which is directly contrary to revelation,—and who wilfully commit sin; for it is evident that they do not at that time believe that there is a God or, if they do believe this, that they regard him not, which is very similar to a not acknowledging of God.

Obs. 195.—*The First Commandment forbiddeth the not worshipping and glorifying the true God, as God, and our God or profaneness.*

We are here informed, that we may worship and glorify the true God, but not *as God,* nor as *our God.*

1. To worship and glorify God, but not *as God,* is to draw near to him with the mouth, and to honour him with the lips, while the heart is far from him.—Matt. xv. 8; Isa. xxix. 13.

2. To worship and glorify God, but not as *our God,* is to be regardless whether or not we have come to the knowledge of him, so as to call him *our God;* or it is to want the habitual exercise of the faith of our covenant relation to him.—Ps. lxxxi. 10, 11.

Obs. 196.—*The First Commandment forbiddeth the giving of that worship and glory to any other which is due to God alone; or idolatry.*

Idolatry is distinguished into *gross* and *spiritual* idolatry.

1. *External* or *gross idolatry* is a paying of religious worship, homage, or adoration, to any person or thing besides the true God.

2. *Internal* or *spiritual idolatry* is a setting up of idols in the heart; or giving of that place in our heart—that affection or regard to any thing whatever, which ought to be given to God alone.- 1 John ii. 15.

Obs. 197.—*Besides those things already mentioned, the First Commandment forbiddeth the following things:—*
1. Bold and curious searching into the secret things of God.—Deut. xxix. 29.
2. All compact and consultation with the devil.—Deut. xviii. 10, &c.; Acts xix. 18, &c.
3. All hearkening to the suggestions of the devil.
4. The making of man the lord of the conscience in things pertaining to religion.—Matt. xxiii. 8, &c.; 2 Cor. i. 24.
5. The charging of God foolishly for the evils which he inflicts upon us.—Ps. xxxvii. 7, 8, and lxxiii.
6. The ascribing of the praise of any good we either have done, are doing, or can do, to fortune or to ourselves. See Deut. viii. 17, 18; Dan. iv. 30.

INFERENCES.

From this subject we learn,—1. That all shall hereafter find that there is a God, whether they now believe it or not. 2. The daring nature of atheism, which levels at the being of God—of the only true God. 3. The necessity of being habitually impressed with the belief of every Divine perfection. 4. The danger of drawing back from following God. 5. That God, who is a Spirit, requireth spiritual worship. 6. That many are idolaters, who believe it not. 7. The necessity of being regulated in all things by God's unerring Word. 8. The danger of imbibing unworthy views of his providence. 9. The necessity of resignation to the will of God in all things. 10. That we are indebted to God for all that we possess.

Of the expression " Before Me."

Q. 48.—What are we specially taught by these words, "Before Me," in the First Commandment?

These words, "Before Me," in the First Commandment, teach us, that God, who seeth all things, taketh notice of, and is much displeased with, the sin of having any other god.

ANALYSIS AND PROOFS.

We are here taught,—
1. That God seeth all things. Heb. iv. 13.—"Neither is there any creature that is not manifest in his sight; but all things are naked and open unto the eyes of him with whom we have to do."
2. That God taketh special notice of the sin of having any other god. Ps. xliv. 20, 21.—"If we have stretched out our hands to a strange god, shall not God search this out?"
3. That God is much displeased with the sin of having any

other god. Deut. xxxii. 16.—" They provoked him to jealousy with strange gods."

EXPLANATION.

Obs. 198.—*God, who seeth all things, taketh special notice of the sin of having any other god before him.*

The strength of the argument implied in the words, " Before me," is, that the sin of having another god is committed in the presence of him who *seeth all things,*—that is, who hath a most intimate, perfect, and comprehensive knowledge of all things.— Ps. cxlvii. 5, and xciv. 8, 9. To deny this, would be to deny one of the glorious perfections of Deity—namely, omniscience. See Ps. cxxxix. If God were not acquainted with the works of his own hands, he could not be the creator, preserver, and governor of the world; nor could he at last judge the world in righteousness. See 1 Cor. iv. 5.

God taketh special notice of *the sin of having any other god*, or of the sin of idolatry; which is to have our minds, wills, and affections set on other objects, as much as, or more than, on God himself.

As this sin strikes more immediately and directly against the authority of God, so he taketh *special notice* of it,—that is, he threatens to resent it with the highest marks of displeasure, not only in the world to come, but even in the present life.—Deut. xxix. 24–29; Rev. xxi. 8.

Obs. 199.—*God is much displeased with the sin of having any other god before him.*

The reason why God is so *much displeased* with idolatry, both external and internal, is, because it sets up a rival in his stead, and that in his very presence; and gives that honour to another which is due to him alone. See his threatenings against those who commit such sins, in Deut. xxix.

INFERENCES.

From this subject we learn,—1. That we cannot be guilty of any sin with which God is unacquainted. 2. That God is particularly displeased with the sin of idolatry. 3. The necessity of examining our hearts, that we may see who sits enthroned there. —whether God, or the world, or self, or any sinful object,—any object loved equally with God, or more than God. 4. That we ought to set our hearts on those things which are above, where Christ sitteth at the right hand of God.

DIV. 2.—THE SECOND COMMANDMENT.

Q. 49.—*Which is the Second Commandment?*

The Second Commandment is, " Thou shalt not

make unto thee any graven image, or any likeness of any thing that is in heaven above, or that is in the earth beneath, or that is in the water under the earth: Thou shalt not bow down thyself to them nor serve them; for I the Lord thy God am a jealous God, visiting the iniquity of the fathers upon the children unto the third and fourth generation of them that hate me; and showing mercy unto thousands of them that love me, and keep my commandments."
Exod. xx. 4–6; Deut. v. 8–10.

Duties Required.

Q. 50.—*What is required in the Second Commandment?*
The Second Commandment requireth the receiving, observing, and keeping pure and entire, all such religious worship and ordinances, as God hath appointed in his Word.

ANALYSIS AND PROOFS.

We are here taught,—
1. That God hath appointed certain religious ordinances to be observed in his worship. Lev. xviii. 4.—" Ye shall do my judgments, and keep mine ordinances, to walk therein: I am the Lord your God."
2. That we are required to accept of and esteem the worship and ordinances of God. Ps. cxix. 103.—" How sweet are thy words unto my taste! yea, sweeter than honey to my mouth." Ps. lxxxiv. 1.—" How amiable are thy tabernacles, O Lord of hosts!"
3. That we are required to observe God's worship and ordinances. Matt. xxviii. 20.—" Teaching them to observe all things whatsoever I have commanded you."
4. That we are required to keep God's worship and ordinances pure and entire. Deut. xii. 32.—" What thing soever I command you, observe to do it; thou shalt not add thereto, nor diminish from it." See also Luke i. 6.

EXPLANATION.

Obs. 200.—*God hath appointed certain religious ordinances to be observed in his worship.*

We may here take notice of the difference between the First and Second Commandment. The First Commandment respects the *object* of worship—the living and true God, and requires that we worship him as our God, and no other. The Second Commandment respects the *means* of worship, and requires that we worship the true God in such a way only, and by such ordinances, as he hath appointed in his Word. The first may be discovered by the light of nature, but the second can be discovered only by revelation.

By *religious worship* we are to understand that homage and respect which we owe to God, and by which we profess subjection to him, and confidence in him, as our God in Christ; and ascribe that praise and glory which are due to him, as our chief good and only happiuess.—Ps. xcv. 6, 7.

The *religious ordinances* of Divine appointment, which ought to be observed by us, are these:—

1. Prayer, which includes thanksgiving.—Phil. iv. 6. Prayer is either public, as in the church,—Acts ii. 42; or private, as in families,—Jer. x. 25; or secret, as by one's self,—Matt. vi. 6.

2. Praise, or singing the praises of God with the voice. This ought to be observed both in public and in private.—Ps. cxlix. 1; James v. 13; Eph. v. 18-20; Col. iii. 16.

3. The reading, the hearing, and the preaching of the Word. The reading and hearing of the Word ought to be observed both in public and in private.—Acts xv. 21; John v. 39; James i. 21-25; Acts x. 33. The preaching of the Word is a public ordinance,—2 Tim. iv. 2; and the hearing of it preached ought to be attended to, that men may become wise to salvation.

4. The administration and the receiving of the sacraments of baptism and the Lord's supper.—Matt. xxviii. 19; 1 Cor. xi. 23, &c.

5. Church government and discipline. See Matt. xvi. 19; 1 Cor. v., and xii. 28; Eph. iv. 11; Matt. xviii. 15-17; 1 Tim. v. 20.

6. The ministry and the maintenance thereof.—Mark xvi. 15; Rom. x. 14, 15; Eph. iv. 11, 12; 1 Cor. ix. 13, 14.

7. Religious fasting,—which is an abstinence from food for a season, so far as bodily weakness and infirmity will permit; and an abstinence from such bodily pleasures and delights as are lawful at other times; together with a ceasing from all worldly employments. This, however, is only designed to fit or to dispose the mind for spiritual and solemn exercises. Fasting is either public, or private, or secret. See Joel ii. 12, &c.; 1 Cor. vii. 5; Matt. vi. 17, 18.

8. Swearing by the name of God. This is to be observed by the people of God, when they devote themselves to him in a perpetual covenant, which shall not be forgotten; or when we are called to declare the truth upon oath.—Deut. vi. 13; Jer. iv. 2.

9. Vowing to the Lord. In all vows God is both a witness and a party; nay, he is the only party and the only witness, both in making and in performing them.—Ps. lxxvi. 11, and cxix. 106.

Obs. 201.—*The Second Commandment requireth us to receive*

to observe, and to keep pure and entire, all such religious worship and ordinances as are of Divine appointment.

1. It requires us to *receive* the worship and ordinances of God. We must approve of and embrace them, just because they bear the stamp of the highest possible authority.

2. It requires us to *observe* the worship and ordinances of God. We must do what is required in them, make use of them, and attend on God in them. By this alone we can prove to ourselves and others, that we really approve of them.—John xiii. 17.

3. It requires us to *keep* the worship and ordinances of God *pure*. We must do what we can to preserve them from all mixture of human invention.

4. It requires us to *keep* the worship and ordinances of God *entire*. We must do what we can to prevent any thing from being taken from them.—Deut. xii. 32.

That the Second Commandment requires "the receiving, observing, and keeping pure and entire all such religious worship and ordinances as God hath appointed," is evident; for although it only forbids us to make and worship any graven image, yet this plainly implies,—That God must be worshipped by some means; that it is a sin to worship God by graven images; that, consequently, it is a sin to worship God by any means which he hath not appointed: and, therefore, that it is a duty to worship God by the means which he hath appointed. These means being his ordinances, they must be received, observed, and kept pure and entire

INFERENCES.

From this subject we learn,—1. That God alone is lord of the conscience; and that we are bound to observe his statutes alone. 2. That God knoweth what ordinances we observe in worshipping him. 3. That he will most highly resent a disregard to his express commands. 4. That every act of religious worship is appointed by God, and ought to be observed just as he commands. 5. That it is dangerous to invent and to introduce into the worship of God, any thing of man's imagination. 6. That in this, as well as in every thing else, the Word of God alone ought to be our guide. 7. That God is jealous, and cannot endure his ordinances to be despised.

Sins Forbidden.

Q. 51.—What is forbidden in the Second Commandment?

The Second Commandment forbiddeth the worshipping of God by images, or any other way not appointed in his Word.

ANALYSIS AND PROOFS.

We are here taught,—

1. That we are forbidden to worship God by images. Deut. iv. 15, 16.—" Take ye, therefore, good heed unto yourselves (for ye saw no manner of similitude on the day that the Lord spake unto you in Horeb), lest ye corrupt yourselves, and make you graven image."

2. That we are forbidden to worship God in any way not appointed in his Word. Deut. iv. 2.—" Ye shall not add unto the word which I command. you, neither shall ye diminish ought from it, that ye may keep the commandments of the Lord your God, which I command you."

EXPLANATION.

Obs. 202.—*The Second Commandment forbiddeth the worshipping of God by images; or idolatry.*

This includes the following things :—

1. The *making of images or of the likeness of any thing* for religious worship; such as images or likenesses of God himself. Father, Son, or Holy Ghost; or of the sun, moon, or stars in the heavens above; or of men, beasts, or trees, &c., in the earth beneath; or of fishes of any kind in the waters under the earth. See Lev. xxvi. 1: Isa. xl. 18; Acts xvii. 29; Rom. i. 22, 23.

2. The *bowing down to graven images or to any likeness of any thing* in the heavens, in the earth, or in the sea. To say (as some do) that bowing down to images is not serving them, is quite absurd; for how can any serve them more effectually than by such acts of religious worship, and by giving to them that honour which belongs to God alone?

The reason why idolatry is prohibited, is because it levels at the very existence of God, and tends to deprive him of his prerogative as God, and to set up others in his place.

The reason why man is so prone to idolatry, is, because he has naturally a desire to set the object of worship before his eyes, that he may see what he worships. This is, indeed, an evidence of man's depravity; for when the mind cannot fix itself upon an unseen God revealing himself in his Word, it shows the want of spirituality of mind, the want of fervency of devotion, and the want of faith in the soul. See Exod. xxxii. 1, &c.; John iv. 24. Moreover, if images could help our devotion, then the work of the Spirit, who helpeth our infirmities and maketh intercession within us, would be unnecessary.

But here it may be asked, If images are forbidden, why do we find that the images of the *cherubim* were placed first in the tabernacle and then in the temple ? To this we answer, that there is a very great difference between the *cherubim* of old, and *images* in the present day. The cherubim were appointed by Jehovah himself; which images by no means are. The cherubim were placed in the most holy place, into which none but the high priest was permitted to enter, and that but once a-year; and being a part of the ceremonial law, they were in time to be abolished; and they are now completely abolished.

The following things are connected with idolatry, and forbidden in this commandment:—

1. The framing of any representation of God in the mind; which is accompanied by the worst of circumstances. See Rom. i. 21, &c.

2. The representation and worship of saints in glory; for however changed, and however glorious they may be, they are but creatures; and, consequently, cannot be the objects of divine worship. Moreover, this is plainly forbidden in Scripture; and representations of them can by no means be formed.

Obs. 203.—*The Second Commandment forbiddeth the worshipping of God in any way not appointed in his Word.*

Of this all those are guilty, who are not pleased with what God hath revealed on this subject, but presumptuously annex their own superstitious inventions to the institutions of Divine appointment; pretending that they are very significant ceremonies, and highly calculated to beautify God's worship, and to excite devotion in his worshippers. By these, however, they have, in a great measure, rendered it carnal and sensible—far from that spiritual worship which God requires.—John iv. 24. Some of the superstitious inventions alluded to are these:—A great variety of office-bearers, of which there is no mention at all in Scripture; kneeling at the sacrament of the Lord's supper; the erection of altars in churches; and the institution and observation of a variety of days, to which a religious veneration is paid; and particularly those days called *Lent*, the observation of which is not only contrary to reason and Scripture, but highly impious—being an imitation or aping of our Lord's *miraculous fast*, in the wilderness. (Christ hath left us an example that we should follow his steps; but he has left no command to attempt to imitate his *miracles*.) They who instituted these days, and they who observe them, are to be reckoned in the number of those who "teach for doctrines the commandments of men,"—Matt. xv. 9. See Col. ii. 16, 17, 20–23; Gal. iv. 9–11; 1 Tim. iv. 1-5; where the distinction of meats under the New Testament dispensation is absolutely condemned.

It may be here objected by some, that there were many ceremonies under the Old Testament dispensation, instituted by the express command of God. To this we answer, that there is a very great difference between ceremonies instituted by God, and the inventions of men. The ceremonies which God appointed of old were no part of the moral law; and they were never designed to be continued in his Church. They were only a shadow of good things to come.—Heb. xi. 1, &c. Worship must now be spiritual, and suited to the gospel dispensation. See John iv. 23, 24.

We may here remark, that this commandment is further violated, when the worship and ordinances of God are neglected, contemned, hindered, or opposed,—Matt. xxiii. 13; Acts xiii. 44, 45; 1 Thess. ii. 15, 16; and likewise when those are tolerated, whether ministers or people, who publish and maintain erroneous opinions and practices. See Deut. xiii. 6–11; Gal. i. 8, 9; Rev. ii. 2, 14, 15, 20.

INFERENCES.

From this subject we learn,—1. That all ought to honour God according to his Word. 2. That acceptable worship must be spiritual, and far removed from the inventions of men. 3. That we are not left to choose the manner in which we are to worship God, any more than the object that we are to worship. 4. That if we do not worship God in spirit, we show that we are unacquainted with his nature and character. 5. That however fond man may be of his own devices, they must be abandoned in the worship of God. 6. That, as members of the Church of Christ, he alone is our head, and we must live by him. 7. The danger of perverting his ordinances more or less; for if we do, we are not blameless. 8. The danger of contemning, neglecting, hindering, or opposing God's worship and ordinances.

Reasons Annexed.

Q. 52.—What are the Reasons annexed to the Second Commandment?

The reasons annexed to the Second Commandment are, God's sovereignty over us, his propriety in us, and the zeal he hath to his own worship.

ANALYSIS AND PROOFS.

We are here taught,—

1. That God is our lord and sovereign. Isa. xxxiii. 22.—" The Lord is our judge, the Lord is our lawgiver, the Lord is our king: he will save us." See also Ps. xcv. 3, 6.

2. That we are the property of God. Ps. xcv. 7.—" He is our God; and we are the people of his pasture, and the sheep of his hand." See also Ps. xlv. 11.

3. That God is very zealous for the purity of his worship. Exod. xxxiv. 14.—" Thou shalt worship no other god; for the Lord, whose name is Jealous, is a jealous God."

EXPLANATION.

Obs. 204.—*We should worship God in the way which he hath appointed, because he is our lord and sovereign.*

By *God's sovereignty over us*, expressed in these words, " I the Lord," we are to understand his absolute power over us, as his creatures; by which he can dispose of us, and prescribe to us, as seemeth good to him. God has no reason to ask what we are willing to do; but what he commands we are bound to do, whatever be the nature or degree of the service to which we are called.

If, then, God has an undoubted and a sovereign prerogative over us, he can appoint such ordinances in his Church as it seemeth good to him; and we are bound to observe them just as he appoints them.

Obs. 205.—*We should worship God in the way which he hath appointed, because we are his property.*

By *God's propriety in us*, expressed in these words, " Thy God," we are here to understand his right in us by redemption: for, as creator, the Lord cannot properly say, " I am thy God," because all have forfeited his favour and love; so that it is as redeemer only that he stands in this most gracious relation to any of the children of men.

If, then, we are among the people of God, we are redeemed by the blood of his Son; and thus his love ought to constrain us to love him, and to show our gratitude to him; which, in a great measure, is manifested by cleaving to all his ordinances, and by observing them exactly in the way which he hath appointed; and if so, then every human invention whatever ought to be rejected as unworthy of a place among Divine institutions.

Obs. 206.—*We should worship God in the way which he hath appointed, because he is very zealous for the purity of his worship.*

This is expressed in these words, " I am a jealous God;" and it intimates that he attentively beholds his worshippers, whether or not they observe all his statutes and ordinances.

Jehovah manifests his *zeal for his worship* in two ways:—by *threatening* and by *promise*.

1. By *threatening*. This is expressed in these words,—" Visiting the iniquity of the fathers upon the children unto the third and fourth generation of them that hate me,"—that is, inflicting punishment upon the children for the iniquity of their parents. See Josh. ix.; 2 Sam. xxi.; 1 Kings xv. 29, 30, and xiv. 11. It must, however, be remembered, that the children who are thus punished, are such only as walk in the ways of their wicked parents, follow their example, and approve of their conduct; or, at least, do not disapprove of it, and mourn on account of it.

2. *By promise.* This is expressed in these words,—" Showing mercy unto thousands of them that love me and keep my commandments." They who *love God*, are such as have an unfeigned pleasure in him as their God, see in him what cannot possibly be found in any besides him, take up their rest in him, and in every thing manifest themselves to be his people. And they who *keep his commandments*, are such as have a universal and a uniform regard to every part of his law, as the only rule of their faith and practice; and, with respect to this commandment, have a particular regard to the institutions of his own appointment.

It may here be remarked, that there is something very observable in the way of expressing the *threatening* and the *promise.* The threatening extends only to the *third* and *fourth* generations of them that hate the Lord; whereas the promise extends to *thousands* of generations of them that love him and keep his commandments. This evidently intimates, that *judgment* is God's *strange work*, and that he has no pleasure in the death of the sinner; but that *mercy* is his *delight*, and that it is manifold and unbounded.

INFERENCES.

From this subject we learn,—1. That God has a right to demand what he pleases. 2. That being his professed people, we are under special obligations to observe what he hath commanded; and likewise the manner in which his commandments ought to be observed. 3. That transgressors shall not escape the due reward of their disobedience. 4. That parents ought to consider well how they act before their children, that they may not plunge them into ruin by their wickedness. 5. That children ought to imitate the example of their parents no further than they follow the Lord. 6. The danger to which those parents expose themselves, who set a bad example before their children. 7. That this will not excuse their children before the Lord, if they do not what he hath commanded. 8. That those children that are brought up in his fear, have much cause to bless the Lord; and likewise, that much will be required from them. 9. The necessity of loving God, and of keeping his commandments.

DIV. 3.—THE THIRD COMMANDMENT.

Q. 53.—*Which is the Third Commandment?*

The Third Commandment is, "Thou shalt not take the name of the Lord thy God in vain; for the Lord will not hold him guiltless that taketh his name in vain."

Exod. xx. 7; Deut. v. 11.

Duties Required.

Q. 54.—What is required in the Third Commandment? The Third Commandment requireth the holy and reverend use of God's names, titles, attributes, ordinances, Word, and works.

ANALYSIS AND PROOFS.

We are here taught,—
1. That God's names are to be used with holy reverence. Ps. xxix. 2.—" Give unto the Lord the glory due unto his name." See also Matt. vi. 9.
2. That God's titles are to be used with holy reverence. Rev. xv. 3, 4.—" Great and marvellous are thy works, Lord God Almighty; just and true are thy ways, thou king of saints. Who shall not fear thee, O Lord, and glorify thy name."
3. That God's attributes are to be used with holy reverence. Rev. iv. 8.—" Holy, holy, holy, Lord God Almighty, who was, and is, and is to come." See also Rev. xv. 4.
4. That God's ordinances are to be used with holy reverence. Eccl. v. 1.—" Keep thy foot when thou goest to the house of God, and be more ready to hear than to give the sacrifice of fools." See also Mal. i. 11, 14.
5. That God's Word is to be used with holy reverence. Prov. xiii. 13.—" Whoso despiseth the Word shall be destroyed; but he that feareth the commandment shall be rewarded." See also Ps. cxxxviii. 2.
6. That God's works are to be used and contemplated with holy reverence. Job xxxvi. 24.—" Remember that thou magnify his work which men behold."

EXPLANATION.

Obs. 207.—*The Third Commandment requireth the holy and reverend use of God's names.*

We may here observe, that by the *name* of God in this commandment, we are to understand every thing by which he maketh himself known,—his names, titles, attributes, ordinances, Word, and works.

The *names* of God are these :—
1. To point him out as absolute, unchangeable, self-existent, &c., he is known by the names, Jehovah, Jah, I Am, God, &c.
2. To point him out as sovereign, he is known by the names, Lord, God, &c.
3. As he is one God, in three persons, in the relation in which these persons stand to one another, they are known by the names of Father, Son, and Holy Ghost.

To make a *holy and reverend use* of God's names, is to think speak, and write of them in faith and fear; having on our minds a holy dread of his majesty, and believing him to be what he calls himself.—Deut. xxviii. 58; Jer. v. 22.

Obs. 208.—*The Third Commandment requireth the holy and reverend use of God's titles.*

As the names of God show what he is in himself, without relation to any; so his *titles* exhibit what he is to the creatures which he hath made.

1. The titles which belong to God as the *God of nature*, are these:—Creator, and Creator of the ends of the earth—Preserver of men—Lord of hosts—King of nations, &c.

2. The titles which belong to God as the *God of grace*, are these:—The Hearer of prayer—the God of Abraham, Isaac, and Jacob—the Holy One of Israel—the Father of mercies—the God of consolation—the King of saints—the God of salvation, &c.; and in a peculiar manner he is known in the New Testament by the endearing title of the God and Father of our Lord Jesus Christ.

3. The persons of the adorable Trinity are also known by distinct titles, according to the part which they act in the work of redemption. The *Father* is known by the title of the Father of Jesus Christ, who is called his Son; the *Son* is known by the titles, Head of the Church, King of kings, and Lord of lords. &c.; and the *Holy Ghost* is known by the titles, Comforter, Sanctifier, &c.

To make a *holy and reverend use* of God's titles, is, to think, and speak, and write of them in faith and fear; viewing them as in Christ, and thus drawing virtue from them, for the increase of our faith and holiness.—Exod. xxiii. 20 21.

Obs. 209.—*The Third Commandment requireth the holy and reverend use of God's attributes.*

By the *attributes* of God we are to understand those excellencies which are ascribed to him, as essentially belonging to his nature, and by which he is distinguished from every creature which he hath made. They are, his infinity, eternity, unchangeableness or immutability, omniscience, omnipresence, omnipotence, &c.; also wisdom and knowledge, power, holiness, justice, goodness and mercy, truth and faithfulness.

To make a *holy and reverend use* of God's attributes, is to think and speak of them in a reverend and spiritual manner, and to use them, both in respect of ourselves and others, for the end for which they were revealed. See Ps. cxxx. 4; 2 Cor. v. 11.

Obs. 210.—*The Third Commandment requireth the holy and reverend use of God's ordinances.*

By ordinances God is known in his Church, as having good-will to the sons of men, as its gracious lord and head, who willeth its salvation for ever, and its comfort amidst its numerous and powerful enemies.

The *ordinances* of God are these:—Prayer and thanksgiving; praise; the administration and the receiving of the sacraments; the reading, and preaching, and hearing of the Word; Church government and discipline; the ministry and the maintenance thereof; religious fasting; oaths, or swearing by the name of God; vows; and lots.

To make a *holy and reverend use* of God's ordinances, is to view God as present in them; and to attend or perform them with a view to his glory.—Matt. xxviii. 20; Ps. lxxxvi. 9. It is to pray in the Spirit, to sing with grace in the heart, to preach and hear in faith, to communicate worthily with grace; in a word, it is to do all that is required in the ordinances after a right manner.

As the name of God is more immediately interposed in *oaths*, *vows*, and *lots*, we shall make a few remarks on each of these.

An *oath* is an act of religious worship, in which God is solemnly called upon as a witness, for the confirmation of the truth formerly doubtful, and for terminating contention among men.—Deut. vi. 13; Heb. vi. 16.

To call on God as a witness in an oath, implies an acknowledgment and belief of the following things:—That he is the infallible searcher of hearts; that he is the powerful avenger of all perjury and falsehood; and that he is infinitely superior to us. See Heb. vi. 16.

But it may be here objected by some, that swearing is unlawful,—that it is said, "Swear not at all;" and, "Above all things swear not."—Matt. v. 34; James v. 12. To this we answer, that these expressions by no means prohibit an oath, when lawfully called upon to swear; but only profane and sinful swearing in common conversation, or a taking of the name of God in vain. See Deut. vi. 13; Jer. iv. 2.

That an oath, which is a most solemn act of religious worship may be used in a holy and reverend manner, the following precept in Jer. iv. 2, must be carefully attended to: "Thou shalt swear in truth, in judgment, and in righteousness."

1. *In truth.* This implies, that what is sworn be strictly conformable to truth,—for, if it be not, God is called upon to witness a lie; that we ourselves be persuaded of its truth; and that it be without fraud or deceit, without any equivocation or mental reservation.

2. *In judgment.* This implies, that what is sworn must be understood, that we may not swear respecting an uncertainty; that we understand the nature of an oath; and that we engage in it with fear and reverence, knowing that it is God with whom we have to do.

3. *In righteousness.* This implies, that the thing concerning which the oath is taken, must be just and lawful in itself; that it must be possible; and that, if we are intimately concerned in the performance of it, it must be in our power; that it must be consistent with our duty to God, and with conscience towards our neighbour; and that we must remember and resolutely determine to perform it.

Here it may be remarked, that the way of appealing to God in an oath, laid down in Scripture, is the lifting up of the hand. See Gen. xiv. 22; Rev. x. 5, 6.

A *vow* is a voluntary and deliberate engagement to the Lord alone, as a party, without regarding any other either as party or as witness. See Ps. l. 14, and cxix. 106. An oath is not always connected with what is religious; but a vow is always connected with what is religious, and with that only. See Deut. xxiii. 21-23.

That vows may be used in a holy and reverend manner, they must be entered into in the exercise of faith, and in the strength of the grace that is in Jesus Christ, without which there can be no performance of them.—John xv. 5; Phil. iv. 13.

A *lot*, or *lotting*, is a laying aside the use of all means, and an immediate and a direct appeal to God, that by his immediate providence he would give a present decision respecting a thing doubtful or questionable. "The lot is cast into the lap, but the whole disposing thereof is of the Lord."—Prov. xvi. 33.

That lots may be used in a holy and reverend manner, they must be used only in affairs of great importance, and in cases of absolute necessity, which cannot be otherwise decided without great inconvenience.—Prov. xviii. 18. It would undoubtedly be a profanation of the name of God, to use the lot in matters of little or no moment, or in trifles; or to call upon him to determine those things which may be easily settled by the use of ordinary means. We must also look to God for the decision, calling at the same time on his name,—Jonah i.; Acts i.; and the matter must be entirely left to the decision of God, without using any deceit to make it tend either to the one side or to the other.

Obs. 211.—*The Third Commandment requireth the holy and reverend use of God's Word.*

By the *Word* of God we are to understand the Scriptures of the Old and New Testaments, called the *Holy Scriptures;* by which alone we can become wise unto salvation, and in which alone we have unfolded to us the various ways in which God hath made himself known, and the way in which we can be happy, both in this world and in that to come.

To make a *holy and reverend use* of God's Word, is to search and believe it as testifying of Christ,—John v. 39; and to take it as a lamp to our feet, and a light to our path,—Ps. cxix. 105

Obs. 212.—*The Third Commandment requireth the holy and reverend use of God's works.*

By the *works* of God we are to understand his work of creation, and his works of providence; in which last is included the work of redemption, the chief of all the ways of God, and that by which he hath revealed to us his glorious grace.

To make a *holy and reverend use* of God's works, is to improve the wonderful displays which he hath made of his glorious excellencies, in creation, providence, and redemption; contemplating therein his infinite greatness, power, wisdom, and goodness; and reverently following and complying with his designs, in all his providential dispensations, blessing and praising him for all his mercies, and submitting to his will in all things.— Rev. xv. 3, 4.

INFERENCES.

From this subject we learn,—1. The necessity of knowing the name sby which the living God is known in his Word, which would lead us to reverence him. 2. That if we are God's, we will study to reverence his great and dreadful name. 3. That, in order to reverence the name of God, we must use his ordinances according to his appointment. 4. That the name of God ought not to be used by us in matters of little moment. 5. That we ought to consider well the nature of an oath, that if called upon in providence to invoke God as a witness by one, we may not be found profaning his name, but glorifying it. 6. The danger of appealing immediately to God by the lot, in matters of little or no moment. 7. The danger of vowing to the Lord, and not performing our vows. 8. The danger of abusing the name of God in any way.

Sins Forbidden.

Q. 55.—What is forbidden in the Third Commandment?

The Third Commandment forbiddeth all profaning or abusing of any thing whereby God maketh himself known.

ANALYSIS AND PROOFS.

We are here taught,—
1. That we are forbidden to profane any thing by which God maketh himself known. Lev. xviii. 21.—" Neither shalt thou profane the name of thy God; I am the Lord." See also Mal. i. 7, 12.
2. That we are forbidden to abuse any thing by which God maketh himself known. Matt. xxiii. 14.—" Woe unto you, scribes and Pharisees, hypocrites! for ye devour widows' houses. and for a pretence make long prayers."

EXPLANATION.

Obs. 213.—*The Third Commandment forbiddeth all profaning or abusing of any thing by which God maketh himself known.*

To "*profane* or *abuse* any thing by which God maketh himself known," is to use his names, his titles, his attributes, his ordinances, his word, or his Works, in a rash, an irreverent, and an unbecoming manner.

The *names, titles,* and *attributes,* of God are profaned or abused by men in various ways:—

1. By entertaining abominable or blasphemous thoughts concerning God; or by not thinking or meditating on him, and on what he hath done for sinners.—Ps. x. 4, and xciv. 11.

2. By blasphemy,—that is, by speaking in a reproachful and reviling manner concerning God, or any thing in which he is concerned.—Lev. xxiv. 16.

3. By perjury,—that is, by asserting a thing to be true which is known to be a gross falsehood; or by asserting upon oath what is known to be doubtful or uncertain; or by promising upon oath what is never intended to be performed.—1 Kings xxi. 13; Mark xiv. 58, 59; Ezek. xvii. 16; Zech. v. 3, 4.

4. By sinful cursings,—that is, by imprecating the wrath and vengeance of God upon ourselves or others; or by invocating the devil in any way for harm.

5. By sinful oaths,—that is, by taking unlawful oaths; or by profane swearing in common conversation.—Matt. v. 34–36, and xxiii. 20–22; James v. 12.

6. By sinful vows,—that is, vows unlawful in themselves, or which, if performed, would involve the makers of them in guilt before God; or by vowing to do what God hath commanded, and to abstain from what he hath forbidden in one's own strength; or by vowing to do what one has no intention to perform.—1 Kings xix. 2; Acts xxiii. 12; Matt. xiv. 3–7; Jer. xlii. 5, 6, 20, 22.

7. By a sinful use of the lot,—that is, by appealing to God by way of diversion, as in playing at cards and dice, when God is most presumptuously invoked to determine who shall be the gainer; or by appealing to God in affairs of little importance, which might otherwise be determined.

8. By using the name of God rashly and irreverently in common conversation, either in a way of exclamation, or of thanksgiving, or of importunity, or of appeal to God.

9. By maligning, scorning, or reviling religion; or by making profession of it in hypocrisy, or for sinister ends; or by backsliding from it; or by committing such enormities and immoralities as dishonour it, and cause the name of God to be evil spoken of.—Acts xiii. 45; Ps. i. 2; 2 Pet. iii. 3; 1 Pet. iv

THIRD COMMANDMENT—REASON ANNEXED.

4; 2 Tim. iii. 5; Heb. vi. 6; Rom. ii. 24; Gal. iii. 1; Heb. x. 38.

The *ordinances* of God are profaned or abused, when they are totally neglected, or when they are attended in a formal, superficial, and customary manner, without seeking to hold communion with God in them, or to derive spiritual nourishment from them.—Acts vii. 42, 43; Isa. xxix. 13, 14.

The *Word* of God is profaned or abused, when it is misinterpreted or misapplied; when any part of it is perverted, either to profane jests, or to curious and unprofitable questions, or to vain janglings, or to the maintaining of false doctrines; or when the purposes and providences of God are misapplied.—Rom. vi. 1; Matt. v. 21, &c.; 2 Pet. iii. 16; Matt. xxii. 24; Isa. xxii. 13; 1 Tim. i. 4, 6, and vi. 4, &c.; 2 Tim. ii. 14; Tit. iii. 9; Eccl. viii. 11.

The *works* of God are profaned or abused, when the creatures are abused to sinful lusts and practices; when, in prosperity, men are forgetful of God, unthankful for mercies, and indulge themselves more in sin on account of the goodness of God; or when, in adversity, they murmur and quarrel at his providences, and become more hardened in sin.—Rom. xiii. 13, 14; Hos. xiii. 6; Rom. ii. 4, 5; 1 Cor. x. 10; Jer. v. 3.

INFERENCES.

From this subject we learn,—1. The necessity of having becoming views of God. 2. The danger of blaspheming the name of God. 3. The sin of perjury, and of cursing and swearing. 4. The necessity of watchfulness, and of avoiding the company of those who fear not God. 5. The necessity of setting a watch upon our lips. 6. The necessity of performing our vows. 7. The danger of appealing to God in matters of little or no moment. 8. That the name of God ought to be spoken of with reverence at all times. 9. The danger of hypocrisy. 10. The danger to which they expose themselves, who offend the children of the kingdom. 11. The sin of which they are guilty, who encourage sinners in their sin. 12. That Divine ordinances are worthy of our regard. 13. The danger of backsliding in religion. 14. That the Word of God should be improved for his glory, and for the good of ourselves and others. 15. That the works of God are wonderful, in creation, providence, and redemption; in mercy and in judgment, &c.

Reason Annexed.

Q. 56.—What is the Reason annexed to the Third Commandment?

The reason annexed to the Third Commandment is, That however the breakers of this commandment may escape punishment from men, yet the Lord our God will not suffer them to escape his righteous judgment; (or will not hold them guiltless that take his name in vain.)

ANALYSIS AND PROOFS.

We are here taught,—

1. That they who take God's name in vain may escape punishment from men.

2. That the sin of taking God's name in vain will be specially punished by God himself. Deut. xxviii. 58, 59.—" If thou wilt not observe to do all the words of this law, that are written in this book, that thou mayest fear this glorious and fearful name THE LORD THY GOD; then the Lord will make thy plagues wonderful."

EXPLANATION.

Obs. 214.—*There are many who hold themselves guiltless of much sin, although they take the name of God in vain.*

1. Many encourage themselves in this sin from its *prevalence* in the world, and from the custom which they themselves have imbibed of profaning the name of God. But the prevalence of profane swearing in common conversation, or a *habit* or *custom* of it, can be no excuse, any more than the prevalence of the crime of murder, or a habit or custom of killing men, can be an excuse of wilful murder.

2. Many conclude that they are at liberty to break out in such language as they would not probably use at another time, when they are hurried into passion by losses, or by crosses, or by disappointments, or by discouragements, &c. But are such guiltless, because they think that they have cause to abuse the name of God? Besides, can any profit or pleasure arise from insulting the great God to his face? This is a crime which we dare not, without danger, be guilty of against a fellow-creature.

3. Many even glory in profaning the name of God by horrid oaths. They not only see no sin in taking the name of God in vain by swearing; but they think that, by doing so, they appear great, and are superior to others. They must have a sort of language to distinguish them from those whom they are pleased to brand with the name of enthusiasts or religious fanatics,—that is, persons who fear the name of the Lord. Such show at once that they do not belong to God, and that they have no part nor lot with those whom they despise.

Obs. 215.—*They who take the name of God in vain may, and often do, escape punishment from men.*

They who are guilty of this sin escape punishment from *magistrates*, partly because human laws do not, or cannot, extend to all profanations of the name of God, and partly because they who re in authority are not unfrequently profane and wicked persons themselves, and consequently cannot with any propriety execute those laws which do extend to blasphemy, perjury, swearing, and the grosser profanations of the name of God. They also escape punishment from *ministers*, when they allow this sin to pass without observation in their public ministrations, and in the exercise of the government of the house of God. They also escape punishment from *parents* and *masters* of families, when such do not reprove and punish those under their charge, who are guilty of this sin. Another reason why the breakers of this commandment escape punishment from men, is because there is so little zeal among them for the honour of the name of God. Were men thus treated, they would soon avenge it as their own interest; but the interest of God's honour appears to be the interest of very few.

Obs. 216.—*Although they who take God's name in vain escape punishment from men, yet the Lord will not suffer them to escape his righteous judgment.*

This is expressed in the commandment itself thus:—" The Lord will not hold him guiltless that taketh his name in vain,"—that is, he will account him very guilty, and will assuredly punish him.

The *judgments* which God inflicts upon such as are profane and abuse his name, are various. This sin destroys families,— Zech. v. 3, 4; brings judgments upon a land,—Hos. iv. 1–5; Jer. v. 7–9; and wonderful plagues upon the body,—Acts xii. 21–23; and it will destroy both soul and body in hell for ever,— Rom. ii. 5.

This, then, must be a *very heinous* sin, seeing the Lord himself undertakes to punish it in such a signal manner, although others may allow it to escape. And its heinousness further appears from the character which is given of such in Scripture, as the open and avowed enemies of God—Ps. cxxxix. 20; and also from the consideration, that there is nothing obtained by the commission of it; that there is no temporal advantage connected with it; but that it is committed out of pure malice against God, and from pure love to the thing itself.

Obs. 217.—*Besides the reason above mentioned, there seem to be other reasons in the commandment itself, why the name of God should not be taken in vain.*

In this commandment God styles himself *the Lord thy God.* "Thou shalt not take the name of the Lord thy God in vain."

1. The consideration, that he is the *Lord* or *Jehovah*, lays us under a strong obligation to use his name with reverence, on account of his essential glory and the excellencies of his nature; and because he has an undoubted right to the obedience of his

creatures: and to fear his name is a part of that obedience which he requires, and which is well pleasing in his sight.

2. The consideration, that he is the *Lord our God*, lays a still stronger obligation upon us to fear his name. If he hath made himself over to us in his Word as reconciled in Christ Jesus, and if he hath revealed himself in the gospel as *our God*, in the endearing relations of the everlasting covenant,—what stronger obligations can we lie under to fear him always, and to beware of offending him by taking his name in vain?

INFERENCES.

From this subject we learn,—1. The necessity of having becoming views of God. 2. The danger of excusing one's self in the commission of sin. 3. That custom or habit will not extenuate any sin; and that passion ought to be avoided, seeing it is not free from sin. 4. The necessity of keeping the door of our lips, that we offend not with our tongue. 5. That God is entitled to our obedience in reverencing his great name. 6. That one distinguishing feature of a child of the devil, is profane swearing. 7. That the blood of Christ alone can cleanse from this sin. 8. The necessity of zeal for the name of God, that the plague of profane swearing may be stayed, and that wrath may be averted from us.

DIV. 4.—THE FOURTH COMMANDMENT

Q. 57.—Which is the Fourth Commandment?

The Fourth Commandment is, "Remember the Sabbath-day to keep it holy. Six days shalt thou labour, and do all thy work; but the seventh day is the Sabbath of the Lord thy God: in it thou shalt not do any work, thou, nor thy son, nor thy daughter, thy man-servant, nor thy maid-servant, nor thy cattle, nor thy stranger that is within thy gates: for in six days the Lord made heaven and earth, the sea, and all that in them is, and rested the seventh day: wherefore the Lord blessed the Sabbath-day, and hallowed it."

Exod. xx. 8–11; Deut. v. 12–15.

Duties Required.

Q. 58.—What is required in the Fourth Commandment?

The Fourth Commandment requireth the keeping holy to God such set times as he hath appointed in his Word, expressly one whole day in seven, to be a holy Sabbath to himself.

FOURTH COMMANDMENT—DUTIES REQUIRED.

ANALYSIS AND PROOFS.

We are here taught,—
1. That God in his Word hath appointed set times for his worship. Lev. xxiii. 37, 38.—" These are the feasts of the Lord which ye shall proclaim to be holy convocations, besides the Sabbath of the Lord."
2. That God requires one whole day in seven, which he hath expressly appointed to be a holy Sabbath to himself. Deut. v. 12, 14.—" Keep the Sabbath-day to sanctify it. The seventh day is the Sabbath of the Lord thy God." Exod. xxxv. 15.— " Whosoever doeth any work on the Sabbath, he shall surely be put to death." See also Exod. xxxv. 2; Lev. xix. 30.

EXPLANATION.

Obs. 218.—*The Fourth Commandment is expressed in a peculiar manner.*

It is expressed both positively and negatively.
1. *Positively.* " Remember the Sabbath-day to keep it holy;" o show what God would have us to do.
2. *Negatively.* " In it thou shalt not do any work;" to show what is forbidden in this commandment, or what God would have us not to do.

Again: the careful observance of this commandment is enjoined on various persons in authority.
1. It is the duty of *parents* to see that their children observe the Sabbath-day. " In it thou shalt not do any work, thou, nor thy son, nor thy daughter."
2. It is the duty of *masters* to see that their servants observe the Sabbath-day. " In it thou shalt not do any work, thou, nor thy man-servant, nor thy maid-servant."
3. It is the duty of *heads of families* to see that all within the gates of their house observe the Sabbath-day to keep it holy. " In it thou shalt not do any work, thou, nor thy stranger that is within thy gates."
4. This commandment may also have a reference to *magistrates*, whose duty it is to see that all within the gates of the city observe the Sabbath, at least externally.

This commandment may have been thus fully expressed, on account of the particular place which the Sabbath holds in religious worship; for, with the observance of the Sabbath, religion must stand or fall.

Obs. 219.—*The Fourth Commandment requireth the keeping holy to God such set times as he hath appointed in his Word.*

By the *set times* here mentioned, we are to understand those stated feasts, and holy convocations for religious worship, which were instituted of old under the ceremonial law, and which the Jews were bound by Divine appointment to observe during the continuance of that ceremonial dispensation. See an account of these stated feasts in Lev. xxiii. But matters are now totally altered; and accordingly, in the New Testament, we do not read of one day to be observed as a stated time for public worship, but the Sabbath. All the Jewish festivals being purely ceremonial, they have been entirely abolished since the resurrection of Christ; so that we have neither a command to observe them, nor an example of observing any of those which in some Churches are called *holidays*. Every thing of this nature we find condemned in the New Testament. See Gal. iv. 10; Col. ii. 16, &c.

But although we are not to observe any stated times of worship, except the Sabbath, under the New Testament dispensation, yet we are undoubtedly called upon at times to worship God publicly on other days, besides that one which he hath appointed for his stated worship. These, however, are not *stated*, but only *occasional* times of worship; and they are to be observed only as his providence calls us. Thus, days of fasting and of thanksgiving are to be observed by us, when we are called in providence to the duty of fasting, or of publicly acknowledging God's mercies with thanksgiving; but these days cannot be called *stated*, but *occasional* times of worship.

Hence it must be a great corruption and innovation in the worship of God, to observe *holidays* of man's appointment; and to observe them as of Divine appointment, and as stated seasons of worship, is as much as to say, that the institutions of God's worship are *imperfect*. Corruption in worship may arise from *adding to* the institutions of Christ, as well as from *taking from* them: and there are not a few who imagine, that they are doing God service when they add to his institutions; whereas it is the greatest dishonour that can be done to him.

Obs. 220.—*The Fourth Commandment requireth us to sanctify one whole day in seven, which God hath expressly appointed to be a holy Sabbath to himself.*

By *one whole day*, as the stated time of worshipping God, we are to understand the same that we are to understand by any other whole day—namely, a period consisting of twenty-four hours, or what is commonly called a *natural day;* and this day we should begin and end at the same time that we begin and end any other day—namely, at midnight.

With respect to the *day* of the week which we are to keep holy, we observe, that the commandment itself enjoins us to keep holy the *seventh day;* but it does not confine us for ever to the observation of the seventh day in order from the creation. Its meaning is, that we must observe *any seventh portion* of our time which God, the object of our worship, shall be pleased to appoint. It is not said, Remember the *seventh* day to keep it holy; but, "Remember the *Sabbath*-day to keep it holy." It is not said, The Lord blessed the *seventh* day and hallowed it; but, " The Lord blessed the *Sabbath*-day and hallowed it."

The day which God hath appointed for his worship is called the *Sabbath*, which signifies *rest*. See Heb. iv. 9, where we read of a rest prepared for the people of God; that is, a *Sabbath* above, of which the weekly Sabbath is a type and foretaste: and it is called a *holy* Sabbath, because it is *set apart* by God for the particular purpose of his worship and service.

It may be here remarked, that it is improper to call this day *Sunday*, as many do. We ought to use those names which are given to it in Scripture. By using the term *Sunday*, instead of *Sabbath* or *the Lord's day*, we show that we prefer the one to the other—a name of our own to a name given in Scripture to this holy day.

Obs. 221.—*Although the commandments which God gave the Israelites, respecting the observation of other Sabbaths or set times, were ceremonial, and abrogated at the death of Christ; yet the Fourth Commandment, concerning the weekly Sabbath, is moral, and binding on all men in all ages.*

This may be proved from the following things:—

1. The time of the first institution of the Sabbath is an argument for its morality, or its binding obligation upon all. See Gen. ii. If Adam, in a state of innocence, required a Sabbath, or a day of holy rest from his worldly employments, that he might hold more intimate communion with his Maker, and worship him with greater solemnity; surely we, who are sinful creatures, and so much engaged in the affairs of this world, require such a day, that our thoughts may be withdrawn from common scenes and occupations, and we more fitted for enjoying communion with the Father of our spirits, and the Author of all good. It may be here observed, that although the Scriptures are entirely silent respecting the observation of the Sabbath from its first institution to the time of Moses—a period upwards of 2000 years, yet it cannot be inferred from this that it was not observed during that period; for it might as well be inferred, that there was no observation of the Sabbath after the time of Moses, during the government of the judges—a period of 450 years, because there is no mention of the observation of that day during all that time. But it cannot be supposed, that the judges, who were pious men, would allow the observation of the Sabbath to fall into neglect. Moreover, the Hebrews well knew that the observation of the Sabbath was a moral duty, before the promulgation of the law; for, before they came to Mount Sinai, we find Moses speaking of the Sabbath as a day well known to them.—Exod. xvi. 23.

2. The place which this commandment has in the moral law is an argument for the binding obligation of the Sabbath upon all. All the commandments of the moral law are evidently of

the same nature; and, consequently, this commandment must be of the same nature with those which precede and those which follow. It was proclaimed by Jehovah from Mount Sinai equally with the rest of the commandments; and, consequently, it ought to be observed by all equally with the rest. It was twice written by the finger of God upon tables of stone, and placed within the ark, as well as the other commandments of the law; and, consequently, it should be obeyed equally with the rest. It is so placed in the moral law, as to connect both tables; and is, as it were, the bond of love to God and man; and it will be found that the breakers or despisers of this commandment are totally void of religion; or, in other words, that they neither love God nor man. Moreover, this commandment is of a nature very different from the ceremonial law, which was never honoured in such a manner, having never been put within the ark, as the moral law was,—which greatly distinguished the one from the other. Hence the Fourth Commandment must be of the same perpetual obligation with the other moral precepts.

3. Another argument in favour of the moral obligation of the Sabbath, is the circumstance, that there was nothing ceremonial or typical in the substance of the Fourth Commandment, with respect to the Jews. In the ceremonial law, every type had a reference to Christ as the antitype; but how could any thing be appointed as a type of that which was altogether unknown? But Christ Jesus, to whom all the types of the ceremonial law refer, was unknown in the capacity of a saviour at the time of the institution of the Sabbath; for man, being then in innocence, stood in no need of one. Moreover, if it had been typical of Christ, it would have been abolished at his death, with all the other types of him. But seeing this is not the case, this commandment must be considered as binding on all till the end of the world.

But it may be here objected, that the children of Israel were commanded to remember the Sabbath-day, from the consideration that they were servants in the land of Egypt; and that their deliverance out of that land was typical of the redemption which Christ accomplished. To this we answer, that the consideration of their being slaves in the land of Egypt was indeed added as a reason why they should keep holy to God the *seventh* day, which was to be observed until the death of Christ. But for this reason, this very *seventh day* was abolished; for the seventh day in order from the creation is not now the Sabbath of the Lord; but the Sabbath is the seventh part of the time given us, which we are now commanded to keep holy. Properly speaking, the substance of the commandment does not rest in observing the same day from the beginning to the end of time; but in observing a seventh part of our time upon earth, according to the will of God: and accordingly, the first day of the week is now the

Sabbath of the Lord; and this day we must sanctify. This, therefore, can be no objection against the moral obligation of the Sabbath.

4. It may be observed, that much as the rigid letter of this valuable institution is now contested, no one precept of the moral law is more frequently or more imperatively enforced. See the following passages:—Exod. xvi. 23–30; Deut. v. 12–14; Exod. xxiii. 12, xxxiv. 21, xxxi. 14–18, and xxxv. 2, 3; Lev. xxiii. 3; Numb. xv. 32–36; Neh. x. 31, and xiii. 15–23; Isa. lviii. 13, 14; Jer. xvii. 21, 22, 24, 27; Ezek. xx. 12, 20, 21, &c.

INFERENCES.

From this subject we learn,—1. The necessity of keeping holy the Sabbath-day. 2. That God is not a hard master; seeing he has given us six days in the week, and only reserved one for himself. 3. That profaners of the Sabbath are grossly ignorant of God, are drowned in worldly cares, and are utterly unfit for heaven. 4. The pleasure which is found in worshipping God on the day which he hath appointed. 5. The danger of giving to other days of man's appointment that honour which belongs to God's day. 6. That we cannot be said to find much pleasure in the worship of God, if we grudge to give him one day in the week. 7. That the Fourth Commandment is binding upon us equally with the rest of the moral law. 8. That, seeing this is a positive commandment which shall be in force to the end of the world, we are guilty of heinous sin against God if we do not observe it.

Change of the Sabbath.

Q. 59.—Which day of the seven hath God appointed to be the weekly Sabbath?

From the beginning of the world to the resurrection of Christ, God appointed the seventh day of the week to be the weekly Sabbath; and the first day of the week ever since, to continue to the end of the world, which is the Christian Sabbath.

ANALYSIS AND PROOFS.

We are here taught,—
1. That the seventh day of the week was at first appointed by God as the weekly Sabbath. Gen. ii. 3.—" God blessed the seventh day and sanctified it." Deut. v. 14.—" The seventh day is the Sabbath of the Lord thy God."
2. That the seventh day of the week continued to be the Sabbath from the beginning of the world till the resurrection of Christ. Matt. xxviii. 1.—" In the end of the Sabbath, as it began to dawn towards the first day of the week."
3. That the change of the Sabbath took place immediately after

the resurrection of Christ. John xx. 19 (compared with ver. 26.) —" Then the same day at evening, being the first day of the week, when the doors were shut where the disciples were assembled for fear of the Jews, came Jesus, and stood in the midst."

4. That the first day of the week is the Christian Sabbath, or Lord's day, and shall continue to be so, without change, till the end of the world. Acts xx. 7.—" Upon the first day of the week, when the disciples came together to break bread, Paul preached to them." Ezek. xliii. 27.—" When those days are expired, it shall be, that upon the eighth day, and so forward, the priests shall make your burnt-offerings upon the altar, and your peace-offerings." See also Rev. i. 10, and xxii. 19.

EXPLANATION.

Obs. 222.—*From the beginning of the world till the resurrection of Christ, the seventh day of the week was appointed by God as the weekly Sabbath.*

During this period, which consisted of 4000 years, the *seventh day of the week*, or the seventh day in order after the creation, was appointed as the Sabbath, in order that, as God rested on that day from the work of creation, men might, after his example, rest from their works, and remember those of the Creator, and celebrate his praises. It was also observed afterwards by the posterity of Abraham, in commemoration of their deliverance from the land of Egypt. See Gen. ii. 2, 3; Exod. xvi. 23-30, xxiii. 12, xxxi. 14-18, xxxiv. 21, and xxxv. 2; Lev. xxiii. 3; Deut. v. 12-15.

That the Sabbath was first instituted at the beginning of the world, and not in the wilderness at the promulgation of the law, will be evident when we consider, that immediately after finishing the creation, God blessed and sanctified the seventh day,— that is, set it apart from a common to a special purpose; that it was observed before the promulgation of the law from Mount Sinai, and spoken of, not as a new, but as an ancient institution; and that, when the law was published to the Hebrews, they were commanded to *remember* the Sabbath-day, which implies, that it was not then first instituted, but that it had been instituted long before, and had been forgotten during their abode in the land of Egypt. See Gen. ii. 2, 3; Exod. xvi. 5, 23.

Obs. 223.—*From the resurrection of Christ till the end of the world, the first day of the week was appointed by God to be the Christian Sabbath.*

During this period, *the first day of the week* is to be observed as the Christian Sabbath or Lord's day; and that in commemoration of an event much more remarkable and glorious than either the creation of the world or the deliverance of the Israelites out of the land of Egypt,—viz., the resurrection of Jesus Christ from the dead, by which the work of redemption was completed.

If it be here asked, why no other event respecting Christ, such as his *incarnation*, or his *death*, or his *ascension*, could have given rise to the observation of the Christian Sabbath, as well as his resurrection; we answer, that if we consider the nature of the Sabbath, we shall find that it is most proper to view his *resurrection* as the proper event from which the Christian Sabbath is to be dated. The word *Sabbath*, as before observed, signifies *rest;* and, consequently, the Christian Sabbath is to be observed because of a state of rest in which Christ was when it was first observed. Heb. iv. 10.—" For he that is entered into his rest, he also hath ceased from his own works, as God did from his." This evidently intimates, that as God rested from the work of creation upon the *seventh* day, which was the reason why this day was observed as the Sabbath; so Christ rested from his work on the *first* day of the week, which is the reason why this day is observed as the Christian Sabbath.

To prove that the Sabbath was actually changed from the *seventh* to the *first* day of the week, and that the first day of the week is to be observed as the Christian Sabbath to the end of the world, the following arguments may be adduced:—

1. The Christian Sabbath was prophesied of under the Old Testament dispensation. See Ps. cxviii. 22, &c., compared with Acts iv. 10, &c. See also Ezek. xliii. 27, where the *eighth* day is mentioned as the day on which spiritual sacrifices were to be offered up to the Lord: and this was to take place after the abolition of the Jewish system of ceremonies—" When these days are expired;" and it was to continue till the end of the world; which is expressed by the words—" And so forward."

2. After Christ's resurrection from the dead, he met with his disciples on the first day of the week. See John xx. 19, 26, where we are informed that Christ appeared twice to his disciples on the *first day* of the week; so that we have reason to conclude, that he appeared to them in this manner during the forty days that he continued with them on earth after his resurrection.

3. When Christ ascended to heaven, he poured out his Spirit in an extraordinary manner on the *first day* of the week. See Acts ii. 1–4, compared with Lev. xxiii. 15, 16; and it will be found that the day of Pentecost was the first day of the week.

4. The apostles and first Christians observed the *first day* of the week, above every other day, for the special worship of God. See Acts xx. 7,—from which it appears, that it was customary for the disciples to *come together* upon this day; for it is not said that they were *called together* on an extraordinary occasion. See also ver. 6, where we are informed that the Apostle Paul abode with them seven days. But it is not said that he met with them in a Church capacity on any of these days, but on the *first day* of the week.

5. There is an apostolical precept for the observation of the *first* day of the week above every other day; and that, too, for the services of the Church. See 1 Cor. xvi. 1, 2.

6. In the New Testament, the *first day* of the week is called *the Lord's day;* which is a good reason why Christians should statedly observe this day for the purposes of Divine worship. See Rev. i. 10. It is called *the Lord's day*, because it was appointed and set apart by him from a common to a sacred use; and to be observed, according to his appointment, in commemoration of the work of redemption, which is a greater and a more glorious work than the work of creation.

INFERENCES.

From this subject we learn,—1. That the Lord has the sole power of our time. 2. That the wisdom of God is conspicuously seen in the change of the Sabbath from the seventh to the first day of the week. 3. That we ought to acquiesce in this change, and remember the resurrection of Christ from the dead, which is the ground of all our hopes. 4. What ought to be our employment on the Lord's day,—viz., assembling of ourselves together for the worship of God.

Sanctification of the Sabbath.

Q. 60.—How is the Sabbath to be Sanctified?

The Sabbath is to be sanctified by a holy resting all that day, even from such worldly employments and recreations as are lawful on other days; and spending the whole time in the public and private exercises of God's worship, except so much as is to be taken up in the works of necessity and mercy.

ANALYSIS AND PROOFS.

We are here taught,—

1. That the Sabbath is to be sanctified by a holy resting all that day. Exod. xx. 10.—" In it thou shalt not do any work." See also Exod. xxxi. 15; Deut. v. 14; Lev. xxiii. 3.

2. That we are to abstain from all worldly employments on the Sabbath. Jer. xvii. 21.—" Thus saith the Lord, Take heed to yourselves, and bear no burden on the Sabbath-day." See also Neh. xiii. 15, 16–22; Luke xxiii. 56.

3. That we are to abstain from recreations and pastimes on the Sabbath, although lawful on other days. Isa. lviii. 13.—" If thou turn away thy foot from the Sabbath, from doing thy pleasure on my holy day; and call the Sabbath a delight, the holy of the Lord, honourable; and shalt honour him, not doing thine own ways, nor finding thine own pleasure, nor speaking thine own words."

4. That the Sabbath is to be employed in the public exercises of God's worship. Isa. lxvi. 23.—" From one Sabbath to another shall all flesh come to worship before me, saith the Lord."

5. That the Sabbath is to be employed in private acts of secret and social worship. Lev. xxiii. 3.—" It is the Sabbath of the Lord in all your dwellings." See also Ps. xcii. title, 1, 2.

6. That works of necessity are lawful on the Sabbath-day. Matt. xii. 1.—" Jesus went on the Sabbath-day through the corn; and his disciples were an hungered, and began to pluck the ears of corn and to eat." See also to ver. 8.

7. That works of mercy are lawful on the Sabbath-day. Luke xiii. 16.—" Ought not this woman, being a daughter of Abraham. whom Satan hath bound, lo, these eighteen years, to be loosed from this bond on the Sabbath-day." See also Matt. xii. 9–13.

EXPLANATION.

Obs. 224.—*The Sabbath is to be sanctified by a holy resting all that day, even from such worldly employments and recreations as are lawful on other days.*

It may be here remarked, that the Sabbath is not a *means* of conveying spiritual blessings, as the Word and sacraments are. It is only a holy season—a time set apart by God for the purposes of his worship, at which he hath promised particularly to bless his people, to meet with them in their assemblies, and to make his goodness pass before them. The Sabbath may, then, be said to be *sanctified*, inasmuch as it is set apart by Divine appointment for the worship of God, that it may be kept holy to him.

The Sabbath is to be sanctified by a *holy rest*, which is the meaning of the word *Sabbath*.

1. On this day we must rest from all *worldly employments*, or from all *servile work;* by which we are to understand any thing done for our worldly gain, profit, or livelihood, which, by prudent management, might have been done the week before, or might be left undone till the end of the Sabbath. See Exod. xxxiv. 21. Connected with worldly employments, from which we must rest on the Sabbath, are ploughing, sowing, reaping, bearing burdens. buying and selling, working at one's ordinary calling; finding one's own pleasure, or speaking his own words; reading newspapers or profane history; studying the arts and sciences; writing letters about worldly business, or making up bills or accounts; unnecessary journeying on this day; walking in the fields and highways for pleasure or diversion, or making use of beasts for pleasure; speaking of the public news of the country, which is a frequent topic of conversation among those who are not spiritually minded; conversing about trade, bargains, profits, and losses, &c.; feasting and visiting of friends; and unnecessary preparation of food. See Neh. xiii.; Exod. xvi. 27, &c.; Numb. xv. 32, &c.; Luke xxiii. 55, 56, and xxiv. 1; Exod. xxxi., xxxv.,

xvi. 23, and xxxv. 3. Now, as this is one of the commandments of the moral law, it must be as strictly binding on us as it was on those who were before us. The law of God is equally holy, just, and good, at all times; and God is as strict in demanding obedience now as he was formerly. See Matt. v. 18.

2. On this day we must also rest from those *worldly recreations* which are lawful on other days. By worldly recreations we are to understand worldly pleasure, unconnected with worldly gain or profit. Those which are unlawful on this day, are such as these:—the visiting of friends: walking in the fields; talking about the news of the day, or about public occurrences; innocent amusements (for there are many which are highly sinful even on other days); travelling about worldly business, and such like things; together with several of those before mentioned, which may be referred to recreations, as well as to worldly employments. See Isa. lviii. 13. We may here remark, that worldly recreations tend to alienate the mind from the true work of the Sabbath, as much as, if not more than, worldly employments. Moreover, if our recreations on the Sabbath are to be the same as they are on other days, why specify the Sabbath as a day of rest?—why make any difference at all between it and the other days of the week?

Obs. 225.—*The whole Sabbath is to be spent in the public and private exercises of God's worship, except so much as is to be taken up in works of necessity and mercy.*

We are here informed, that the Sabbath is to be sanctified by *holy exercises.*

1. On the Lord's day we are to be engaged in the *public exercises of God's worship.* Such are, hearing the Word read and preached, joining in prayer and praise, and partaking of the sacraments, according to Divine appointment. See Rom. x. 17; 1 Cor. i. 21; Acts xvi. 13, and xx. 7; Ps. xcii. title. And these exercises are to be engaged in with that frame of mind which ought to characterise the Lord's day. See Rev. i. 10.

2. On the Lord's day we are likewise to be engaged in the *private exercises of God's worship.* Under these are comprehended secret and family duties. By *secret* duties we are to understand, secret prayer; reading the Scriptures by one's self, and other religious books which tend to lead the soul to God; meditation on divine subjects; and self-examination. And by *family* duties we are to understand, family worship, family examination, and family conference. See Jer. x. 25; Lev. xxiii. 3; Gen. xviii. 19; Josh. xxiv. 15; 2 Sam. vi. 20; Job i. 5; Acts x. 2; Matt. xxvi. 30; Ps. xcii. 1, 2.

In these exercises the *whole day* must be spent, *except so much as is to be taken up in works of necessity and mercy,*—that is, in such works as could neither have been done on the day before the Sabbath, nor deferred until the end of it. *Works of necessity* are such as these:—defending one's self, or fleeing from an enemy; quenching fire; working a vessel at sea; and other things of a similar nature. And *works of mercy* are such as these:—refreshing the body; visiting the sick, and ministering to their comfort and necessities: feeding cattle, and preserving them from danger when exposed to it; making collections for the poor; and other things of a similar nature.—Matt. xii. 1, &c.; Luke xiii. 10, &c., and xiv. 3, &c.; 1 Cor. xvi. 1, 2. It may be here remarked, that if a field of corn is in danger of being carried down by the sudden and unexpected overflowing of a river, it is lawful to preserve as much of it as possible, because it is not an ordinary dispensation of providence. But in the case merely of unseasonable weather, it is neither necessary nor lawful to cut down and gather in on the Sabbath-day, because the dispensation of providence is ordinary, and the promise of God ought to be depended upon,—that seed time and harvest shall continue until the end of the world.—Gen. viii. 22.

INFERENCES.

From this subject we learn,—1. That God is the same now that he was in ancient times; that his law is equally binding now as formerly; and that holiness is as acceptable now as it was formerly. 2. That they who think that God will dispense with any part of obedience to his law, are ignorant both of him and of it. 3. That all who love God will give him the honour which is due unto his name on the Sabbath-day. 4. That the Sabbath is not our own; and that we dare not do what we please on this day, without offending God. 5. That a mere resting from worldly employments and recreations is of no moment in the sight of God, unless we are engaged in holy exercises.

Sins Forbidden.

Q. 69.—What is forbidden in the Fourth Commandment?

The Fourth Commandment forbiddeth the omission or careless performance of the duties required, and the profaning the day by idleness, or doing that which is in itself sinful, or by unnecessary thoughts, words, or works, about our worldly employments or recreations.

ANALYSIS AND PROOFS.

We are here taught,—
1. That we are forbidden to omit any of the duties required on the Sabbath. Ezek. xxii. 26.—" Her priests have violated my law, and have profaned mine holy things; they have put no difference between the holy and profane, neither have they showed

difference between the unclean and the clean, and have hid their eyes from my Sabbaths, and I am profaned among them."

2. That the duties of the Sabbath are not to be performed carelessly. Deut. x. 12.—" Serve the Lord thy God, with all thy heart, and with all thy soul." See also Mal. i. 13.

3. That the Sabbath is not to be profaned by idleness. Exod. xx. 8.—" Remember the Sabbath-day, to keep it holy."

4. That sinful acts are aggravated by being committed on the Sabbath. Ezek. xxiii. 38.—" They have defiled my sanctuary in the same day, and have profaned my Sabbaths."

5. That unnecessary thoughts about our worldly concerns are forbidden on the Sabbath. Amos viii. 5.—" When will the new moon be gone, that we may sell corn? and the Sabbath, that we may set forth wheat?"

6. That unnecessary conversation about our worldly affairs is forbidden on the Sabbath. Isa. lviii. 13.—" Not doing thine own ways, nor finding thine own pleasure, nor speaking thine own words."

7. That unnecessary works for forwarding our worldly concerns are forbidden on the Sabbath. Jer. xvii. 21.—"Thus saith the Lord, Take heed to yourselves, and bear no burden on the Sabbath-day."

EXPLANATION.

Obs. 226.—*The Fourth Commandment forbids the omission of the duties which God requires on the Sabbath.*

The duties of which this commandment forbids the *omission*, are these:—Attendance on the public ordinances of religion, prayer, both private and secret; and meditation, which may be exercised about the works of creation and providence, about the work of redemption in its various parts and consequences, about the holiness of God, about that heavenly rest which remaineth for the righteous, and about other things of a similar nature. The neglect of these duties on the Sabbath is an evidence of the neglect of all religious duties through the week; and, consequently, of atheism, profaneness, and apostasy.

Obs. 227.—*The Fourth Commandment forbids the careless performance of the duties required on the Sabbath.*

The duties of the Sabbath are performed *carelessly*, when they are performed in a *partial* way,—that is, when some of them are observed, and others equally important and necessary are totally omitted; for example, when the public duties are attended to, and the private and secret ones neglected; or when they are performed in a *formal* way,—that is, without any regard to the principle from which obedience should flow, and to the end to which it should be directed; or when they are performed in a *cold*, and a *lifeless*, and an *indifferent* manner,—that is, without any vigour, and spirit, and pleasure. See Rev. iii. 15, &c.

Obs. 228.—*The Fourth Commandment forbids the profaning of the Lord's day by idleness.*

The Sabbath is profaned by *idleness*, when it is spent idly, either in whole or in part; not employing ourselves in the duties of God's worship, but loitering away the time at home or in the fields, either in vain and idle thoughts, or in vain and idle conversation, or the like. This day is also profaned by idleness, when we endeavour to shorten the day as much as possible, by rising later on the morning of this day than of other days, or by retiring to rest sooner at night, in order to get up in due time for worldly business.

Obs. 229.—*The Fourth Commandment forbiddeth the profaning of the Lord's day by doing that which is in itself sinful.*

Sin committed on any day is hateful to God; but *sin committed on the Sabbath* aggravates guilt, and exposes to severer punishment from the Lord; and this is the reason why there is a prohibition of doing on the Sabbath what is unlawful at any time. See Neh. xiii. 15, &c.; Jer. xvii. 27.

Obs. 230.—*The Fourth Commandment forbiddeth the profaning of the Sabbath by unnecessary thoughts, words, or works, about our worldly employments or recreations.*

The thoughts, words, and works, which are here forbidden on the Sabbath, are these :—unnecessary thoughts and contrivances about worldly affairs, unnecessary words and conversation respecting earthly employments, unnecessary works in any worldly business, or those pleasures and recreations which are lawful on other days; or they are all those thoughts, words, or works, which are not unavoidably used about the works of necessity and mercy, which are lawful on the Lord's day. It is only by not thinking, or speaking, or working about our worldly employments, and by employing ourselves in holy exercises, that we distinguish the Sabbath from every other day. See Isa. lviii. 13.

INFERENCES.

From this subject we learn,—1. That divine ordinances, as means of salvation, ought to be observed by all in the due order. 2. That when they are not performed in the due order, the end of their appointment is lost. 3. That if we would worship God in truth, we must imbibe the spirit of true worshippers.

Reasons Annexed.

Q. 62.—**What are the Reasons annexed to the Fourth Commandment?**

The reasons annexed to the Fourth Commandment are, God's allowing us six days of the week for our own employments, his challenging a special propriety in the seventh, his own example, and his blessing the Sabbath-day.

ANALYSIS AND PROOFS.

We are here taught,—
1. That God allows us six days of the week for our own employments. Exod. xxxi. 15.—" Six days may work be done." See also Exod. xx. 9.
2. That God claims the seventh day or the Sabbath as his own property. Lev. xxiii. 3.—" Ye shall do no work therein; it is the Sabbath of the Lord in all your dwellings." See also Exod. xx. 10.
3. That God hath set us an example of resting on the Sabbath, which he requires us to follow. Exod. xxxi. 17.—" It is a sign between me and the children of Israel for ever; for in six days the Lord made heaven and earth, and on the seventh day he rested, and was refreshed." See also Exod. xx. 11.
4. That God requires the Sabbath to be observed by us, because he himself blessed and sanctified it. Gen. ii. 3.—" God blessed the seventh day and sanctified it." See also Exod. xx. 11.

EXPLANATION.

Obs. 231.—*We should keep the Sabbath holy, because God has allowed us six days of the week for our own employments.*

This is expressed in these words:—" Six days shalt thou labour and do all thy work." And the force of this reason is, that it is highly unreasonable and ungrateful to grudge a seventh part of our time in the immediate worship of God, when he hath allowed us six days for our own employments.

Obs. 232.—*We should keep the Sabbath holy, because God challenges a special propriety in the seventh,—that is, in the seventh part of our time.*

This is expressed in these words:—" But the seventh day is the Sabbath of the Lord thy God." And the force of this reason is, that as God represents himself as in covenant with his people, they ought to observe this day, in which he challenges a special propriety, or which he claims as his own in a peculiar manner, for the social and public worship of this covenant God; which they ought to reckon a high privilege, seeing he condescends to hold communion with them in the ordinances of his grace.

Obs. 233.—*We should keep the Sabbath holy, because God himself hath set us an example of resting on this day.*

This is expressed in these words:—" For in six days the Lord made heaven and earth, the sea, and all that in them is, and rested the seventh day." Although God could have made all things in an instant of time, as perfect and as beautiful as they were after he had spent six days in the work, yet he was pleased to take that time to create all things, to fix the morality of six days for worldly employments, and of a seventh for holy rest; and both these by his own example. If it be asked here, how God's example of resting on the *seventh* day can be any reason for our resting on the *first ;* we answer, that although the observation of a particular day in seven be *changeable,* yet the duty of observing a seventh part of our time is *moral,* both by God's precept and example. Now, to despise God's own example, is to despise his works; and to despise the Christian Sabbath, is to despise the work of Christ; and, consequently, this is to pour contempt upon the wisdom, and power, and goodness of God in the works of creation and redemption.

Obs. 234.—*We should keep the Sabbath holy, because God hath blessed the Sabbath-day and sanctified it.*

This is expressed in these words:—" Wherefore the Lord blessed the Sabbath-day and hallowed it,"—that is, set it apart for the worship of his name, and for calling to mind his holiness, and the arduous undertaking of his dear Son. And they who observe this day according to his appointment, and who worship him on it in spirit and in truth, may, according to his promise, expect much spiritual comfort on this day. See Isa. lvi. 6, 7, and lviii. 13, 14. We may here observe, that the particle *wherefore,* used towards the end of this commandment, teaches us, that God's resting on the Sabbath was the great reason why he set it apart as a day of rest to us, that we might thereon contemplate his works both of creation and of grace.

INFERENCES.

From this subject we learn,—1. That the reasons for remembering the Sabbath-day to keep it holy, are very weighty and satisfactory. 2. That we should endeavour to prepare for the Sabbath before its approach. 3. That we should make conscience of attending the public ordinances of Divine appointment. 4. That we ought to prepare for the public ordinances, by spending the morning of the Lord's day in secret and private exercises, such as prayer, reading the Scriptures, and meditation. 5. That when the public worship of God is over, we should meditate and converse about spiritual things, and what we have heard. 6. That when we are necessarily detained from the public ordinances our hearts should be there.—Ps. lxiii. 1 2.

SECT. III.—THE DUTIES WHICH WE OWE TO MAN—CONTAINED IN THE LAST SIX COMMANDMENTS OF THE LAW.

DIV. 1.—THE FIFTH COMMANDMENT.

Q. 63.—*Which is the Fifth Commandment?*

The Fifth Commandment is, " Honour thy father and thy mother, that thy days may be long upon the land which the Lord thy God giveth thee."
Exod. xx. 12; Deut. v. 16.

Duties Required.

Q. 64.—*What is required in the Fifth Commandment?*

The Fifth Commandment requireth the preserving the honour, and performing the duties belonging to every one in their several places and relations, as superiors, inferiors, or equals.

ANALYSIS AND PROOFS.

We are here taught,—

1. That there are several stations in society which are ordained by God. Rom. xiii. 1.—" The powers that be are ordained by God."

2. That we are required to preserve the honour due to every one in their several stations. 1 Pet. ii. 17.—" Honour all men."

3. That we are required to preserve the honour due to our superiors. Lev. xix. 32.—" Thou shalt rise up before the hoary head, and honour the face of the old man, and fear thy God; I am the Lord."

4. That we are required to preserve the honour due to our inferiors. Rom. xii. 16.—" Condescend to men of low estate."

5. That we are required to preserve the honour due to our equals. Rom. xii. 10.—" Be kindly affectioned one to another, with brotherly love; in honour preferring one another."

6. That we are required faithfully to perform the duties which belong to every one in their several stations. Rom. xiii. 7.— " Render therefore to all their dues."

7. That we are required to perform the duties which we owe to our superiors. Rom. xiii. 1. -" Let every soul be subject to the higher powers." See also Eph. vi. 1, 5.

8. That we are required to perform the duties which we owe to our inferiors. Eph. vi. 9.—" And ye masters, do the same things unto them, forbearing threatening; knowing that your master also is in heaven." See also vi. 4.

9. That we are required to perform the duties which we owe

to our equals. Eph. v. 21.—" Submitting yourselves one to another in the fear of God."

10. That all our social duties must be performed with a due regard to the authority of God. Eph. vi. 7.—" With good will doing service, as to the Lord, and not to men."

EXPLANATION.

Obs. 235.—*There are various stations and relations among mankind in this world.*

This must be evident to every one; and it is the work of God, who alone is the supreme sovereign of the universe. Had it pleased him, he could have made all equal; and could have so ordered things, that this equality should have continued for ever. But as this was never designed by him, so it is impossible that this should take place in the world. The inequality, however, which exists, is no deformity in the creation of God; nay, it is the reverse, for it constitutes one of the beauties of the universe, and is much calculated for the purposes of external peace and order. As all the members of the body have not the same office, so all the members of the family, of the Church, or of the State, have not the same office; some are superiors, and others are inferiors, for the purposes of mutual good.

The consequence of this inequality is, that there are various duties incumbent on men in their respective stations and relations; and it is only by the performance of these duties that they can be said to answer the end for which God has fixed them in certain relations in the world.

Obs. 236.—*The general scope of the Fifth Commandment is, the performance of those duties which we mutually owe to one another, in our several relations, as superiors, inferiors, and equals.*

By *father* and *mother* in this commandment, we are to understand, not only natural parents, but all superiors in age and gifts, and especially such as are, by the ordinance of God, over us in places of authority, whether in the family, or in the Church, or in the State. And superiors are so called, both to teach them in all duties towards their inferiors, like natural parents, to express love and kindness towards them, according to their several relations; and to lead inferiors to a greater willingness and cheerfulness in performing their duties to their superiors, as to their parents.

All men stand related to one another in the relation either of superiors, inferiors, or equals.

1. *Superiors* are all those who are above us in station, office, dignity, or gifts; and their duties to their inferiors are these:—
1. To adorn their superiority by a holy and an exemplary conversation.—Tit. ii. 1–3. 2. To take every opportunity of warn

ing and instructing them, and of recommending to them Christ and his religion. 3. To bear their infirmities, and thus to encourage them.—Rom. xv. 1.

2. *Inferiors* are all those who are under us in station, office, dignity, or gifts; and their duties to their superiors are these:— 1. To give them due honour and respect,—Lev. xix. 32; 2 Kings ii. 23. 2. To desire earnestly their counsel and instructions, and to submit to them readily.—1 Pet. v. 5. 3. To imitate them in that which is good.—James v. 10, 11; 1 Cor. xi. 1. 4. To judge favourably of them in those things in which they have a greater liberty than themselves.—Rom. xiv. 3.

3. *Equals* are all those who are of like age, station, or condition in the world; and their duties to one another are these:— 1. To cultivate the most affectionate love and peace with one another.—Rom. xiv. 19; 2 Cor. xiii. 11. 2. To prefer one another in honour and esteem.—Rom. xii. 10; Phil. ii. 2, 3. 3. To be courteous and affable to one another, and to be ready to promote and to rejoice in the welfare of one another.—1 Pet. iii. 8, and iv. 8; Rom. xiv. 19; Eph. iv. 32; Rom. xii. 15; 1 Cor. x. 24. 4. To reprove and warn one another faithfully.— Lev. xix. 17; Ps. cxli. 5; 1 Thess. v. 14; Gal. vi. 1; Matt. xviii. 15. 5. To vie with one another in tender sympathy under trouble.—Gal. vi. 2; Matt. vii. 12, and xxv. 36; Heb. xiii. 3. 6. To provoke one another to love and good works, and to a holy and circumspect behaviour.—Heb. x. 24.

It may here be remarked, that we are not left to perform these duties according to the dictates of our own minds. If we allow ourselves to be ruled by this opinion, we shall perform none of them, at least none of them in a right manner. But we are laid under an obligation to perform them from a variety of considerations; and the right performance of them is a great evidence of that holiness without which no man shall see the Lord. Accordingly, they are enjoined in the New Testament, on gospel principles—viz., faith in the authority of the Lawgiver, and love to his service. And we may further remark, that they who are wanting in the performance of relative duties, or in the practice of relative religion, cannot be called religious; for this is the grand test of the sincerity of love to God, and of the reality of faith, which. if real, will work by love in the practice of relative duties. 1 John iv. 20.—" He that loveth not his brother whom he hath seen," saith the beloved disciple, " how can he love God whom he hath not seen?" See also verses 7, 8, 12, 21.

Besides the duties of superiors, inferiors, and equals, above mentioned, we may notice more particularly the duties which belong to the several relations among mankind; such as husbands and wives, parents and children, masters and servants, ministers and people, and magistrates and subjects.

Obs. 237.—*The Fifth Commandment requireth the perfor-*

mance of the various duties which husbands and wives owe to one another.

The duties which belong to husband and wife are these:—
1. To love one another most tenderly and affectionately.—Eph v. 28, 31, 33: Tit. ii. 4.
2. To adhere with the strictest fidelity to the marriage covenant.—1 Pet. iii. 7; 1 Cor. vii. 15; Heb. xiii. 4.
3. To desire to please one another.—1 Cor. vii. 33, 34; Gen. xvi.
4. To use every means to preserve domestic peace.—Matt. v. 9.
5. To use the utmost care that they be not a disgrace to one another. This includes a regard to propriety of conduct, in whatever circumstances they may be placed.—1 Pet. iii. 4; Prov. xxxi. 28.
6. To sympathize with one another amidst all the ills of life, and to share in one another's joys.—1 Sam. i. 8.
7. To watch over one another's souls.—1 Pet. iii. 7; 1 Cor vii. 16.
8. As the husband is the head of the wife, he is bound to defend her from every harm and danger to the utmost of his power; and the wife must place herself under the guardianship of her husband.
9. As the wife may stand in need of direction in a variety of things, she must consult her husband; and he must be willing to impart to her that instruction of which he is capable; and both must walk in the fear of the Lord.—1 Cor. xiv. 35.
10. To provide for the family is a very important part of the duty of the husband, who is the head of the family,—1 Tim. v. 8; and with this the duty of the wife is intimately connected.—Prov. xxxi. 27.
11. Both husband and wife are equally concerned in the religious instruction of the children of the family, and of servants. For this Abraham was highly commended by God. See Gen. xviii. 9.

Obs. 238.—*The Fifth Commandment requireth the performance of the various duties which parents and children owe to one another.*

The duties of *parents* to their children are these:—
1. To pray for them before they are born; for if they are sinners in the womb (which they are, if we believe the Scriptures), their sanctification ought to be pleaded with God, and likewise their interest in the everlasting covenant; and this should be more attended to by parents than it generally is, seeing we read of some who were sanctified from the womb.
2. To bless the Lord for them, seeing every child is a gift from God.—Luke i. 64.

3. To pray for them when they are born, and to plead the promise of the covenant for them, taking God as their God, and the God of their seed, according to his promise—" I will be your God, and the God of your seed;" and, "The promise is to you and to your children."

4. To take all possible care of them by day and by night, in their helpless state, that they may show their regard for the gifts of God.—Isa. xlix. 15.

5. To make suitable provision for them when their reason and understanding begin to appear, and while they are immediately under their care.—1 Tim. v. 8.

6. To maintain that authority over them which God has given them.

7. To correct and reprove them when necessary.—Prov. xxix. 15, xix. 18, and xxiii. 13, 14. This ought to be done in love; and the child should be informed of the reason of his being corrected, for if he is not, he cannot be the subject of correction.

8. To bring them up in the nurture and admonition of the Lord.—Prov. xxii. 6; 2 Tim. iii. 15; Prov. i. 8, and iv. 3, 4; Deut. vi. 6, 7. They who neglect this neither love God nor their children.

9. To pray with them and for them.—Job i. 5. They who live without family prayer, live without God in the world, and live like the beasts that perish.

10. To set before them a good example.—Ps. ci. 2.

11. To act impartially towards them, and not show more kindness to one than to another.

12. To lay no command upon them, but what they may obey without sinning against God.—Acts iv. 19.

13. To take good heed that they be no dishonour to their children.

14. To place them, at a proper age, in some lawful employment.—Gen. iv. 2.

15. To dispose of them seasonably in marriage, suited to their temper, station, and consent; and their temporal, but especially their spiritual and eternal welfare.—Ruth iii. 1; Gen. xxiv. and xxviii.

16. To make such an arrangement and settlement of their temporal affairs in their favour in due time, as shall prevent all contention and alienation of affection among them.—Isa xxxviii. 1.

17. When dying, to charge them solemnly, and to encourage them to fear the Lord, to bless them, and to commend them into the hand of a covenant God.—Gen. xlix. 1, &c.; Jer. xlix. 11.

The duties of *children* to their parents are these:—

1. To love them.—Gen. xlvi. 29.
2. To fear them.—Lev. xix. 3; 1 Kings ii. 20; Prov. xxxi. 28.
3. To obey them.—Eph. vi. 1. 4; Gen. xxxvii. 13; Luke ii. 51

4. To be impressed with a sense of their inferiority to their parents.—1 Kings ii. 19; Deut. xxvii. 16; Gen. xxxi. 35.

5. To hearken to their counsel and advice.—Prov. i. 8, and iv. 1. And this should be the case both in temporal and spiritual concerns.—Gen. xxvii. 46, and xxviii. 1, 2.

6. To conceal their infirmities, and to bear with them.—Gen. ix. 22. &c.; Prov. xxiii. 22.

7. To supply their wants to the utmost of their power, when they are old and stand in need of it. 1 Tim. v. 4; Gen. xlvii 12; John xix. 27; Matt. xv. 4, &c.

8. To pray for them.

9. To show respect for them after their death.

Obs. 239.—*The Fifth Commandment requireth the performance of the various duties which masters and servants owe to one another.*

The duties of *masters* to their servants are these:—

1. To be careful whom they hire, lest they bring the curse of God into their family with a wicked servant.—Ps. ci. 6; Gen. xxxix. 3, 4.

2. To consider carefully the abilities of their servants, and to proportion their work accordingly.

3. To give them proper directions for the work assigned them.—Prov. xxxi. 27.

4. To assign them proper maintenance and wages for their work.—Prov. xxvii. 27; James v. 4; Deut. xxiv. 14. &c.

5. To keep them in their proper station with respect to familiarity and power, and such like things.—Prov. xxix. 21.

6. To treat them with gentleness, and to be ready to hea. what they say in excuse for their conduct.—Eph. vi. 9; Job xxxi. 13.

7. Not to hearken willingly to evil reports respecting their servants.—Ps. xv. 3; Prov. xxix. 12.

8. To take care of them when sick and infirm.—Matt. viii. 6, 1 Sam. xxx. 11, &c.

9. To be particularly kind to those who are remarkably faithful and diligent.—Prov. xiv. 35; Deut. xv. 12, &c.

10. To be anxious to train them up in the fear of the Lord.—Gen. xviii. 19; Josh. xxiv. 15; Ps. ci.

11. To allow them sufficient time for the secret and public exercises of religion.

The duties of *servants* to their masters are these:—

1. To hire themselves, if possible, with such as fear the Lord.

2. To esteem, and reverence, and honour their masters, both internally and externally.—1 Pet. ii. 18; 1 Tim. vi. 1, &c.; Eph vi. 5.

3. To maintain the honour of the family carefully and conscientiously.—Gen. xxiv. 34, &c., and xxxix. 8, 9.

4. To adhere strictly to their own allotted provision, and wages, and rest.—Gen. xxx. 33; Prov. xxxi. 15.

5. To submit with meekness to rebukes and corrections.—Tit. ii. 9; 1 Pet. ii. 18; Gen. xvi. 9.

6. To perform the business or work assigned them conscientiously, honestly, cheerfully, singly, faithfully, readily, and diligently.—Tit. ii. 9, 10; Matt. xxiv. 45, 46; Gen. xxxi. 38; Col. iii. 22-24; Prov. xviii. 9; Gen. xxxi. 6; Prov. xxii. 29; Rom. xii. 11.

7. To attend conscientiously to family worship, and to receive with readiness such family instructions as may be tendered to them.—Prov. iv 7.

Obs. 240.—*The Fifth Commandment requireth the performance of the various duties which ministers and people owe to one another.*

The duties of *ministers* to their people are these:—

1. To provide a proper stock of knowledge for their work.—2 Cor. iv. 13. There should be an experience of what is said in the beginning of 1 John i.

2. Not to enter among a people, unless properly called.—Rom. x. 15; 1 Pet. v. 3; Jer. xxiii. 21. &c.

3. To acquaint themselves with the state of their people, that they may regulate their ministrations accordingly.—Phil. ii. 19, 20.

4. To exercise the most tender love and care for their souls.—1 Thess. ii. 7, 8.

5. To administer divine ordinances among them faithfully, impartially, and diligently, in a manner answerable to their condition, without respect of persons.—Gal. vi. 6; 2 Tim. iv. 2.

6. To watch over their behaviour for the good of their souls.—Rev. xix. 17; Ezek. iii. 17. &c.. and xxxiii. 7, &c.

7. To pray for them habitually and fervently.—Eph. i. 15, &c., and iii. 14, &c.

8. To set before them a holy and shining example of divine truth in their Christian practice.—Heb. xiii. 7; Tit. ii. 7; 1 Tim. iv. 12; 1 Thess. ii. 1-10.

The duties of *people* to their ministers are these:—

1. To reverence them highly as the ambassadors of Christ, the King of kings and Lord of lords.—1 Cor. iv. 1.

2. To love them highly for their work's sake.—1 Thess. v. 12, 13; Gal. iv. 14.

3. To pray for them fervently and habitually.—Rom. xv. 30, 31; Eph. vi. 19, 20; 1 Thess. v. 25.

4. To attend diligently to the means of grace as dispensed by them.—Heb. x. 25; Luke x. 16.

5. To submit to them, as Christ's deputies, in warnings, reproofs, and censures, &c.—Heb. xiii. 17; Gal. vi. 1; Matt. xviii 15, &c.; 2 Tim. iv. 2.

6. To beware of taking up an ill report concerning them, without scriptural evidence.—1 Tim. v. 19.

7. To render them comfortable, with respect to maintenance and support.—1 Tim. v. 18; 1 Cor. ix. 13, &c.; Gal. vi. 6; 1 Cor. ix. 11.

Obs. 241.—*The Fifth Commandment requireth the performance of the various duties which magistrates and subjects owe to one another.*

The duties of *magistrates* to their subjects are these:—

1. To establish good and just laws, and to see them faithfully executed.—Zech. viii. 16; 2 Chron. xix. 5, &c.; Ps. lxxii. and lxxxii.

2. To govern their subjects with wisdom, equity, and affection.—2 Chron. i. 10; Prov. xviii. 5, xxv. 5, and xxix. 2, 4, 14.

3. To protect them in their just privileges and rights, both temporal and spiritual, which have been conferred on them by God.—1 Tim. ii. 2.

4. To punish evil doers, and to encourage them that do well.—Rom. xiii.; Deut. i. 16, &c.

5. To promote the interests of true religion by their good example.—Isa. xlix. 23.

The duties of *subjects* to magistrates are these:—

1. To respect them as the deputies and ordinance of God.—Rom. xiii.; 1 Pet. ii. 13, 17; 1 Sam. xxvi. 16, 17.

2. To put a charitable construction on their conduct, so far as it will bear, in consistency with the honour of God.—Exod. xxii. 28; Eccl. x. 20; 2 Pet. ii. 9, 10.

3. To be subject to their just laws.—Rom. xiii. 1, &c.; Tit. iii. 1, 2.

4. To pay tribute or just taxes cheerfully.—Rom. xiii. 6; Luke xx. 25; Matt. xvii. 25, &c.

5. To defend them from their enemies.—1 Sam. xxvi. 15; 2 Sam. xviii. 3.

6. To pray for them frequently and fervently.—1 Tim. ii. 1, 2.

7. To endeavour carefully to live under their government an honour, a comfort, and a blessing, both to them and to others.

INFERENCES.

From this subject we learn,—1. That we ought to be content with our lot, and resigned to the will of God, who assigns to all their station in this world. 2. The various duties which belong to superiors, inferiors, and equals; and the dispositions which Christians ought to exercise towards one another. 3. The danger of hatred in husband or wife; the direful consequences of it; and that all have cause to mourn over their sins in this relation. 4. The importance of the charge committed to parents, and that they cannot divest themselves of this charge; that the command

of God, and the vows which they have vowed, are upon them;
that the consequences of doing or of not doing their duty, are of
the utmost importance; that parents may be the means of saving
or of damning the souls of their children; and that parents and
children shall at last meet before the judgment-seat of Christ,
either to acquit or to condemn one another. 5. That it is the
duty of children to reverence and obey their parents; that disobedience to parents is a great sin, and deserves the judgment of
God; and that children must give an account to God of their
conduct towards their parents. 6. That the place of masters is
very important; that God secureth the rights of inferiors; and
that masters should remember that Christ is the judge of all,
and that on earth they themselves are but servants. 7. That servants cannot plead ignorance of their duty; that they are bound
by God to do that of which they probably do not often think;
that their own engagements bind them to faithfulness in all
things; and that they are to obey, lest they be found liars, and
their own tongues condemn them. 8. That the office of a minister in the Church of Christ is very important; that his work is
very important, and the consequences of it momentous; that
much good may be done to the souls of men by the right discharge of this office; and that an account must soon be given by
all who are invested with it. 9. That, as the work of ministers
of the gospel is arduous, and requires encouragement, it is the
duty of the people to do what they can to assist them and
strengthen their hands; and that ministers and people ought to
be comforts to one another. 10. That the duty of magistrates is
very important; that it is an ordinance of God; that they are
accountable for the discharge of the trust committed to them;
and that many eyes are upon them, and also the eyes of the King
of kings and Lord of lords. 11. That it is the duty of subjects to
obey magistrates; and that they who disobey them, sin against
God, by whom they are ordained.

Sins Forbidden.

Q. 65.—What is forbidden in the Fifth Commandment?

The Fifth Commandment forbiddeth the neglecting
of, or doing any thing against, the honour and duty
which belongeth to every one in their several places
and relations.

ANALYSIS AND PROOFS.

We are here taught,—

1. That we are forbidden to neglect the honour due to any one,
whether our superior, our inferior, or our equal. 1 Pet. ii. 17.
—" Honour all men." See also Rom. xiii. 7; Gen. xxiii. 7;
Rom. xii. 16; 1 Pet. iii. 8; Eph. vi. 2.

2. That we are forbidden to do any thing against the honour belonging to any one, whether our superior, our inferior, or our equal. Rom. xii. 10.—" Be kindly affectioned one to another, with brotherly love; in honour preferring one another." See also Eccl. x. 20; Matt. xxiii. 11; Phil. ii. 3; 1 Cor. xix. 22.

3. That we are forbidden to neglect the duties which are due to any one, whether our superior, our inferior, or our equal. Rom. xiii. 8.—" Owe no man any thing, but to love one another." See also Tit. iii. 1; Eph. vi. 1, 5; Col. iv. 1; Eph. vi. 4; Gal v. 13; 1 Pet. iii. 8.

4. That we are forbidden to do any thing against the duties which we owe to any one, whether our superior, our inferior, or our equal. 1 Thess. v. 15.—" Follow that which is good, both among yourselves, and to all men." See also 1 Pet. iii. 6 Matt. xxiii. 4; Phil. ii. 3.

EXPLANATION.

Obs. 242.—*The Fifth Commandment forbiddeth superiors inferiors, and equals, to neglect the honour and duty which belong to any one, or to do any thing against that honour and duty.*

To *neglect the honour and duty* which we owe to any one whether our superior, or our inferior, or our equal, is not only to omit the performance of such relative duties altogether, but also when they are performed, to do them without any regard to the command and authority of the Lawgiver.—Isa. xxix. 13.

To *do any thing against the honour and duty* which we owe any one, whether our superior, our inferior, or our equal, is to commit those sins which are the very opposite of the relative duties which are incumbent upon us.—Rom. ii. 22.

1. This commandment is violated by *superiors* when they trample upon their inferiors; when they seek their own glory and ease, and profit, and pleasure; when they command things unlawful, or things which their inferiors cannot perform; when they counsel, and encourage, and favour them in what is evil, or dissuade, and discountenance, and discourage them in what is good; when they disgrace their superiority by a careless behaviour before their inferiors; or when they enrage or provoke them to anger. It is violated by those who are *superior in age* when they seek not opportunities of establishing the younger in the faith as it is in Jesus; when, by their wickedness, they are a disgrace to the hoary head, which ought to be a crown of glory; or when they do not set before the young an example of faith and holiness in all manner of conversation. It is violated by *superiors in gifts and grace*, when they despise the weak, and will not bear with them; when they do not study to instruct them; or when they take advantage of their weakness and inferiority.

2. This commandment is violated by *inferiors*, when they envy, despise, or rebel against their superiors, in their lawful counsels, commands, and corrections. It is violated by *inferiors in age*, when they do not respect the man of gray hairs; when they reproach the hoary head; when they contemn the advice, and hate the example of the aged; when they do not seek to be instructed by them; or when they mock them, and avoid them, and will have none of their service. It is violated by *inferiors in gifts and grace*, when they envy and grieve at the gifts of superiors; when they despise their instruction; when they misrepresent them; or when they do not imitate them, or learn of them.

3. This commandment is violated by *equals*, when they envy the gifts of one another; when they grieve at the advancement or prosperity of one another; when they usurp pre-eminence over one another; when they undervalue or despise one another; when they do not prefer one another in love; or when they do not live as brethren in love.

Besides the sins of superiors, inferiors, and equals, above enumerated, we may notice more particularly the sins which are committed by mankind in the various relations in which they stand to one another; as husbands and wives, parents and children, masters and servants, ministers and people, and magistrates and subjects.

Obs. 243.—*The Fifth Commandment forbiddeth those sins by which it is violated in the relation of husbands and wives.*

1. It is violated by both *husband* and *wife*, when they do not always act towards one another under impressions of the nearness of the relation; when they speak disdainfully to one another; when they appear so morose, that they will scarcely exchange words; when they take offence at each other's conduct, although in a mere trifle; when they do not seek to please one another; when they do not submit to one another's judgment; when they refuse to hearken to one another, as helpers of spiritual joy; when they grieve each other by word or deed; when their affections are in any respect alienated from one another; or when they give one another cause to suspect any unfaithfulness in the marriage covenant.

2. It is violated by the *husband*, when he indulges in idleness, and does not provide for his household, but spends in rioting and drunkenness what should be laid out for the comfort of his wife and family; when he keeps from his wife more than is meet; when he ceases to be her guardian; when he lords it over her, not considering that she is his own flesh; or when he stretches out his hand against her, whom he ought to love as himself.

3. It is violated by the *wife*, when she has no respect for her husband; when she is not careful to lay out frugally what he provides; or when she usurps the place of her husband, not re-

membering the nature of that superiority which is given him ovei her.

Obs. 244.—*The Fifth Commandment forbiddeth those sins by which it is violated in the relation of parents and children.*

1. It is violated by *parents*, when they are careless about their children in their earlier years; when they do not pray much for them and with them; when they are careless about their education; when they have no anxiety to train them up in the fear of the Lord; when they encourage them in idleness; when they do not teach them to pray to God; when they do not deter them from sin, or when they correct them for transgressing against themselves, while sin against God is overlooked; when lying, swearing, cheating, and profanation of the Lord's day, &c., are not checked, nor the evil of such sins pointed out to them; when they do not correct them in due time, and when necessary; or when they prefer one child to another, as if not equally related to them.

2. It is violated by *children*, when they lose their love and affection for their parents; when they do not fear and reverence them; when they are disobedient to them in their just and lawful commands; when they do not submit to their counsel and direction, and reproofs and admonitions; when they cease to requite their kindness towards them; when they give them cause of sorrow; or when they do not pray for them, but curse them, although only in their hearts. Wicked and disobedient children are in that black catalogue of sinners who are excluded from the kingdom of heaven. See Rom. i. 29, &c.

Obs. 245.—*The Fifth Commandment forbiddeth those sins by which it is violated in the relation of masters and servants.*

1. It is violated by *masters*, when they refuse their servants proper maintenance and wages; when they deprive them of any part of their due upon any pretence; when they treat them unmercifully; when they believe a bad report against them without reason; when they exercise no care over them; when they do not seek their spiritual welfare, provided they get their own work done by them; when they deprive them of necessary rest; when they prevent them from attending public ordinances; when they do not allow them sufficient time to attend to their eternal concerns; when they set a bad example before them; or when they do not correct them when they sin against God.

2. It is violated by *servants*, when they show no respect for their masters; when they do not study to maintain the honour of the family; when they are disobedient; when they are slothful, or negligent, or idle, and not diligent in business; or when they show no desire to follow the way of peace and holiness, without which they cannot see the Lord in mercy.

Obs. 246.—*The Fifth Commandment forbiddeth those sins by which it is violated in the relation of ministers and people.*

1. It is violated by *ministers*, when they enter among a people contrary to their will; when they are careless about the knowledge of their people's state; when they are careless about their eternal welfare; when they do not dispense ordinances among them in due order; when they are slothful in their work; when they do not frequently pray for their people; when they do not set an example of faith and holiness before them; when they do not declare the whole counsel of God, respecting the only way of a sinner's acceptance; when they preach smooth things, and not the great things of God's law; when they study to please men more than God; or when they do not study to show themselves approved in all things, as those who must give an account.

2. It is violated by the *people*, when they do not reverence their ministers; when they do not esteem them very highly for their work's sake; when they speak evil of them; when they do not pray for them; when they do not wait on the ordinances of Christ when dispensed by them; when they despise their counsel, and direction, and reproofs; when they are not careful to strengthen their hands in their great work; when they slander them unjustly; when they judge rashly concerning them; or when they do not allow them a sufficiency of the world's good things.

Obs. 247.—*The Fifth Commandment forbiddeth those sins by which it is violated in the relation of magistrates and subjects.*

1. It is violated by *magistrates*, when they establish unjust or unequal laws; when they are partial in the administration of justice, or take bribes; when they oppress the poor; when they do not study to promote the interests of true religion by precept and example; when they do not protect the rights and privileges of their subjects; when they do not endeavour to restrain vice and immorality; when they do not punish evil-doers; in a word, when they do not act according to the spirit of their important office.

2. It is violated by *subjects*, when they do not respect magistrates as the ordinance of God; when they judge uncharitably respecting their conduct; when they disobey their just laws; when they refuse the payment of just taxes and tribute; when they do not pray for them; when they are not careful to be an honour to them; when they do not protect them from danger; or when they rebel against them.

INFERENCES.

From this subject we learn,—1. That we ought to consider whether we answer the design of God in the various relations in which we are placed. 2. That all have come short of the glory of God in these relations. 3. That relative religion is a very important part of that holiness without which no man shall see the Lord; and therefore it is necessary to consider whether our obedience to God, and our love to man in our respective relations, arise from that faith which is the work and the gift of God.

Reason Annexed.

Q. 66.—What is the Reason annexed to the Fifth Commandment?

The reason annexed to the Fifth Commandment, is a promise of long life and prosperity (as far as it shall serve for God's glory and their own good) to all such as keep this commandment.

ANALYSIS AND PROOFS.

We are here taught,—
1. That long life is promised to those who honour their parents Eph. vi. 2, 3.—" Honour thy father and mother, that thou mayest live long on the earth."
2. That temporal prosperity is promised to those who honour their parents. Eph. vi. 2, 3.—" Honour thy father and mother, that it may be well with thee."
3. That long life and temporal prosperity are always regulated by a regard to the glory of God. John xi. 4.—" This sickness is not unto death, but for the glory of God."
4. That temporal prosperity is always limited to what is best for the people of God. Prov. xxx. 8.—" Give me neither poverty nor riches; feed me with food convenient for me."

EXPLANATION.

Obs. 248.—*To all those who keep the Fifth Commandment God hath promised long life and prosperity on earth.*

In Eph. vi. 2, this commandment is called *the first commandment with promise*, not because there is not a promise annexed to the other commandments of the law (for, " in keeping of God's commandments there is great reward"), but because there is a peculiar promise made to those who observe this commandment. The promise made in the Second Commandment extends in general to all those who love God and keep his commandments; but the promise here annexed extends only to those who observe this commandment in particular.

The blessing promised in the Fifth Commandment is *long life*, expressed in these words:—" That thy days may be long upon the land which the Lord thy God giveth thee;" together with temporal *prosperity*, or the blessings and comforts of life; without which, long life would be only a burden. See Rev. ix. 6. We may here remark that long life is only a real blessing when men grow in grace as they grow in days and in years; when they retain the use of their reason, together with some degree of bodily strength; and when they continue to be useful to those around them. See Ps. xcii. 13, 14; Deut. xxxiv. 7; Josh. xxiv. 25, 29.

The *place* where the life promised in this commandment is to be enjoyed, refers to the *Gentiles* as well as to the *Jews*. As it respects the Jews, it is called "the land which the Lord gave them,"—that is, the earthly Canaan; but as it respects the Gentiles, it is any place of the earth where their lot may be cast; and hence it is said in Eph. vi. 2, 3, "Honour thy father and thy mother, that it may be well with thee, and that thou mayest live long on the earth."

It may be here remarked, that this commandment cannot be kept perfectly, any more than the other commandments of the law; and that obedience to it does by no means entitle to the reward promised, as a reward of *debt*. The reward here promised is as much of *grace*, as is the reward of eternal life promised by God. We ought to view God's own excellencies as the chief motive to obedience; and also to meditate on what he is in himself; and this will lead us to love *him* for what he is in himself, as well as for what he is to us, and for what he hath promised us.

Obs. 249.—*The promise of long life with prosperity, in the Fifth Commandment, is not absolute, but limited,—that is, long life with prosperity is promised, as far as it shall serve for God's glory and his people's good*

This is a very comfortable limitation; and no believer will desire long life and prosperity, or any temporal blessing, but as it is for *the glory of God and his own good*. And hence, although we frequently see some who conscientiously perform relative duties, live but a short and an afflicted life; yet there is no unrighteousness in this part of the Divine procedure; for God may see defects in the obedience of his own children, with respect to relative duties, which others may not; or he may take them away from the evil to come, and bestow upon them a blessed and eternal life in heaven: for it must always be remembered, that the promise of long life and prosperity is restricted in a way to promote the glory of God, and the best interests of his people.—Isa. lvii. 1, 2.

And we may here remark, on the other hand, that, although many, who neglect the duties of this commandment, live long and enjoy much worldly prosperity, and consequently appear on a level with those who conscientiously observe relative duties; yet there is a real difference in the way in which the two characters referred to enjoy long life and prosperity. The observers of this commandment have a *promise* of long life and prosperity; whereas those who neglect the duties of it have no promise of these things at all. To the former, long life comes in virtue of a promise, which is infallible,—so far as it shall serve for God's glory, and their good; but to the latter it does not come in virtue of any promise at all, for such have no interest in the promise; on the contrary, they are under the curse of God; for it is written, " Cursed is every one that continueth not in all things which are written in the book of the law to do them."—Gal. iii. 10. See Ps. lxxii.

INFERENCES.

From this subject we learn,—1. The necessity of relative religion. 2. That, if the life of those who observe this commandment be short and afflicted here, it will be long and blessed hereafter. 3. The misery of all those who pay no regard to the duties required in this commandment: they are under the curse of God in this life, and they will be miserable through eternity.

DIV. 2.—THE SIXTH COMMANDMENT.

Q. 67.—Which is the Sixth Commandment?

The Sixth Commandment is, " Thou shalt not kill."
Exod. xx. 13; Deut. v. 17.

Duties Required.

Q. 68.—What is required in the Sixth Commandment?

The Sixth Commandment requireth all lawful endeavours to preserve our own life, and the life of others.

ANALYSIS AND PROOFS.

We are here taught,—
1. That we must use all lawful endeavours to preserve our own lives. Eph. v. 29.—" No man ever yet hated his own flesh; but nourisheth and cherisheth it." See also 1 Tim. v. 23.
2. That we are to use no unlawful endeavours for the preservation of our own lives. Matt. xvi. 25.—" Whosoever will save his life, shall lose it."
3. That we must use all lawful endeavours to preserve the lives of others. Prov. xxiv. 11, 12.—" If thou forbear to deliver them that are drawn unto death, and those that are ready to be slain; if thou sayest, Behold, we knew it not; doth not he that pondereth the heart consider it?" See also Job xxix. 13.
4. That we are to use no unlawful endeavours to preserve the lives of others. Numb. xxxv. 31.—" Ye shall take no satisfaction for the life of a murderer."

EXPLANATION.

Obs. 250.--*The Sixth Commandment requireth us to use all*

lawful endeavours to preserve our own natural life, and to promote the life of our souls.

1. We are required to promote the life of our souls, or our *spiritual* and *eternal life*, by the following means:—

(1.) By carefully studying the Scriptures, which contain the words of eternal life; and by diligently improving the ordinances of the gospel, which are the means of promoting this life.—John v. 39, and xvii. 3; 1 Pet. i. 23, and ii. 1, 2.

(2.) By receiving Jesus Christ into the soul by faith, as the resurrection and the life.—John vi. 27, and xi. 25.

(3.) By avoiding all manner of sin, and every appearance of evil and temptation to it.—Prov. viii. 36, xi. 19, and iv. 23.

2. We are required to preserve our own *natural life*, by the following means:—

(1.) By instating it in a new-covenant relation to God. See Ps. xvi. 1, and xvii. 8; 1 Sam. xxv. 29.

(2.) By just and necessary defence of it from such as seek to destroy it. See 2 Cor. xi. 32, 33; Acts xxiii. 12, &c.

(3.) By furnishing our body with proper food, medicine, raiment, labour, rest, and recreation.—Eph. v. 29.

(4.) By avoiding gluttony, and drunkenness, and lasciviousness, which tend gradually to ruin the body.—Luke xxi. 34; Prov. v., vii., vi. 26, &c., xxiii. 26, &c., and ix. 18.

(5.) By keeping our inward passions in a proper temper of meekness, peaceableness, patience, gentleness, kindness, and humility.—Prov. xv. 13, 15, xvii. 20, 22, and xviii. 14.

Obs. 251.—*The Sixth Commandment requireth us to use all lawful endeavours to preserve the natural life of others, and to promote the life of their souls.*

1. We are required to promote the *spiritual* and *eternal life* of others, by the following means:—

(1.) By setting before them such an example of gospel holiness, as may gain them to Christ.—Matt. v. 16; Zech. viii. 23; 1 Pet. iii. 1, 2.

(2.) By diligent instruction, and excitement to faith and holiness, according to our station, accompanied with fervent prayer for them.—1 Thess. v. 14; 2 Tim. iv. 2; Gen. xliii. 29.

(3.) By earnest desire to prevent them from sinning, or from being tempted to sin.—Jude 23.

2. We are required to preserve the *natural life* of others, by the following means:—

(1.) By endeavouring to protect them from every unlawful attempt to take away their life.—Prov. xxiv. 11, 12; Ps. lxxxii. 3, 4; 1 Sam. xiv. 45.

(2.) By giving them the necessaries of life, as equity or charity requires.—1 Kings xviii. 4; Prov. iii. 27. &c., and xix. 17; James ii. 15, 16; 1 John iii. 17.

(3.) By manifesting to them those Christian graces which are so much calculated to excite to the preservation of life,—viz., love, compassion, meekness, gentleness, and kindness.—Prov. x. 12; Luke x. 33, &c.; Prov. xiv. 29; Col. iii. 13; 1 Pet. iii. 4; Rom. xii. 10.

We may here remark, that there are several *motives* which should influence us to save life. 1. By preserving life, we honour God; and when we part with any of our substance for the relief of the wants of the poor and needy, we lend to him; and we may well trust him for future payment.—Prov. xix. 17. 2. Our neighbour has a claim upon us, when he is in danger or in need; he has a right to our aid—to our every attempt to preserve his life, and his comforts, &c., that he may not suffer through our neglect of the lawful means which are put in our power. 3. If we are wanting in this duty to our neighbour, we condemn ourselves, and virtually say, that we deserve not that our neighbour should use any lawful means for our preservation.

INFERENCES.

From this subject we learn,—1. That we are not to do evil for the greatest good. 2. That the soul is infinitely valuable, and that the promotion of its life is as necessary as the preservation of the life of the body. 3. That health is a precious blessing. 4. That we are only to use the means of Divine appointment, or lawful means, for the preservation of life.

Sins Forbidden.

Q. 69.—What is forbidden in the Sixth Commandment?

The Sixth Commandment forbiddeth the taking away of our own life, or the life of our neighbour unjustly, or whatsoever tendeth thereunto.

ANALYSIS AND PROOFS.

We are here taught,—

1. That we are forbidden to destroy our own lives. Acts xvi. 28.—" Paul cried with a loud voice, saying, Do thyself no harm."

2. That we are to avoid every thing which would tend to take away our own lives. Job xiv. 14.—" All the days of my appointed time will I wait till my change come."

3. That we are forbidden to take away the life of another person unjustly. Gen. ix. 6.—" Whoso sheddeth man's blood, by man shall his blood be shed." See also Lev. xxiv. 17.

4. That we are to avoid every thing which would tend to take away the life of another. Deut. xxiv. 6.—" No man shall take the nether or the upper millstone to pledge; for he taketh a man's life to pledge."

EXPLANATION.

Obs. 252.—*The Sixth Commanament forbidaeth the taking away of our own life, or whatever tendeth to this end.*

1. We are forbidden to murder our own *souls*,—which is done, (1.) By neglecting and despising the means of salvation.—Prov. viii. 34, &c. (2.) By quenching or opposing the strivings of God's Spirit.—Prov. xxix. 1; Heb. x. 26, &c.; 2 Pet. ii. 20, &c. (3.) By continued unbelief, and impenitence, and progress in sin.—Ezek. xviii. 30, 31; Rom. ii. 4, 5.

2. We are forbidden to take away our *natural life*,—which is done by laying violent hands upon ourselves.—1 John iii. 15. They who have been guilty of this awful crime were the worst of characters,—such as Saul, Ahithophel, and Judas.—1 Sam. xxxi. 4, 5; 2 Sam. xvii. 23; Matt. xxvii. 4, 5.

3. Whatever *tends* to destroy our natural life, is expressly forbidden according to the spirit of this commandment. Under this may be comprehended the following things :—(1.) Every indulgence of thoughts or designs against our life.—Jonah iv. 3; Job vii. 15. (2.) Indulgence of envy and rage, which tends to the killing of the body.—Job v. 2; Prov. xiv. 30. (3.) Impatience and discontent under trouble.—Ps. xxxviii. 1, 8. (4.) Immoderate worldly sorrow.—Prov. xvii. 22. (5.) Anxious care about worldly things.—Matt. vi. 31, 34; Ps. iv. 6. (6.) Neglect of our body, with respect to food, raiment, medicine, rest and recreations, through superstition, carelessness, covetousness, churlishness, outrageous passion, or temptations of Satan.—Col. ii. 23; Eccl. vi. 2, and x. 18; 1 Kings xxi. 4. (7.) Intemperance, gluttony, and drunkenness.—Luke xxi. 34; Phil. iii. 19; Prov. xxiii. 21, 29, and xx. 1; Luke xvii. 27; Rom. xiii. 13; 1 Cor. vi. 9; 1 Pet. ii. 11. (8.) Immoderate labour.—Eccl. ii. 22, &c. (9.) Exposing ourselves to dangers unnecessarily.—Matt. iv. 5–7; 2 Sam. xxiii. 16, 17.

Obs. 253.—*The Sixth Commandment forbiddeth the taking away of the life of another unjustly, or whatever tendeth to this end.*

1. We are forbidden to murder the *soul* of another person,—which is done, (1.) By setting before him a sinful or an imprudent example.—Matt. xviii. 6, 7. (2.) By neglecting to prevent him from sinning, or by not endeavouring to reform him from it.—Ezek. iii. 18; 1 John iii. 15. (3.) By co-operating with him in sin,—which is done when we command him to sin,—1 Kings xii. 28; when we advise him to sin,—2 Sam. xiii. 5; Hab. ii. 15; when we provoke him to sin,—1 Kings xxi. 25; Job ii. 9; when we tempt him to sin,—Prov. vii. 10, &c.; when we teach him to commit sin; when we assist him to commit sin, —Acts viii. 1; or when we delight in and approve of his sin.—

dom. i. 32; Ps. xlix. 32; Prov. xiv. 9. (4.) By hardening our heart against him on account of his sin, and not lamenting it and his danger by it.—Ezek. ix. 4; Lam. i. 8; Ps. cxix. 136.

2. We are directly forbidden by this commandment to *take away the life of another unjustly*,—which is done, (1.) When life is taken away without law, or under pretence of law. See two remarkable instances of this in 2 Sam. xi. 15; 1 Kings xxi. (2.) When an unjust war is undertaken and prosecuted, in which many are slain.—Hab. ii. 12. (3.) When a private duel or single combat is undertaken; which arises from pride, passion, and an insatiable desire to revenge an injury or wrong received or supposed.—Matt. v. 44; Prov. xvi. 32.

3. Whatever *tends* to take away the life of another unjustly, is forbidden by this commandment. Under this may be comprehended the following things:—(1.) Sinful anger and wrath, which, on account of their direful effects, are so frequently forbidden.—Matt. v. 22; Eph. iv. 26, 27. (2.) Envy or grieving at the prosperity of another. Prov. xiv. 30; Job v. 2. (3.) Hatred and malice against him.—1 John iii. 15. (4.) Revengeful thoughts, desires, and joys.—Matt. vi. 15; Prov. xxiv. 17, &c. (5.) Indifference to his distress.—Prov. xii. 10; Obad. 10, &c.; Amos vi. 6. (6.) Quarrelling, bitter railing, reproachful or disdainful scoffing or deriding, and angry cursing.—James iii. 5, &c.; Prov. xviii. 21, and xxiii. 29. (7.) False accusation.— Luke xxiii. 2; Acts xxiv. 5. (8.) Fierce, sullen, or enraged looks; which denote inclination to mischief or pleasure in it.— Gen. iv. 5; Obad. 12; Acts vii. 54. (9.) Withholding from another the means by which his life may be supported.—Luke x. 31, &c.; James ii. 15, &c.; Job xxxi. 16, &c.; Matt. xxiv. 41, &c. (10.) Injuring his body, or his trade, labour, or property, by which life and health are maintained.—Exod. xxi. 18, 22; Ezek. xxii. 7; Isa. iii. 14, 15; Mic. iii. 3; Isa. v. 8; Matt. xxiv. 9, 10.

We may here remark, that the life of another may be *justly* taken away in the following cases:—1. When he forfeits it to the laws of his country, or in the case of public justice.—Gen. ix. 6; Lev. xxiv. 17; Numb. xxxv. 31, &c. 2. In the case of necessary self-defence,—that is, when there is no way of escaping from the aggressor, but we must either lose our own life, or deprive him of his.—Exod. xxii. 2, 3. 3. In the case of lawful war,—that is, when it is undertaken in defence of civil liberty, or to ward off unprovoked invasion of foreign enemies, after every other means taken to prevent bloodshed have proved vain.

INFERENCES.

From this subject we learn,—1. The necessity of cherishing convictions, and of faith and repentance. 2. To beware of what tends to deprive us of life. 3. The necessity of letting our ligh* shine before men. 4. The danger to which we expose ourselves by sinning before our neighbour; or by allowing sin in him; or by taking part with him in any respect; or by not lamenting his sin. 5. The necessity of having respect to the spirit of the law and gospel, both in our words and actions. 6. That we are guilty of our own blood, if we neglect Christ and his salvation.

DIV. 3.—THE SEVENTH COMMANDMENT.

Q. 70.—Which is the Seventh Commandment?

The Seventh Commandment is, "Thou shalt not commit adultery."

Exod. xx. 14; Deut. v. 18.

Duties Required.

Q. 71.—What is required in the Seventh Commandment?

The Seventh Commandment requireth the preservation of our own and our neighbour's chastity, in heart speech, and behaviour.

ANALYSIS AND PROOFS.

We are here taught,—

1. That we are required to preserve our own chastity. 1 Thess. iv. 4.—"That every one of you should know how to possess his vessel in sanctification and honour."

2. That we are required to avoid all occasions of temptation. Prov. v. 8.—"Remove thy way far from her, and come not nigh the door of her house."

3. That we are required to be chaste in our thoughts. 2 Tim. ii. 22.—"Flee also youthful lusts."

4. That we are required to be chaste in our words. Eph. iv. 29.—"Let no corrupt communication proceed out of your mouth." See also Eph. v. 4.

5. That we are required to be chaste in our actions. 1 Pet. iii. 2.—"While they behold your chaste conversation coupled with fear."

6. That we are required to preserve our neighbour's chastity as well as our own. Eph. v. 11.—"Have no fellowship with the unfruitful works of darkness, but rather reprove them."

EXPLANATION.

Obs. 254.—*The Seventh Commandment requireth the preservation of our own chastity, in heart, speech, and behaviour.*

For preserving our own chastity, the following things are necessary:—

1. An earnest desire to have our whole man instated in a new covenant relation to Christ, and to God in him, and to have his Spirit dwelling in us.

2. Daily and earnest application of the Word of God, of the blood of Christ, and of the gracious influences of the Spirit, for mortifying our inward lusts, and filling our hearts with true holiness in opposition to them. See John xv. 3, and xvii. 17; 1 Pet. i. 23; Heb. ix. 14; Rom. viii. 13.

3. An habitual and earnest recommendation of ourselves to the preservation of God.—Ps. xvi. 1, xvii. 8, and xix. 11, 12.

4. A lively exercise of our implanted graces.—2 Pet. i. 5; 2 Cor. vii. 1; Phil. iii. 12.

5. Watchfulness over the heart, the eyes, and the ears.—Prov. v. 23; Job xxxi. 1; Prov. xix. 27, and vii. 21, &c.

6. Temperance in eating and drinking.—Rom. xiii. 13.

7. A careful avoiding of light and unchaste company.—Prov. ix. 6, and v. 8, 9; Ps. i. 1; Eph. v. 11, 12; Prov. iv. 14, &c.

8. Diligence in lawful business.—Ezek. xvi. 49; 2 Sam. xi. 2.

9. An early and earnest resistance of temptations to unchastity or impurity, or occasions thereof.—Rom. vii. 5; Gen. xxxix.; 1 Cor. vi. 18.

10. Marrying in the Lord, when necessary; and mutual love between married persons.—1 Cor. vii. 2; Heb. xiii. 4.

Obs. 255.—*The Seventh Commandment requireth the preservation of the chastity of others as well as our own.*

We are to preserve the chastity of others by the following means:—

1. By taking care to do nothing which tends to ensnare or to defile them.—Gen. xxxviii. 14, 15, 26; Eph. iv. 29.

2. By doing every thing that we can by example, instruction, warning, reproof, and prayer for them, to preserve and promote their chastity. See Prov. ii., v., vii., and ix.; where much is said upon this subject, and according to which we ought to act.

INFERENCES.

From this subject we learn,—1. That the law of God reaches the heart as well as the life. 2. The necessity of prayer for the sanctifying influences of the Holy Spirit, seeing he will not dwell in the unclean.

Sins Forbidden.

Q. 72.—*What is forbidden in the Seventh Commandment?*

The Seventh Commandment forbiddeth all unchaste thoughts, words, and actions.

ANALYSIS AND PROOFS.

We are here taught,—
1. That all unchaste thoughts are forbidden. Matt. v. 28. "Whosoever looketh on a woman to lust after her, hath committed adultery with her already in his heart."
2. That all unchaste conversation is forbidden. Eph. iv. 29. —" Let no corrupt communication proceed out of your mouth." See also Eph. v. 4.
3. That all unchaste actions are forbidden. Eph. v. 3.—" Fornication and uncleanness, let it not once be named among you." See also Rom. xiii. 13.

EXPLANATION.

Obs. 256.—*The Seventh Commandment forbiddeth all unchaste thoughts, words, and actions.*

1. It forbids *all unchaste or unclean thoughts.*—Matt. v. 18. These are dangerous; and, if lodged in the heart with pleasure, may, like a hidden spark, break forth into a vehement flame. They are the nearest approach to open wickedness, and require only a proper opportunity.
2. It forbids *all unchaste conversation.* By this, as well as by actions, is the law of God violated. See Matt. xii. 37. Much is spoken contrary to the spirit of this commandment, although it does not break forth into action.
3. It forbids *all unchaste actions.* To these may be referred all unnatural pollutions, which can scarcely be named,—Rom. i. 24, &c.; Lev. xviii. 6, 23; polygamy, or having more wives or husbands than one at the same time,—Gen. ii. 22, &c.; adultery, when one or both of the parties are married; fornication, which is the sin of unmarried persons; concubinage,—1 Kings xi. 1, &c.; and immoderate and unseasonable familiarity between married persons,—1 Thess. iv. 3, 4; Deut. xxii. 25.

Obs. 257.—*The Seventh Commandment forbiddeth whatever tendeth to unchastity.*

Under this may be comprehended the following things:—1. Speaking, hearing, reading, or writing unchaste expressions.—Eph. iv. 29. 2. All unchaste looks. 3. Receiving temptations into the heart, or enticing others.—2 Pet. ii. 14; Isa. iii. 16, &c. 4. Light and immodest behaviour, together with wanton embraces and dalliances.—Prov. vii. 13. 5. All stage plays and lewd pictures.—Ezek. xxiii. 14, &c. 6. All immodest apparel. —Prov. vii. 10; Isa. iii. 7. The company of vain persons.— Prov. v. 8, &c. 8. All idleness.—Ezek. xvi. 49. 9. Intemperance in eating and drinking.—Prov. xxiii. 30; Jer. v. 8. 10 Undue delay of marriage.—1 Cor. vii. 7, &c. 11. Unjust divorce.—Matt. v. 32. 12. Wilful desertion.—1 Cor. vii. 12, &c. 13. Unkindness between married persons.—1 Cor. vii. 5. 14.

Vows of perpetual celibacy, and prohibitions of marriage.—Matt. xix. 10, 11. 15. Dispensing with unlawful marriages.—Mark vi. 18. 16. The allowing of places of uncleanness to exist.—Deut. xxiii. 17.

Obs. 258.—*The sins forbidden by the Seventh Commandment should be avoided, for the following reasons:*—

1. Because pollution or uncleanness exceedingly dishonours God. See Gen. xxxix. 9; Ps. li. 4; Job xxxi. 11; 1 Cor. iii. 17.

2. Because falls into this sin are not unfrequently the punishment of some other sin.—Prov. xxii. 14; Rom. i. 26, &c.; Hos. iv. 14; Amos vii. 17.

3. Because few persons truly repent of this sin; and these with great difficulty. Hos. iv. 11; Prov. ii. 19.—" None that go unto her return again, neither take they hold of the paths of life,"—that is, not many do so in truth. And yet we read of some among the Corinthians to whom repentance was given,—1 Cor. vi. 9-11; but this, as it were, requires a greater than ordinary share of Divine grace. See Prov. xxiii. 27, 28; Eccl. vii. 26; Acts xxiv. 25.

4. Because this sin dishonours and frequently murders the body.—Prov. v. 11, 12, and vii. 22; 1 Cor. vi. 18.

5. Because it frequently leaves a stain upon the character.—Prov. vi. 33. David's sin, although pardoned, is handed down as a blot upon his character; and it shall continue to be so till the latest posterity.

6. Because it wrathfully consumes the outward estate.—Prov. v. 10, and vi. 26; Job xxxi. 12.

7. Because in a fearful manner it secures the eternal ruin of those who are guilty of it. See Prov. vi. 32, vii. 26, 27, and ix. 18; Heb. xiii. 4; 1 Cor. vi. 9, 10; Gal. v. 19, &c.; Rev. xxi. 8, and xxii. 15; Col. iii. 5, 6; Eph. v. 5, 6. These passages clearly show the danger to which this sin exposes the soul for ever.

INFERENCES.

From this subject we learn,—1. The necessity of watchfulness. 2. The necessity of reflecting upon the omniscience of God,—as Joseph did. 3. The necessity of walking after the Spirit, that we may not fulfil the lusts of the flesh. 4. The necessity of shunning all occasions of unchastity by the senses. 5. The necessity of fervent prayer to be preserved from this sin, and from all temptations to it.

DIV. 4.—THE EIGHTH COMMANDMENT.

Q. 73.—Which is the Eighth Commandment?

The Eighth Commandment is, "Thou shalt not steal."

Exod. xx. 15; Deut. v. 19.

Duties Required.

Q. 74.—What is required in the Eighth Commandment?

The Eighth Commandment requireth the lawful procuring and furthering of the wealth and outward estate of ourselves and others.

ANALYSIS AND PROOFS.

We are here taught,—

1. That we are to endeavour by lawful means to procure wealth. Rom. xiii. 17.—" Provide things honest in the sight of all men." See also Prov. vi. 6.

2. That we are to endeavour by lawful means to promote and further our outward estate. Prov. xxvii. 23.—" Be thou diligent to know the state of thy flocks, and look well to thy herds."

3. That we are to endeavour by lawful means to assist others in procuring wealth. Gal. vi. 10.—" As we have therefore opportunity, let us do good unto all men."

4. That we are to endeavour by lawful means to further and promote the outward estate of others. Phil. ii. 4.—" Look not every man on his own things, but every man also on the things of others."

EXPLANATION.

Obs. 259.—*The Eighth Commandment requireth the lawful procuring and furthering of our own wealth and outward estate.*

This may be done in the following ways:—

1. By claiming a new covenant right to all things, through a spiritual union to Christ, who is the heir of all things.—Matt. vi. 33; 1 Cor. iii. 21, &c. A little enjoyed by a believer, in virtue of union with Christ and of the promise of the covenant, is incomparably superior to all that the worldling can enjoy without the promise.

2. By depending on God and praying to him, as our new covenant Father, to bestow upon us, and keep for us, such things as are necessary and convenient.—Deut. viii. 18; Ps. cxxvii. 1, and cxxviii. 1, 2; Prov. xxx. 8; Matt. vi. 11.

3. By prudent foresight and care to have every thing answerable to our station and ability.—1 Tim. v. 8. Keeping at a dis-

tance from anxious care and sinful indifference, every lawful mean ought to be used, otherwise we are guilty of presumption; for the means and the end are intimately connected in the ways of God; and in his ways we are to walk.

4. By due exercise of our ability or stock in some lawful calling, which is calculated to glorify God, and to profit ourselves and others.—Gen. iv. 2; Eph. iv. 28; Prov. x. 4, xiii. 4, and xiv. 8; Ps. cxii. 5; Isa. xxviii. 26; 2 Thess. iii. 10.

5. By cheerfully allowing ourselves a moderate enjoyment of the fruits of our lawful industry.—Eccl. ii. 24, iii. 12, 13, and ix. 9; Ps. cxxviii. 2.

6. By frugal management of what we have, to the best advantage, not from a churlish disposition, but as stewards of God's property; taking care to waste nothing upon trifles, and to lose nothing useful.—John vi. 12; Prov. xxi. 20, compared with chap. xi. 24.

7. By carefully avoiding unnecessary law-suits, and every other thing which tends to embarrass our outward estate, or shame our profession.—Prov. xi. 5; Matt. v. 40; 1 Cor. vi. 1-8.

8. By never idolizing, but by moderating our affections towards all earthly enjoyments.—1 Tim. vi. 17.

9. By carefully avoiding all haste to be rich, and all mingling of unjust gain with our lawful property, as a curse upon it.—Prov. xxviii. 22; 1 Tim. vi. 9; James v. 3, &c.

10. By liberal and prudently directed donations to the poor, and to pious purposes.—Prov. iii. 9, 10, and xix. 17; Matt. xxv. 40.

Obs. 260.—*The Eighth Commandment requireth the lawful procuring and furthering of the wealth and outward estate of others.*

This may be done in the following ways:—

1. By praying that both they and it may be secured in a new covenant relation to God; for while they are out of Christ, they have only a common, and not a covenant right, to any blessing whatever.—Phil. ii. 4.

2. By carefully endeavouring to prevent their loss and damage. See Exod. xxiii. 4, 5; and Deut. xxii. 1, &c.; where we have some instances of the way in which we may be instrumental in preventing the loss and damage of others.

3. By universal honesty in dealing with others; rather hurting our own property than theirs.—Matt. vii. 12; Ps. xv.; Zech. vii. 9, 10.

4. By conscientious restitution of every thing which we may have found, or unjustly taken away.—Luke xix. 8; Lev. v. 2, &c.; Deut. xxii. 2, 3; Job xx. 10, 18; Ezek. xviii. 8, and xxxiii. 15; Exod. xxii. 3, 4; Numb. v. 8.

5. By charity and equity in cheerfully but prudently lending

to others for their assistance, even without interest, or hope of payment, if their circumstances require it.—Deut. xxiii. 19, 20; Lev. xxv. 35, &c.; Ps. xv. 5; Matt. v. 42; Luke vi. 35, &c.

6. By charitable donations of that which is truly our own, and with a real desire to help the poor, and to promote the religious service of God.—Luke xi. 41, and xvi. 9; 1 Tim. v. 8; Eph. iv. 28; Eccl. xi. 1; 1 John iii. 17; Gal. vi. 10; Prov. xxxix.; 2 Cor. ix. 7; Matt. vi. 3, 4. What we give must be from an honourable regard to Christ and his poor members, or brethren of mankind. And when donations are thus given, they are most reasonable, as we hold all that we have from God as his stewards,—Luke xvi. 10; 1 Tim. vi. 17, 18; Ps. cxii. 9; Prov. x. 2; they are most honourable, conforming us to the pattern of God in Christ,—Luke vi. 35; 2 Cor. viii. 9; Acts xx. 35; they are most conducive to secure proper necessaries for ourselves and our posterity,—Prov. xi. 24, &c., xix. 17, and xxviii. 27; Eccl. xi. 1, 2; Ps. xxxvii. 25, &c.; they are a most remarkable means of preventing trouble, or of securing comfort under it.—Ps. xli. And they who confer them will be most honourably proclaimed by Christ in the last judgment,—Matt. xxv. 34, &c.; and they will be abundantly but graciously rewarded in heaven to all eternity. —Matt. v. 7, and vi. 4; Luke xvi. 9.

INFERENCES.

From this subject we learn,—1. That God prospers means used; such as prayer, prudence, and foresight, dependence and diligence. 2. That the world is not our portion. 3. The danger of indifference respecting those in need. 4. That love to the poor is an evidence of a state of life.—1 John iii. 14. 5. The danger of withholding from the poor what it is in our power to bestow upon them. See Matt. xxv. 42, &c.

Sins Forbidden.

Q. 75.—What is forbidden in the Eighth Commandment?

The Eighth Commandment forbiddeth whatsoever doth or may unjustly hinder our own or our neighbour's wealth or outward estate.

ANALYSIS AND PROOFS.

We are here taught,—
1. That we are forbidden to neglect lawful means for procuring wealth for ourselves and families. 1 Tim. v. 8.—" If any provide not for his own, and especially for those of his own house, he hath denied the faith, and is worse than an infidel."
2. That we are forbidden to do that which may hinder the increase of our wealth and outward estate. Prov. xxiii. 21.—" The

drunkard and the glutton shall come to poverty, and drowsiness shall clothe a man with rags." See also Prov. xxi. 17.

3. That we are forbidden to neglect the furtherance of the wealth of others, when it is in our power. Deut. xv. 8.—" Thou shalt open thy hand wide unto him, and shalt surely lend him sufficient for his need, in that which he wanteth."

4. That we are forbidden to do any thing which may hinder the furtherance of the wealth of others. Zech. viii. 17.—" Let none of you imagine evil in your hearts against his neighbour." See also Eph. iv. 28.

EXPLANATION.

Obs. 261.—*The Eighth Commandment forbiddeth whatever doth or may unjustly hinder our own wealth or outward estate.*

We may be guilty of this in the following ways:—

1. By idleness.—2 Thess. iii. 10, &c.; 1 Tim. v. 13; 1 Thess. v. 11, &c.

2. By carelessness and sloth.—Prov. xiii. 4, vi. 10, 11, xxiii. 21, xxiv. 30, &c., and xxviii. 19.

3. By not depending upon God and acknowledging him in all our worldly business.—Deut. viii. 28; Ps. cvii. 38.

4. By prodigal wasting of that which God bestows upon us.—Prov. xxi. 17·; Luke xv. 13, 30.

5. By rash engagements in law-suits and suretyship.—Matt. v. 40; 1 Cor. vi. 1, &c.; Prov. vi. 1, &c., and xxii. 26, &c.

6. By foolishly giving to such as have no need, or to sluggards, or to spendthrifts; and by imprudently lending to rash projectors, or to prodigal wasters, or the like.—Ps. cxxv. 5.

7. By distrustful anxiety in procuring and retaining earthly things.—Matt. vi. 31, &c.; Prov. xxviii. 22; Eccl. iv. 8.

8. By sordid churlishness—wanting a heart to enjoy, in a proper manner or degree, that wealth which we have; or to lay out proper expenses on our affairs.—Eccl. vi. 1, &c.

9. By the exercise of unlawful callings; such as gambling, stage-playing, smuggling, &c., &c.; and grasping at excessive gains, by which the curse of God is brought upon what we have. On these things the blessing of God cannot be sought; because they are calculated to deprive the thoughtless of their substance, by laying temptations in their way. And hence such occupations fall under the name of stealing; and we deprive ourselves of our wealth by encouraging them.—Zech. v. 4; Hag. i. 6.

Obs. 262.—*The Eighth Commandment forbiddeth whatever doth or may unjustly hinder the wealth or outward estate of others.*

Among the ways by which our neighbour's wealth may be unjustly hindered, the following should be remembered:—

1. Besides direct theft, we hinder our neighbour's wealth by

240 EIGHTH COMMANDMENT—SINS FORBIDDEN.

a covetous inclination to have his property, and by idleness.—Heb. xiii. 5; Col. iii. 5; Josh. vii. 21, &c.; Eph. iv. 28; Matt xx. 6.

2. By base gain procured by sordid or unlawful means, and by enabling persons to earn their subsistence by unlawful amusements.—Hab. ii. 15.

3. By simoniacal merchandize of spiritual gifts, pardons censures, church livings, or other sacred things; giving or procuring them for money, or through favour, or the like.—Jo xv. 34.

4. By family frauds, either by husbands or wives, or children or servants.—1 Tim. v. 8; Prov. xxviii. 24, and xxxi. 12; Tit ii. 9, 10.

5. By taking advantage of our neighbour's ignorance or necessity in buying or selling; which is done, (1.) By improper or false commendation of that which we sell, or dispraise of that which we intend to buy.—Prov. xx. 14. (2.) By adulterating goods, or selling one kind and delivering another.—Amos viii. 5, 6. (3.) By using false weights or measures in merchandize.—Amos viii. 5; Mic. vi. 10, 11; Prov. xi. 1; Lev. xix. 35, &c. and xxiv. 14.

6. By bad payment of debts—neither early nor fully enough nor in current money.—Ps. xv. 4; Acts v. 1, &c.; Gen. xxiii. 15

7. By dishonest partnership—taking as much or more of th gain, when we have less of the stock, or less labour in procuring it.—Matt. vii. 12; 1 Thess. iv. 6.

8. By removing our neighbour's landmarks; injuring his corn, grass, goods, or conveniences; decoying his servants or customers from him; screwing ourselves into his business; or such like.—Heb. xiii. 1; Prov. xxii. 28, and xxiii. 10; Mic. ii. 2 and vii. 2, &c.

9. By dishonesty in trust,—particularly to the poor, the fatherless, or widows.—Prov. xxiii. 10, &c.; Luke xvi. 1, &c., and ix. 47.

10. By dishonesty in loans.—Exod. xxii. 14, 25, &c.; Ps. xv. 5; Matt. v. 42. Connected with this, is the contracting of debt in a dishonest manner; which arises either from a want of intention, or a probable appearance of ability, to keep our promise of payment in due time; or when there is no real necessity on our part; or when it is done to the hurt of others,—purchasing things which we might well enough want.—Ps. xxxvii. 21; 1 Thess. iv. 6; Isa. lix. 14.

11. By fraudulent bankruptcy.—Luke xv. 13; Jer. ix. 4, &c.

12. By uncharitable or sinful use of our own property: such is the practice of engrossing corn, and the other most necessary commodities, which cannot be wanted,—Prov. xi. 26; the depopulation of villages by the enclosure of commons, or unjust enclosures.—Isa. v. 8; and Micah ii. 2. Connected with this sin

is that of oppression, or bearing down our neighbour by our superior wealth, or power, or influence, or by vexatious lawsuits, or by retaining pledges, or such like.—Mic. iii. 2,3; Ezek. xxii. 7; Mal. iii. 5; Exod. xxii. 26, &c.; Deut. xxiv. 6; 1 Cor. v. 11, and vi. 10.

13. By partnership with thieves—by tempting and encouraging others to steal,—Ps. xxix. 24; by not checking this abominable practice when we have it in our power, or not punishing it as it deserves; or by resetting stolen goods, or concealing them.

14. By unmercifulness to the poor.—Eph. iv. 28. This is perfidious ingratitude to God,—Matt. xviii. 23, &c.; Luke xvi. 10; it is murder of the poor,—1 John iii. 15; James ii. 16, &c.; and an evidence that we are destitute of the grace of God.—1 John iii. 17. It provokes God to deal unmercifully with us,—James ii. 13, and v. 4; Prov. xxi. 13; imperceptibly wastes our substance,—Prov. xi. 24, &c.; James v. 2, 3; and, if persisted in, it will at last condemn us.—Matt. xxv. 41-46.

15. By a sacrilegious deficiency in that good example, religious instruction, fervent prayer, and other important usefulness, which we owe to our neighbour, for promoting his temporal as well as his eternal good.—Heb. x. 24.

16. By withholding from the support of the gospel, or not giving in a manner answerable to our income. See Matt. iii. 8; Neh. x. 32, and xiii. 10; Hag. i. 4; 1 Cor. ix. This sin is considered by God as levelled at himself; and it is a very great evidence, that they who are guilty of this have never yet received the gospel in the love of it—let man say what he will. They who have really experienced the value of the glad tidings of salvation in their own case, will do what they can to send them to others. See our Lord's command to all his disciples respecting this.—Matt. xxviii. 19, 20; Mark xvi. 15, 16.

INFERENCES.

From this subject we learn,—1. That we ought to use the world, but not abuse it. 2. That we ought to acknowledge God in the procuring of our substance, and in the giving of it away. 3. The evil of the sin of stealing,—it curses, reproaches, brings to an untimely end, and excludes from the kingdom of heaven, if unrepented of.—Zech. v. 3,4; Job xxx. 5; 1 Cor. v. 10. 4. The necessity of contentment with our lot. 5. That we ought to beware of a covetous spirit, and of idleness. 6. That the sins forbidden in this commandment cannot be concealed from an omniscient God. 7. That we ought to be strictly just in all things.—Matt. vii. 12. 8. That there is no religion where in justice dwells. 9. The necessity of watchfulness.

DIV. 5.—THE NINTH COMMANDMENT.

Q. 76.—*Which is the Ninth Commandment?*

The Ninth Commandment is, "Thou shalt not bear false witness against thy neighbour."
Exod. xx. 16; Deut. v. 20.

Duties Required.

Q. 77.—*What is required in the Ninth Commandment?*

The Ninth Commandment requireth the maintaining and promoting of truth between man and man, and of our own and our neighbour's good name, especially in witness bearing.

ANALYSIS AND PROOFS.

We are here taught,—

1. That we must at all times speak and maintain the truth. Zech. viii. 16.—" Speak ye every man the truth to his neighbour."
2. That we must endeavour to promote the truth. Phil. iv. 8.—" Whatsoever things are true—think on these things."
3. That we must endeavour to preserve our own good name. Matt. v. 16.—" Let your light so shine before men, that they may see your good works, and glorify your Father who is in heaven." See also 2 Cor. xi. 16, 18, 23; 1 Pet. iii. 16.
4. That we must endeavour to preserve our neighbour's good name. Tit. iii. 2.—" Speak evil of no man." See also Ps. ci. 5.
5. That we are required in a special manner to speak truth in witness bearing. Prov. xiv. 5.—" A faithful witness will not lie; but a false witness will utter lies."

EXPLANATION.

Obs. 263.—*The Ninth Commandment requireth the maintaining and promoting of truth among men.*

We must maintain and promote the truth in the following ways:—

1. By speaking nothing but the truth, as we think, and as things really are; for it is impossible to speak the truth indeed, if there is not an agreement between the tongue and the heart.—Ps. xv. 2; 2 Thess. ii. 11, &c.
2. By declaring that which is true on every proper occasion.—Zech. viii. 16, 19.
3. By bearing witness, when necessary, in judicature; and freely, plainly, fully, sincerely, and unbiassedly declaring the truth, and nothing but the truth.—Jer. iv. 2; Prov. xix. 5; 1

Sam. xix. 4, &c.; 2 Sam. xiv. 18, &c.; 2 Chron. xix. 9; Josh. vii. 19.

Obs. 264.—*The Ninth Commandment requireth the maintaining and promoting of our own good name.*

We must maintain and promote our own good name in the following ways:—

1. By taking hold of God's covenant of grace, that we may have his new name put upon us, and his honour engaged in support of our character.—Isa. lvi. 5, and lxii. 4, 12.

2. By entertaining only such thoughts as are honourable to truth, and to our character.—Phil. iv. 8.

3. By speaking nothing of ourselves but what is real truth, either in praise or dispraise; and that only when we are duly called to it.—Prov. xxvii. 2, xxv. 14, and xxvi. 16. Connected with this is a prudent concealing of our secret sins and infirmities, which we have no Divine call to confess to men.—Prov. xxv. 9, &c. In connection with this also, we are meekly to defend our character when it is unjustly attacked.—John v., vii., viii., and x.; Acts xxii., xxiv., and xxvi.

4. By avoiding every thing sinful or imprudent in our behaviour, and all appearances of it; and by constantly following every thing good and answerable to our station.—Eccl. x. 1; 1 Thess. v. 22; Phil. iv. 8; 2 Pet. i. 4, &c.

Obs. 265.—*The Ninth Commandment requireth the maintaining and promoting of our neighbour's good name.*

We must maintain and promote the good name of our neighbour in the following ways:—

1. By an earnest desire to have him vested with the honourable character of a friend and a child of God.—James v. 20; Rom. x. 1; 1 Pet. iv. 8.

2. By charitably esteeming him.—Rom. xii. 10; Phil. ii. 3.

3. By kindly covering his infirmities.—James v. 20; 1 Pet. iv. 8.

4. By readily acknowledging his gifts and graces, and good behaviour.—Col. iv. 12; Phil. ii. 19, &c.; 1 Cor. i. 4, &c.

5. By defending his character when it is unjustly attacked.—1 Sam. xxii. 14.

6. By readily receiving a good report concerning him, and by being averse to hear what tends to his dishonour.—1 Cor. xiii. 6, &c.; Ps. xv. 3; 1 Sam. xxii. 14, 15.

7. By earnestly discouraging talebearers, backbiters, and slanderers; and by endeavouring to bring them to due disgrace and punishment.—Ps. ci. 5; Prov. xxv. 23; 2 Cor. xii. 20.

8. By watching over our neighbour, from true love to him; and by proper advice, warning, and reproof.—Lev. xix. 16, &c.; Matt. xviii. 15, &c.; 1 Thess. v. 14; 2 Thess. iii. 14.

INFERENCES.

From this subject we learn,—1. That they who do not love the truth are not yet born again. 2. That the truth is worthy to be told. 3. That all liars and dissemblers are hateful to God. 4. The value of a good name.

Sins Forbidden.

Q. 78.—What is forbidden in the Ninth Commandment?

The Ninth Commandment forbiddeth whatsoever is prejudicial to truth, or injurious to our own or our neighbour's good name.

ANALYSIS AND PROOFS.

We are here taught,—
1. That we are forbidden to do any thing which is prejudicial to truth. Eph. iv. 25.—" Putting away lying, speak every man truth with his neighbour." See also Col. iii. 9; Rom. iii. 13.
2. That we are forbidden to do any thing which is injurious to our own good name. Job xxvii. 6.—" My righteousness I hold fast, and will not let it go; my heart shall not reproach me so long as I live." See also ver. 5.
3. That we are forbidden to do any thing which may be injurious to our neighbour's good name. Exod. xxiii. 1.—" Thou shalt not raise (margin, *receive*) a false report: put not thine hand with the wicked to be an unrighteous witness."

EXPLANATION.

Obs. 266.—*The Ninth Commandment forbiddeth whatever is prejudicial to truth.*

1. In *judicial processes*, this commandment is violated in the following respects:—

(1.) The *pursuer* is guilty of a breach of truth, when he makes an unjust demand upon the defender; or when he lays to his charge things which he knows not, or of which he believes him to be innocent; or when he suborneth false witnesses.—Acts xxiv. 5, and xxv. 7; Luke xix. 8; Acts vi. 13.

(2.) The *defender* is guilty of this sin, when he denies a charge which is just, when called to make confession; or when he makes use of artful evasions, by which the pursuer or complainer is put to unnecessary trouble and expense in obtaining justice.—Prov. xxviii. 13.

(3.) *Witnesses* are guilty of this sin, not only when they bear testimony to a downright falsehood, but also when they deny or keep back any part of the truth, which is the highway to prevent justice from being executed.—Prov. xix. 5, 9, and xxv. 18; Mal. iii. 5; Deut. xix. 15.

(4.) *Advocates* are guilty of this sin, when they undertake to plead or to maintain a bad cause; considering it as a part of their profession to defend what is wrong, as well as what is just and right.—Acts xxiv. 2.

(5.) *Judges* are guilty of this sin, when they pronounce a rash, partial, and unjust sentence; thereby perverting justice, justifying the wicked, and condemning the righteous; which is abominable, —Matt. xxvii. 24, &c.; Mic. vii. 3; Isa. lix. 13, &c.; which last passage is too often verified in the present day.

2. In *extrajudicial cases*, or in common life, this commandment is violated in the following ways:—

(1.) By unfaithfulness,—paying no due regard to promises, rashly making them, or entering into stations and relations which imply them; and want of due concern to remember and fulfil them.—Rom. i. 31; 2 Tim. iii. 3; Jer. ix. 3, &c.; Hos. iv. 1.

(2.) By undue silence,—when iniquity requires either that we should reprove it ourselves, or complain of it to rulers.—Lev. v. 1, and xix. 17; Deut. xiii. 6, &c.; Mark viii. 38; Eph. v. 7; Matt. xviii. 15.

(3.) By speaking the truth unseasonably or maliciously, or perverting it to a wrong meaning.—Prov. xxix. 11; 1 Sam. xxii. 8, &c.; Ps. lii. 2, &c.; Matt. xxvi. 60, &c.

(4.) By equivocation, or using words of a double signification, in a sense different from that in which we expect another will understand them; and by mental reservation, or concealing some words in our own mind, which give our expressions a meaning different from that which they appear to have.—Gen. xx. 2, 12, and xxvi. 6, 7.

(5.) By hypocrisy or dissimulation,—that is, by appearing to be or to do what we neither are nor do.—Matt. xxiii.; Isa. xxix. 13; 2 Tim. iii. 5; Tit. i. 16. Connected with this is forgery of all kinds, counterfeiting of money, forging writs, &c.; and every thing which is opposed to the truth, and which tends to the injury of society.—Ps. cxix. 69.

(6.) By simple falsehood, or uttering that which is really false, although we ourselves believe it to be true.—Zech. viii. 16, 19.

(7.) By rash judging, or affirming and denying without proper certainty.—1 Cor. xiii. 6.

(8.) By gross lying, or uttering what we know to be false with an intention to deceive our neighbour.—Hos. iv. 2; Jer. ix. 3, &c.; Isa. lix. 18; 1 Kings xiii. 18; Gen. iii. 4, &c.; Eph. iv. 25. Of this there are many kinds; such as lying for jest,—Hos. vii. 8; lying for profit,—2 Kings v. 22, &c.; Rom. iii. 8; lying for concealment of guilt,—Gen. xviii. 15; Acts v. 3, &c.; lying for preventing danger,—Gen. xii. 11, xx. 2, and xxvi. 7; Mark xiv. 68, &c.; lying for the purpose of doing mischief,—Prov. vi. 16, &c.; Acts vi. 11, &c., and xxiv. 5; and lying from custom or rashness,—2 Sam. xiii. 30. All these kinds of lying are highly sinful.

Obs. 267.—*The Ninth Commandment forbiddeth whatever is injurious to our own good name.*

Our own reputation may be injured in the following ways:—

1. In our *heart*—by thinking too highly or too meanly of ourselves, reckoning ourselves less indebted to God for his gifts and graces than we really are.—Exod. iv. 10, &c.; Prov. xxv. 14, and xxvi. 12, 16.

2. In our *words*—by unjustly, or at least unseasonably, accusing ourselves of a variety of miscarriages and faults, when we have no due call in providence for so doing,—Prov. xxv. 9, &c.; Job xxvii. 5, 6; or by denying truth, or affirming falsehood in our own favour.—Prov. xxviii. 13; 2 Kings v. 25; Acts v. 8.

3. In our *conduct*—by doing what is sinful in itself, or even imprudent,—1 Sam. ii. 24; or by joining ourselves with infamous company,—Prov. v. 8, 9; or by thrusting ourselves into stations and circumstances in life, in which we cannot conduct ourselves to our own honour, and to the honour of God.—2 Kings viii. 13.

Obs. 268.—*The Ninth Commandment forbiddeth whatever is injurious to the good name of others.*

We may injure our neighbour's reputation in the following ways:—

1. In our *heart*—by evil surmisings,—1 Tim. vi. 4; by uncharitable and rash judging,—Matt. vii. 1, &c.; 1 Cor. xiii. 7; by making ourselves a standard for judging others,—Rom. xiv. 3, 10; by judging their conscience, state, or intentions, as if we were in God's place,—Rom. xiv. 4; by misinterpreting their purposes, words, or actions,—Rom. iii. 8; by secret contempt of them,—2 Sam. vi. 16; Luke xviii. 9, &c.; by envying their just fame,—Matt. xxi. 15; by taking pleasure in their disgrace,—Jer. xlviii. 27; or by fond admiration of them,—Jude 16.

2. In our *speech*—by speaking truth in order to dishonour them, —Luke xv. 2; Mark vi. 3; by unnecessarily divulging their infirmities,—Gen. ix. 22; by aggravating their real faults,—Matt. vii. 3, &c.; by reviving the infamy of former faults of which they had repented, and which had been forgotten,—2 Sam. xvi. 7; by betraying their secrets,—Prov. xvii. 9; 2 Tim. iii. 4; by endeavouring to wound their reputation,—Ezra iv. 12, &c.; Matt. xii. 22, &c.; by raising, spreading, or receiving false reports concerning them,—Exod. xxiii. 1; Neh. vi. 6; Jer. xviii. 18; by falsely slandering them,—Ps. l. 20; by false or malicious accusation of them to rulers,—Acts xxiv. 5; Jer. xxxviii. 4; by backbiting or wounding their character in their absence,—Rom. i. 29; 2 Cor. xii. 20; by tale-bearing between different families,—Lev. xix. 16; 2 Thess. iii. 11; by encouraging tale-bearers, or by not bringing them to due punishment,—Prov. xxix. 12; by scornful derision,—Gal. iv. 29; Heb. iv. 36; by reviling and calling bad

names,—Matt. v. 22; or by passionate railing and brawling,—Ps. lii. 2, and lxiv. 3, &c.; Jude 10.

3. In our *conduct*—by suspicious or contemptuous gestures,—Ps. xxii. 7; Prov. vi. 12, 13; by turning our back upon others without sufficient ground,—Gal. ii. 12; by neglecting to warn them, or prevent them from doing what is sinful or imprudent, and by advice, encouragement, or example, drawing them into it, to the injury of their character,—1 Sam. ii. 13, and iii. 13; Ezek. xxxiii. 6, &c.

Obs. 269.—*The Ninth Commandment forbids whatever tends to injure truth, or the reputation of ourselves or of others.*

Here the following things may be enumerated:—1. Excessive readiness to speak in company, by which we manifest the pride and vanity of our heart, and show ourselves fools.—Eccl. v. 3, and x. 14; Prov. x. 19. 2. Idle talk, which has no tendency to promote any good end, either civil or religious.—Matt. xii. 36; Eph. v. 4. 3. Inordinate jesting.—Eph. v. 4. 4. Flattery, which includes much baseness, falsehood, deceit, and treachery in the giver, and marks much baseness and self-conceit in the receiver. See Ps. xii. 3, xxxvi. 3, and Acts xii. 22, 23, which is one instance of the basest flattery.

INFERENCES.

From this subject we learn,—1. That truth ought to be sacred in every circumstance of life. 2. That God is a God of truth. 3. The danger of lying. 4. The necessity of watching over our tongue. 5. The necessity of wisdom from above, and of much prayer.

DIV. 6.—THE TENTH COMMANDMENT.

Q. 79.—*Which is the Tenth Commandment?*

The Tenth Commandment is, "Thou shalt not covet thy neighbour's house, thou shalt not covet thy neighbour's wife, nor his man-servant, nor his maid-servant, nor his ox, nor his ass, nor any thing that is thy neighbour's."

Exod. xx. 17; Deut. v. 21.

Duties Required.

Q. 80.—*What is required in the Tenth Commandment?*

The Tenth Commandment requireth full contentment with our own condition, with a right and charitable frame of spirit toward our neighbour, and all that is his.

ANALYSIS AND PROOFS.

We are here taught,—
1. That we are required to be contented with our condition in life. Heb. xiii. 5.—" Let your conversation be without covetousness, and be content with such things as ye have."
2. That we are required to cultivate a right and charitable disposition towards the person of our neighbour. Rom. xii. 15. —" Rejoice with them that do rejoice, and weep with them that weep."
3. That we are required to cultivate a right disposition towards the property of our neighbour. Luke xii. 15.—" Take heed, and beware of covetousness." See also 1 Cor. xiii. 4.

EXPLANATION.

Obs. 270.—*The Tenth Commandment requireth full contentment with our condition in life.*

The *full contentment* which this commandment requires with respect to that condition in which Providence hath placed us, includes the following things:—

1. A hearty reconcilement to the will of God, as the only and universal standard for regulating our lot, both in its form and degree.—Ps. xlvii. 4.
2. An absolute resignation and entire submission to the will of God, as wise and holy, and just and good, and gracious in all his providential disposals of us, or of any thing belonging to us.— Matt. xvi. 24; Phil. iv. 11, 12.
3. An inward calmness under his denial of outward comforts, and a satisfaction in our lot, as good—as the best for us.—Hab iii. 17, 18; 2 Sam. xv. 25, 26, and xvi. 10, &c.

Besides those things just mentioned, this commandment also requires a due weanedness of affection from every created enjoyment; because, if we set our heart immoderately on what we at present enjoy, we are guilty of a kind of covetousness. And here we may observe the following things:—1. Our hearts must be habitually indifferent towards created enjoyments.—Luke xiv. 26; Ps. cxxxi. 1, &c. 2. We must expect nothing from them but what God puts in them.—Isa. xvii. 10, and lvii. 10. 3. We must derive all our comfort from God himself, in the midst of plenty, as well as in poverty.—Ps. xviii. 46; 1 Sam. ii. 1, &c.: Ps. cxlii. 4, 5; Hab. iii. 17, 18. 4. We must use all created enjoyments as fading and transitory, and mortify every degree of lustful desire after them.—1 Sam. xiv. 32; 1 Cor. vii. 29, &c.

In order that this full contentment with our lot, which so much glorifies God, and prevents sin in thought, and word, and action, may be obtained, the following things are necessary:—1. We must receive a God in Christ, as our God, as he is offered in the gospel, as the source and sum of all that good which is to be found in the creatures.—Ps. xxiii., lxxiii. 23-26, and lxxxi. 8

&c. We must believe that God, as the new covenant God of his people, and as their friend and father, is the maker, manager, and disposer of all things. Job xxxiv. 33; Isa. xlvi. 3, 4, and lii. 7; Matt. vi. 30.

When this state of contentment is attained, it may be *strengthened* and *promoted* by considering these things:—1. That we ourselves are dependent on God's mere grace and bounty.—Gen. xxxii. 10; Isa. lxiii. 7; Ps. xxxv. 6, 7. 2. That the wants and afflictions of our own outward lot are likely to be its most useful part to our precious souls.—2 Cor. iv. 17; Ps. cxix. 67, 71; Mic. vii. 14; Rev. iii. 19; Heb. xiii. 5, &c. 3. That worldly enjoyments are always very empty, and often very hurtful.—Prov. xxiii. 5; Deut. xxxii. 15; Hos. xiii. 6, and the whole Book of Ecclesiastes. 4. That our temptations, burdens, services, and final account, are proportioned to our enjoyments.—Matt. xxv. 14, &c.; Luke xix. 12, &c., and xii. 47, 48. 5. That the more we enjoy in this world, the more dangerous is our situation.—Mark x. 23. 6. That Jesus Christ has marked our way through every trouble, and attends us to bear, and to carry, and to deliver us.—Isa. xlvi. 3, 4, and lxiii. 9. 7. That death and eternity, in which earthly enjoyments can do us no service whatever, and in which we shall reap the happy fruits of our troubles, are at hand.—John xvi. 33; Acts xiv. 22; Matt. xix. 29; Rom. viii. 17, 18; 2 Cor. iv. 17, &c.

It may here be remarked, that if we have a view to legal perfection, it is utterly impossible, in this life, to attain to that full contentment which this commandment requires. This is no more possible in our present fallen state, than obedience to any other Divine commandment. Perfection in any grace whatever is not to be looked for here. The perfection, however, may be full as to its parts, although not so in degree. See Phil. iv. 11. And although it is difficult to attain the contentment here required, yet, being a duty, we ought to seek after it; for by it God is highly honoured, and the peace of the soul is greatly promoted.

Obs. 271.—*The Tenth Commandment requireth a right and charitable frame of spirit towards our neighbour and all that is his.*

This right and charitable disposition towards the person and property of our neighbour, may include the following things:—

1. A hearty love to his person for the sake of God his maker.—Rom. xiii. 9, &c.

2. A kind regard to his property for his own sake, but chiefly for the sake of God.—Deut. xxii. 1.

3. An earnest desire for, and a cordial delight in, his welfare, both temporal, and spiritual, and eternal.—Rom. xii. 15; Heb. xiii. 3; Ps. xxxv. 13, &c.; Rom. xii. 30, &c.

It must, however, be remembered, that this right and chariable disposition cannot be attained without faith; nor can our duty in this respect be performed, if the affections are not influenced by grace; which alone will sway and determine us to promote and to rejoice in our neighbour's welfare, in whatever light we view it.

INFERENCES.

From this subject we learn,—1. That we should be moderate in all our enjoyments. 2. That we receive all our comforts from God. 3. That all things are at the disposal of God, the righteous governor of the universe. 4. That God is not unjust, although all are not equal. 5. That we ought to avoid anxious care, which is unprofitable. 6. That there is enough in God for all.

Sins Forbidden.

Q. 81.—What is forbidden in the Tenth Commandment?

The Tenth Commandment forbiddeth all discontentment with our own estate, envying or grieving at the good of our neighbour, and all inordinate motions and affections to any thing that is his.

ANALYSIS AND PROOFS.

We are here taught,—

1. That we are forbidden to be discontented with our condition in life. 1 Cor. x. 10.—" Neither murmur ye as some of them also murmured, and were destroyed of the destroyer."

2. That we are forbidden to be envious at the good of others. Gal. v. 26.—" Let us not be desirous of vain-glory—envying one another."

3. That we are forbidden to grieve at the good of others. James v. 9.—" Grudge not one against another."

4. That we are forbidden to indulge inordinate motions or affections towards any thing that belongs to our neighbour. Col. iii. 5.—" Mortify, therefore, your members which are upon the earth; inordinate affection, evil concupiscence, and covetousness which is idolatry."

EXPLANATION.

Obs. 272.—*The Tenth Commandment forbiddeth all discontentment with our condition in life.*

Discontentment with the condition in which Providence hath placed us, includes the following things:—1. Inward rebellion against God's providential will.—Hos. iv. 16. 2. Fretfulness or grief at the disposal of our lot.—1 Kings xxi. 4. 3. Inward displeasure against that condition which God has allotted us.—Job xviii. 4; Jonah iv. 4. Inward blasphemy against God, as if he had been guilty of injustice or cruelty in ordering our lot.—Job ix. 17 18, x. 16. and xxx. 21; Mal. iii. 13, &c.

The *aggravations* of this sin of discontentment are these:—1. It argues an unwillingness to be at the disposal of God,—which is to oppose our own comforts, both here and hereafter.—Gen. xxx. 1, and xlii. 36. 2. It argues that we deem ourselves more competent judges of what is best for us, than God himself.—1. Kings i. 5. 3. This sin must be very heinous, inasmuch as it unfits for glorifying God in this world, and also for duty to all around us.—Esth. v. 11, &c. 4. This sin has many of the most forbidding sins in its train: such as blasphemy against God; atheism,—1 Sam. xxviii.; murder,—1 Kings xxi. 4, &c.; Esth. iii.; suicide,—2 Sam. xvii. 23; and even death and hell follow it.

This sin of discontentment with our condition arises from *want of faith* in the Divine procedure—from not viewing God as a God of faithfulness.

Some of the *remedies* which ought to be used, in order that this dangerous disease may be healed, are the following:—1. The only sovereign remedy is, to take God as our portion and as our reconciled God and Father in Christ, and to give Christ the chief place in our hearts.—Ps. lxxiii. 25, 26, and lxxvi. 4. 2. We must take a view of our mercies amidst all our miseries. 3. Gratitude to God for all his mercies, and a sense of our unworthiness of the least of them, tend much to curb this spirit which possesses so many, and by which they torment themselves and all around them. 4. As the discontented cannot be eminently holy while this spirit reigns in them, it is necessary that it be checked by faith and repentance.

Obs. 273.—*The Tenth Commandment forbiddeth all envying or grieving at the good of our neighbour.*

By *envying or grieving at the good of our neighbour*, we are to understand a repining or grudging at his prosperous circumstances, or any superior privilege which he possesses above ourselves. The advantages which he may have over us, and which may excite repining, envying, and grieving or grudging, are such as these:—gifts, graces, relations, wealth, honour, pleasure, &c. But to such as acknowledge an overruling Providence, these things will be no occasion to sin.

We may here remark, that *covetousness*, the sin here forbidden, is an excessive thirst after what we have not, and what God in his providence does not see meet that we should possess: and this thirst is so great that it cannot be satisfied. See Prov. i. 19. Its *nature* may be thus briefly described:—1. It is diametrically opposite to that spirit of love which we ought to manifest to our neighbour. 2. It is a fostering of pride, to allow the desires to go out after what belongs to our neighbour. 3. It is a continual enemy to one's peace.—Gen. xxxvii.; Isa. iii. 16. 4. This disposition will restrain all in whom it dwells from aiding their neighbour in any respect, and thus they cannot love their neighbour as themselves.

Obs. 274.—*The Tenth Commandment forbiddeth all the inordinate motions or affections which may be in the soul.*

By the *inordinate motions or affections*, which are the source or spring of covetousness, we are to understand not only every unlawful purpose, intention, or desire, which is actually formed in the heart, but even the first motions or risings of corruption in the soul, which appear there before there is any actual commission of the sin here forbidden. See Col. iii. 5.

This commandment, then, forbids the following things:—

1. Covetousness of created enjoyments, in inordinate lusting after the things which we *ourselves* possess. (1.) In respect of having the heart immoderately set upon them.—Luke xii. 21, and xiv. 18–20, 26. (2.) In respect of desiring them for themselves, or for a wrong end.—James iv. 3. (3.) In respect of using them with too much avidity, without regard to necessity or experience, as if we were under their power.—1 Cor. vi. 12; 1 Sam. xiv. 32. (4.) In respect of using them to the hurt of our souls, and to the dishonour of God.—1 Cor. x. 31.

2. Covetousness of created enjoyments, in inordinate lusting after the things which belong to *our neighbour*. (1.) In respect of desiring what God hath put out of our power.—Josh. vii. 21; 2 Sam. xxiii. 15. (2.) In respect of desiring that which is attainable by lawful means, by such as are unlawful, or for an unlawful end.—James v. 3; Jer. xvii. 11. (3.) In respect of desiring it so violently as to disturb our mind until we enjoy it, and render us fretful if we must want it.—Gen. xxx. 1.

This commandment also forbids the *corrupt frame of our fallen nature*, from which all sinful lustings proceed. 1. As existing in the heart, but not consented to.—Rom. vii. The principle or habit from which sinful actions proceed, is doubtless here forbidden, as well as the actions themselves which proceed from such corruption; for the law hath for its province the thoughts of the heart, as well as the actions of the life. 2. As consented to in itself, but not in the execution of its desires.— Matt. v. 28; Eccl. vi. 9. 3. As conceiving, contriving, and bringing forth actual sin, in thought, word, and deed.—Matt. xv. 19, 20; James i. 15. 4. As having brought forth continued acts of wickedness to the very point of execution.—1 Sam. xiv. 24, &c., and xxiii. 26; Esth. iii., v., and vi.; Isa. xxxvii.; Acts xvi. 27, and xxi. 31, 32.

We may here remark, that in Scripture *lusts* are variously denominated. 1. They are called *deceitful lusts*,—Eph. iv. 22; because, although they appear to be dormant, they are always waiting an opportunity. 2. They are called *hurtful lusts*,— 1 Tim. vi. 9: because they are exceedingly dangerous, seeking always to destroy. 3. They are called *worldly lusts*,—Tit. ii. 12; because they are not of God, but of the world, and of the devil, the god of this world. 4. They are called *former lusts*,—1 Pet. i. 14; because they reign in every natural man without control. 5. They are said to *war against the soul*,—1 Pet. ii. 11; because they all conspire to destroy the whole man. 6. They are said to *war in our members*,—James iv. 1; because they are not harmonious among themselves, but like those who compose an army, who may join together to destroy an enemy, although they are not harmonious among themselves.

INFERENCES.

From this subject we learn,—1. The duty of resignation to the Divine will. 2. That we ought to love our neighbour as ourselves. 3. That, as the world is fading, we ought to set our affections on things above. 4. That the soul is more valuable than all earthly things. 5. The necessity of the blood of Christ to cleanse from original sin, which is the spring of all actual sin. 6. That sin is still in the best, and will continue to be until death. 7. The necessity of the application of Jesus Christ by faith.

CHAPTER II.

SPECIAL DUTIES WHICH GOD REQUIRES OF MAN UNDER
THE GOSPEL DISPENSATION.

INTRODUCTION—SHOWING MAN'S INABILITY TO KEEP THE MORAL LAW
—THAT THERE ARE VARIOUS DEGREES OF GUILT IN BREAKING IT—
AND THE DESERT OF EVERY TRANSGRESSION OF IT.

Man's Inability to Keep the Law.

Q. 82.—Is any man able perfectly to keep the Commandments of God?

No mere man since the fall is able in this life perfectly to keep the commandments of God, but doth daily break them in thought, word, and deed.

ANALYSIS AND PROOFS.

We are here taught,—
1. That no mere man since the fall is able, in this life, to keep the commandments of God perfectly. Eccl. vii. 20.— " There is not a just man upon earth that doeth good, and sinneth not."

2. That all men, in this life, break the commandments of God daily. Gen. vi. 5.—" Every imagination of the thoughts of his heart was only evil continually."

3. That we all daily break the commandments of God in our thoughts. Gen. viii. 21.—" The imagination of man's heart is evil from his youth."

4. That we all daily break the commandments of God in our words and conversation. James iii. 8.—" The tongue can no man tame; it is an unruly evil, full of deadly poison."

5. That we all daily break the commandments of God in our actions. Rom. vii. 19.—" The good that I would, I do not; but the evil which I would not, that I do." See also James iii. 2.

EXPLANATION.

Obs. 275.—*Since the fall, no mere man is able, in this life, to keep the commandments of God perfectly.*

The perfection which the law of God requires must be *absolute perfection*, both in heart and life, without the least failure in any respect whatever; and it must flow from a nature perfectly holy, without which a constant and uninterrupted obedience cannot be given to the exceeding broad demands of the law. See Matt. xxii. 37-39. Man, indeed, may please his fancy with a *sincere obedience*, but this will never save his soul. " Thou shalt love the Lord thy God." How? Imperfectly, though sincerely? No: this will by no means satisfy the law; but " with all thy heart, with all thy soul, with all thy strength, and with all thy mind." And whatever the law requires, there must be the highest perfection in degree; for any thing less than this would be disobedience.

This absolute perfection was attainable for the short period which preceded the fall of man; for the ability was stamped upon him at his creation. Eccl. vii. 29.—" God made man upright." And it will be attained by the saints in heaven; for there God's servants shall serve him.

It is said that *no mere man* is able to keep the commandments of God perfectly, in order that Christ may be excepted, who is not a mere man, but infinitely more than a man, being *Immanuel* —God with us—God in our nature: and he is excepted, not only because he was able to yield perfect obedience to the law, but because he actually yielded it; and such an obedience, too, as was meritorious of life eternal for all his spiritual seed.—Rom. v. 17-19.

That no mere man can keep the commandments of God perfectly, may be thus proved:—

1. Scripture directly proves it in numberless places. See Eccl. vii. 20; I John i. 8; James iii. 2; Rom. iii. 9-19; Ps. xiv. and viii., where the corruption and sin of all are largely expressed.

2. We have the testimony of the saints themselves, the excel-

lent of the earth, to their sin. Even the most eminent of them acknowledge their sin and corruption; as Abraham, David, Peter, and many others. Now, if their sins are upon record, where is their perfection?

3. We find in the best a principle of corruption, as well as of grace, between which there is a continual struggle,—a struggle which shall last until death put an end to it.—Gal. v. 17.

4. Prayer would be unnecessary, if legal perfection could be attained.

5. Legal perfection is not attainable in this life, because there is no such measure of grace promised as would enable any to keep the commandments of God perfectly. This would be inconsistent with the present state, and with the nature of spiritual growth in grace, which is gradual; for the saints do not attain the full stature of perfect men in Christ Jesus until they arrive at glory.

6. All were included in the covenant made with Adam; and, consequently, all sinned in him and fell with him in his first transgression.

7. Experience attests the universal corruption of mankind.

We may here remark, that there are two very *dangerous mistakes* into which some fall, from the consideration of this subject:—

1. They accuse God of injustice in commanding what is impossible. It is, indeed, now impossible; but once it was not. The sin, however, is man's; and God is most just: for, although man has by sin lost his power of obeying, yet God has not lost his right of commanding.

2. They suspend their endeavours after perfection. Because they cannot be perfect, they think that they need not study to be holy; that, seeing perfection is unattainable, they may suspend their endeavours after holiness. But such conduct evinces a total ignorance of the nature of true holiness; for, whenever there is a true knowledge of holiness, there will be an increasing desire after perfection.

Obs. 276.—*In this life all men, without exception, daily break the commandments of God, in thought, word, and deed.*

1. We daily break them in our *thoughts*. This is done when our thoughts are sinfully employed, either with reference to God, or to our neighbour, or to ourselves.

2. We daily break them in our *words* and conversation. This is done when our words are idle and unprofitable; when they dishonour God, and are hurtful to ourselves and to others; when those are spoken which ought not to be uttered; when those are restrained which ought to be spoken; or when they are not delivered in due order.

3. We daily break them in our *actions* This is done when

sins are committed which have been conceived in thought, or which have been uttered by the tongue,—which are more than can be numbered. See Ps. xl. 12.

But it may be here objected, that we read of some who were *perfect* in their generation; such as Noah,—Gen. vi. 9; Job,-i. 8; Hezekiah,—Isa. xxxviii. 3; and Zecharias and Elizabeth —Luke i. 6. To this we answer, that by perfection in these saints we are to understand, not *absolute perfection*, which is unattainable in this life, but only *comparative perfection*,—that is, when compared with others, they may be styled *perfect*. They were more holy and circumspect than those around them; but absolute perfection they by no means attained in this life; for their sins are upon record. See Gen. ix. 21; Job iii. 2; 2 Chron. xxxii. 25; Isa. xxxix.; Luke i. 20.

But here, again, it may be said, that the Scriptures affirm, that "Whosoever is born of God, doth not commit sin."—1 John iii. 9. This is, indeed, a truth; but it is no proof of absolute perfection. The meaning of the expression is, that they who are born of God have obtained a real view of sin, and have seen it in all its hatefulness; the consequence of which is, that they cannot *delight* in sin,—they cannot take pleasure in it,—they do not make a trade of sin, as natural men do, who are called *workers of iniquity.*—Ps. cxxv. 5.

INFERENCES.

From this subject we learn,—1. That all men are equally miserable by nature, and equally need a Saviour. 2. That there is no life by the law. 3. The necessity of an interest in Jesus Christ. 4. That the saints must continue their spiritual warfare until death. 5. That we must place all our dependence on the grace of God. 6. That there is no hope from any other quarter. 7. That believers are much obligated to the grace of God. 8 That the saints shall be perfect in due time.

Different Degrees of Guilt in Breaking the Law.

Q. 83.—Are all Transgressions of the Law equally heinous?

Some sins in themselves, and by reason of several aggravations, are more heinous in the sight of God than others.

ANALYSIS AND PROOFS.

We are here taught,—

1. That some sins are in themselves more heinous in the sight of God than others. 1 John v. 16.—" There is a sin unto death. I do not say that he shall pray for it." See also Ezek. viii. 13.

2 That aggravations make sin more heinous in the sight of

God. Matt. xxiii. 14.—" Woe unto you, scribes and Pharisees. hypocrites! for ye devour widows' houses, and for a pretence make long prayer; therefore ye shall receive the greater damnation." See also James iv. 17.

EXPLANATION.

Obs. 277.—*Some sins are in themselves more heinous in the sight of God than others.*

By the *heinousness* of sin, we are to understand its hatefulness in the sight of God, or its offensiveness to him.

Some sins are *in themselves* more heinous or hateful in the sight of God than other sins are,—that is, they are so in their own nature, even although no aggravating circumstance whatever attend them. Thus, blasphemy against God, idolatry, unbelief, profanation of the name of God, &c.,—sins against the first table of the law;—and murder, oppression, theft, bearing false witness, &c.,—sins against the second table,—are very great in themselves, or in their own nature, without considering any o. the circumstances attending them.

Obs. 278.—*Some sins are, on account of several aggravations more heinous in the sight of God than others.*

Sins receive their *aggravations* from the following things :— From the persons offending, from the parties offended, from th nature and quality of the offence, and from the circumstances o time and place.

1. Sins receive their aggravations from the *persons offending* who may be viewed either with respect to their age, their gifts, or their office. The more distinguished a person is on any of these accounts, the more aggravated is the sin committed by him See Job xxxii. 7, &c.; Eccl. iv. 13; 2 Sam. xii. 14; 1 Kings xi 9; 1 Cor. v. 1; James iv. 17; Luke xii. 47; Ps. lxxviii. 17; Jer. xxiii. 11, &c.; Gen. ii. 13.

2. Sins receive their aggravations from the *parties offended.* (1.) Sins committed against God, his attributes, and worship, are more heinous than sins committed against man, and the institutions of man; for, as the difference between the objects is infinite, so the difference between the sins must be so too.—1 Sam. ii. 25; Ps. li. 4; Rom. ii. 4; Mal. i. 14. The same may be said of Christ and his grace,—Heb. ii. 3, and xii. 25; Acts iv. 12; and of the Holy Spirit and his witness and working,— Eph. iv. 30; 1 Thess. v. 19. (2.) Sins committed against superiors, and those to whom we stand especially related and engaged, are more aggravated than sins committed against those who are upon a level with ourselves.—Numb. xii. 8, &c.; Prov. xxx. 17; Ps. lv. 12, &c. (3.) Sins committed against the people of God are more heinous than sins committed against others.—Zeph. ii. 8; Luke x. 16; Matt. xviii. 6; 1 Cor. viii. 12; Rom. xiv. 13

(4.) Sins committed against the soul are more aggravated than sins committed against the body.—Ezek. xiii. 19; Matt. xxiii. 15. (5.) Sins committed against the common good of all men, or of many, are more heinous than sins committed against an individual, or a few,—1 Thess. ii. 15, 16; from which it is evident who they are that sin against the common good of mankind, viz., they who do what they can to hinder the propagation of the gospel where it is not, and to mar its success where it is; for there is nothing which tends more to the common good of mankind than to send to them the Word of salvation. They who do not what they can for this end, cannot be said to love God with all their heart, and their neighbour as themselves. See also Josh. xxii. 20.

3. Sins receive their aggravations from the *nature* and *quality* of the offence. (1.) Sin is aggravated, if committed against the express letter of the law.—Rom. i. 32; Ezra ix. 10. (2.) Sin is aggravated, if by its commission many sins are committed, or if by it many commandments are violated,—Prov. v., where the sin forbidden is accompanied with a complication of evils. See also 2 Sam. xii. 9. (3.) Sin is aggravated, when it breaks forth into words and actions.—Matt. v. 22. (4.) Sin is aggravated, when it admits of no reparation.—Numb. xxxv. 31; Prov. vi. 35. (5.) Sin is aggravated, when committed against convictions of conscience.—Numb. xv. 30, &c.; Rom. i. 32; Dan. v. 22; Tit. iii. 10. (6.) Sin is aggravated, when committed deliberately, frequently, obstinately, with delight, &c.—Ps. xxxvi. 4; Numb. xiv. 22; Zech. vii. 11, 12; Prov. ii. 14. (7.) When sin is committed against mercies, judgments, public or private admonition, reproofs, the censures of the Church, against our prayers, our purposes, our vows, and our engagements to be the Lord's,—when it is committed imprudently, boastingly, maliciously,—when it is persevered in, or relapsed into after repentance, it must be highly aggravated.

4. Sins receive their aggravations from the circumstances of *time* and *place*. Although sin is sin at any time and in any place, yet there are times when it becomes most dangerous to commit sin, and places in which sin committed becomes very aggravated. (1.) Sin committed on any day is sin; but sin committed on the Sabbath, or the Lord's day, is a greater sin; for if we are to watch against sin on any day, it ought surely to be on this day. (2.) When sin is committed on a day set apart for humiliation or thanksgiving, it is more heinous than the same sin committed on the same day not set apart for such necessary services, according to the calls of Providence. (3.) When sin is committed immediately before or after the public worship of God, it becomes a heinous sin; for it argues both a total indifference about the preparation of the heart to wait upon God, and a disregard to the exercises of his worship, in which we may have been

engaged.—Ezek. xxiii. 37, &c. (4.) Sin committed in Britain is more aggravated than the same sin committed in a heathen land; because the one is a land enlightened by the gospel, while the other is sitting in the region and shadow of spiritual darkness.—Isa. xxvi. 10. (5.) Sin is more aggravated when committed by one who dwells in a religious family, than it is when committed by one who lives in one of the families of Satan. (6.) Sin committed in public is more aggravated than sin committed in private, because many may be led astray.—1 Sam. ii. 22-24; 2 Sam. xvi. 22.

INFERENCES.

From this subject we learn,—1. The necessity of abasement before God, under a deep sense of our aggravated sins. 2. The greatness of pardoning mercy, which is extended to the chief of sinners. 3. The necessity of self-examination, that we may see how aggravated our sins are; for without this we must be ignorant of sin. 4. That our sins are very great in a land enlightened by the gospel. 5. That we ought not to think any sin of a trifling nature, for it shall not be found so at last. 6. That, as there are degrees of sin, so there are degrees of punishment in hell.

Desert of every Breach of the Law.

Q. 84.—*What doth every sin deserve?*

Every sin deserveth God's wrath and curse, both in this life and that which is to come.

ANALYSIS AND PROOFS.

We are here taught,—
1. That every sin deserves the wrath and curse of God in this life. Gal. iii. 10.—" Cursed is every one that continueth not in all things which are written in the book of the law to do them."
2. That every sin deserves the wrath and curse of God for ever in the world to come. Rom. vi. 23.—" The wages of sin is death; but the gift of God is eternal life through Jesus Christ our Lord." See also Matt. xxv. 41.

EXPLANATION.

Obs. 279.—*Every sin deserves the wrath and curse of God, both in this world and in the world to come.*

By the *desert* of sin we are to understand that which is in the nature of sin, and which of itself deserves all the wrath which God has denounced against it, and which shall assuredly be inflicted upon all impenitent sinners. As sin respects the holiness of God, so it is the opposition, the contrariety of sin to this holiness, as discovered in his law. in which the desert or demerit of sin consists.

By the *wrath* of God, we are to understand his anger in the dreadful effects of it, whether manifested in a more visible or in a more secret way,—Ps. xi. 6; or, it is a most pure, unlimited, and undisturbed act of the Divine mind, which produces the most dreadful effects against the sinner.—Isa. xxxiii. 14; Nah. i. 2.

The *curse* of God has a reference particularly to his law; and by it we may understand the sentence of his law denouncing all evil against the transgressor.—Gal. iii. 10.

Every sin deserves the wrath and curse of God both here and hereafter; for, although there are different degrees of punishment in the world to come, yet the smallest sin deserves this punishment as well as the greatest. And this is evident from what the law saith, Gal. iii. 10,—" Cursed is every one that continueth not in all things which are written in the book of the law to do them;" and James ii. 10,—" He that offendeth in one point is guilty of all." If the law will not overlook one transgression, then the least must be punished; but, strictly speaking, the law knows no punishment less than the curse. If so, then every sin deserves the curse; and the law can do no wrong to the sinner when the curse is executed. But we have a direct testimony that sin deserves death: Rom. vi. 23,—" The wages of sin is death." Now, it is not said that the wages of a *great sin* is death, or that the wages of *many sins* is death, or that the wages of a little sin is not death; but in plain language it is said, that " Death is the wages of sin,"—that is, of every sin, great or small; and this must be so in the very nature of the thing. But further, if Christ endured the wrath and curse of God in the room of his people, it must be evident that their sin deserves the same. See Tit. ii. 14.

The reasons why every sin, however small, deserves the wrath and curse of God, are the following:—

1. When sin is committed, it is against the sovereignty of God. It is a setting up of one's own will and authority in direct opposition to the will and authority of God—which, surely, is no mean guilt; and in the very nature of the thing it deserves an adequate recompense. But no suitable recompense can be given in this world; and in the world to come, none is given less than the wrath and curse of God, which are justly due to sin

2. Sin is committed against the holiness of God.—Heb. i. 13. There is nothing that God hates but sin. If sinners, then, delight in sin with their whole heart, it cannot be trifling guilt; and consequently, it deserves a most exemplary punishment.

3. Sin is committed against the *goodness* of God. It is a rendering of evil for good, cursing for blessing, the worst we have for the best which God can give. And surely this conduct deserves a punishment suited to the nature of the offence committed

against a good and gracious God; and this punishment is the curse.

4. Sin is committed against the righteous law of God, the rule by which all ought to be governed. He, then, who can transgress God's law without remorse, is a rebel against the Majesty of heaven; and, consequently, deserves punishment.

5. It is a well known fact, that the more eminent the person is against whom the sin is committed, the greater is the punishment which it deserves. If, then, God is in every respect infinite, the offence committed against him must deserve infinite punishment; but a finite creature cannot bear infinite punishment any other way than by infinite duration,—that is, for ever.

6. Sin is an infinite evil,—that is, it is an evil for which the sinner himself can never make atonement; and, consequently, his sin must remain until it be taken away by Him who gave His life a ransom for many. But if this ransom is despised, there remaineth no more sacrifice for sin, but a certain fearful expectation of the wrath and curse of God for evermore.

INFERENCES.

From this subject we learn,—1. That the least sin deserves death. 2. That God is righteous when he taketh vengeance. 3. That the least sin cannot be expiated but by the blood of Christ. 4. The love of God in making his Son a sin-offering for us. 5. That we have reason for ever to admire redeeming love.

Special Duties required of Man under the Gospel Dispensation.

Q. 85.—What doth God require of us, that we may escape his wrath and curse due to us for sin?

To escape the wrath and curse of God due to us for sin, God requireth of us faith in Jesus Christ, repentance unto life, with the diligent use of all the outward means whereby Christ communicateth to us the benefits of redemption.

ANALYSIS AND PROOFS.

We are here taught,—

1. That God himself has devised a way of escape from the effects of sin. John iii. 16.—" God so loved the world, that he gave his only begotten Son, that whosoever believeth in him should not perish, but have everlasting life."

2. That faith in Jesus Christ is necessary for escaping the wrath and curse of God. Acts xvi. 31.—" Believe in the Lord Jesus Christ, and thou shalt be saved."

3. That true repentance is necessary for escaping the wrath and

curse of God. Luke xiii. 3.—" Except ye repent, ye shall all likewise perish."

4. That a diligent use of the means of grace is required of all who would escape the wrath and curse of God. Phil. ii. 12, 13. —" Work out your own salvation with fear and trembling; for it is God who worketh in you both to will and to do of his good pleasure." See also Prov. ii. 1, 5, and viii. 34.

5. That the benefits of redemption are usually communicated to sinners by means of the ordinances. Rom. x. 14.—" How then shall they call on him in whom they have not believed? and how shall they believe in him of whom they have not heard? and how shall they hear without a preacher?"

EXPLANATION.

Obs. 280.—*Faith and repentance, and the diligent use of the means of grace, are not required to give us a right or title to eternal life, or to the possession of it; but only as the means of conveying and improving the purchased salvation, and as evidences of interest therein.* See 1 Cor. i. 21.

It might, indeed, appear from the proposition stated above, that faith, and repentance, and the diligent use of the means of grace, are to be viewed as the conditions of escaping the wrath and curse of God; but it must ever be remembered, that eternal life is the *gift of God* through Jesus Christ our Lord.—Rom. vi. 23. Faith and repentance are, indeed, absolutely necessary in order to salvation; but they are not the conditions on which God promises eternal life, or they are not the procuring cause of it; for he could have required these duties from his creatures although he had never promised them any thing at all.

In order, then, to prevent some dangerous mistakes which may be committed, and which might lead us to build our hopes of acceptance with God on a false foundation, we shall make the following remarks:—

1. The only ground of pardon of sin and acceptance with God, is the *imputed righteousness of Jesus Christ*. Duties, however spiritual, by no means merit deliverance from the curse of the law, and from the wrath of God. See Rom. v. 18, 19. Salvation by grace, and a covenant of works, are quite incompatible.

2. The way of acceptance under the gospel dispensation is *not a more easy way of salvation* than what was known from the beginning. They who imagine that the gospel is a new law, and an easy law, to be obeyed in order to obtain life before God, must, in order to be consistent with themselves, maintain that the law is not so strict now as it was formerly; which idea is not very honourable either to the law or to the Lawgiver. In opposition to this absurd idea, it must be maintained, that the law is the same in all ages; for, saith the great Lawgiver, " One jot or one tittle shall not pass from the law, till all be fulfilled."

By all that would be saved, it must be fulfilled in the person of the Surety of sinners; and he knew experimentally that the law will not depart from any of its demands, however small. Never, indeed, could it possibly do so, seeing it is the law of Him who is the same yesterday, to-day, and for ever.

3. Faith, and repentance, and the diligent use of the means of salvation, are not the *procuring cause* of our escaping the wrath and curse of God. To suppose this to be the case, would be to make a saviour of our duties. It would be a renouncing of the satisfaction of Christ; which, doubtless, is a most dangerous and foolish imagination. See Rom. iii. 20. If deliverance can be obtained in any other way than by the obedience and satisfaction of Christ, then Christ hath died in vain—man is his own saviour —and no thanks to Christ for salvation, at least for a whole salvation. Such an opinion betrays consummate ignorance of the covenant of grace, and of the Scriptures where this covenant is revealed; and it is accompanied with the utmost danger.

Obs. 281.—*Faith in Jesus Christ, and repentance unto life, are necessary in order to escape the wrath and curse of God due to us for sin.*

1. *Faith in Jesus Christ* is necessary for the following reasons:—(1.) Because, until we believe, we are dead in trespasses and sins.—Eph. ii. (2.) Because " without faith it is impossible to please God."—Heb. xi. 6. (3.) Because faith is the hinge upon which salvation and misery turn.—Mark xvi. 16; John iii. 16, 36. (4.) Because without faith there can be no union with Christ.—2 Cor. v. 17; John xv. 4, &c. (5.) Because, by way of eminence, " to believe " is the command of God.—1 John iii 23; John vi. 29.

2. Repentance unto life is necessary, for the following reasons: —(1.) Because the Scriptures enjoin it.—Acts xvii. 30; Ezek. xviii. 30, &c., and xxxiii. 11; Acts ii. 38. (2.) Because it is not only enjoined, but enjoined with certification, that whosoever doth not repent shall assuredly perish.—Luke xiii. 3,'5; Rev. ii. 5. (3.) Because there is no unrepented guilt in heaven; and, consequently, without repentance we cannot enter into the kingdom of heaven. (4.) Because Christ is exalted to bestow repentance.—Acts v. 31. (5.) Repentance is necessary as a concomitant of faith. For without faith there can be no repentance and without repentance there can be no faith.—Zech. xii. 10. Faith gives a view of what Christ is, and what he hath done, that iniquity might not be our ruin; and repentance is the suitable exercise of a soul convinced of this work of Christ in its lawroom and place.

But here it may be asked, Are not faith and repentance represented in Scripture as *gifts of God?* How, then, can they be required of us? Are we to conclude that we can believe and repent of ourselves? Or, how can God require of us what is not in our power to perform? To this we answer, that God requires of us what it is beyond our power to perform, to show us the necessity of that grace which is promised, and which Christ, as our exalted Saviour, is empowered and commissioned to bestow.—Phil. i. 29; Eph. i. 19; Acts v. 31, and xi. 18; John vi. 44, and xv. 5; Jer. xiii. 23.

The connection of faith with salvation consists in this, that it is the hand which receives Christ with all the benefits of the redemption which he hath purchased for sinners.—Ps. lxviii. 31; John i. 12.

The connection of repentance with salvation consists in this, that it is the exercise which natively flows from faith in Jesus Christ; discovering that sorrow for sin without which there can be no salvation for sinners, and which is habitual in all those who shall see the kingdom of heaven; and reminding them of him who was a made a sin-offering for them, that they might be made the righteousness of God in him.

Obs. 282.—*The diligent use of all the outward means by which Christ communicates to sinners the benefits of redemption, is necessary in order to escape the wrath and curse of God due to us for sin.*

The diligent use of the means of salvation is necessary for the following reasons:—1. The appointment of them shows their necessity. 2. They are necessary, because by rejecting them we ascribe folly to God, and pour contempt upon him. 3. They are necessary, because we cannot expect salvation without the due use of them; and this is an idea which is uniformly insisted on in Scripture.—Prov. viii. 33, 34; Rom. x. 17. 4. The use of them is most necessary, because we are commanded by God to make use of them. Every thing which he hath commanded is most necessary, both with respect to himself and with respect to us;—with respect to himself, to show his authority and his love; and with respect to us, to show our love to him, and our regard for his word and authority.

By a *diligent use* of all the outward means of grace, we are to understand, an embracing of every opportunity offered in the course of Divine providence for waiting upon God in the way of commanded duty; and a looking up to him for his blessing upon them, by which alone they can be profitable to us, or advance our spiritual concerns.—1 Cor. iii. 6, &c.

The means of grace are commonly distinguished into *external* and *internal*. The external, or outward means, are mentioned above, as those by which the benefits of redemption are communicated; and the internal means, which are produced by the use of the outward means, are faith and repentance, and the other graces of the Spirit which accompany or flow from them.

The connection of all the outward means with salvation consists in this, that "by them Christ communicates to us the benefits of redemption."

We may here observe, that if we regard only the mere observance of ordinances, it is in man's own power to observe them, without any supernatural grace; but to observe them with profit man of himself is utterly unable. Thus, to hear with profit, the Word must be mixed with faith; but we are told in Scripture that "faith is the gift of God." A man may read the Scriptures, may attend the house of God, may call upon his name, may converse about the concerns of his soul, may reprove sin, &c., without any special grace from on high. But there is a great difference between the observance of these means in the strength of nature, and the observance of them in the strength of new covenant grace.

INFERENCES.

From this subject we learn,—1. The importance of right views of a sinner's acceptance in the sight of God; that the ground of it is not duties, but Christ's righteousness received by faith, without which we must perish. 2. The necessity of true repentance. 3. The value of the means of salvation. 4. The necessity of seeking a blessing upon these means.

SECT. 1.—OF FAITH IN JESUS CHRIST.

Q. 86.—*What is Faith in Jesus Christ?*

Faith in Jesus Christ is a saving grace, whereby we receive and rest upon him alone for salvation, as he is offered to us in the gospel.

ANALYSIS AND PROOFS.

We are here taught,—
1. That faith in Jesus Christ is a saving grace. John xx. 31.—" That believing ye might have life through his name." See also Heb. x. 39.
2. That Jesus Christ is received as a Saviour by faith. John i. 12.—" As many as received him, to them gave he power to become the sons of God, even to them that believe on his name."
3. That by faith we depend on Christ for salvation. Acts xv. 11.—" We believe that, through the grace of the Lord Jesus, we shall be saved."
4. That by faith we depend on Christ alone for salvation. Gal. ii. 16.—" We have believed in Jesus Christ, that we might be justified by the faith of Christ, and not by the works of the law."
5. That by faith we receive Christ as offered in the gospel. Eph. i. 13.—" In whom ye also trusted, after that ye heard the word of truth, the gospel (or glad tidings) of your salvation."

EXPLANATION.

Obs. 283.—*Faith is neither more nor less than belief; and saving faith is a belief of the gospel, or of God's testimony concerning his Son.*

It has been supposed by many that there are several kinds of faith mentioned in the Sacred Writings; such as historical faith, temporary faith, the faith of miracles, and saving faith. But a careful examination of the subject would convince such, that whatever be the thing believed, there can be no difference with respect to the *manner* of believing; and that the only distinction that can take place is with respect to the *object* or *thing believed*. "The inspired writers never give the least hint that they had any uncommon idea annexed to the term (pistis) *faith* or *belief;* nor did they give any directions *how* to believe or to act faith, though they insist much on *what* men are to believe, and upon the divine evidence of its truth. It is also remarkable, that we do not find any of the first converts inquiring what faith is, or in what manner they were to believe. Hence we may reasonably infer, that the apostles used the word *faith* in its ordinary meaning, which required no explanation, and that their hearers did in fact so understand them."

"In the Epistle to the Hebrews (chap. xi. 1), faith is thus defined by the apostle: 'Now faith is the *confidence* of things hoped for, the *conviction* of things not seen.' Faith is here expressed by the two words *confidence* and *conviction;* and its objects are *things hoped for—things not seen.*[*] Things hoped for must be future good things revealed and promised; and *confidence* in relation to such things must be a *confidence of persuasion*, founded on God's faithfulness and power, that what he hath promised he will undoubtedly perform; for it is thus explained: a being *persuaded* of the promises,—Heb. xi. 15; a *judging him faithful* who hath promised,—Heb. xi. 11; a being *fully persuaded* that what God hath promised he is able also to perform,

---

[*] Although the word *substance* comes nearer to the etymology of the original word, yet its use in Scripture must chiefly be consulted. The LXX. frequently use it to express *confidence* or *confidence of expectation*.—Ruth i. 12; Ps. xxxix. 7; Ezek. xix. 5. In the New Testament it occurs five times; in three of which it is translated *confidence*, viz., 2 Cor. ix. 4, and xi. 17; Heb. iii. 14; and even in this place the translators have so rendered it in the margin. The word translated *evidence* occurs only twice in the New Testament, viz., in this place and in 2 Tim. iii. 16, where it is translated *reproof*, but without any necessity. The word *conviction* agrees best with the original verb, which is generally translated *convince*, as in John viii. 9; Acts xviii. 28; 1 Cor. xiv. 24; Tit. i. 9; James ii. 9; Jude 15, as it should also be in John xvi. 8; 2 Tim. iv. 2. Although the original word sometimes signifies the *evidence, proof,* or *demonstration* which produces conviction; yet, when expressive of faith, it must necessarily mean *conviction* itself, which is the effect of evidence upon the mind.

—Rom. iv. 21. This confidence of faith in the Divine promises is inseparable from *hope;* for it is the confidence of things hoped for, and it is said to be a *believing in hope* (Rom. iv. 18), viz., of obtaining the good things promised. Again, faith is here defined more generally—the *conviction of things not seen.* Things not seen include not only things promised, but things testified,—John iii. 33; 2 Thess. i. 10; not only good things to be hoped for, but evil things to be dreaded,—Heb. xi. 7; not merely things future, but things past and present,—Heb. xi. 3, 6. They must all, however, so far as they are the objects of faith, be *things not seen;* for faith is opposed to sight,—2 Cor. v. 7; it being a conviction of the truth and reality of things made known by revelation, and grounded on the authority of that revelation, considered as the Word of God."—1 Thess. ii. 13.

" This simple notion of faith may be illustrated and confirmed by the following observations :—

1. " The gospel is held forth as a *witness, record,* or *testimony* concerning this great truth, that Jesus is the Christ, the Son of God, and that God hath given eternal life in him to all who believe.—1 John v. 5–13. Those who were sent to testify the gospel of the grace of God, are termed *witnesses.* John the Baptist ' came for a witness to bear witness of the Light.'—John i. 7. The apostles were ' chosen witnesses' to testify this truth to the world.—John xv. 27; Acts x. 39, 41. And the Father, the Word, and the Holy Spirit are represented as three concurring witnesses to the same important truth,—1 John v. 7; and hence it is termed the *witness* or *testimony of God,*—1 John v. 9; 1 Cor. ii. 1.

2. " The immediate design of all testimony or witness-bearing is, to *produce a belief* of the truth of what is testified. This is the declared design of testifying the gospel. John ' came to bear witness of the Light, that all men through him might believe.'—John i. 17. ' He that saw it bear record, that ye might believe.'—John xix. 35. This is also the design of the miraculous works by which the gospel testimony was confirmed.—John x. 36–38, v. 36, and xx. 31.

3. " Agreeably to these observations, faith is described to be a belief corresponding to that which is spoken, testified, or preached. Abraham, whose faith is set before us as an example, ' believed according to that which was spoken.'—Rom. iv. 18. Such also was the faith of the Thessalonians : ' Our testimony among you was believed,'—2 Thess. i. 10; and of the Corinthians : ' So we preach, and so ye believed.'—1 Cor. xv. 11. We all know what it is to receive or believe the witness of men in the most important affairs of human life; and by this the Apostle John gives us an idea of that faith which the gospel requires, without making any difference whatever in the nature of believing, but only substituting the testimony of God in place of that of men. ' If

we receive the witness of men, the witness of God is greater.'—1 John v. 9. We receive men's testimony by believing that they are true in what they declare; so, 'he that *receiveth* His testimony, hath set to his seal that God is true.'—John iii. 33. In the former case, we believe *men;* in the latter, we believe *God;* but this difference respects only the *object;* the nature of *believing* being the same in both cases. The witness of God is *greater* than that of men; but this does not alter the nature of belief, but only increases the degree of it, by giving us greater assurance; for men are fallible, and may be deceived themselves; but neither of these is possible with God, to whom omniscience and faithfulness are absolutely essential. That by *receiving* the witness of God, the apostle means nothing more than simply *believing* it, is evident; for he expresses its opposite thus: 'He that *believeth not* God hath made him a liar, because he *believeth not* the record that God gave of his Son.'—1 John v. 10. It is, therefore, evident from the whole, that faith is neither more nor less than *belief;* and that saving faith is a *belief of the gospel*, or of God's testimony concerning his Son."

We may here remark, that the general personal object of faith is *God* essentially considered as Father, Son, and Holy Ghost; but the special personal object is *Jesus Christ*. Again, the general object is the *whole Word of God*, in which his name, and nature, and perfections are revealed; but the particular object is the *promise* in the Word, or the *offer of Christ* in the gospel.

Obs. 284.—*By faith the sinner receives and rests on Christ alone for salvation.*

1. By faith we are said to *receive Christ*, because he is exhibited under the notion of a *gift*, which is presented to the children of men, who are spiritually wretched and poor in the extreme.—2 Cor. ix. 15; Rev. iii. 17, 18. It also shows the part which the Father acts in the work of salvation. "He gave the Son." He presents the gift; which, if we do not receive, we incur his displeasure, because we reject his grace; and thus make him a liar, by not believing the record or testimony which he hath given concerning his Son,—that is, by not crediting what he testifies, viz., "That he hath given us eternal life through him."—1 John v. 10, 11.

2. By faith we are said to *rest on Christ*, because he is exhibited to us as the sure foundation which God hath laid in Zion, upon which we may rest the burden of all our spiritual and eternal concerns with the fullest satisfaction.—Isa. xxviii. 16; Ps. cxvi. 7. It may be here observed, that there is an expression frequently used in the Old Testament, which seems to be exactly of the same import with *resting upon*, viz., *trusting in*,—that is, an implicit reliance or dependence upon God, or upon the righte-

ousness of his Son, for acceptance with him. See Isa. xxvi. 4, xlv. 24, and innumerable passages in the Book of Psalms.

It is said that we must receive and rest on *Christ alone* for salvation, in order to exclude every thing else but Christ and his righteousness, as the ground of our acceptance with God, and our title to eternal life; and this is done in opposition to those who substitute other things in the room of the perfect righteousness of the Redeemer.

1. There are some who trust in the *general mercy* of God, and place their hope in it. This is done by those who have never seen the necessity of a satisfaction for sin. Such would exalt mercy at the expense of justice. If they could be saved at all, they do not care whether it were in an honourable way or not—whether it were in a way consistent with the Divine attributes or not. This is quite dishonourable to God, and not at all agreeable to what we read in Exod. xxxiv. 6, 7. Let such remember, that without a satisfaction for sin there can be no remission.

2. There are others who rest upon the *works of the law* as the ground of their hope and confidence. This is done by those who have never seen the spirituality and extent of the law; who have never found themselves under the curse; and who have never seen their utter inability to obey the law perfectly in any thing whatever.—Gal. iii. 10–12. Let such remember, that if our first parents, while in innocence, could not gain life in this way, much less can they who have lost all ability to obey the law perfectly.

3. There are others, again, who join together the *righteousness of Christ and their own works*, as the ground of their hope and confidence. This is waxing still worse and worse; and it is done by those who have seen neither the perfection of Christ's atonement nor their own sinfulness. Such imagine that Christ will make up their deficiency; but this is a most preposterous idea. and highly dishonourable to the blessed Trinity, inasmuch as it intimates, that they cannot save without the sinner's doings, or that their work is imperfect without his. See Rom. ix. 31–33. Here there must be extreme ignorance respecting the method of salvation revealed in the Scriptures.

The end of faith is *salvation*,—that is, salvation from sin and from wrath.—Matt. i. 21; 1 Pet. i. 8, 9. 1. *Salvation from sin* includes salvation from the *guilt* of sin, or that in sin which exposes us to the punishment due to it.—Rom. vi. 23. Salvation from the *pollution* or *defilement* of sin, or that in sin which renders us altogether as an unclean thing, and consequently unfit for the kingdom of heaven; for nothing unclean can enter the New Jerusalem. Salvation from the *dominion* or *power* of sin, or that in sin by which we are rendered incapable of serving the Lord acceptably, or with reverence and godly fear.—Rom. vi. 12, &c. And salvation from the very *being* of sin, which becomes more and more visible as we improve the atonement, and which is entirely removed at death, but not till then. 2. *Salvation from wrath* is the consequence of salvation from sin; and hence, salvation from sin must doubtless be a greater salvation than salvation from wrath. In a word, the salvation for which we rest upon Christ, consists of a life of holiness here, as well as of happiness hereafter.—Matt. i. 21; 2 Tim. i. 9; Rev. iii. 21. Hence, "If any one is conscious that he is contented if his faith can only deliver him from future punishment and secure the possession of heaven, he has too much reason to suspect that he has yet to learn the nature of faith as described in the gospel. An habitual feeling of this sort is a sure evidence of an unregenerate mind, deceiving itself with something far short of faith in the Redeemer."

Faith in Jesus Christ, then, is a feeling of trust in him for salvation in all its parts. The believer trusts in Christ for pardon of sin, sanctification of soul, and eternal glory. He believes, that on account of what Christ hath done for sinners, his past sins are already pardoned; that the Spirit of Christ, which now dwells in him, shall enable him to purify his soul in obeying the truth to the end; and that in due time he shall obtain the promised glory.

Obs. 285.—*Jesus Christ is to be received by us for salvation as he is offered in the gospel.*

1. Jesus Christ is offered *freely*, in opposition to any thing that the sinner can bring as a price for Christ or his salvation. The gift of God is above all price—infinitely valuable, bestowed on sinners of mankind out of the sovereign and boundless love of the Father.

2. Jesus Christ is offered *wholly*. God hath given his Son to us, not for one purpose only, but for every purpose; not in one character or relation, but in every character and relation which he sustains. To receive Christ wholly, then, is to receive him in his person and in all his offices, which are all necessary for us, —it is to receive him as our prophet, as our priest, and as our king.

3. Jesus Christ is offered *particularly*. It is not enough to believe that Christ is offered to all in general, because there can be no benefit by a belief of the general offer of Christ, without a particular application of him by the person himself to whom he is offered. It is not enough to believe and be persuaded of the mercy of God in Christ,—that he is able and willing to save sinners; but he must be persuaded that Christ is able and willing to save us in particular. As the law condemns not only all in general, but every one in particular; so nothing can relieve the sinner thus condemned in particular, but the particular application of Jesus Christ by faith. "The general truth, that God so loved the world, that he gave his only begotten Son, who is able

and willing to save to the uttermost all that come to him, will prove perfectly inadequate to call forth the sinner's love. He must embrace and rest upon Christ for his own individual salvation, before this can possibly take place. Never will a sinner be able sincerely to say, *I love God*, till he can likewise add. *because he first loved me*. The Psalmist gives a just account of the manner in which love to God is produced, when he says, ' I love the Lord, because he hath heard the voice of my supplication; and hath delivered my soul from death, mine eyes from tears, and my feet from falling.'—Ps. cxvi. This must every sinner be able to say, with more or less confidence, regarding his eternal salvation, before he can be rationally expected to experience any cordial love to God.''

Should the trembling sinner feel any hesitation to make this application of the doctrine, which every individual must make to himself, in order to possess faith in Christ, he might be argued with in the following manner:—" Doubt not that the blood of Christ the Son of God cleanseth from all sin; and that by him all who believe are justified from all things from which they could not be justified by the law.—1 John i. 7; Acts xiii. 39. This is the record which God hath given of his Son. If, therefore, thou believest not that God is now willing to receive thee for his Son's sake, thou makest God a liar, and deniest that Jesus is the Christ.—1 John ii. 12, and v. 10. Thou believest, it is true, that he died for the sins of the world; but believing this, thou believest not that his atonement is sufficient for thy sins. Thus thou wouldst rob him of his peculiar character, and render him no more the Lamb of God that taketh away the sins of the world, and whose blood justifieth from all things all that believe. Thou sayest that thou art a wicked creature, and that thou art unworthy of so great a mercy; and it is true. Thou art indeed a most guilty and polluted sinner, who deservest the wrath of God to be poured out upon thee; but if the blood of Christ cannot justify thee *now*, when shall it become more powerful, and when shalt thou become less guilty? Will thy future conduct atone for thy sins for which the blood of Christ is unable to atone? Wilt thou not rather add guilt to thy former iniquity, and daily become more deserving of the fiery indignation which shall devour the adversaries? Reject not, then, the counsel of God against thyself. Thou believest that Christ died for our sins, and rose again for our justification; be assured, then, that thy sins are forgiven thee for his sake. Believe the Word of God when he tells thee, ' That whosoever believeth shall not perish, but have everlasting life.' He is not a man that he should lie. Hath he promised, and will he not bring it to pass? If, however, thou wilt not believe, thou shalt remain in thy sins, and the curse of God shall abide upon thee. But still be assured, that though thou perish, it is not the less true that there is nothing wanting on the part of Christ to forgive thy sins, and to bestow on thee everlasting glory. Whether thou believe or not, this is true now, and will be true throughout eternity. Thy belief alone is wanting to put thee in actual possession of what Christ is able and willing to confer, and is now offering freely to bestow. Let not, then, thy unbelief prove thy ruin. Add not to the former amount of thy transgressions this only unpardonable sin—that of doing despite unto the Spirit of grace, in trampling under foot the blood of the Son of God."

Obs. 286.—*The gospel offer of salvation is made to all men, but the promise of salvation is made to those only who believe.*

1. "The *declaration* and *call* of the gospel are, to all of every nation, condition, and character, without any limitation or restriction whatever.—Mark xvi. 16; Rom. x. 12; Gal. iii. 28; Matt. ix. 13; Luke vii. 37–50, and xxiii. 43; Acts ii. 37–40; 1 Cor. vi. 9–12; 1 Tim. i. 13. The gospel holds forth a *free* salvation, without any consideration of men's good works or qualifications, either to merit it, or to prepare and fit themselves for it. Salvation is everywhere ascribed to the sovereign free grace of God.—Eph. ii. 5; Tit. iii. 5; Rom. xi. 5, and iii. 24; Eph. i. 5, 6; Rom. iv. 16, xi. 6, and iv. 5, 16; Eph. i. 8. The gospel also *calls* all men everywhere to faith and repentance, and *invites* them in the most earnest manner to partake of a full and free salvation.—Isa. lv. 1–8; Matt. xi. 28; John vii. 37, 38; Luke xiv. 16–24. The apostles not only declared the gospel testimony, but called every one to believe it to their salvation; and they urged this call by every motive and argument with which the gospel furnished them; and which are the strongest that can be proposed to the human mind.—2 Cor. v. 18–21; Acts xvii. 30, 31 iii. 19, xx. 21, and xxvi. 20. But,

2. "Although the gospel declaration and call are universal, yet the *promise* of salvation is only to him who *believeth.*—Mark xvi. 16; Rom. x. 9. The gospel does not declare that *all* shall be saved; nor, indeed, that any shall be saved who do not believe It declares the testimony of God concerning his Son, and the salvation that is in him; calls upon all mankind to believe that testimony; and promises salvation to every one that believeth it, but to none else. Hence, the gospel promise of salvation is not universal, but restricted to him who believeth.—John iii. 16. Further, as the gospel does not promise salvation to any but believers, nor tells any particular person expressly and directly that he himself is a believer, so the assurance of a man's own justification is founded, not merely upon the *direct testimony* of God, but also upon the testimony of his own conscience, bearing him witness in the Holy Spirit, *that he believes* the gospel testimony concerning Christ, and so *is justified* according to the tenor of the gospel promise."

Obs. 287.—*No sinner can believe of himself; or, in other words, faith is the gift of God.*

"Although the knowledge and belief of the truth is a duty incumbent on all who hear the gospel; yet this belief is the special gift of God, being the effect of Divine teaching by means of the Word, and peculiar to the elect."—Eph. ii. 8; Phil. i. 29; John vi. 45; Rom. x. 17; 1 John v. 1. For a sinner, dead in sin, to begin the exercise of faith, or of any of the graces of the Spirit, before the promises of these graces have begun to be performed to him, is absolutely impossible; and hence faith is here called a *saving grace*. It is called a *grace*, because it is freely bestowed on the sinner, without any thing going before, or any thing to recommend him to the notice of God; and it is called a *saving grace*, not because it is saving as it is an act of ours, or as if it were a condition, by the fulfilment of which we shall be saved (for this would be salvation by works, entirely opposed to the plan of salvation revealed in the gospel), but because salvation accompanies it wherever it is found of Divine operation. See Col. ii. 12. Whatever appearances of faith, then, there may be in false professors, they have not radically that perception of the truth, nor that persuasion of it on its proper evidence, which real believers have.

But here a caution is necessary with respect to the doctrine of Divine influence. "We must beware of misapplying this doctrine, by neglecting to believe in Christ till we feel the distinct operation of his Spirit enabling us to do so; or of neglecting to comply with the gospel call, on pretence of allowing God to accomplish his work by implanting the grace of faith. God bestows the gift of faith, by imperceptibly enabling men to consider and embrace his Word as rational creatures. We are not, then, to look for any sudden sensible impulse of Divine grace, as seamen wait for the flowing of the tide before they attempt to leave the harbour; nor are we to suppose it necessary, that we should in all cases be able to distinguish between the gracious operations of the Spirit, and the natural exercise of our own intellectual and active powers. We should trust entirely in the effectual aid of Divine grace, and ascribe all our salvation to Almighty power; and yet we are to attempt to believe and obey the gospel, as if we were able to do so of ourselves." We may further remark, that in our attempts to believe in Christ, we should not fix our attention on the operations of our mind, but on those external and heavenly objects which are exhibited to us in the gospel,— on "the facts and doctrines, the invitations and promises of the gospel—the divine person and mediatorial offices of Christ—his vicarious satisfaction on the cross, and his glorious ministry in the heavenly temple—his boundless compassion and mighty power—his unsearchable riches and enduring faithfulness"—in a word, on "the Lamb of God that taketh away the sins of the world."

Obs. 288.—*As we cannot discern the difference between the real believer and the mere professor by the confession of the mouth, when that confession accords with the form of sound words, it is necessary that true faith should be distinguished by its genuine effects upon the heart and life.*

This must be evident to every one. "And such is the important, interesting, and salutary nature of the saving truth testified in the gospel, with its suitableness and freeness for the chief of sinners, that it is no sooner *perceived* and *believed*, than it takes possession of the will and affections, and becomes in the soul the ground of its hope, trust, and reliance,—the object of its desire, acceptance, esteem, and joy,—and the principle of every holy, active, and gracious disposition of heart."

Here a caution is necessary. "These *effects*, of faith or of the truth believed, ought not to be confounded with *faith itself*, as is commonly done. Although faith is the confidence of *things hoped for*, and also worketh by *love;* yet it is neither hope nor love, for the apostle distinguisheth it from both: 'And now abideth faith, hope, love, these *three.*'—1 Jo.. xiii. 13. The same may be said of all its other effects upon the heart; for whatever is more than belief is more than faith, and ought to go by another name." We may here observe, that faith, hope, and love, are thus accurately distinguished: "The gospel presents a *faithful* testimony to be believed, exhibiting an *amiable* object to be loved, and *good things to come* to be hoped for. *Faith*, then, respects the truth of the testimony; *love*, what is amiable in it; and *hope*, the good things in prospect."

"But (it may be here asked) what necessity is there to make such a nice distinction? Can any harm arise from including in the nature of faith such holy dispositions, affections, and exercises of heart, as are confessedly inseparable from it?" To this we reply in the following considerations:—

1. "Unless we carefully distinguish faith from its effects, particularly on the point of a sinner's acceptance with God, the important doctrine of free justification by faith alone will be materially affected. The Scriptures pointedly declare, that God justifies sinners '*freely by his grace*, through the *redemption* that is in Jesus Christ,' and that this justification is received 'through *faith* in Christ's blood.'—Rom. iii. 24, 25. Faith in this case is always distinguished from, and opposed to, the works of the law; not merely of the ceremonial law, but of that law which respects the heart as well as the life.—Rom. iii. 20, 27, 28, and ix. 32; Gal. ii. 16, and iii. 9–15; Matt. xxii. 37–41. If, then, faith is not distinguished from, and opposed to, our conformity to the law, both outwardly

and inwardly, it cannot be said that we are 'justified by faith without the deeds of the law,' or that God 'justifieth the *ungodly*.'— Rom. iii. 28, and iv. 5. Faith, indeed, as a principle of action, 'worketh by love;' but it is not as thus working that it is imputed for righteousness; for it is expressly declared, that righteousness is imputed 'to him that *worketh not*, but *believeth* on him that justifieth the *ungodly*.'—Rom. iv. 5. 'It is of *faith*, that it might be by *grace*,'—Rom. iv. 16; and grace and works are represented as incompatible with each other,—Rom. xi. 6; for 'to him that *worketh* is the reward not reckoned of *grace*, but of *debt*,'—Rom. iv. 4. Now, when men include in the very nature of justifying faith such good dispositions, holy affections, and pious exercises of heart, as the moral law requires, and so make them necessary to a sinner's acceptance with God, it perverts the apostle's doctrine on this important subject, and makes justification to be at least 'as it were by the works of the law.'

2. "The effect of such doctrine upon the mind of an awakened sinner is obvious. He who conceives that, in order to his pardon and acceptance with God, he must first be possessed of such good dispositions and holy affections as are commonly included in the nature of faith, will find no immediate relief from the gospel, nor any thing in it which fully reaches his case, while he views himself merely as a guilty sinner. Instead of believing on Him who justifieth the ungodly, he believes, on the contrary, tha' he cannot be justified till he sustains an opposite character. Though Christ died for *sinners*—for the *ungodly;* yet he does not believe that Christ's death will be any benefit to him as a mere sinner, but as possessed of holy dispositions; nor does he expect relief to his conscience purely and directly from the atonement, but through the medium of a better opinion of his own heart or character. This sentiment, if he is really concerned about the salvation of his soul, must set him upon attempts to reform his heart, and to do something, under the notion of acting faith, that he may be justified; and all his endeavours, prayers, and religious exercises, will be directed to that end. The religion of thousands consists in a train of successive attempts of this kind, while they are agitated by alternate hopes and fears, according as they apprehend they have been successful or not in such self-justifying labours; and should any work themselves up to some degree of hope and peace by exertions of this kind, such hope does not arise from the work finished by the Son of God, as alone sufficient to justify the ungodly, but from some supposed change wrought upon their own hearts, entitling them to trust in him. So that the effect of this principle is either tormenting fear, or self-righteous confidence; and, therefore, it is equally inimical to true peace and real gospel holiness."

Obs. 289.—*The first and principal evidence of faith is consciousness.*

"All who really believe the gospel must be instantly more or less conscious of it. We are so constituted, that we cannot hear, or feel, or see objects without knowing it. The impressions which objects make upon our senses, and our consciousness of these impressions, are inseparable. Our minds are also so framed, that we cannot believe the truth of any report, without being immediately conscious that we do so. Whatever produces belief, excites at the same instant an inward consciousness of it; and in all ordinary cases we cannot be more sure that *a thing is true*, than that we ourselves *perceive it to be so*. This every man knows by experience. When, therefore, the light of the glorious gospel shines into the heart of a sinner with divine evidence, so as to produce conviction that it is the truth and testimony of God, it must necessarily be accompanied with a present consciousness in the mind of him who believes it and is affected by it. The Scriptures suppose that a believer is immediately conscious of his faith; for it calls him at the very first to confess it with his mouth unto salvation.—Rom. x. 9. Jesus asked the man whom he had cured of blindness, "Dost thou believe on the Son of God?'—John ix. 35. He also asks his disciples, ' But whom *say ye* that I am?'—Matt. xvi. 15 ; and Philip saith to the eunuch, 'If *thou believest* with all thine heart.'—Acts viii. 37. The confession demanded is that of a man's *own belief*, which no man could make in sincerity and truth without knowing that he believes. Accordingly, the Scripture confessions run in this manner : ' *We believe*, and are sure that thou art that Christ, the Son of the living God.'—John vi. 69. ' By this *we believe* that thou camest forth from God.'— John xvi. 30. ' Lord, *I believe*, —John ix. 38. '*I believe* that Jesus is the Son of God,'—Acts viii. 37. These confessions express not only their *belief*, but also their *consciousness* of it; and if we allow them to be sincere, and not spoken in ignorance or hypocrisy, they clearly prove, that those who believe the gospel know immediately that they do so, and can say, *I believe*. The most of these confessions were made on their first believing, and before their faith had been evidenced by their works. They could not, perhaps, answer all the metaphysical questions which men have agitated about the nature of faith, any more than the blind man could philosophize upon the nature of light and vision, or tell how Jesus opened his eyes; yet like him they could say, and with the like consciousness, ' One thing I know, that whereas I was blind, now I see.'—John ix. 25. The power of Jesus in giving sight to the blind man made him instantly sensible that he saw, and left no room for reasoning upon the subject; even so, when the import and evidence of the truth shines into the heart by the enlightening

Spirit, it has at once the double effect of producing *belief* and the *consciousness* of it. This consciousness of faith is the first and radical evidence to a man that he is justified according to the gospel promise, and upon this must all additional and succeeding proofs of it ultimately rest; for good works cannot prove to him that he is justified, unless he is at the same time conscious that they are the fruits of faith and love."

This may be made further evident from the following remarks:—

1. " It is recorded as matter of fact, that the first converts to Christianity were filled with *peace* and *joy*, as soon as they believed the gospel.—Acts ii. 24, viii. 39, x. 43, 46, xiii. 48, and xvi. 31-35; 1 Thess. i. 5, 6. Peace with God, and rejoicing in the hope of his glory, are immediately connected with being justified by faith.—Rom. v. 1, 2. The ' belief that they *may* be justified,' or ' the hope of being made just,' though a relief from despair, will not fully account for this peace and joy.* Believers enjoy peace with God in proportion to the evidence they have that their sins are forgiven them; and their joy is described to be a joy in God through the Lord Jesus Christ, by whom they have now received the reconciliation.—Rom. v. 11. The conscience is said to be purged or made perfect by the blood of Christ.— Heb. ix. 14, and x. 2. The sense of guilt in the conscience is a *sure* and *personal* thing, and the pain occasioned by it is the fear of Divine wrath upon the individual. The atonement *alone*, or *without more*, is sufficient to remove this fear, perfect the conscience, and give peace with God; but it does not produce this effect upon the conscience while the sinner views it only as a *possible* relief, or that by which he *may* be justified, and remains entirely uncertain whether he *is*, or ever *shall be*, justified by it or not. A concealed pardon cannot fully relieve or cleanse the conscience. A purged conscience, and the conscious sense of being purged, are one and the same thing. This is stated as a prerequisite to our serving the living God with freedom and acceptance, and supposes that we both believe the truth and are conscious that we do so.—Heb. ix. 14.

* To show that a believer, even in the full assurance of faith, has no evidence that God is *willing* to save him, some produce the faith of those who applied for bodily cures, which appears to be only a persuasion of Christ's *ability*. But the answer is easy. There was no universal declaration made, that Christ *would* heal all the diseased who believed his *power*. Such a declaration would have removed all doubts of his *willingness* from those who believed his *ability*, and would have left no room for saying, " If thou *wilt*, thou canst make me clean." But the gospel openly declares it to be the *will* of God, " That every one that seeth the Son, and believeth on him, should have everlasting life."—John vi. 40. And Jesus saith, " Him that cometh unto me, I will in no wise cast out," ver. 37. This gives the believer a claim on his *faithfulness*, and leaves him no room to suspect his *willingness*.

2. "The *Spirit of adoption* is also represented as the common privilege of all believers; for as they are 'all the children of God by faith in Christ Jesus' (Gal. iii. 26), so, 'because they are sons, God hath sent forth the Spirit of his Son into their hearts.' —Gal. iv. 6. By this Spirit they know their filial relation to God; for it witnesseth with their spirits that they are the children of God, and emboldens them to cry, 'Abba, Father.'—Rom. viii. 15, 16. Agreeably to which, Christ hath taught his disciples to pray, 'Our Father,' &c.

3. "Another immediate effect of believing the gospel is *love to God*, which supposes the knowledge of his love to us. It is indeed admitted, that when we perceive his good-will towards sinners in general, as manifested in the gospel, and know that there is forgiveness with him, so as to hope in his mercy, it will *reconcile* us to his character, and lead us to *esteem* and *reverence* him, and to *desire* his favour above every thing, though we should not yet be assured of his love to ourselves in particular; and this, no doubt, is love. But that love which is of the nature of *gratitude*, cannot take place without some degree of persuasion that we ourselves are beloved or benefited by the object of it. Accordingly, the apostle says, 'We love him because he first loved us' (1 John iv. 19),—*i. e.*, because we *know* this; for he had said before, 'We have known and believed the love that God hath to us.'

4. "*Obedience* is another effect of the belief of the truth. But believers are exhorted to obedience from the consideration of their being redeemed, and already in a justified state. They are commanded to *love* one another, and to *walk* in love, because God hath loved them, and even as Christ loved them, and gave himself for them,—John xiii. 34; 1 John iv. 11; Eph. v. 2; to *forgive* one another, because God, for Christ's sake, hath forgiven them,—Eph. iv. 32; Col. iii. 13; to *liberality* in alms-giving, because they know the grace of the Lord Jesus Christ, that though he was rich, yet for their sakes he became poor, that they through his poverty might be rich,—2 Cor. viii. 9; to *glorify* God in their body and spirit, which are God's, because they are not their own, but bought with a price,—1 Cor. vi. 20; and to be *holy* in all manner of conversation, passing the time of their sojourning here in *fear;* forasmuch as they know that they were redeemed with the precious blood of Christ, as of a lamb without blemish and without spot,—1 Pet. i. 15–20. These motives evidently suppose, that believers know that they are in a state of salvation; and that not as a *consequence* of their obedience, but as a *ground* or *reason* of it; for motives, in the order of nature, must be known and believed previous to the conduct which is influenced by them. The knowledge of their salvation, therefore, must originate in, and be constantly supported by, the gospel itself standing true in their minds, and so drawing forth the testimony of

their conscience that they believe it. This testimony will be more or less explicit, according to the degree of faith which is the subject of it; even as faith itself is weak or strong, in proportion to the degree of light and evidence with which the gospel by the Spirit shines into the mind, which is the foundation of both."

Obs. 290.—*Although consciousness is the first and radical evidence which a man has of his own salvation in believing the gospel, yet this does not supersede other proofs of it to his own conscience.*

" This principal evidence still leaves room for additional evidence, not, however, that God is true, but that the person himself is a true believer;* and for this the Scripture refers him to the genuine effects of the gospel on his heart and life. The Word of God supposes that men may deceive themselves in this important matter,—Gal. vi. 3; and repels the vain pretensions of such as say they believe and know God, and have fellowship with him, whilst they walk in darkness and keep not his commandments,—1 John i. 6, and ii. 4, 5; James ii. 20. Nay, it supposes that men may be enlightened, receive the word with joy, for a while believe, know the way of righteousness, and even escape the pollutions of the world through the knowledge of the Lord and Saviour, and yet fall away irrecoverably.—Luke viii. 13; Heb. vi. 4–6, and x. 26; 2 Pet. ii. 20, 21. These things are set before believers with a view to guard them against presumption, and to awaken in them a cautious fear lest they should grow barren and unfruitful in the knowledge of Christ, and depart from the living God through unbelief.—John xv. 2, 6; Rom. xi. 19–28; 1 Cor. x. 11, 12; Heb. iii. 12; 2 Pet. iii. 17; 2 John viii. On the other hand, Jesus said to those who believed on him, ' If ye continue in my word, then are ye my disciples indeed.'—John viii. 31. ' If ye keep my commandments, ye shall abide in my love.'—John xv. 19. His beloved disciple writes in the same strain : ' But whoso keepeth his word, in him verily is the love of God perfected: hereby know we that we are in him. We know that we have passed from death unto life, because we love the brethren. Hereby know we that we are of the truth, and shall assure our hearts before him. And he that keepeth his commandments dwelleth in him, and he in him ; and hereby we know that he abideth in us, by the Spirit which he hath given us.'—1 John ii. 5. and iii. 14, 19, 24. These and such passages clearly show that believers know their connection with Christ, not merely by con-

---

* No doubt the truth of God is more and more confirmed to a believer as he experiences the effects of his Word, and the accomplishment of his promises ; but the point in hand is the evidence of a man's own salvation : and it is one thing to know *that God is true*, and another to know *that I am a true believer*.

scious belief, but also by faith working by love, and influencing them to keep his commandments. Accordingly, they are exhorted to give diligence to make their calling and election sure, by adding to their faith virtue, knowledge, temperance, patience, godliness, brotherly-kindness, and charity; and to show the same diligence to the full assurance of hope unto the end.—2 Pet. i. 5–12; Heb. vi. 11.* When the gospel first shines into a man's mind with Divine light and evidence, making itself manifest in his conscience as the Word of the living God, it does not leave him in painful uncertainty, either as to his faith or state, though he be not as yet conscious of all these effects by which he must afterwards try his faith. But when his faith works with his works, and brings forth the fruits of the gospel, and purifies his soul to the unfeigned love of the brethren, he sees it distinguished from that faith which is dead, being alone.—James ii. 17, 20, 26. When it overcomes the world, and raises him above the prevailing influence of the cares, riches, and pleasures of this life, his conscience bears him witness that he does not class with the thorny-ground professors.—Luke viii. 14. When it supports him under tribulations and trials, so that he does not faint or give way, this trial of his faith working patience, and being attended with Divine support and consolation, gives him experience that God is with him, and that he is distinguished from those who receive the word with joy, and for a while believe, but in time of temptation fall away.—James i. 3, 4; Rom. v. 3, 4; Luke viii. 13. By this his hope is confirmed that he shall endure unto the end, and that his faith will be found unto praise, and honour, and glory at the appearing of Jesus Christ.—I Pet. i. 5, 7. So that, as he continues in Christ's word, and grows in conformity to him, his experience of the love of God is enlarged, and the testimony of his conscience strengthened, by the Holy Spirit, the Comforter, giving him additional manifestations, and more abundant fellowship with Christ in his joy, as the earnest of the heavenly inheritance."—Rom. v. 5; John xiv. 21, 23, and xv. 9–12; Eph. i. 13, 14.

We may here remark, that we should not begin immediately, on our first believing, to look for those fruits of faith which distinguish the genuine disciples of Christ. "Before doing this, we should persevere for some time in applying to Jesus by the prayer of faith. Although the word of the Lord works effectually in them who cordially receive it, by bringing forth good fruit; yet

* When the apostle exhorts believers to give all diligence to make *their calling and election sure*, &c., some are of opinion that he means that we are to make them *sure to others;* but if we look to the end of the 10th verse, we shall find that he means that we are to make them sure to *ourselves*, to *our own consciences* in the sight of God: for it by no means follows, that because *others* may think our calling and election sure, therefore we shall *never fall*, but obtain the heavenly kingdom.

it works gradually, like the earth which produces ' first the blade, then the ear, and after that the full corn in the ear.' If we suddenly withdraw our attention from the object of faith, to search for the fruits of it, its influence in purifying our heart will thereby be greatly weakened, our spiritual joy will be interrupted, and our unbelieving fears revived. We should, therefore, hold fast the beginning of our confidence, by frequently renewing our application to Christ; that our faith may grow exceedingly, and that we may attain the full assurance of hope as the result of our experience."

Obs. 291.—*There are various evidences of the strength and weakness of faith.*

1. Faith appears to be *strong*, when it rests upon the word of a faithful God—faithful to the word upon which he hath caused us to hope, not when sense and reason seem to favour our hopes, but even when there is no evidence of hope from that quarter,—when we wait on the Lord and cleave to him in the midst of many and great difficulties,—Matt. xv. 21, &c.; when we commit ourselves to God in the most troublesome times, reposing ourselves on him with the utmost confidence,—Ps. cxii. 7; when we are found walking in all the commandments and ordinances of the Lord, notwithstanding the temptations, and reproaches, and sufferings to which we may be exposed from the world around us; and when we are found in love with those duties which appear disagreeable to flesh and blood, which we do not consult,—Heb. xi. 24, &c.

2. Faith appears to be *weak*, when we do not see the Divine word to be always a sure ground of hope; when we can suspect the favour and love of God to us,—Isa. xl. 27; when we murmur and complain if our prayers are not immediately answered,—Isa. xxxviii. 14; when we are more addicted to a life of sense than to a life of faith,—John xx. 27; and when we are much afraid of reproach, and suffering, and persecution for the sake of Christ and his gospel, &c. But if we have an inward hatred at sin as such—as contrary to the holiness of God; if we love Christ above all things, and account all things but loss for the excellent knowledge of him; and if we are well pleased with the plan of salvation appointed by God, and would be saved by Christ alone and his imputed righteousness; then, although weak, faith appears to be accompanied with salvation.

INFERENCES.

From this subject we learn,—1. The value and necessity of Christ. 2. The value and extent of the gospel. 3. The greatness of the love of God. 4. That Christ is in every respect a suitable Saviour. 5. That unbelief is the greatest sin, and the crowning one which excludes any man from the kingdom of heaven. 6. That the salvation which Christ offers, consists of deliverance from sin here, as well as from wrath hereafter. 7. The happiness of believers, or of those who receive the testimony of God concerning his Son; and the misery of unbelievers, or of those who reject this testimony.—Mark xvi. 16; 1 John v. 10–12.

SECT. 2.—OF REPENTANCE UNTO LIFE.

Q. 87.—What is Repentance unto Life?

Repentance unto life is a saving grace, whereby a sinner, out of a true sense of his sin, and apprehension of the mercy of God in Christ, doth, with grief and hatred of his sin, turn from it unto God, with full purpose of, and endeavour after new obedience.

ANALYSIS AND PROOFS.

We are here taught,—

1. That repentance unto life is a saving grace. 2 Cor. vii. 10. "Godly sorrow worketh repentance to salvation, not to be repented of." See also Acts xi. 18.

2. That in repentance there must be a true sense of sin. Ps. xli. 4.—"Against thee, thee only, have I sinned, and done this evil in thy sight." See also Ezek. xvi. 61.

3. That in repentance there is an apprehension of mercy in God. Rom. ii. 4.—"The goodness of God leadeth thee to repentance." See also Joel ii. 13.

4. That the mercy of God to the sinner is exhibited only in Christ. 2 Cor. v. 19.—"God was in Christ reconciling the world to himself." See also Rom. iii. 25.

5. That in true repentance there is a sincere grief for sin. Jer. xxxi. 19.—"I was ashamed, yea, even confounded, because I did bear the reproach of my youth." See also ver. 18.

6. That in true repentance there is a sincere hatred of sin. Ezek. xxxvi. 31.—"Then shall ye remember your own evil ways, and your doings that were not good, and shall loathe yourselves in your own sight, for your iniquities, and for your abominations." See also Ps. cxix. 128.

7. That in true repentance the sinner turns from his sin. Ezek. xviii. 30.—"Repent, and turn yourselves from all your transgressions." See also Jer. xxxi. 18.

8. That in true repentance the sinner returns to God. Lam. iii. 40.—"Let us search and try our ways, and turn again to the Lord."

9. That in true repentance there is a full purpose of obedience to God. Ps. cxix. 59.—"I thought on my ways, and turned my feet unto thy testimon   See also ver. 8

10. That in true repentance there is an anxious endeavour to obey God. Jer. xxxi. 18.—" Turn thou me, and I shall be turned, for thou art the Lord my God."

11. That the obedience which follows true repentance is new obedience. Rom. vii. 6.—" That we should serve in newness of spirit, and not in the oldness of the letter."

EXPLANATION.

Obs. 292.—*Repentance is commonly distinguished into legal repentance and evangelical repentance.*

1. *Legal repentance*, or what the apostle calls " the sorrow of the world, which worketh death " (2 Cor. vii. 10), is that legal sorrow or horror of conscience which the men of the world have, or may have, from the fear of God, not as a reconciled God, but as a vindictive judge, ready to take vengeance upon them, by pouring out the vials of his wrath. There may, indeed, be a sort of mourning for sin, a sight and sense of it, and a kind of turning from it to God, &c.; but the subjects of it are never conversant about sin as such, or as it is sin—offensive to God, and contrary to his spotless purity. This is the case only with those who have received the gift of repentance from God.

2. *Evangelical repentance*, here called *repentance unto life*, is that in which there is a true sight and sense of sin, and faith in the Divine mercy, or an apprehension of the mercy of God in Christ, whatever be the sin and its aggravations; and in which there is chiefly a view of sin, as committed against God, and as contrary to his holy nature and law,—Ps. li.; or, in a word, it is that " godly sorrow which is not to be repented of."

This true repentance is here called a *saving grace*. It is called a *grace*, because it is the *gift* of God. Acts xi. 18.—" Then hath God also to the Gentiles *granted* repentance unto life." Acts v 31.—" Christ is exalted a prince and a saviour to *give* repentance unto Israel, and remission of sins." Jer. xxxi. 18.— " Turn thou me, and I shall be turned." This would not be a very correct request, if repentance were not the *gift of God.* See also Zech. xii. 10. It is called a *saving grace*, because, wherever it is found, the subject of it is in a state of salvation; or because it is accompanied with salvation.—Luke xiii. 5.

With respect to the *subjects* of repentance, we may here remark, that, in a strict sense, the proper subjects are, not only those who are under the guilt of sin, or in an unjustified state, but also those who are justified, and to whom there is no condemnation, being in Christ Jesus; for although believers are not in sin, properly speaking, yet, not being wholly freed from it, it still cleaving to them while here, they also are the subjects of repentance as long as they continue in this world.

Obs. 293.—*True repentance is wrought in the heart of a sinner by the Spirit of God.*

That man cannot produce in himself that godly sorrow which is not to be repented of, is evident from the striking language of the Prophet Jeremiah (xxii. 23): "Can the Ethiopian change his skin, or the leopard his spots?" This must be deemed an impossibility. In like manner, it is equally impossible for a sinner to turn himself from sin unto God; and, accordingly, it is added, "Then may ye also do good that are accustomed to do evil." It is true, indeed, that man may depart from some gross sins; but the voice of Scripture is, that the Spirit of God is the author of this grace.—Jer. xxxi. 18; Zech. xii. 10.

The *means* by which the Spirit works the grace of repentance in the heart of a sinner, is *the Word of God;* which must be here viewed in a twofold light—the *law* and the *gospel*, both of which are necessary. 1. The *law* serves as a hammer to break in pieces the hard and stony heart.—Jer. xxiii. 29.—"Is not my Word like a hammer that breaketh the rock in pieces?" 2. The *gospel* is the Word which accomplishes what the law cannot do. The law is like a hammer to break, but we may view the gospel as a fire to melt the hard heart. Jer. xxiii. 29.—"Is not my Word like a fire, saith the Lord?" It is the gospel that is the power of God to salvation—to every part of salvation; and without it no part of salvation can be accomplished. Hence, we must view the gospel as alluring to the soul—as drawing with the cords of love—as constraining to approach unto God—and as the still small voice in which a reconciled God speaks peace to the soul: and if this does not prove effectual for the purposes of salvation, nothing else will; for surely this is revealed for this very thing. All the thunders of the law will not bring one soul to God, or make it truly part with one beloved sin; but the gospel will make it forsake all and follow Christ, who died for our sins, and rose again for our justification.

Obs. 294.—*The springs of true repentance are, a true sense of sin, and an apprehension of the mercy of God in Christ.*

1. True repentance implies *a true sense of sin;* a sight and sense, not only of the danger, but also of the filthiness and odiousness of sin, as contrary to the spotless purity of God, and, consequently, as highly offensive to him.—Ps. li. 4. And from this it is evident, that there must be a sight of sin, before there can be a sense of its filthiness and odiousness. The eyes must be opened to behold this evil thing, and how it has pervaded the whole man; how it has dishonoured every part of the Divine law; what it has done with respect to its danger; and what Jehovah himself thinks of it.

2. True repentance supposes *an apprehension of the mercy of God in Christ;* or faith by which we can lay hold upon his

mercy—a conviction that there is forgiveness with him that he may be feared, and plenteous redemption through Christ, and in no other way; and this will excite repentance, and make tears of godly sorrow flow. And it is for this reason that mercy is said to be apprehended in Christ, because God was in Christ reconciling the world to himself, not imputing unto men their trespasses. —Zech. xii. 10.

With respect to the *order* of faith and repentance, we may here remark, that in respect of *time*, all the blessings of salvation are bestowed *at once;* but, in the order of *nature*, faith must precede repentance. This is evident from the nature of repentance itself. Repentance is a turning from sin to God; but there can be no turning to God but through Christ; and there can be no coming to Christ but by faith.—John xiv. 6, and vi. 35.

Obs. 295.—*In true repentance, which flows from faith, there must be grief for sin, hatred of sin, and a turning from sin unto God, with full purpose of, and endeavour after new obedience.*

1. In true repentance there must be *grief for sin*. This, if it flow from faith, will rest upon sin as such, and will be a true and an abiding sorrow on account of sin.

2. In true repentance there must be *hatred of sin*. This is a part of repentance nearly allied to the former; for we cannot be said to be affected with grief on account of sin, without being filled at the same time with a hatred of it. And wherever this hatred of sin is genuine, it will fill the soul with shame, and a loathing and an abhorring of ourselves on account of it.—Isa. vi 5; Job xl. 4, 5; 2 Cor. vii. 11. Hatred of sin is not genuine, if it is not universal and irreconcilable:—universal, against all sin; and irreconcilable to any known sin.

3. In true repentance there must be *a turning from sin unto God, with full purpose of new obedience and endeavour after it*. Properly speaking, this is what completes that repentance which is not to be repented of. And it consists chiefly in this; for it is this that evidences that sin is the object of our grief and hatred.

Turning from sin implies a turning from all sin, both in heart and life,—Ps. cxix. 113; a turning away from sin, and a resisting of its outbreakings; a turning from the sin that most easily besets us; a turning from all temptations to sin; and a watching against all occasions of sin, from a conviction that unwatchfulness is sinful in itself, and accompanied with the worst of consequences.—Prov. iv. 14, &c.

Returning to God implies, that the sinner must return to his love to God, as his lord and master, who has a claim upon his love to his person; and this by an unfeigned and a voluntary choice of him as his only lord.—Isa. xxvi. 13; Acts ix. 6; Hos. ii. 7.

Full purpose of new obedience implies, that the true penitent resolves to turn immediately to the practice of every known duty required of him by his Lord and Master, without gainsaying; and that he will serve him in spirit and in truth.—Ps. cxix. 6, and li. 6; Phil. iii. 3; Ps. cxix. 60.

But this is not all. There must be some evidence that the sinner acts according to his purpose; there must be an *endeavour after new obedience*. This, however, does not imply that the true penitent can perform the obedience required of him; but that he is not discouraged from making the attempt, seeing this is commanded, and is done by the children of God. The cause of a sinner's turning unto God, is his being turned by God; and if he performs the obedience required, it is in the strength of grace promised to him, by which he is encouraged to make the attempt.—Phil. iii. 14; 2 Cor. xii. 9; Deut. xxxiii. 25.

The obedience which follows true repentance is *new obedience;* and it is so called for the following reasons:—1. It proceeds from *new principles,*—faith in the authority of the Lawgiver, and love to his service.—John xiv. 15. 2. It is influenced by *new motives,* which are the grace of God, and the love of his Son; higher than which no motives can be named.—Tit. ii. 11, &c.; 2 Cor. v. 14, &c. 3. It is performed in a *new manner.* Formerly, the sinner trusted in himself for strength to perform obedience; now, he does all in the strength of Christ. Formerly, he had no dependence on the grace of the covenant; now, he rests upon the covenant, doing all things through Christ strengthening him. Formerly, his obedience was forced; now, he delights in the law of God after the inward man. Formerly, his heart was not placed upon God; now, he serves the Lord with his whole heart.—Ps. cxix. 69. 4. It is directed to a *new end.* Formerly, the sinner had not—could not have the glory of God in view; but now, the glory of God is the ultimate end of his new obedience.—1 Cor. x. 31.

INFERENCES.

From this subject we learn,—1. That salvation is by grace. 2. That all need repentance, but that it is not genuine in all. 3. That sin is the object of Heaven's abhorrence. 4. The necessity of prayer for the gift of repentance. 5. That repentance must be habitual and universal. 6. The danger of impenitence; that all who continue impenitent shall perish.—Luke xiii. 3, 5.

SECT. 3.—OF THE DILIGENT USE OF THE MEANS OF GRACE, VIZ.:— THE WORD OF GOD, THE SACRAMENTS, AND PRAYER.

Q. 88.—*What are the outward means whereby Christ communicateth to us the benefits of Redemption?*

The outward and ordinary means whereby Christ

communicateth to us the benefits of redemption, are his ordinances, especially the Word, sacraments, and prayer, all which are made effectual to the elect for salvation.

ANALYSIS AND PROOFS.

We are here taught,—
1. That there are certain means of grace to be observed by the people of God. Acts ii. 42.—" They continued stedfastly in the apostles' doctrine and fellowship, and in breaking of bread and in prayers."
2. That the means of grace have been appointed by Christ. Matt. xxviii. 20.—" Teaching them to observe all things whatsoever I have commanded you."
3. That the benefits of redemption are communicated by the means of grace. Eph. iv. 11, 12.—" He gave some, apostles; and some, prophets; and some, evangelists; and some, pastors and teachers; for the perfecting of the saints, for the work of the ministry, for the edifying of the body of Christ."
4. That the Word of God is a special means of grace. John xx. 31.—" These are written that ye might believe that Jesus is the Christ, the Son of God; and that, believing, ye might have life through his name."
5. That the sacraments are special mean of grace. 1 Cor. x 16.—" The cup of blessing which we bless, is it not the communion of the blood of Christ? The bread which we break, is it not the communion of the body of Christ?"
6. That prayer is a special means of grace. Mark xi. 24.— " What things soever ye desire when ye pray, believe that ye receive them, and ye shall have them."
7. That the means of grace are, by the Spirit, rendered effectual to the salvation of God's people. 1 Thess. i. 5.—" The gospel came not unto you in word only, but also in power, and in the Holy Ghost, and in much assurance." See also 1 Tim. iv. 16.

EXPLANATION.

Obs. 296.—*The outward and ordinary means of grace are the ordinances or institutions of Christ.*

A *means*, in general, is something which goes before the end in view; which end cannot be obtained if this something be neglected. A *means of salvation*, then, is *that through which salvation flows* into the soul from the God of salvation. It is something in which God exhibits himself with all that he is, and all that he hath. It is something, if we may so speak, which comes between God and the soul, in which the best interests of the soul are exhibited, and by which that is conveyed to the soul which is necessary for grace and glory.

The means of salvation are, the ordinances or institutions of Divine appointment, by which Christ communicates to sinners the benefits of redemption; and they have been distinguished into *outward* and *inward* means of grace. The *outward* means are, the Word, the sacraments, and prayer; and the *inward* means are, faith and repentance, and such like, and particularly the inward and powerful influences of the Holy Spirit. And these are necessary to accompany the outward means in order to salvation, and are wrought by their instrumentality.—Heb. iv. 2; Rom. x. 17. We may here remark, that what makes an ordinance a means of salvation, is just the *Divine warrant*—the appointment of Christ the King and Head of the Church. Matt. xxviii. 19, 20.

The ordinances are called *ordinary* means, to distinguish them from any thing extraordinary which may be in the salvation of any: but which we have no reason to expect, because we have no promise of this, and, consequently, no foundation on which our faith may rest, that it shall be so with us; or, in other words, they are called *ordinary*, because they are the stated method by which Christ communicates the benefits of his purchase to sinners of mankind. Rom. x. 14, &c.

The means of grace are called *Christ's* ordinances, because they are all instituted by him as the Head of the Church, and the King of Zion; and, consequently, they are to be observed in the Church until the end of the world.

Obs. 297.—*The special means of grace are, the Word, the sacraments, and prayers.*

1. The *Word* read and preached is a special means of salvation. Salvation must be heard of before it can be embraced, and in whatever way we hear of it, that way is doubtless a means of salvation. And if it be read or preached, the same blessings are exhibited; and the same God addresses us, and beseeches us to receive Christ for all the purposes of eternal life.—John xx. 31; 1 Pet. i. 23; John v. 39; Deut. xvii. 18-20; Acts xv. 21; 2 Tim. iv. 2; James i. 21; Acts x. 33. The reading of the Word is an ordinance of Divine institution which is most shamefully neglected, both in private and in public; notwithstanding that God has promised to accompany the reading of it with his blessing. How small a portion of the Scriptures is read in the course of a year, in most places of public worship! No wonder that so little good is done in the present time, when the divinely-inspired and life-giving oracles are thus neglected!

2. The *sacraments*, baptism and the Lord's supper, are special means of salvation. It must, however, be remembered, that they are not converting, but confirming and sealing ordinances. They represent to our senses what the Word represents to our faith: and they are designed to confirm and strengthen

our faith and the other graces of the Spirit. And they to whom they are administered (we speak particularly of the Lord's Supper) are supposed to have felt the powerful efficacy of the former means of salvation, viz., the reading and preaching of the Word.

3. *Prayer* is a special means of salvation. This is a peculiar mode of communion between Christ and the soul; and it brings home to one's self all the good which the Word exhibits, and which the sacraments represent.—Matt. xi. 24. Every one that is at all concerned about his best interests, will use this means, and that for ever,—not only until he know in whom he has believed, but until he actually come and appear before his God in his holy habitation.

Obs. 298.—*The means of salvation instituted by Christ are made effectual to all the people of God.*

The ordinances are made effectual to the *elect* for salvation.— Acts ii. 47, and xiii. 48. That they are not made effectual to all for salvation, is evident both from the Word of God and from observation. The complaint of the ancient prophet (Isa. liii. 1), "Who hath believed our report, and to whom is the arm of the Lord revealed?" was likewise made by Christ in the days of his flesh, and by the Apostle Paul, expressive of their sense of the disregard which is generally manifested to the means of salvation. And it has been the uniform complaint of the faithful in all ages, that the report of the servants of Christ has not been believed; the greater part walking in their own ways, unmindful of their best interests. But, although multitudes reject Christ, and finally neglect his great salvation, yet they have the offer of it, to show the infinite value of Christ's satisfaction—that in it there is enough for all, and that none are excluded who do not exclude themselves; and, at the same time, to render those the more inexcusable, who slight the precious privileges that are conferred upon them.

It must ever be remembered, that the ordinances of Christ's appointment have no efficacy *in themselves*. It is the *divine blessing* alone that can make them effectual to salvation. Without this, any heavenly institution would be but a dead letter, sounding brass, and a tinkling cymbal. This happens in the case of too many, who rest merely in the form, without seeking after the power of godliness.

Obs. 299.—*By the ordinances of his own appointment, Christ communicates to sinners the benefits of redemption.*

By the *benefits of redemption* we are to understand all the blessings of Christ's purchase, which may be summed up in grace here and glory hereafter.—Ps. lxxxiv. 11. And, agreeably to Scripture, the communication of the benefits of redemption is here ascribed to *Christ*, who has every thing of this nature wholly at his own disposal: according to what he himself saith,—Luke

xxii. 29, and Matt. xxviii. 18. This power Christ does not usurp; for of right it belongs to him, and that in consequence of the gift of the Father,—John iii. 35; and also in consequence of his own purchase; and hence the benefits of redemption are called a *purchased possession.*—Eph. i. 14.

INFERENCES.

From this subject we learn,—1. How comfortless they are who have not the means of salvation; and that it is our duty to send these means where they are not. 2. That, as there are degrees of favour, so there will also be degrees of punishment. 3. The necessity of observing the ordinances of Christ, without which we cannot expect salvation. 4. That they who despise them are not in the way of salvation. 5. The peculiar importance of having them purely dispensed. 6. That something more is necessary than a mere formal observance of them.

DIV. 1.—OF THE WORD OF GOD AS A MEANS OF GRACE.

Effects of the Word of God.

Q. 89.—How is the Word made effectual to Salvation? The Spirit of God maketh the reading, but especially the preaching of the Word, an effectual means of convincing and converting sinners, and of building them up in holiness and comfort, through faith unto salvation.

ANALYSIS AND PROOFS.

We are here taught,—

1. That the Holy Spirit alone makes the Word effectual to salvation. 1 Pet. 1. 22.—" Ye have purified your souls in obeying the truth, through the Spirit." See also 2 Cor. iii. 18.

2. That the reading of the Word is made an effectual means of convincing sinners. 2 Kings xxii. 10, 11.—" Shaphan read it before the king. And it came to pass, when the king had heard the words of the book of the law, that he rent his clothes."

3. That the reading of the Word is made an effectual means of converting sinners. Ps. xix. 7.—" The law of the Lord is perfect, converting the soul."

4. That the reading of the Word is an effectual means of building up God's people in holiness. Acts xx. 32.—" I commend you to God, and to the word of his grace, which is able to build you up, and to give you an inheritance among all them that are sanctified."

5. That the reading of the Word is an effectual means of comforting God's people. Rom. xv. 4.—" Whatsoever things were written aforetime, were written for our learning, that we, through patience and comfort of the Scriptures, might have hope."

6. That the reading of the Word is made effectual to salvation, through faith. 2 Tim. iii. 15.—" From a child thou hast known the Holy Scriptures, which are able to make thee wise unto salvation, through faith which is in Christ Jesus."

7. That the preaching of the Word is especially an effectual means of convincing sinners. Acts ii. 37.—" When they heard this, they were pricked in their heart, and said unto Peter and to the rest of the apostles, Men and brethren, what shall we do?"

8. That the preaching of the Word is especially an effectual means of converting sinners. Acts xxvi. 17, 18.—" The Gentiles, unto whom I now send thee, to open their eyes and to turn them from darkness to light, and from the power of Satan unto God."

9. That the preaching of the Word is especially an effectual means of building up God's people in holiness. Col. i. 28.— " We preach, warning every man, and teaching every man in all wisdom, that we may present every man perfect in Christ Jesus."

10. That the preaching of the Word is especially an effectual means of comforting God's people. 1 Thess. iii. 2.—" And sent Timothy to establish you, and to comfort you concerning your faith."

11. That the preaching of the Word is made effectual to salvation, only through faith. Heb. iv. 2.—"The Word preached did not profit them, not being mixed with faith in them that heard it."

EXPLANATION.

Obs. 300.—*The reading of the Word, but especially the preaching of it, is made, by the Spirit, an effectual means of salvation.*

1. The *reading of the Word*, or of the Scriptures of the Old and New Testaments, is a means of salvation appointed by God.

The Word of God is to be read by all sorts of people in secret. —Deut. xvii. 19; John v. 39; Isa. xxxiv. 16; and in their families,—Deut. vi. 6-9; Gen. xviii. 17-19; Ps. lxxviii. 5-7, and lxxix. 6; Jer. x. 25. It is also to be read by ministers in the public assemblies of the people of God.—Deut. xxxi. 9, &c.; Neh. viii. 2, &c., and ix. 3, &c. But this is a duty much neglected in the present day; notwithstanding that the reading of the Word is appointed as a means of convincing and converting sinners.— 1 Tim. iv. 13. If Moses was publicly read in the synagogue every Sabbath-day, ought not Christ to be publicly read in the congregation every Lord's day?

The Holy Scriptures are to be read,—(1.) With a high and reverend esteem of them, because they are the Word of God given by inspiration of the Holy Ghost, and able to make men wise unto salvation.—Ps. xix. 10; Isa. lxvi. 2. (2.) With a firm persuasion that they are the very Word of God; because, unless fully convinced of this, we shall never view them as a sufficient foundation, upon which we may build our hopes of salvation,—in them we shall never hope, nor in them shall we ever trust, as containing the words of eternal life.—1 Thess. ii. 13; 2 Pet. i. 19, &c. (3.) With a firm persuasion that God alone can enable us to understand them; because, being a revelation from God, they are too spiritual to be understood by any exertion of the natural powers of man.—1 Cor. ii. 14, and iii. 13, &c.; Luke xxiv. 45.

2. The *preaching of the Word* is especially an effectual means of salvation appointed by God.

The Word of God is to be *preached* only by such as are sufficiently qualified, and also duly approved, and called to that office. —Eph. iv. 8, &c.; Mal. ii. 7; Rom. x. 15; 1 Tim. iv. 14. The epistles of the Apostle Paul to Timothy and Titus, fully show what the character of a preacher of the Word of God should be.

They who are called to preach the gospel, are to preach sound doctrine,—that is, they must declare the whole counsel of God respecting the plan of salvation; they must preach the whole of revealed truth contained in the Scriptures of the Old and New Testaments, and what is evidently implied in it, although not expressed. And this they must do,—(1.) *Diligently.*—2 Tim. iv. 2. Every opportunity must be seized, that the souls of men may be profited, and that God may be glorified. (2.) *Plainly.* —1 Cor. ii. 4, and xiv. 9. The gospel must be preached with plainness and simplicity, and in language level to the capacities of all. Some seem to forget that all have souls to be saved, when they adapt their language to the capacities only of a few. (3.) *Faithfully.*—Jer. xxiii. 28; 1 Cor. iv. 1, 2; Acts xx. 27. To preach faithfully is to make known, or not to shun to declare, the whole counsel of God, or every part of the will of God necessary for salvation. (4.) *Wisely.*—1 Cor. iii. 2; Heb. v. 12; Luke xii. 42. A minister may be said to preach wisely, when, in studying, he suits himself to the necessities and capacities of his hearers. (5.) *Zealously.*—Acts xviii. 25. The motive to zeal in the ministers of the gospel is the highest possible; and if they feel its constraining influence they cannot but be zealous in His cause; and this motive is the love of Christ, by which Paul was always actuated.—2 Cor. v. 14, and xii. 15. A want of zeal in preaching the gospel bespeaks no great desire to save the sinner; which is one of the great designs of the ministry; and they who are not actuated in this work by love to the souls of men, bear the name, but want the essentials which constitute the character of a minister of Christ.—2 Cor. v. 13, &c.; Col. iv. 12. (6.) *Sincerely.*—2 Cor. ii. 17, and iv. 2; 2 Thess. ii. 4, &c.; John vii. 18; 1 Cor. ix. 22; 1 Tim. iv. 16. Sincerity is a most necessary feature in the character of a minister of the gospel. Unsound doctrine is of the most dangerous tendency, and most dishonouring to Christ; for his glory is not promoted, nor can the conversion, and edification, and salvation of sinners take place.

The Word of God is made effectual by the sole agency of the *Holy Spirit.* The Word may be read and preached, as commanded; but it is the Spirit of God who is the life of the Word read and preached, and who alone can make it the power of God unto salvation.—1 Cor. ii. 11, and iii. 5; Ezek. xxviii. The prophet might prophesy to the dry bones, as he was commanded; but it was the Spirit alone that could put life into them, and make them stand up and praise the Lord.

It is said that "the Spirit of God maketh the reading, but *especially the preaching* of the Word, an effectual means" of salvation, because the *preaching* of the Word is the more *common means*; and we have full evidence that it is the most *effectual.*—Acts ii. 41, iv. 4, and xi. 20, 21. And in 1 Cor. i. 21, we read, that it nath pleased God to save, by the foolishness of *preaching,* them that believe; and in Rom. x. 17, we read, that faith cometh by *hearing,* and hearing by the Word of God.

Obs. 301.—*The ends for which the Spirit makes use of the Word read, but especially of the Word preached, are, to convince and convert sinners, and to build up saints in holiness and comfort, through faith unto salvation.*

1. The Spirit makes use of the Word to *convince and to convert sinners.* For *convincing* sinners, the Spirit makes use of the law; for, saith the Scripture, "by the law is the knowledge of sin." By him the sinner is convinced, both of the *nature* of sin, which consists in its being a want of conformity to God's law, or in its being a transgression of it; and of the *desert* of sin, which includes the wrath and curse of God, both in this life and in that which is to come. The Spirit also makes use of the Word as an effectual means of *converting* sinners.—Ps. xix. 7. Conversion is a spiritual motion of the whole man to a God in Christ, as the immediate and certain effect of the spiritual change which is effected in regeneration (Jer. iii. 22); which is inseparably connected with conversion as its cause. Of this supernatural change the Word is the means, but not in the hand of man himself; for he can neither prepare himself for it, nor can he cooperate with the Spirit in producing such a change.

2. The Spirit makes use of the Word to *build up saints in holiness and comfort.* He builds up the saints in *holiness,* by giving them clear and repeated discoveries of the glory of Christ, so that they are more and more transformed into the same image with him.—2 Cor. iii. 18. And he builds them up in *comfort,* by conveying with power into their souls the exceeding great and

precious promises which convey every ground of lasting and satisfying comfort to them; by which they are made very joyful in the God of their salvation.—Eph. iv. 12, &c.; Rom. xvi. 25; 1 Thess. iii. 11, &c.; Rom. xv. 4; 1 Thess. iii. 2, &c.; Is. xl. 1, 2.

Agreeably to Scripture, we are here informed, that the instrument by which the Spirit makes these means effectual for building up the saints in holiness and comfort, is *faith*. And the instrumentality which faith has, in the hand of the Spirit, in accomplishing this, is, that it rests on the faithful Word of their God for the promoting of both these ends.—1 Thess. ii. 13; Ps. cxxxviii. 8.

The end for which all this is done, is the complete and eternal *salvation* of the saints. And hence the gospel is called " the power of God unto salvation,"—that is, deliverance from sin and from wrath—from the guilt and punishment, and the power and pollution of sin—from the curse of the law—and from the power of death and of the grave.

INFERENCES.

From this subject we learn,—1. The value of the Bible. 2. The necessity of the Word of life. 3. That the ministry is an arduous work, and most important in its consequences. 4. The necessity of the reading and preaching of the Word. 5. The danger of despising or omitting it. 6. That the Spirit is most necessary to make the Word effectual. 7. The necessity of faith, without which the Word read or preached cannot profit. 8. The necessity of using the means of salvation; and that without this we are not in the way to obtain the blessing.

Proper use of the Word of God.

Q. 90.—How is the Word to be read and heard, that it may become effectual to Salvation?

That the Word may become effectual to salvation, we must attend thereunto with diligence, preparation, and prayer; receive it with faith and love; lay it up in our hearts, and practise it in our lives.

ANALYSIS AND PROOFS.

We are here taught,—
1. That the Word of God must be attended to, and understood. Acts viii. 30.—" Understandest thou what thou readest?"
2. That the Word of God must be attended to with diligence. Acts xvii. 11.—" And searched the Scriptures daily, whether these things were so." See also Prov. viii. 34.
3. That the Word of God must be attended to with preparation. James i. 21.—" Lay apart all filthiness and superfluity of

naughtiness, and receive with meekness the ingrafted Word, which is able to save your souls." See also Luke viii. 18.

4. That the Word of God must be attended to with prayer. Ps. cxix. 18.—" Open thou mine eyes, that I may behold wondrous things out of thy law."

5. That the Word of God must be received with faith. 1 Thess. ii. 13.—" For this cause also thank we God, without ceasing, because when ye received the Word of God which ye heard of us, ye received it not as the word of men, but (as it is in truth) the Word of God, which effectually worketh also in you that believe." See also Heb. iv. 2.

6. That the Word of God must be received with love. Ps. cxix. 97.—" O how love I thy law!" See also 2 Thess. ii. 10.

7. That the Word of God must be meditated upon. Col. iii. 16.—" Let the Word of Christ dwell in you richly in all wisdom."

8. That the Word of God must be laid up in the heart. Deut. xi. 18.—" Ye shall lay up these my words in your heart and in your soul." See also Ps. cxix. 11.

9. That the truths of the Word of God must be reduced to practice in our lives. James i. 22.—" Be ye doers of the Word, and not hearers only, deceiving your own selves."

EXPLANATION.

Obs. 302.—*That the Word may become effectual to salvation, we must attend to it with diligence, preparation, and prayer.*

When it is said that we must *attend* to the Word, it intimates that the Word must become our chief study while we live; and that it must be deeply engraven on the heart; and that for this good reason, that it contains that good part which shall never be taken away.

1. We must attend to the Word with *diligence*. Every opportunity of reading the Word, and of hearing it read and preached, must be embraced.

2. We must attend to the Word with *preparation*. This includes various things. We must consider well—(1.) The authority of God stamped upon the Word.—Acts x. 33; Ps. lxxxix. 6, 7. (2.) That the preaching of the Word is the ordinance of God for our salvation. (3.) That the preaching of the Word will be to us either the savour of death or the savour of life.— 2 Cor. ii. 15, 16; Luke viii. 18. (4.) The necessity of laying aside all filthiness of the flesh and spirit.—Gen. xxxv. 2, 3; 1 Pet. ii. 1, 2. (5.) The necessity of banishing from the heart the cares of the world, when we hear the Word.—Matt. xiii. 22. (6.) The necessity of being washed in the blood of Christ, when we hear the Word; for an unholy soul can hold no communion with God in the ordinances of his grace.—Ps. xxvi. 6. (7.) Our

own peculiar circumstances, when we hear the Word read or preached.—1 Kings viii. 38.

3. We must attend to the Word with *prayer*. This is necessary, because God alone can dispose our hearts to perform aright the exercises of his worship; and, consequently, it is our duty to address him for this very purpose, that our exercises may not be in vain as to ourselves.—Ps. cxix. 18; 2 Thess. iii. 1. Before reading or hearing the Word, we should pray that it may become the power of God to our salvation; or an effectual means in his hand for convincing, converting, and edifying our souls.—Rom. i. 16; John vi. 63.

But notwithstanding all our preparation that the Word may become effectual, we must disclaim all dependence upon it; and rest upon the promise of the Spirit to render it subservient to the important purposes for which it is designed.

Obs. 303.—*That the Word may become effectual to salvation, we must receive it with faith and love.*

To *receive* the Word, is to accept of it with all readiness of mind, as the Word of God indeed—the dictates of the Holy Spirit, directed to the soul for the purposes of salvation; and the right improvement of the Word during the reading and hearing of it, is called a *receiving* of it, because we can derive no real benefit to our souls from the free offer and exhibition of all the blessings contained therein, unless we receive them as the free gift of God.—John iii. 27.

1. We must receive the Word in *faith*. Here the following things may be observed:—(1.) We must believe the Divine authority of every part of the book called the Bible, and credit it as God's testimony of himself to man. There must be no doubt in our minds with respect to this subject; for there is abundant evidence of its truth within itself; and if we doubt, we cannot be said to receive the Word in faith. (2.) As it contains every thing necessary, not only for the salvation of sinners in general, but for that of ourselves in particular, we must not only receive it as true, but we must receive it with particular application; for it contains the message of God to us individually, as if there were none but ourselves to whom it is directed.—Lam. iii. 24; Ps. cxix 20. (3.) If we would have any respect to our own progress in the Divine life, and to our comfort, we must examine the effects which the Word has upon us.—Ps. cxix. 9, 50; Dan x. 19.

2. We must receive the Word with *love*. This is the natural consequence of its being received with faith; for wherever faith is, it worketh by love, and purifieth the heart. If the Word come home with power in the experience of any, as in the case of the Thessalonians, it will be accompanied with love. Compare 1 Thess. i. 5, and ii. 13. with 2 Thess. i. 3, &c., and it will

be evident that their faith was not alone; for their love is spoken of in the highest terms. To all who do not receive the Word in love, it is the savour of the second death.—2 Thess. ii. 10.

Obs. 304.—*That the Word may become effectual to salvation, we must lay it up in our hearts, and practise it in our lives.*

1. We must *lay up the Word in our hearts.* The understanding must be exercised about the knowledge of it; the will must be exercised about complying with it in all its parts; the affections must be fixed upon it; and the memory must retain it. Without all this, it cannot be said to be laid up in our hearts.—Ps. cxix. 11; Heb. ii. 1. Closely connected with laying up the Word in our hearts, is the exercise of *meditation* upon what has been spoken, or upon what we may have read or heard read.—Ps. i. 2.

2. We must *practise the Word in our lives.* This is the great end of the former exercises. To practise the Word in our lives, is to have a conversation in word and deed becoming the gospel —to have the outward and inward man regulated according to the unerring Word of God.

INFERENCES.

From this subject we learn,—1. The value of the Word of God, and the respect which we ought to pay to it. 2. The danger of disregarding it. 3. That there is much necessary on our part that we may understand the Word, but that nothing will prove effectual without the Spirit. 4. The necessity of fear and reverence in reading the Word, and the danger of the want of these. 5. The necessity of faith and love when we read or hear the Word. 6. The necessity of laying it up in our hearts, meditating upon it, and reducing it to practice. 7. That the outward performance avails nothing, if the heart is not engaged.—Isa. xxix. 13.

DIV. 2.—OF THE SACRAMENTS AS MEANS OF GRACE.

Of the Efficacy of the Sacraments.

Q. 91.—How do the Sacraments become Effectual Means of Salvation.

The sacraments become effectual means of salvation, not from any virtue in them, or in him that doth administer them, but only by the blessing of Christ, and the working of his Spirit in them that by faith receive them.

ANALYSIS AND PROOFS.

We are here taught,—

1. That the sacraments possess no virtue in themselves. Acts viii. 13, 23.—" Simon himself believed also, and was baptized. But Peter said to him, I perceive that thou art in the gall of bitterness, and in the bond of iniquity."

2. That the sacraments are not rendered effectual by any virtue in the administrator. 1 Cor. iii. 7.—" Neither is he that planteth any thing, neither he that watereth; but God that giveth the increase."

3. That the sacraments are rendered effectual by the blessing of Christ. Matt. iii. 11.—" He shall baptize you with the Holy Ghost and with fire."

4. That the sacraments are made effectual by the operation of the Spirit of God. John vi. 63.—" It is the Spirit that quickeneth; the flesh profiteth nothing."

5. That the sacraments become effectual to those only who receive them by faith. Mark xvi. 16.—" He that believeth, and is baptized, shall be saved."

EXPLANATION.

Obs. 305.—*The sacraments are effectual means of salvation.*

A *means of salvation* is an appointment of Jesus Christ, the king and head of the Church, in the use of which salvation is begun, carried on, and perfected. See Acts ii. 37, &c.; 1 Cor. x. 16.

The difference between the *Word of God* as a means of salvation, and the *sacraments* as means of salvation, is this: the Word of God is a means which respect both saints and sinners; but the sacraments are means which respect the saints alone, in the sight of God. The Word is designed as a means of convincing and converting sinners; the sacraments, of comforting saints and confirming them in their most holy faith. The Word must precede the sacraments, which are designed only for those who believe; and faith cometh by hearing the Word of God read or preached. The Word must appear to be an effectual means of salvation, before we ought to meddle with the sacraments.

The sacraments are not only *means*, but they are *effectual means* of salvation to all whom they concern: and this is verified in the experience of not a few who hold sensible communion with Christ in the breaking of bread, which is a season of great joy to their souls; and the comfort thus received through them, is a pledge of a full salvation and of full communion with Christ in the Church triumphant.

Obs. 306.—*The sacraments possess no virtue in themselves.*

The sacraments of themselves have no virtue or efficacy to confer salvation, being only among the outward and ordinary means by which the benefits of redemption are communicated to sinners. They can confer no saving benefit of themselves, any more than the rainbow can prevent a second deluge; it being only a pledge given by God that he will not again drown the world. That they cannot confer saving grace is evident; for if they had this power in themselves, all that partake of them would have grace, which we know is not the case.—1 Pet. iii. 21. This clause seems to have been inserted in opposition to those who hold it as a favourite tenet, that the sacraments of the New Testament are the true, and proper, and immediate causes of grace; and that the efficacy of them flows from the sacramental action of receiving the external elements; or, in other words, who foolishly imagine that the sacraments are converting ordinances. But see the state of Simon Magus after baptism.—Acts viii. 13, 23.

Obs. 307.—*The sacraments are not rendered effectual by any virtue in the administrator.*

The best of men cannot render efficacious any Divine ordinance which can be administered by them, nor was it ever designed that this should be the case. Man is only an instrument in the hand of God, to do what he hath commanded; but the virtue of any ordinance rests entirely upon God himself. See 1 Cor. iii. 6, 7. If the administrator of Divine ordinances could confer grace, or withhold it, with respect to the receivers of them, it would place the administrator in God's stead, whose prerogative alone it is to render the means of salvation effectual for the purposes designed by them. And this idea seems to have been inserted in opposition to that most dangerous tenet maintained by the Church of Rome, which asserts, that the efficacy of the sacraments depends upon the intention of the priest or administrator; thus ascribing to him the power of conferring or withholding grace, which belongs to God alone. But were this the case, it could not be known whether the sacraments would be accompanied with any benefit at all, because none can be absolutely certain about the intention of another, seeing the secrets of the heart are known to God alone.—Acts i. 24.

Obs. 308.—*The sacraments are rendered effectual only by the blessing of Christ and the operation of his Spirit.*

1. The sacraments derive their efficacy from *the blessing of Christ.* Without this, or without that Divine life and power with which he has promised to accompany the sacraments, they are but a dead letter in themselves; having no life, until spirit and life be put within them by Him who taketh of the things of Christ and showeth them unto us.

2. The sacraments derive their efficacy from *the working of Christ's Spirit.* By this we are to understand, not his work in

implanting grace in the soul in a day of effectual calling, which also is his work; but particularly his calling forth this implanted grace into lively exercise when the sacraments are dispensed. And when the graces of the Spirit are thus drawn forth into lively exercise, and fixed on the objects exhibited in the sacraments, then the Spirit may be said to work in them that receive them.

The sacraments are effectual means of salvation to those only who *receive them by faith*,—to those only who apply to themselves those things which are exhibited in them, or Christ and the benefits of his redemption.

INFERENCES.

From this subject we learn,—1. That the sacraments are valuable means of salvation. 2. That they are useful and necessary. 3. The necessity of faith and of the Spirit. 4. That the sacraments receive their virtue or efficacy from Christ and his Spirit. 5. That we must not rest in the sacraments, but look to the end of them.

Of the Nature of the Sacraments.

Q. 92.—What is a Sacrament.

A Sacrament is a holy ordinance instituted by Christ, wherein by sensible signs, Christ, and the benefits of the new covenant, are represented, sealed, and applied to believers.

ANALYSIS AND PROOFS.

We are here taught,—

1. That the sacraments are holy ordinances. 1 Cor. x. 21.—"Ye cannot drink of the cup of the Lord and the cup of devils; ye cannot be partakers of the Lord's table and of the table of devils."

2. That the sacrament of baptism was instituted by Christ. Matt. xxviii. 19.—"Go ye, therefore, and teach all nations, baptizing them."

3. That the sacrament of the supper was instituted by Christ. Matt. xxvi. 26, 27.—"And as they were eating, Jesus took bread and blessed it, and brake it, and gave it to the disciples, and said, Take, eat; this is my body. And he took the cup, and gave thanks, and gave it to them, saying, Drink ye all of it."

4. That Christ is represented by sensible signs in the sacrament of baptism. Rom vi. 3, 4.—"Know ye not, that so many of us as were baptized into Jesus Christ, were baptized into his death? Therefore we are buried with him by baptism into death."

5. That Christ is represented by sensible signs in the sacrament of the supper. 1 Cor. xi. 24.—"This is my body which is broken for you; this do in remembrance of me."

6. That the benefits of the new covenant are represented in the sacraments. John vi. 53, 54.—"Except ye eat the flesh of

the Son of Man, and drink his blood, ye have no life in you. Whoso eateth my flesh, and drinketh my blood, hath eternal life."

7. That Christ and the benefits of the new covenant are sealed to believers in the sacraments. Rom. iv. 11.—"He received the sign of circumcision, a seal of the righteousness of the faith which he had, yet being uncircumcised."

8. That Christ and the benefits of the new covenant are applied to believers in the sacraments. John vi. 56, 57.—"He that eateth my flesh, and drinketh my blood, dwelleth in me, and I in him. As the living Father hath sent me, and I live by the Father; so he that eateth me, even he shall live by me."

EXPLANATION.

Obs. 309.—*The sacraments are holy ordinances instituted by Christ.*

The word *sacrament* is of Latin origin; and it was anciently used by the Romans to signify their military oath, or that oath by which their soldiers bound themselves to be true and faithful to their generals, and not to desert their standard in the day of danger. This oath, then, implied obedience to their superiors in all things connected with the military art; and disobedience no sooner appeared in any of those who had taken this oath, than they discovered to all around them that they had perjured themselves. In this view, a *sacrament* signifies not only something that is sacred, but also, on our part, a solemn engagement to be the Lord's. And if the ancient oath, denoted by the word *sacrament*, was reciprocal or mutual,—that is, if the Roman generals bound themselves to be true to their soldiers, as they did to be faithful to them,—we have exactly the same thing pointed out to us with reference to the captain of our salvation, Jesus Christ. He engages himself to us as such; and we also engage to be his— to be for him, and not for another.

The author of the ordinances, called sacraments, is *Jesus Christ*. Every ordinance in the Christian Church, that is a means of salvation or of comfort, must derive its origin from him, because he alone is the king and the head of the Church— 'given to be head over all things to the Church, which is his body, the fulness of him that filleth all in all." That, then, which makes a sacrament, is *his word of institution.*

It is necessary to have the *express and immediate warrant of Christ* respecting a sacrament, for the following reasons:—1. Because otherwise it would not deserve the name of a sacrament; and hence we find that the apostle told the Corinthians, that he received the institution of the Lord's Supper immediately from Christ himself.—1 Cor. xi. 23. 2. The sacraments have a respect unto the covenant; but none can appoint the seals of the covenant, which the sacraments are, but Christ, who is the representative of the covenant, and who, as such, hath fulfilled its condition. All the promises of the covenant are in Him yea and amen, to the glory of God the Father; but who can seal the promises but Christ? 3. The sacraments have a respect to the house of God, the worship of God, and the Divine glory. None, therefore, can appoint them but Christ, who above all things sought his Father's glory; and hence we find that his authority is visibly stamped upon both the sacraments of the New Testament.—Matt. xxviii. 19, 20, and xxvi. 26, 27; 1 Cor. xi. 23.

Obs. 310.—*The sacraments consist of two parts—an outward and sensible sign, and an inward and spiritual grace.*

1. The *outward and sensible sign* is something that we can see or perceive by our senses; and it must be of Christ's own appointment. Thus, the element used in baptism is *water*, which is visible to us; and the elements used in the Lord's Supper are *bread and wine*, which are also visible, and which we can handle and taste. And this is one of the principal parts of a sacrament, immediately appointed by Christ. But connected with the elements, there are also what are called *sacramental actions*, which cannot properly be considered as distinct from the elements, because they are exercised about them; and both constitute but one outward sign or part of a sacrament.

2. The *inward and spiritual grace* is that which is signified by the visible or sensible signs; and without a participation of this spiritual grace, the sacraments are but a mere shadow without a substance. See Matt. iii. 11; Rom. ii. 28, 29.

Obs. 311.—*The end or design of the sacraments is, to represent Christ and the benefits of the new covenant, and to seal and apply them to believers.*

1. The sacraments are designed to *represent Christ and the benefits of the new covenant*. As Christ is the great spiritual blessing represented in the sacraments, there must be a spiritual relation between the sign and the thing signified thereby; the consequence of which union is, that the names and effects of the one are applied to the names and effects of the other. Without such a spiritual relation, there would be no sacrament. And this union is effectual in those who partake of the sacraments, when, together with the signs, the spiritual blessings represented by them are received by faith.

2. The sacraments are designed to *seal* Christ and the benefits of the new covenant to believers. By the sacraments, Christ and the benefits of his redemption are made infallibly sure to believers; and they hereby engage that they will be for Christ, and not for another, and that they will serve him with reverential fear all their days

3. The sacraments are designed to *apply* Christ and the benefits of the new covenant to the souls of the worthy receivers of them. This must necessarily follow from a due participation of the symbols, or from eating and drinking by faith; which cannot be done without an actual possession or application of the benefits of the new covenant, which are signified by the signs.

The sacraments are designed only for *believers.* None have a right to the seals of the covenant but believers, or they who are within the bond of the covenant—who have fled to Christ for refuge from sin and from wrath—who see none like Christ—who follow him whithersoever he goeth—who have no confidence in the flesh—and who rest upon the finished atonement of Christ as the sole ground of their hopes, both in time and through eternity.

INFERENCES.

From this subject we learn,—1. The love of Christ in giving the means of comfort to the Church. 2. The privilege of the saints. 3. The happiness of those who are interested in the new and everlasting covenant. 4. The danger of despising the sacraments, which are the seals of the covenant.

Of the New Testament Sacraments.

Q. 93.—*Which are the Sacraments of the New Testament?*

The sacraments of the New Testament are Baptism and the Lord's Supper.

ANALYSIS AND PROOFS.

We are here taught,—

1. That baptism is a sacrament of the New Testament. Matt. xxviii. 19.—" Go ye, therefore, and teach all nations, baptizing them."

2. That the Lord's Supper is a sacrament of the New Testament. 1 Cor. xi. 23-25.—" I have received of the Lord that which also I delivered unto you, That the Lord Jesus, the same night in which he was betrayed, took bread: and, when he had given thanks, he brake it, and said, Take, eat; this is my body, which is broken for you; this do in remembrance of me. After the same manner also he took the cup when he had supped, saying, This cup is the New Testament in my blood; this do ye, as oft as ye drink it, in remembrance of me."

EXPLANATION.

Obs. 312.—*The sacraments of the Old Testament, which exhibited the same blessings that those of the New Testament exhibit, were circumcision and the passover.*

1. *Circumcision* was instituted about 1900 years before the incarnation of Christ: and doubtless looked forward to him who

was to come. It was the sign of the covenant which God made, or rather renewed, with Abraham his friend, in the hundredth year of his age.—Gen. xvii. Circumcision represented our *natural pollution and depravity*, together with the necessity of *regeneration*, or of being cut off from the first Adam, as a federal head and representative, and of being ingrafted into Christ, the second Adam, and washed in his all-cleansing blood.—Rom. ii. 28, 29. It was the initiatory sacrament under the Old Testament dispensation, as baptism is under the New. Both substantially represent the same thing: the one, the putting off of the sins of the flesh; and the other, the washing of them away in the blood of Jesus.

2. The *passover* was instituted on the occasion of the deliverance of the children of Israel out of the land of Egypt; and it had a most important meaning with respect to Christ, who was to come.—Exod. xii. No sooner did the destroying angel observe the blood sprinkled where it ought to be, according to the Divine command, than he viewed it as their refuge; so that this evidenced obedience to the Divine command, and faith in the blood of Christ which was to be shed. And without doubt this sprinkling of blood typified, that it is only in virtue of the blood or satisfaction of Christ, that the danger arising from sin can be averted,—namely, the curse of the law and the wrath of God, which shall assuredly overtake all those who are not under the sprinkling of the blood of Jesus.—Rom. v. 9.

The following are some of the things which it was necessary to observe in eating the passover; and they showed it to be at that time an ordinance of a very peculiar nature, and typical of Christ, our passover.

1. It was necessary that the passover lamb should be "without blemish."—Exod. xii. 5. This showed, that although our sins were imputed to Christ, yet he himself was holy, and harmless, and undefiled; and hence he is called "a lamb without blemish and without spot."—1 Pet. i. 19.

2. It was necessary that the passover lamb should be "kept for a season before it was killed."—Exod. xii. 3, 6. During this period, according to the Jewish writers, the lamb was tied to their bed-posts, that, by its continual bleating, the Israelites might be called to remember their severe bondage in Egypt, and the great mercy of deliverance from it; and, moreover, to excite them to look forward by faith to the sufferings which Christ was to endure. And with respect to the Lord's Supper, we are to prepare for it by frequently considering our misery by sin, and what Christ suffered that it might not be our ruin.

3. It was necessary that the passover lamb should be "slain," or killed by blood shedding.—Exod. xii. 6. In like manner, it behoved Christ to suffer a violent death; his blood must be shed to satisfy Divine justice —Luke xxiv. 26.

4. It was necessary that the passover lamb should be "roasted with fire."—Exod. xii. 8, 9. This represented, in a very significant manner, the exquisite sufferings of Christ, which he endured without the least abatement or intermission, until all was over. And we may here remark, that the spit, on which the passover lamb was roasted, was in the form of a *cross*. How wonderfully did the type correspond with the antitype!

5. It was necessary that the passover lamb should be "eaten entirely or wholly," and none of it left.—Exod. xii. 10. This represented Christ as a complete Saviour; that faith must apply a whole Saviour in all his offices, as made of God unto us wisdom, and righteousness, and sanctification, and redemption.—1 Cor. i. 30.

6. It was necessary that the passover lamb should be "eaten with bitter herbs and unleavened bread."—Exod. xii. 18. This represents to us, that Christ must be received with the exercise of genuine repentance.

7. It was necessary that the passover lamb should be "eaten the same night in which it was slain."—Exod. xii. 8. This clearly shows, that Christ ought to be received and applied to the soul without delay, as soon as we hear of him as a sacrifice slain for sin.

8. It was necessary that the passover lamb should be "eaten with the loins girded, shoes on the feet, and the staff in the hand."—Exod. xii. 11. This clearly represents the necessity of accounting ourselves strangers and pilgrims on the earth; and shows, that Christ is to be improved for the purposes of salvation to the very last moment of our life, and that we are to be always ready for our departure, as the Israelites were commanded to be for their departure out of the land of bondage.

9. It was necessary that the passover lamb should be "eaten by all the families of Israel at one and the same time."—Exod. xii. 8. This represents, in the clearest manner, the fulness which is in Christ Jesus and his atonement for all, that all may apply to him, and he will satisfy them, and that at once.—Col. ii. 9.

10. It was necessary that the blood of the passover lamb should be "sprinkled on the door-posts and lintels of the houses of the Israelites," for securing them from the stroke of the destroying angel. This represents the necessity of having the soul sprinkled with the blood of Christ by faith, that it may be secured from the effects of Divine wrath; and, moreover, it is necessary that our conversation, which is visible to the world, be also sprinkled with blood, that we may be a new lump; for even "Christ our passover is sacrificed for us."—1 Cor. v. 7.

Thus it is evident, what a striking resemblance there is between the type and the antitype; and it is also evident that the passover and the Lord's Supper are substantially the same. Both exhibit deliverances,—spiritual mercies in and through Jesus

Christ. And it may be here remarked, that there never was a deliverance which more fully exhibited the salvation of Christ in substance, than that of the Israelites from the land of Egypt.

Obs. 313.—*The sacraments of the New Testament, or those which have come in the room of circumcision and the passover, are baptism and the Lord's Supper.*

1. *Baptism* was appointed by Jesus Christ himself after his resurrection, when all power both in heaven and on earth was given unto him; and it comes in the room of circumcision. The particular passage of Scripture which proves this, is Col. ii. 10–12, —" And ye are complete in him " (viz., Christ), &c. If there is nothing under the gospel to correspond with circumcision under the law, how could the apostle say to the Colossians that they were *complete in Christ?* They would have certainly found out the deception.

2. *The Lord's Supper* was appointed by Jesus Christ on the same night in which he was betrayed into the hands of sinners; and it comes in the room of the passover; as may be justly inferred from what has been said above respecting the resemblance between the passover and its antitype.

The sacraments of the Old Testament differ from those of the New Testament in the following respects:—While the former represented *Christ as to come*, the latter represent him *as already come*. By the former, spiritual mercies were not so clearly exhibited as they are by the latter.

Obs. 314.—*Besides baptism and the Lord's Supper, there are no other ordinances of Christ's appointment which may be called sacraments.*

This will be evident from the following things:—

1. No other ordinances consist of two parts—an outward sensible sign and an inward spiritual grace, but baptism and the Lord's Supper.

2. There were no more than two sacraments under the Old Testament dispensation; and we may readily believe that the New Testament Church is not more burdened with ceremonies than the Old was. As the gospel is most simple, so the Christian Church is most simple in its various services. Circumcision under the Old Testament had respect to children—was the initiating seal of the covenant—and was not to be repeated. In like manner, baptism under the New Testament has respect to children—is the initiating seal of the covenant—and is not to be repeated. The children of the Jews were first to be circumcised, and afterwards to eat the passover. In like manner, the children of Christians are first to be baptized, and afterwards to sit down at the Lord's Table. The passover was to be repeated; and so is the Lord's Supper. Circumcision represented the putting away

of the sins of the flesh; baptism refers to their being washed away in the blood of Christ. The passover typified the redemption by Christ, and the sufferings which he was to endure; the Lord's Supper represents his actual sufferings, and the atonement which he made thereby. Thus the number and nature of the sacraments are the same now that they were formerly.

3. Baptism and the Lord's Supper are fully sufficient to seal the new covenant to believers. If two sacraments were sufficient, under the dark dispensation, for all the purposes of grace, surely a greater number is not required now when we enjoy the true light. Two witnesses are accounted sufficient to attest or confirm a deed. And accordingly, by the two sacraments, the believer has confirmed to him all grace and all glory. Baptism is the seal of being brought within the covenant; and the Lord's Supper is the seal of being kept within it. The one is the sign of life given him from above; and the other is the sign of the nourishment received from the fulness of the covenant.

INFERENCES.

From this subject we learn,—1. That the way of salvation has always been the same; but that it is clearer now than it was formerly. 2. That our privileges are greater than those of the Jews were; and to whom much is given, of them shall much be required. 3. That our obligations to redeeming love are very great. 4. That the believer's comfort and happiness are sure.

Of the Nature and Use of Baptism.

Q. 94.—What is Baptism?

Baptism is a sacrament, wherein the washing with water, in the name of the Father, and of the Son, and of the Holy Ghost, doth signify and seal our ingrafting into Christ, and partaking of the benefits of the covenant of grace, and our engagement to be the Lord's.

ANALYSIS AND PROOFS.

We are here taught,—

1. That water is the sign to be used in baptism. Acts x. 47.—" Can any man forbid water, that these should not be baptized?"

2. That baptism is to be administered in the name of the Father, and of the Son, and of the Holy Ghost. Matt. xxviii. 19.—" Go ye, therefore, and teach all nations, baptizing them in the name of the Father, and of the Son, and of the Holy Ghost."

3. That baptism signifies the ingrafting of believers into Christ. 1 Cor. xii. 13.—" By one spirit are we all baptized into one body." See also Rom. vi. 3.

4. That baptism seals the ingrafting of believers into Christ. Gal. iii. 27.—" As many of you as have been baptized into Christ have put on Christ."

5. That baptism signifies our having a right to the benefits of the covenant of grace. Acts ii. 38.—" Repent and be baptized every one of you in the name of Jesus Christ, for the remission of sins ; and ye shall receive the gift of the Holy Ghost."

6. That baptism seals our right to the benefits of the covenant of grace. Rom. iv. 11.—" And he received the sign of circumcision, a seal of the righteousness of the faith which he had."

7. That baptism signifies and seals our engagement to be the Lord's. Rom. vi. 4.—" We are buried with him by baptism into death ; that like as Christ was raised up from the dead by the glory of the Father, even so we also should walk in newness of life."

EXPLANATION.

Obs. 315.—*Baptism is a washing or sprinkling with water.*

In Scripture there is mention made of several kinds of baptism. 1. *Levitical washings*,—Heb. ix. 10 ; where the word in the original is " baptisms "—divers baptisms. See also ver. 13, where we read of sprinkling. 2. *The baptism of blood*,—Matt. xx. 22, 23, and Luke xii. 50; with which Christ and the greater part of his apostles, and all martyrs were baptized. 3. *The baptism of the Holy Ghost*, or the conferring of his gifts.—Matt. iii. 11; Acts i. 5. 4. In Acts xviii. 25, it may signify the *doctrine of baptism*. But, 5. It chiefly signifies the *sacrament of baptism ;* or baptism with water, according to Christ's appointment.—Acts xix. 4, 5.

Baptism had a Divine warrant before it was formally appointed by Christ; for we read of the baptism of John, who doubtless received a command to baptize with water. See John i. 33, where we read of John speaking of " him who sent him " to baptize with water.

Between the baptism of John and that of Christ there was no essential difference, for the same blessings were exhibited by both. A difference, however, may be discovered with respect to *time* and *objects*. 1. With respect to *time*. The baptism of John was dispensed before the work of Christ was finished ; but the baptism which Christ committed to the apostles, was mostly after his work was finished, and after he himself had entered into his glory. Or, the baptism of John was a sign of faith in Christ as about to come ; whereas the baptism of Christ is an expression of faith in him as already come. 2. With respect to their *objects*. The baptism of John was confined to Judea, or to the Jewish nation ; whereas the baptism of Christ is extended to all to whom the gospel is preached.—Mark xvi. 15, 16.

The *sign* to be used in baptism is *water;* which represents the *cleansing efficacy or virtue* both of the *blood* and of the *Spirit of Christ.*—Rev. i. 5; Tit. iii. 5. By the former, the soul is cleansed *meritoriously ;* and by the latter, it is cleansed *effica ciously.*—1 John i. 7; Ezek. xxxvi. 27. By the former, the guilt of sin is removed in justification; and by the latter, the pollution of sin is gradually removed in sanctification.

The *analogy* or *resemblance* between the sign and the thing signified in baptism, or between water and the blood and Spirit of Christ, may be seen from the following remarks:—1. Water has a *cleansing* virtue, for removing filth and pollution from the body, and from other things. In like manner, the fountain of Christ's blood, which is opened for sin and for uncleanness, removes the filth of the soul, and cleanses the conscience from dead works to serve the living God. 2. Water has a *refreshing* virtue on the weary traveller, and on the parched ground. And what more refreshing to the weary traveller towards Zion, than to drink at the fountain of living water? What more calculated to make the barren soul bud forth abundantly, than to be refreshed with the pure water of life?—Ps. xlii.; John vi. 35. 3. Water has an *extinguishing* virtue. And how efficacious are the blood and Spirit of Christ to extinguish the flames of Jehovah's wrath, and the fire of our lusts which war against the soul! 4. Water has a *softening* virtue; mollifying the hardened ground, and making it abundantly fruitful. In like manner, the blood of Christ softens the most hardened heart, when applied to it by the Holy Spirit; causing tears of godly sorrow to flow, and the fruits of repentance to spring forth, and bringing the whole man into a ready compliance with the Divine will. 5. Water is absolutely *necessary*. In like manner, the blood and Spirit of Christ are absolutely necessary; for without them sinners must perish eternally.—John vi. 53; Rom. viii. 9. 6. Water is *common* and *free* to all. In like manner, the blood and Spirit of Christ are freely offered to all without exception.—Isa. lv. 1, &c. 7. Water, although necessary, is of no use, unless it is applied to the various purposes for which it is designed. In like manner, the blood of Christ is of no use to any, unless it is applied to the soul by the Holy Spirit through faith.

With respect to those by whom the ordinance of baptism is to be dispensed, we observe, that the command to baptize being connected with preaching, it is evident, that none but those who are lawfully called to preach, have a right to baptize.—Matt. xxviii. 19, 20.

With respect to the *mode* or *manner* of administration, there are various opinions,—whether it ought to be performed by plunging or dipping, or by pouring or sprinkling. But without entering into the various arguments on both sides, we shall only make the following remarks:—When we consider the way in which the thing signified by baptism is expressed (Tit. iii. 5, 6; Heb. x. 22), and that the pouring out of the Holy Spirit is expressly called baptism (Acts x. 44, 45, compared with chap. xi. 15, 16); when we consider the divers washings of which the apostle speaks in Heb. ix. 10; or, as it is in the original, divers baptisms; referring probably to the various liquids which were used,—viz., water, and oil, and blood, into which it is not very likely that the people and various things were plunged; and that Christ speaks of a baptism of blood, with which he was to be baptized; when we consider also the instances of the administration of this ordinance by the apostles (Acts ii., where we read of 3000 being baptized in one day); the baptism of the jailor and his family, and of the Apostle Paul (Acts xvi. and ix. 18); the one in prison, and the other in a private house, where it is probable they had not much water, and as probable that the administrators would not have brought them forth to the nearest water—the one at midnight, which was dangerous, and the other in the weak state in which he then was, after three days' fasting (Acts x. 47, 48); and, moreover, when we consider, that the yoke of Christ is easy and his burden light ; and that his religion is adapted for all parts of the world—the coldest as well as the hottest; and for all constitutions—the weakest as well as the strongest; when we consider all these things, we must conclude, that baptism may be administered by sprinkling as well as by plunging,—nay, that sprinkling or pouring is most agreeable to the general tenor of Scripture.

Obs. 316.—*Baptism is to be administered in the name of the Father, and of the Son, and of the Holy Ghost.*

To be *baptized in the name of the Father, Son, and Holy Ghost*, implies, that we are to be baptized in virtue of the will, and authority, and command of the Father, Son, and Holy Ghost; and that ministers have authority from the Father, Son, and Holy Ghost to baptize. And this intimates, that the blessed Trinity have not only appointed and authorised baptism to be a sacrament of the New Testament, and to be dispensed by ministers lawfully called; but that they become jointly engaged tc make good all the blessings of the covenant of which baptism is a seal, as they are represented, and sealed, and applied to believers in this ordinance. It also implies, that by baptism we are solemnly dedicated and devoted to the Father, Son, and Holy Ghost, as our God and portion for ever; that we enter into a solemn covenant with this God; that we choose God the Father as our Father, God the Son as our Redeemer, and God the Holy Ghost as our Sanctifier, and Guide, and Comforter; and that we come under engagements to the faith, and profession, and obedience of the blessed Trinity, and solemnly renounce the devil, and the world, and the flesh, the great enemies of God and man. —1 Pet. iii. 21.

In administering baptism, it is necessary to use the *express words* of institution—" In the name of the Father, and of the Son, and of the Holy Ghost." For ministers are commanded to baptize in this manner; and it is the making use of the express words of institution, that constitutes a sacrament according to Christ's appointment.

Obs. 317.—*Baptism is designed to signify and seal the ingrafting of believers into Christ, their having a right to the benefits of the covenant of grace, and their engagement to be the Lord's.*

1. Baptism is designed to *signify and seal our ingrafting into Christ.* Ingrafting in general expresses the idea of a close union between two things, which, if they had not been brought together by some power, would have remained for ever separate.—Rom. xi. Ingrafting into Christ expresses union with him; and had not his power been exerted in cutting us off from the old stock, the first Adam, of whom we are branches by nature, this spiritual union could have never been effected.—John xv. 5. And in consequence of this union, which is signified and sealed by baptism, the imputation of Christ's righteousness is also sealed. —Gal. iii. 27.

2. Baptism is designed to *signify and seal the benefits of the covenant of grace.* And these are:—(1.) Remission of sins by the blood of Christ; which is clearly signified by baptism. As water washes away all outward pollution, so Christ's blood cleanses from all sin. (2.) Regeneration by the Spirit of Christ; which is also exhibited in baptism.—Tit. iii. 5; John iii. 5. (3.) Adoption into the family of God; which implies our former distance from God, as strangers to him and to the privileges of his family. (4.) A resurrection to eternal life,—1 Cor. xv. 26, which seems to intimate that baptism has a reference to the resurrection, as a privilege of the children of God included in the benefits of the new covenant.

3. Baptism is designed to *signify and seal our engagement to be the Lord's.* And this may well be considered as a consequence of the benefits of the new covenant being sealed to us; for if God engages on his part that he will be our God, that he will receive us as members of the visible Church, and give us a right to its privileges, and that he will take us into his family, &c., we may readily believe, that we are, in like manner, to *engage to be the Lord's;* which implies, that we will be his and for him, now, wholly, and for ever, in soul, and body, and spirit, and in all that we are and have, whether gifts or graces, or worldly comforts.—1 Cor. vi. 19, 20; 1 Chron. xxix. 14. This engagement on our part also implies, that we have firmly resolved to renounce all other lords and masters whatever, as the devil, and the world, and the flesh, and sin in whatever shape it may appear. And this engagement is not to be in word only, but in deed and in truth,—that we will be the Lord's by practice as well as by profession, that we will be what he would have us to be, and that we

will study conformity to him in all things.—Rom. vi. 4. If we are baptized in the name of the Father, Son, and Holy Ghost, we must view this as a dedicating ordinance; and seeing God makes himself over to us, as our all in all through the redeeming death of his Son, it is surely meet that we should give ourselves to him in a perpetual covenant that shall never be forgotten. In a word, by baptism we declare, that we are well pleased with the scheme of salvation through the righteousness of Jesus Christ,—with the new covenant as it is exhibited in the Scriptures as the wisdom of God unto salvation. We may also observe the following things, in addition to what is expressed above:—

4. Baptism is designed as a *mark* or *badge* between Christians and the enemies of Christ; although it is to be lamented that too many of those who have received the outward sign live as his open and avowed enemies.

5. Baptism is designed as a *solemn admission* of the party baptized into the visible Church, and to all its privileges.—1 Cor. xii. 13. Baptism does not *constitute* any one a *member* of the Church; for it is supposed that all who are baptized *are* Church members; and if they are children of professing parents, they are born members of the visible Church.—1 Cor. vii. 14. But by it they who were members before, have their membership sealed to them; for "by one Spirit are we all baptized into one body."—1 Cor. xii. 13. And this shows how inaccurately *they* speak upon this subject, who talk of *Christening* their children, as if by baptism they were *made Christians.*

We may here remark, that new covenant blessings are not sealed to all that are baptized. The Holy Spirit will not seal an unbeliever to redemption, however flaming his profession may be; for such in the sight of God have nothing to do with the seals of the covenant. But in the sight of the Church they may have a right, if there is nothing against them with respect to their knowledge and conduct before the world,—Rom. ix. 4; where it is said, that to the seed of Abraham pertain the adoption, and the glory, and the covenants, and the giving of the law, and the service of God, and the promises; although at this time (generally speaking) they had no part nor lot in Christ. And such may be the case with many of those who are none of God's.

Obs. 318.—*The efficacy of baptism consists neither in the removal of original sin, nor in giving a right to new covenant blessings, but in ratifying or sealing the right to these blessings.*

1. The efficacy of baptism consists not, as some imagine, in the *removal of original sin.* This opinion shows consummate ignorance of what this sin is, of the workings of the human heart, and of what takes place in the world. If original sin, which is the spring or source of all actual sin, were removed by baptism, there would be *no actual sin* in the world. Moreover, we see children

diseased, and afflicted, and subjected to death after baptism, and before they are guilty of any actual sin; which cannot be accounted for but upon the supposition of sin still existing (Rom. vi. 23); for when sin is fully removed, there will be no more death.

2. The efficacy of baptism consists not, according to others, in *giving a right to the blessings of the new covenant.* This is not, and cannot be, the case; for it is the *promise* of the covenant that is made to the children as well as to the parents.—Acts ii. 39. And baptism is only a sign and seal of its blessings, as circumcision formerly was.—Rom. iv. 11. But,

3. The efficacy of baptism consists in effectually *ratifying or sealing the right to the blessings of the covenant;* which are in the promise so certain, that they shall all be obtained in due time, according to the will of a promising God.

Obs. 319.—*Although baptism is not absolutely necessary to salvation, yet it is necessary that it should be observed by all the followers of Christ.*

Baptism is not absolutely necessary to salvation, as if the mere want of it would hinder the salvation of the soul; but it is necessary *in virtue of Christ's command.* What he hath appointed in his Church ought to be had in reverence; and as baptism is a seal of the covenant, it ought to be observed as a means of salvation. It is not, then, the *want* of this ordinance, but the *contempt* of it, that exposes to condemnation. That it is not absolutely necessary to salvation, is evident from the case of Cornelius, who was accepted by God before he was baptized; and also from that of the thief on the cross, who was not baptized at all.—Acts x.; Luke xxiii.

Obs. 320.—*It is the duty of Christians to improve their baptism, especially when present at the administration of it to others.*

As it is the duty of Christians to improve all the instituted ordinances of religion; so it is their duty also to improve this ordinance of baptism; which may be done in the following manner:—

1. By serious and thankful consideration of its nature, and the uses and ends for which Christ instituted it; of the privileges and benefits of the new covenant, which are conferred and sealed by it; and of our solemn vow made therein.

2. By being humbled on account of our spiritual defilement, and our falling short of, and walking contrary to, the grace of baptism and our engagements.

3. By growing up to assurance of pardon, and all the blessings sealed to us in this sacrament.

4. By drawing strength from the death and resurrection of Jesus Christ, into whom we are baptized, for the mortifying of sin and the quickening of grace.

5. By endeavouring to walk by faith; to have our conversation in holiness and righteousness, as those that have therein given themselves to Christ; and to walk in brotherly love as being baptized into one body by the same Spirit.

INFERENCES.

From this subject we learn,—1. That baptism is a very simple, but a very important ordinance. 2. That what is signified by water is most necessary. 3. The necessity of adhering to the command of Christ in administering this ordinance. 4. The importance of being well acquainted with the nature of baptism. 5. The danger of neglecting and contemning it.

Of the Subjects of Baptism.

Q. 95. To whom is Baptism to be administered?

Baptism is not to be administered to any that are out of the visible Church, till they profess their faith in Christ, and obedience to him; but the infants of such as are members of the visible Church are to be baptized.

ANALYSIS AND PROOFS.

We are here taught,—

1. That baptism is not to be administered to any who are not members of Christ's Church, till they profess their faith in him. Acts viii. 36, 37.—" What doth hinder me to be baptized? And Philip said, If thou believest with all thine heart, thou mayest."

2. That a profession of future obedience to Christ is necessary, before any who are not members of his Church be baptized. 1 Pet. iii. 21.—" The like figure whereunto even baptism doth also now save us (not the putting away of the filth of the flesh, but the answer of a good conscience towards God) by the resurrection of Jesus Christ."

3. That children of believing parents are proper subjects of baptism, as God bestows on many of them the blessings which it signifies. Luke xviii. 16.—" Suffer little children to come unto me, and forbid them not; for of such is the kingdom of God."

4. That children of believing parents are entitled to the sign of the covenant, as God has given them the promise of it. Acts ii. 39.—" The promise is unto you and to your children."

5. That children are to be considered ceremonially holy, and are entitled to the sign of the covenant, by the profession and membership of only one of their parents. 1 Cor. vii. 14.—" The unbelieving husband is sanctified by the wife, and the unbelieving wife is sanctified by the husband; else were your children unclean; but now are they holy."

6. That the infants of a family are entitled to the sign of the

covenant, on the profession and baptism of their parent. Acts xvi. 33.—" And was baptized, he and all his, straightway."

EXPLANATION.

Obs. 321.—*Baptism is not to be administered to any that are out of the visible Church, until they profess faith in Christ and obedience to him.*

By the *visible Church* we are to understand a society composed of all those, together with their children, who, in all ages and places of the world, profess the true religion. The *visible* Church is opposed to what is called the *invisible* Church, which is composed of all the elect that have been or shall be gathered into one under Christ the head.—Eph. i. 10, &c.; John x. 16, and xi. 52.

There are various descriptions of people, who are obviously without the visible Church, and who, of course, have no right to the seals of the covenant; such as Jews, Mahometans, pagans, infidels, and scandalous persons, &c. As such, neither they nor their children are to be baptized, for they are without the covenant—they are visibly far from righteousness, and they want even a name to live. To baptize such while they continue in that state, would be a prostitution of the ordinance.—Eph. ii. 12.

Baptism, however, is not to be withheld from these for ever. We are here told, that it is only not to be administered to them, *until they profess faith in Christ and obedience to him.* To " profess faith in Christ," is to profess a belief of the whole system of revealed truth. And to " profess obedience to Christ," is to yield an external subjection to all his ordinances and institutions, and to promise future obedience to his laws. Acts viii. 37, and ii. 46. It must, however, be remembered, that such a profession respects those only who have come to years of understanding. If any continue without the covenant, they exclude themselves for ever from the seal of the covenant.

But seeing the Church is viewed as *visible* and *invisible*, profession may be considered both with respect to *God* and with respect to *man*. With respect to *man*, a visible and public profession of faith in Christ and obedience to him, is all that is necessary to give a right, before the visible Church, to all its privileges. But with respect to *God*, none but they who are truly within the bond of the covenant, have a right to baptism, or to any of the privileges of the Church.

Obs. 322.—*The children and infants of believing parents have a right to baptism.*

That the *infants of believing parents* have a right to baptism, may be proved from the Abrahamic covenant, or the covenant which God made with Abraham; provided it was the covenant of grace—the same in substance, and containing the same blessings as that one under which believers now are. Now, that this covenant was the *covenant of grace*, is evident from a comparison of Gen. xvii. 7, where the covenant made with Abraham is expressed, with Heb. viii. 10, where the new covenant is expressed. In the one, the promise is, " To be a God unto thee, and to thy seed after thee;" and in the other, it is, " I will be to them a God, and they (the house of Israel, which must surely include infants) shall be to me a people." But God cannot be said to be the God of any, and of their seed, in the natural sense of the expression, but in Christ Jesus his Son, or through the covenant of grace. Therefore, as the covenant of grace promises every thing, when God promises to be our God ; so the Abrahamic covenant, which promises the same thing in the same manner, must be the covenant of grace. But the covenant made with Abraham included his seed, and gave them a right to circumcision, the seal of it. Hence, in like manner, it must follow, that children are now also included in the covenant blessings, or have a right to baptism, the seal of the covenant. See also Luke i. 54, &c., where we learn that the Old Testament saints were under the same covenant of grace under which believers now are.

That the children of believing parents ought to be baptized, may also be proved from various other passages of Scripture :—

1. It may be proved from Luke xviii. 16.—" Suffer little children to come unto me, and forbid them not; for of such is the kingdom of God, or of heaven."—Matt. xix. 14. From these words of our Saviour it is evident, that little children are capable of Church membership, or of being in the kingdom of heaven ; and if so, they are surely capable of baptism, the initiatory seal of the covenant.

2. It may be proved from Mark x. 14-16, where we read, that Jesus " took up little children in his arms, and put his hands upon them, and blessed them." By this he evidently declared to his apostles, that children were capable of receiving spiritual blessings; and, consequently, the visible sign of their being members of the kingdom of God. And it is further evident, that at the very moment in which Christ blessed them, they were members of the Church ; for, said he, " Of such *is* the kingdom of heaven."

3. It may be proved from Matt. xxviii. 19.—" Go ye therefore, and teach all nations, baptizing them in the name of the Father, and of the Son, and of the Holy Ghost." From this, in connection with the preceding passages, it is evident, that little children were to be baptized, being a part of the nations which Christ commissioned his apostles to teach and baptize. If there are any little children in the kingdom of God above, (and who can say that there are not ?) it will not be very easy to prove, that in this world baptism ought not to be administered to them as such.

4. It may be proved from 1 Cor. vii. 14.—" The unbelieving

husband is sanctified by the wife, and the unbelieving wife is sanctified by the husband; else were your children unclean; but now are they holy." This is a passage which shows in a very clear light, notwithstanding the inconsistent objections of opponents, the right of children to baptism in virtue of their relation to their believing parents. The *holiness* here spoken of must be something which flows from the holiness of one or both of the parents, and without which the children would be unclean; and surely this can mean nothing more than what is called a *federal* or a *covenant holiness,* which entitles the children to the privileges of the covenant. And if children are thus holy, who can deny them the seal of the covenant?

5. It may be proved from Acts ii. 38, 39.—" Then Peter said unto them, Repent and be baptized every one of you in the name of Jesus Christ, for the remission of sins, and ye shall receive the Holy Ghost; for the promise is to you and to your children." Whatever the promise is to which the apostle here alludes, nothing is more obvious than that he uses it as a *motive* why they and their children should be baptized, or submit by this external sign to the dispensation of Christ. If, then, the promise was any reason why the parents should be baptized, it was as good a reason why the children should be baptized; the promise being made to both. This is as plain as language can make it. The promise is to you, parents; therefore be ye baptized: the promise is to you, children; therefore be ye also baptized. If the apostle were made to speak a different language, according to the Baptists, a Jew might with the utmost propriety argue thus:—" I see that the promise—the motive now urged—is made to my children as well as to myself; if, therefore, it is no reason why *they* should be baptized, it can be no reason why *I* should be baptized." But with respect to the *promise* here alluded to,—that it is not (as the Baptists maintain) the *Prophecy of Joel,* before referred to by the apostle (ver. 17-21), is evident; because, were this the case, it would follow, either that baptism belonged to the age of miracles, which continued but a short time after the ascension of Christ; or that all who have been baptized, have been baptized in the faith of a promise which has not been fulfilled; which would be a gross insult upon the faithfulness of a promising God. But, on the other hand, that it is the covenant made with Abraham, is evident from Gal. iii. 14, 29, where this covenant is expressly called *the promise.* And it is said, " If ye be Christ's, then are ye Abraham's seed, and heirs according to *the promise.*" To what promise?—not surely the Prophecy of Joel, but *the promise* which God made with Abraham; which, moreover, is put beyond all doubt by considering Acts iii. 25, 26. And the covenant made with Abraham may well be called *the promise* made to him; and as believers are called his children and heirs according to *the promise,* we may safely rely upon it, that the

promise in the passage before us is the very same as the covenant of grace. If, then, this is urged as a motive to baptism, it must doubtless respect children as well as their parents; for the promise respected Abraham and his seed, who were both circumcised.

6. It may be proved from Rom. xi. 16, 17.—" If the first fruit be holy, the lump is also holy; and if the root be holy, so are the branches. And if some of the branches be broken off, and thou, being a wild olive tree, wert graffed in among them, and with them partakest of the root and fatness of the olive tree, boast not against the branches," &c. From this passage we learn that many Jews believed in Christ; and likewise, that these believers were still the natural branches in the root, Abraham, and partook of the fatness of the true olive. The natural branches, then, or the believing Jews, must have enjoyed the same privileges that ever they did; and, consequently, they must have had something answering to circumcision; and this could be nothing but baptism. Hence, the ingrafted branches, or the believing Gentiles, were entitled to the same; otherwise it could not be said, " Thou, being a wild olive tree, wert graffed in among them, and with them partakest of the root and fatness of the olive tree." That the children of Jewish parents were included in the covenant made with Abraham, is beyond a doubt; but if the same privileges are not enjoyed by the children of believing Gentiles that were enjoyed by Jewish children, they cannot be said to *partake of the root and fatness of the olive tree;* which would at once overthrow the apostle's argument; and, in fact, what he affirms would not be true. But, moreover, what can be more evident than that the children of believing Gentiles are federally holy, as much as the Jewish children are, seeing they are ingrafted in among them without any restriction as to their enjoyment of the same privileges?

But finally, there is the highest probability that the apostles baptized infants; for we find that they baptized whole households or families at once. Thus we read of the baptism of the family of Lydia, and of the family of the jailer at Philippi, in Acts xvi., and of the family of Stephanas, in 1 Cor. i. In these passages there is no mention made of *adults* more than of *infants;* and, consequently, it will be as difficult to prove that all were adults, as that there were some children. But the whole were baptized; and may we not suppose that there were some young ones or infants, as well as adults, among them? That in all these families there was not one infant, is scarcely credible. Now, if there were infants, and if, according to our opponents' view of the subject, they were excepted, we should naturally expect to see such an exception recorded, as something new in the visible Church. But no such thing is upon record,—an evidence that no infants were excluded from baptism We may here remark, that the Book of Acts contains the history of the Church for upwards of thirty years; in which time the infants of those who were first baptized must have reached the years of maturity. If they were not baptized in infancy, how comes it to pass, that, among the numerous baptisms recorded in the New Testament, no reference is made to the baptism of any of them in an *adult* state? From the silence of Scripture on this head, taken in connection with the instances of the baptism of whole families above referred to, we conclude that they must have been baptized in infancy or childhood, or along with their parents.

Obs. 323.—*Baptism is not be administered oftener than once.*

There is no command to dispense this ordinance oftener than *once;* nor does its nature admit of its being oftener administered. By baptism we are admitted into the Church; and this admission can take place but once; and as it signifies and seals our ingrafting into Christ, we are to be baptized but once; because, if once in Christ, we can never be broken off.

Obs. 324.—*The naming of a child at baptism is no part of the ordinance.*

That the giving of a *name* at baptism is no part of this institution, is evident from the commission which Christ gave to his apostles.—Matt. xxviii. 19, 20. There are many, indeed, who maintain that naming a child is a part of baptism; but no one who is taught from above will maintain such an absurd opinion. Every thing connected with the ordinance was appointed by Christ; but it was never mentioned by him, that a child should be named then, as if it could not be named before. It is the parent who names his child, and who ought to do it; but it would be altogether absurd to say, that what is done by the parent in this respect constitutes an essential part, or even any part of the ordinance. Baptism, then, is not the giving of a name to a child, but the *dedication* of a child to God, whose gift it is, together with a promise or vow on the part of the parent, that he will "train up his child in the nurture and admonition of the Lord;" which, if he neglect to do, he becomes guilty of perjury, and thus renders himself obnoxious to the punishment threatened against the breakers of the Third Commandment.

Obs. 325.—*None but the immediate parents have a right to present any child for baptism.*

This is evident; for it is only in the right of the immediate parents that children ought to be baptized; and no conscientious parent, who knows the nature of baptism, will make application for it on any other right or ground whatever. They who do so, or they who have their children baptized in the right of a sponsor or godfather, cannot be supposed to be much acquainted with the great things designed by this ordinance. Such require it merely to serve a purpose (perhaps to conceal the wickedness of the parents, who are conscious that they have no right to receive baptism for their children, or for some other end equally bad), and when their children are baptized, they care no more about the ordinance, and frequently as little about their children, with respect to bringing them up for God. That children should be baptized on the right of another, who is a member of the visible Church, whether relation by blood or acquaintance, is most absurd. No one can give a right to his brother to the privileges of the Church; how, then, can he give a right to his brother's children for baptism? or, how can one relation give a right to another, except that of parents and children? They can no more do this, than Abraham, Isaac, or Jacob, could have given a right to the descendants of Esau to all or any of the privileges of the Jewish Church. But, notwithstanding this, many who undertake to be sponsors for children in baptism, and who vow to Jehovah, the heart-searcher of all, that they will bring up the children for whom they engage in the fear of the Lord, are as ignorant of them, and pay as little attention to them, with respect both to this world and the world to come, as one on the other side of the globe.

INFERENCES.

From this subject we learn,—1. That the way of salvation has always been the same; and that the grace of God has been visible in all ages. 2. The fulness of our privileges, and of those of our children. 3. That when baptism is administered to any in our presence, it ought to excite our gratitude that we were born in a Christian land, and within the visible Church, so as to have a right to all its privileges. 4. That we have reason to bless God that we live under the New Testament dispensation. 5. That parents ought to consider how they have paid their vows to the Lord,—whether they make conscience of praying for and with their children—of bringing them up in the fear of the Lord—and of informing them of the necessity of an interest in Christ, and of true godliness, &c.

Of the Nature and Use of the Lord's Supper.

Q. 96.—What is the Lord's Supper?

The Lord's Supper is a sacrament, wherein, by giving and receiving bread and wine, according to Christ's appointment, his death is shewed forth; and the worthy receivers are, not after a corporal and carnal manner, but by faith, made partakers of his body and blood, with all his benefits, to their spiritual nourishment and growth in grace.

OF THE NATURE AND USE OF THE LORD'S SUPPER. 321

ANALYSIS AND PROOFS.

We are here taught,—
1. That the sensible signs to be used in the Lord's Supper are bread and wine. Matt. xxvi. 26, 27.—" Jesus took bread, and blessed it, and brake it, and gave it to them, saying, Take, eat ; this is my body. And he took the cup, and gave thanks, and gave it to them, saying, Drink ye all of it."
2. That by giving and receiving bread and wine in the sacrament of the Supper, according to Christ's appointment, his death is shewed forth. 1 Cor. xi. 26.—" As often as ye eat this bread, and drink this cup, ye do shew the Lord's death till he come."
3. That it is not in a corporal and carnal manner that Christ's body and blood are received in the sacrament. 1 Cor. x. 16.—" The cup of blessing which we bless, is it not the communion of the blood of Christ? The bread which we break, is it not the communion of the body of Christ?"
4. That in the sacrament the body and blood of Christ are received by faith. John vi. 35.—" I am the bread of life; he that cometh to me shall never hunger; and he that believeth on me shall never thirst."
5. That in the sacrament, believers are made partakers of Christ and all his benefits. John vi. 51.—" I am the living bread which came down from heaven. If any man eat of this bread, he shall live for ever; and the bread that I will give is my flesh, which I will give for the life of the world."
6. That spiritual nourishment is conferred in the sacrament. John vi. 55.—" My flesh is meat indeed, and my blood is drink indeed."
7. That by worthily partaking of the Lord's Supper, the Christian is enabled to grow in grace. John iv. 14.—" The water that I shall give him, shall be in him a well of water springing up into everlasting life."

EXPLANATION.

Obs. 326.—*The Sacrament of the Lord's Supper is known by various names.*
1. It is called *the Sacrament;* the meaning of which word was formerly explained ; and although it is not found in Scripture, yet its import is.
2. It is called *the Lord's Supper;* which is a scriptural expression, and therefore unexceptionable.—1 Cor. xi. 20. It is called a *Supper*, because it was appointed immediately after eating the last Passover, which feast was always eaten at night.—Exod. xii. ; Matt. xxvi. And it is called the *Lord's* Supper, because Jesus Christ, the constituted head and king of Zion, was the author of it. And it is highly requisite that it should derive its authority from him; because all the grace therein exhibited i

treasured up in him, and applied by him to the soul. Its appointment was an act of dominion; and by observing it in obedience to his command, and in remembrance of him, who is the substance of it, we acknowledge this dominion.

3. It is called *the Communion*,—1 Cor. x. 16; and that, too, with great propriety. In this ordinance we hold communion both with Christ and with one another. And hence it is evident, that we must first be united to Christ, or brought within the bond of the covenant, before any real communion can be held with him in the breaking of bread.

4. It is called *the Feast*,—1 Cor. v. 8; and that very properly, seeing the import of this ordinance leads us to this idea. This is a term which is not often applied to it among us, although it is far more proper than some of those that are generally used. Gospel privileges and preparations are called by this name, both in the Old and in the New Testament.—Isa. xxv. 6; Matt. xxii. 2, &c.; Luke xiv. 16, &c. The Lord's Supper is a feast of remembrance, as the Passover was of old; and at it we dedicate ourselves to the Lord.—1 Kings viii. 65.

5. It is called *the Eucharist;* which is a word of Greek origin, and signifies *thanksgiving*. When Christ instituted the ordinance, we read that he *gave thanks;* and this he did before he broke the bread (1 Cor. xi. 24); no doubt very joyful that the time was come when he was actually to redeem his Church from sin and all its consequences. And surely, when we are called to celebrate this ordinance, we ought to be employed in giving thanks; for here we have abundant reason for testifying our gratitude to our redeeming Saviour, who gave himself for us while we were his enemies.

6. It is also called *the Breaking of Bread*,—Acts ii. 42, because this is one of the actions performed in its celebration; Christ's *Testament*,—Luke xxii. 20, because it is one of the seals of the covenant of grace; the *Cup of Blessing*,—1 Cor. x. 16; and the *Lord's Table*,—1 Cor. x. 21. From its being called the Lord's Table, we may infer, that it should be received in a *sitting posture*, which appears to be most agreeable to the practice of our Lord and his apostles at the first institution of this ordinance. —Matt. xxvi. 20, 26.

We may here observe, that our Saviour instituted this ordinance on the same night in which he was betrayed, or on the night preceding his death. By this we discover the wonderful love and regard which he had for his Church at this time. Although he was to suffer from every quarter, and that in the room of sinners, yet he had the comfort of his people so much at heart, that he appointed this memorial of his love to be observed by them until he come again.—1 Cor. xi. 23–26.

Obs. 327.—*The elements or sensible signs to be used in the celebration of the Lord's Supper, are bread and wine.*

These were appointed by Christ himself as symbols or representations of his body and blood ; by which we are to understand in general, his incarnation, his meritorious obedience, and his satisfactory death ; all which are necessary for the accomplishment of that redemption for which he appeared in this world. And hence there must be some *analogy* or *resemblance* between the signs and the things signified, or between bread and wine, and the body and blood of Christ.

1. The analogy or resemblance between the *bread* and *body of Christ*, may be traced in the following particulars :—(1.) Bread is *most necessary* for the preservation of the natural life, for none can exist without it ; and hence it is called the *staff of life*. In like manner, nothing is so necessary for the soul as Christ, the bread of life, which came down from heaven ; of which, if a man eat, he shall live for ever.—John vi. 32–58. (2.) Bread is most calculated for the *nourishment*, and *strengthening*, and *satisfying* of the body. In like manner, nothing is more calculated for oui spiritual nourishment, and strength, and satisfaction, than the broken body of the Son of God. This is the means provided by God for preserving the life of the soul, and for satisfying the sinner's need. (3.) Bread is the *common* provision of all. In like manner, the salvation of Christ is a salvation offered to all. and suited for all.—Rev. xxii. 17 ; Matt xi. 28. (4.) Bread must be *prepared* in various ways before it can be useful to man. Corn must be thrashed, bruised or ground, and baked, before it is bread fit for man. In like manner, that Christ might be man's Saviour, he must be bruised (so to speak) between the wrath of his Father, and our sins and the enmity and malice of men and of devils against him. He must be scorched, as it were, in the furnace of incensed justice.—Psal. xx. 14 ; Isa. liii. 4, 5. (5.) Bread is food which is *never loathed* by those who are in health. In like manner, the bread of life which came down from heaven is always pleasant and agreeable to the believer; for to such Christ is precious ; although the greater part of mankind loathe and abhor the heavenly manna. (6.) Bread, before it can be of any service to man, must be *used* by him and *incorporated* with him. In like manner, the body of Christ must be broken, and received and fed upon by faith, before it can be of any spiritual advantage to the soul.—John vi. 56.

2. The analogy or resemblance between *wine* and the *blood of Christ*, may be traced in the following particulars :—(1.) Wine. in order to be used, must be forcibly *squeezed* out of the grape, which must be bruised for this purpose. In like manner, the blood of Christ was forcibly separated from his body. He was bruised in the wine-press of Divine wrath, that his blood might be drink to our perishing souls.—John vi. 53. (2.) Wine is of a *refreshing*, and *cheering*, and *strengthening* nature.—Prov. xxvi. 6. And what can be more refreshing to the spiritual tra-

veller to the Zion above, and to the soul harassed by Satan's temptations, than the application of the blood of Christ to the soul by faith? (3.) Wine is of a *medicinal* virtue.—1 Tim. v. 23; Luke x. 34. In like manner, the blood of Christ, when applied by the Divine Spirit, cleanses and cures; and the soul is made to rejoice in the Lord. (4.) Wine is of no advantage *without being used*. In like manner, the blood of Christ is of no profit at all to the soul, unless it is applied by the agency of the Holy Spirit, and unless there is an habitual use of it by faith for the purposes for which it was shed, and for which it is exhibited to the believer's faith in this sacrament.

Obs. 328.—*In the sacrament of the Lord's Supper, there is a giving and receiving of bread and wine.*

Under this we may consider the *sacramental actions* on the part of the administrator, and on that of the receivers of this ordinance.

1. The sacramental actions on the part of the *administrator* are four; and Christ having set the example, his ministers are to follow his steps. (1.) He *took* the bread and the cup. This action implies the Father's designation of his Son to be the saviour of a lost world; according as it is said, "I have laid help upon One that is mighty," &c.—Ps. lxxxix. 19. (2.) He *blessed* the bread and the cup, or the wine in the cup. This action seems to imply, that Christ hath appointed bread and wine to be the visible signs or symbols of his body and blood; and that by his example he hath warranted ministers to set apart, by prayer and thanksgiving, from a common to a sacred use, so much of the elements as shall be used in the celebration of the ordinance. And it may also imply God's sending his Son into the world every way suited and qualified, with all gifts and graces, for being the saviour of sinners, and for meeting the wants of his people in every time of need. (3.) He *broke* the bread. This is an action so necessary to the ordinance, that it is sometimes called *the breaking of bread*.—Acts xx. 7. It plainly points out the exquisite sufferings of the Son of God, and their absolute necessity, as the only channel through which mercy can flow to sinners. It also exhibits Christ's willingness to suffer; being as willing to suffer as he was to break the bread in the presence of his disciples. And although we do not read of his pouring out the wine, which represents his blood shed; yet the bruising of his body was intimately connected with the shedding of his blood; for the one could not take place without the other. (4.) He *gave* the bread and the cup to the disciples. Taking this action in connection with the command, "Take, eat—drink ye all of it," it is by no means the least important. It denotes, in general, that Christ is the free gift of God for life and salvation to sinners of mankind; that God the Father makes over his Son to us, with all the bless-

ings of his purchase, to be ours both now and for ever. And it may be here remarked, that Christ did not give the cup out of his own hand to each of his disciples individually, but to those that were nearest to him, to be given to one another, or to be divided among themselves. This is evident from his own words —" Take, eat; drink *ye all* of it." And it is most like a communion feast, and most expressive of love to one another, when communicants thus divide among themselves the symbols of the bread and water of life.

2. The sacramental actions on the part of the *receivers*, are these:—(1.) They *take* the bread and the cup into their own hands. This implies, that our receiving of Christ is founded upon the gift and grant which is made of him in the Word. And this is the comfort of sinners, that, in virtue of this grant in the Word, they have a right to receive Christ for a whole salvation. Here, then, faith is absolutely necessary; for Christ and all the benefits of his redemption are received only by the hand of faith; and the soul of the believer cheerfully complies with the offer that is made of him, by eating and drinking at his table. (2.) They *eat* the bread and *drink* the wine. This implies, in general, that there must be a particular application of Jesus Christ to the soul, in virtue of the gospel offer being made to every one.—Acts ii. 39. It likewise implies the great pleasure which the believer enjoys in thus feeding by faith upon Christ and all the benefits of his redemption.

Obs. 329.—*The Lord's Supper was designed to shew forth his death, and to be a memorial of him until he come again.*

1. This ordinance was instituted, that by it *the Lord's death might be shewn forth.* As it is from the death of Christ that all our hopes in time and through eternity do flow; and as we here behold his love, which passeth all understanding, covering every sin and appearing in the sinner's room, that it might not be his ruin; it well becomes us to *shew forth the Lord's death.* This is a term expressive of a profession of faith in the death of Christ in our room, not only as having actually taken place, but as having been most acceptable to God; and it is also expressive of our acquiescence in it together with his obedience, as the only ground of our hope before God. We may here remark, that, although this ordinance is not absolutely necessary to salvation, yet all the followers of Christ who have arrived at the years of knowledge and understanding, lie under an obligation to observe it. There are circumstances which may occur to prevent some true believers from observing it; in which case it is not necessary to salvation. But if any who have it in their power neglect the celebration of it, they are guilty of much sin. They reject the commandment of Christ, express the highest degree of ingratitude to him for the best of mercies, and despise their own best

interests, which should lie so near their hearts in this world; they are guilty of a wilful contempt of the words of life and of a dying Saviour; they show the highest disrespect for the love of Christ, which passeth all understanding; and they wilfully reject the blessings which most intimately concern their immortal souls.

2. This ordinance was instituted as a *memorial of Jesus Christ until he come again.* " Do this," said the Saviour, "in remembrance of me." At this ordinance we must remember that he actually did and suffered all that was written in the Law, and the Prophets, and the Psalms concerning him—all that the hand or counsel of God had determined. We must remember that, unless Jehovah himself had found a ransom, we must have assuredly perished eternally. We must remember the infinite value of his death, its precious nature, and how it secures the everlasting salvation of an innumerable multitude out of every nation, and kindred, and tongue, and people. And we must remember how willing he was to stand in the breach, that wrath might be averted—to suffer and to die, the Just One for the unjust, that he might bring us back to God, and give us the pleasant land—the land of Immanuel. But this must not be a bare remembrance of his death; it must be such a remembrance as will excite to adoration of that display of justice and holiness which took place when the Son of God was suspended on the cross—when the Lord spared him not, but was pleased to bruise him, and to put him to grief. And hence it must be accompanied with humiliation on our part, seeing our sins were the procuring cause of his death—with detestation of sin, and with thankfulness; because his death was in our stead, and finished the work which was assigned him to do. It must also be remembered in such a manner as to place our whole dependence on it for justification and life before God; for Jesus was delivered for our offences, and raised again for our justification, that our faith and hope might be in God.—1 Pet. i. 21.

Obs. 330.—*In the Lord's Supper, the worthy receivers are made partakers of Christ's body and blood, with all his benefits.*

By *worthy receivers* we are here to understand *true believers.* But these are not called *worthy* receivers, on account of any worthiness in themselves, or because they have any thing of which they may glory; for no one, not even the highest archangel, has any thing to boast of before God. But this term may be applied to them on account of their union with Jesus Christ, from whom they derive all that is necessary for partaking of this ordinance in a right and becoming manner.—2 Cor. iii. 5.

Believers, then, who alone observe this ordinance in a worthy manner, are made partakers of *Christ's body and blood, with all his benefits.* The expression. " Christ's body and blood," points out his work and labour of love—all that he did, as Mediator, and all that was done upon his person—which is set before us at his table as the true food of the soul.—John vi. 53. And the "benefits" of which believers are made partakers, are such as these:—the Holy Spirit to teach, to guide, and to comfort them; an ample indemnity of all sin, for Christ's blood is shed for the remission of the sins of many; peace with God, and peace of conscience; together with many more, the number and value of which cannot be named. They are called *his* (*i.e.*, Christ's) benefits, because he purchased them,—Tit. ii. 14; because the Father hath given all things into his hand,—John iii. 35; and because he dispenses them; "he giveth gifts unto men."—Eph. iv. 8. And worthy partakers are said to receive, not only *his benefits*, but *all his benefits;* because when Christ himself is received, all good things are received along with him.—1 Cor. iii. 21-23.

Obs. 331.—*Believers are made partakers of Christ's body and blood, not in a corporal and carnal manner, but by faith.*

It is here said that believers are made partakers of Christ and his benefits, *not in a corporal and carnal manner*, in opposition to the Popish abomination of *transubstantiation;* by which they understand, that the bread and wine, after consecration or blessing, are changed into the real body and blood of the Lord, or into the substance of his body and blood. This opinion is repugnant not only to Scripture, but also to reason and to our senses; and it destroys the very nature and end of a sacrament.

1. It is contrary to *Scripture*, which expressly affirms that, after blessing, the elements are called by the same names as before. This is surely an intimation, that there is no such change made upon them as is here supposed.—Matt. xxvi. 26-29; 1 Cor. xi. 23-28.

2. It is repugnant to *reason*, which informs us that a body can occupy but one place at one time, and cannot possibly be in different places at one and the same time. But the advocates for this horrid doctrine must admit, that the body of Christ is at the same time in ten thousand places, nay, in millions of places, even in as many as there are consecrated wafers; that it must be dead and alive at once; that it must be in heaven and on earth at once; and that accidents may be without a substance, and a substance without accidents;—all which is replete with the greatest absurdity.

3. It is repugnant to our *senses*, which inform us that, after blessing, the elements are still bread and wine. We can only be said to *hear* that this change takes place, which however is fully contradicted by all the other senses. Such a change as this would destroy all moral certainty; would destroy the proof of all the miracles by which the Word of God is confirmed; and, in a word we could not be certain of any thing whatever.

4. This blasphemous doctrine *destroys the very nature and end of a sacrament.* The design of this ordinance is to *commemorate* an absent Christ: " Do this in remembrance of me." But this opinion would really present him before our eyes; notwithstanding that we are assured by Scripture, that the heavens must retain his manhood till he come again.—Acts iii. 21. And, moreover, there would be no difference between the sign and the thing signified.

But it may be here asked, Is there no change at all made upon the bread and wine in the Lord's Supper? To this we answer in the affirmative. But the change which takes place is not a *physical*, but only a *moral* change,—a change as to their use and signification. They are set apart from a common to a sacred use; and we are no longer to deem what may be used of them as ordinary food, but as symbols of Christ's body and blood, and of the benefits of his redemption. And this change takes place, not by destroying their substance, but by Divine appointment.

The only way, then, in which believers are made partakers of Christ's body and blood, with all his benefits, is spiritually, or by *faith*,—that is, by applying and appropriating him and his righteousness, and all that he hath, to themselves.—Ps. xvi. 5, 6.

We may here observe that, although Christ is not corporeally present in the Lord's Supper, yet he is as really and spiritually present to the faith of believers in this ordinance, as the elements themselves are to their outward senses.—1 Cor. xi. 29. If it be objected to this, that Christ said " This is my body," we answer, that this expression must be understood, not in a *literal*, but in a *figurative* sense; as if he had said, " This bread is the *sign* or *symbol* of my body." It must ever be remembered that, when the strict literal sense would involve a manifest absurdity, we must have recourse to the figurative sense. Thus, when the apostle saith (1 Cor. x. 4), " That Rock was Christ," we cannot understand it literally, as if that rock, materially considered, was *really* Christ; but figuratively, that rock signified Christ. And this will be found to be the case with a great many other Scripture expressions, as when Christ is called a *way*, a *door*, a *vine*, &c.—John x. and xv.

Obs. 332.—*By worthily partaking of the Lord's Supper, the believer receives spiritual nourishment, and is enabled to grow in grace.*

This is the consequence of being made partaker of Christ and all his benefits by faith; and it implies, that this sacrament is not a converting, but a *nourishing* ordinance, and that the worthy receivers are already *in a state of grace.* Whenever faith is in right exercise, it cannot fail to receive strength and spiritual nourishment; and the soul, of course, must go on its way rejoicing, being thus made strong in the Lord. and in the power of his might. And these effects take place when the believer has a greater desire after the sincere milk of the Word. that his soul may grow thereby; when he is enabled to live more by faith, and less by sense; when he discovers more opposition to sin in its various workings; and when he is enabled more and more to adorn the doctrine of God our Saviour in all things, by a life and conversation becoming his gospel.—1 Pet. ii. 2; 2 Cor. v. 7; Ps. lxvi. 18; Tit. ii. 10; Phil. i. 27.

Obs. 333.—*The ordinance of the Lord's Supper is not a sacrifice for sin.*

This is the opinion of the Church of Rome, and of many others who are nearly allied to her. But it may be observed, that there are many, even among Protestants, who, although they do not speak of it as such, nevertheless appear to act upon the principle of its being so. Accordingly, when they sit down at the Lord's Table, and eat and drink there, they imagine that their sins are pardoned, and that they cannot come short of eternal life. This is ascribing to the ordinance the same merit that is ascribed to the death of Christ; which is as much as saying with the Papists, that the Lord's Supper is a sacrifice for the remission of sins. So far from being a sacrifice for sin, this ordinance is designed only to be a commemoration of that *one sacrifice*, which Jesus Christ offered to God once for all. It reminds us of the sacrifice of Christ; and at his table we may plead this sacrifice for the remission of sins. But surely the elements cannot be this sacrifice, but only a sign and a seal of it, designed for the best of purposes connected with the comfort of the soul for ever.

INFERENCES.

From this subject we learn,—1. That the Church is precious in the sight of Christ, and that he remembers her. 2. The love of God and his Christ to sinners of mankind. 3. That there is much done by Christ for the comfort of the saints. 4. The danger of not complying with the command of Christ in this ordinance. 5. That there is no sacrifice for sin, but the atoning death of Christ. 6. The necessity of having right ends in view in partaking of the ordinance of the Supper, and the danger of partaking from improper motives.

Of the Proper Observance of the Lord's Supper.

Q. 97.—What is required to the worthy receiving of the Lord's Supper?

It is required of them that would worthily partake of the Lord's Supper, that they examine themselves of their knowledge to discern the Lord's body, of their faith to feed upon him, of their repentance, love, and new obedience, lest coming unworthily, they eat and drink judgment to themselves.

ANALYSIS AND PROOFS.

We are here taught,—

1. That self-examination is required of all who would worthily partake of the Lord's Supper. 1 Cor. xi. 28.—"Let a man examine himself, and so let him eat of that bread, and drink of that cup."

2. That communicants should examine themselves respecting their knowledge to discern the Lord's body. 1 Cor. xi. 29.—"He that eateth and drinketh unworthily, eateth and drinketh damnation (or judgment) to himself, not discerning the Lord's body."

3. That communicants should examine themselves respecting their faith to feed upon Christ. 2 Cor. xiii. 5.—"Examine yourselves whether ye be in the faith." See also John vi. 57.

4. That communicants should examine themselves respecting their repentance. Lam. iii. 40.—"Let us search and try our ways, and turn again to the Lord."

5. That communicants should examine themselves respecting their love. 1 John iv. 8.—"He that loveth not, knoweth not God: for God is love."

6. That communicants should examine themselves respecting their new obedience. 1 Cor. v. 8.—"Let us keep the feast, not with old leaven, neither with the leaven of malice and wickedness, but with the unleavened bread of sincerity and truth."

7. That it is dangerous to neglect the duty of self-examination. 1 Cor. xi. 31.—"If we would judge ourselves, we should not be judged."

8. That communicating unworthily exposes us to the judgments of God. 1 Cor. xi. 29.—"He that eateth and drinketh unworthily, eateth and drinketh damnation (or judgment) to himself."—Ver. 30.

EXPLANATION.

Obs. 334.—*Self-examination is required of all who would worthily partake of the Lord's Supper.*

With respect to those who have a right to partake of this ordinance, we may observe, that, *before men*, all have a right who appear to be true Christians; who have been baptized into the name of Christ; who profess their faith in him, and show their love to him; and who have a competent knowledge of the doctrines of Christianity; or, in other words, who seem to fear God and keep his commandments, or who seem to have a conversation becoming the gospel. But, *before God*, none but truly gracious persons, who have been converted and are within the bond of the covenant, and who have fled for refuge to Christ, have a right to sit down at his table. Nay, we may advance a step further and say, that, unless such come in a state of preparation, even they may approach the Lord's Table unworthily. And thus it is that believers may communicate unworthily, merely because they come unmindful of the duty here enjoined.

The worthiness which is here required, is not worthiness in a *legal* sense; for, before God, no saint, however eminent, has the least merit, or any thing on which he may found his plea for any of the blessings exhibited in this ordinance. After all that we are or can do, we are but unprofitable servants, having done no more than our duty. All that is meant, then, by this worthiness, is a *gospel suitableness*—a proper state and frame,—Matt. xxii. 8, where *worthiness* is taken nearly in the same meaning.

In order, then, to discover whether we have this worthiness—this gospel suitableness—this proper state and frame, we must apply ourselves to the duty of *self-examination*. To *examine one's self* is to make strict inquiry into one's own state, and to pass an impartial sentence upon one's self, according to a proper rule; and this is an exercise which very nearly concerns one's own salvation. Nor does it concern some persons only; but it is unquestionably the indispensable duty of every one without exception; and it is a duty, too, which ought to be practised habitually,—2 Cor. xiii. 5, but particularly in the view of approaching the Lord's Table.

The *only rule* which we can observe with safety in this duty of self-examination, is the *Word of God.*—Isa. viii. 20. This alone informs us what we ought to be, and what we ought to do; and likewise what are the true marks and evidences of a gracious state.

That respecting which all ought to examine themselves, is the state or condition of their souls in the sight of God. This is evident from 2 Cor. xiii. 5.—" Examine yourselves, whether ye be *in the faith;*" whether in Christ or in a state of nature; whether born of God, born again, born from above, or still without God, and without Christ, and without hope in the world; whether believers or unbelievers; whether translated into the kingdom of God's dear Son, or still in the kingdom of Satan; whether passed from death to life, or still in a state of spiritual death, &c. But there are five things in particular, respecting which we must examine ourselves; and these are knowledge, faith, repentance, love, and new obedience; which may, with great propriety be called *sacramental graces,* because absolutely necessary to worthy communicating. Self-examination respecting these graces is absolutely necessary, for without it we cannot discover whether or not we possess them; and, consequently, whether or not we have any right to partake of the ordinance of the Supper. We must, however, remember, that, after all we can do in this respect, we must not depend upon ourselves or upon our prepara tion, but trust in the grace that is in Christ Jesus, and commit ourselves into his hand to work all our work in us and for us, and to bear all the glory. It is he alone who can thoroughly search us and try our hearts; he alone who can see if there be any wicked way in us, and who can lead us in the way everlasting.—Ps. cxxxix.

Obs. 335. *All those who would worthily partake of the Lord's Supper, must examine themselves respecting their knowledge to discern the Lord's body.*

1. They must examine whether their knowledge be *competent in degree;* whether they have a knowledge of the fundamental doctrines of Christianity, so far as to be acquainted in some measure with the nature and perfections of God as revealed in Scripture; with the doctrine of the Trinity, and the part which each person has to act in the plan of salvation; with the wisdom, power, holiness, justice, goodness, and truth of God as harmoniously displayed in the work of redemption; with the fall of man, and the misery of the present state; with the person, and offices, and righteousness of Jesus Christ; with the fulness, freeness, and stability of the covenant of grace, and the application of its benefits by the Holy Spirit; with the necessity of faith and repentance, and all the other graces of the Spirit; with the nature, and the uses, and ends of the Lord's Supper; and likewise with their own manifold sins and wants; without which, knowledge cannot be said to be competent.

2. They must examine whether their knowledge *be saving in its kind;* whether it be an experimental knowledge; whether the soul feels the truth of what it knows; whether it be a knowledge that exalts Christ and debases self; whether it influences its possessor to place an implicit confidence in the Lord Jesus, from a heartfelt experience of his worth, and of his being the only way to the Father; whether it has such an influence on the heart as to make it better, as to make it love Christ and holiness more, and hate sin more, even with a perfect hatred, and to make us run with alacrity and cheerfulness in the ways of God's commandments; in a word, whether it be such a knowledge as influences the whole of our conduct; for, saith Christ, "If ye know these things, happy are ye if ye do them."—John xiii. 17.

Such knowledge as that now described, is absolutely necessary to worthy communicating; because they who are ignorant, or who have a mere speculative knowledge, who know nothing of themselves, of their sins, of their need of Christ, and of what he can bestow in virtue of his promise, cannot discern the things of the Spirit, which must be "spiritually discerned;" and, consequently, they cannot apprehend the true meaning and design of the holy things in this ordinance—they cannot "discern the Lord's body."

To *discern the Lord's body* is to perceive and understand that the symbols of bread and wine represent the broken body and shed blood of Jesus Christ. As the elements of bread and wine are in themselves common things, and only representations of the body and blood of Christ, but nevertheless true representations of the same, so we must truly distinguish them from common bread and wine—as designed wholly for holy purposes. Through the elements we must look to the great things designed by them, even to Christ offering himself a sacrifice for sin, and making atonement for the sins of many; and we must do this in such a manner as to discern him as spiritually present in this ordinance, making offer of himself, with all that is his, to the worthy receivers; and we must so discern him as to trust in him for ever, having in some measure seen his incomparable beauties and excellencies at his own table.

Obs. 336.—*All those who would worthily partake of the Lord's Supper, must examine themselves respecting their faith to feed upon Christ.*

They who would communicate worthily, must examine whether their faith be a true or a false faith; whether they place a full, a real, and a lasting dependence upon Christ alone for life and salvation, rejecting every other confidence; or whether they give no more than a bare assent to what is written concerning him, with respect to the truth of his having been in the world, and of his having been crucified and raised from the dead; whether their faith be such a faith as purifieth the heart, worketh by love, overcometh the world, and saveth the soul; or whether it be only what is called a dead faith—a faith which produces none of the fruits of love to God.

Some of the marks or evidences of that faith which is wrought in all the children of God, are these:—They whose faith is of the operation of God's Spirit, do not rest in their present attainments of knowledge respecting the person and work of Christ, but desire to follow on to know the Lord more and more; they cordially embrace Jesus Christ in all his offices, being fully persuaded that he is the only Saviour of sinners, and that he is able and willing to save to the uttermost all who come to him; they receive him as their prophet, to teach them by his Word and Spirit; as their priest, who hath atoned for their guilt and is interceding for them; and as their king, to defend them from their enemies and to govern them by his laws; they are deeply humbled under a sight and sense of sin, as that abominable thing which the Lord hateth; they are not only weaned from the practice of sin, but purified from the love of sin; they account all things but loss for Christ, that they may win him and be found in him; they are careful to maintain good works, knowing that faith works by love to Christ and his people; they are encouraged to approach unto God in prayer for the performance of his promises, which are all in. Christ yea and amen (*i. e.*, absolutely certain), to the glory of God the Father (Heb. iv. 16; 2 Cor. i. 20); in a word, they desire Christ above all—they desire him supremely for himself, and not only for what he is to them.

In partaking of the Lord's Supper, faith is absolutely necessary, because without it we cannot *feed upon Christ*,—that is, without faith we cannot receive into our souls from his fulness all that spiritual good which is exhibited to us in the promise; without faith we cannot look above the symbols, and contemplate the crucified Redeemer as our Saviour, in such a manner as that our souls shall be refreshed and strengthened. It is also necessary, because without it, we are not in covenant with God, and consequently, have no right to the seal of the covenant; without it we cannot become united to Christ; without it, we cannot be brought into the family of God, and consequently, can have no right to sit down at his table; without it, we cannot become the Lord's peculiar treasure; and, moreover, without it, the other graces of the Spirit cannot be excited, nor work to the Divine glory.

Obs. 337.—*All those who would worthily partake of the Lord's Supper, must examine themselves respecting their repentance.*

They who would communicate worthily, must examine whether their repentance be true repentance, or whether it be only that sorrow of the world which worketh death.

They whose repentance is *genuine*, or wrought by the Spirit of God, are grieved for sin, because it is offensive and dishonouring to God, as well as hurtful to themselves (Ps. li. 4); they are more affected with the evil of sin, than with the afflictions which may follow it (Luke xv. 18); they are grieved on account of their remaining sin, and mourn over a corrupt heart, the root of sin; they are concerned not only to have the guilt of sin removed by the blood of Christ, but also its power and pollution removed by the Holy Spirit, for both these are inseparable; they do not rest merely in the pardon of sin, without sanctification of nature (Acts ii. 38); they turn from sin both in heart and life (Hos. xiv. 8); they hate not only some sins, but all known sin; they forsake sin not only for a time, but with a fixed resolution never to return to its indulgence; they are deeply affected with the sin of unbelief, which too much cleaves to the best (John xvi. 9); they bring forth fruits of holy obedience meet for repentance (Matt. iii. 8); and they experience something of what the Apostle Paul says on this subject in 2 Cor. vii. 11.

In partaking of the Lord's Supper, repentance is absolutely necessary, because without it there can be no mourning for sin, which is an inseparable concomitant of faith's looking to and improving a crucified Saviour in this ordinance (Zech. xii. 10); because it is only to the penitent that the Lord hath promised to look (Isa. lvii. 15); because, although believers receive the seal of the pardon of sin at the Lord's Table, yet God will not there seal the impenitent with the forgiveness of sin; because none but the truly humble see any thing in the blood of Christ exhibited at his table, for the stony heart careth not for the Fountain opened for sin and uncleanness; because, without repentance, sin is in the soul in its full strength and vigour; because, in this ordinance, God designs to discover the bitterness of sin, as well as his love to us in Christ; and because, without true repentance, there can be no suitable remembrance of a crucified Jesus at his table.

Obs. 338.—*All who would worthily partake of the Lord's Supper, must examine themselves respecting their love.*

They who would communicate worthily, must examine whether they possess that love to God, to Jesus Christ, to their Christian brethren, and to all mankind, which is characteristic of all believers.

1. Our love to *God* is genuine, if we love him supremely for his own excellencies; if we endeavour always to please him by keeping his commandments; and if we are sincerely grieved when we at any time offend him.

2. Our love to *Jesus Christ* is genuine, if we love him above every other object; if we love him on account of what he is in himself, or on account of his excellencies, which render him altogether lovely (Cant. v. 10, &c.); if we love him, not only for what he hath done for sinners in general, but also for what he hath done for us in particular; if our meditation of him is sweet, and our hearts fixed upon him as our chief joy; if we delight in his Word and ordinances (Ps. cxix. and lxxxiv.); if we delight in communion with him; if we cleave fast to him at all times; if we embrace him in all his offices, and obey him in all his commands, as well as rely upon his promises; if the objects of his love are the objects of our love, and the objects of his hatred the objects of our hatred; if we are desirous of promoting his cause and interest in the world; if we can hate and willingly forego what is most precious to us in this world, rather than forsake him; if we are grieved that we love him so little, and are desirous to love him more; if we are habitually looking forward to his second coming, and in the meantime relying on his Spirit, that we may have grace to glorify him while we live, and to think of death and the grave without dismay; and, in a word, if we account him all our salvation and all our desire, and give up ourselves to him, to be his now, wholly, and for ever, in a covenant not to be forgotten.

3. Our love to the *people of God*, which must be a love of *complacency* and *delight*, is genuine if we see more in them than in others, why they ought to be loved; if we love them because

God loves them, and because they belong to Christ and bear his image; if we make no distinction in our love to the saints, but love them all, whether they be rich or poor; if we not only love all the saints, but love them at all times, in adversity as well as in prosperity; if we prefer and delight in their company and religious conversation, esteeming them the excellent ones of the earth; if we study to rejoice with them, to soothe their sorrows, and to do them good in the time of need (Rom. xii. 15; 1 John iii. 16, &c.); and if we cover their sins, forgive injuries done by them, and are not bitter against them.

4. Our love to *all men* in general, or to the men of the world and even our enemies, whom we must love with a love of *benevolence* and *beneficence*, is genuine, if we sincerely wish them well; if we pray for them; and if we do them all the good we can. Our love to our enemies especially is genuine, if in it we are moved by the example of Christ, who died for his enemies; if we do not manifest a desire of revenge, but commit them to the Lord who judgeth righteously; if we do not rejoice, but are sorry when evil overtakes them (Prov. xxiv. 17, &c.); if we desire to forgive them and to seek their good, notwithstanding what they have done to us (Luke xi. 4); and if we pray for them, and relieve their distresses.—Matt. v. 44; Luke xxiii. 34; Acts viii. 60; Rom. xii. 20, 21.

In partaking of the Lord's Supper, love to *Christ* is necessary, because without it we cannot hate sin; without it we cannot delight in the Lord Jesus; without it we can take no pleasure in any thing that he hath done, or commands us to do; and without it we cannot love his people, although they are the objects of his esteem and delight. Love to *all men*, but especially to those who are of the *household of faith*, is absolutely necessary, because strictly enjoined in Scripture.—Matt. v. 23, 24; 1 Cor. v. 8; Gal. vi. 10; 1 John iv. 20. Faith and love go hand in hand; and brotherly love is an evidence of having passed from death to life,—1 John iii. 14; and Christ frequently gave this as a mark by which his disciples might be known,—see 1 John. Love to our *enemies* is necessary, because it is commanded by God,—Matt. v. 44; Rom. ii. 14; and also, because we are bound to follow the example of Christ, who forgave us when we were enemies and ungodly.—Eph. iv. 34; Col. iii. 13.

Obs. 339.—*All who would worthily partake of the Lord's Supper, must examine themselves respecting their new obedience.*

They who would communicate worthily, must examine whether their obedience proceeds from new principles, is performed according to a new rule and in a new manner, and directed to a new end.

1. New obedience springs from *new principles,*—that is, it is

performed, not from fear of future punishment, but from faith in the authority of the great Lawgiver, and from love to his service.

2. New obedience is performed according to a *new rule*,—that is, the rule which the believer observes in the course of his obedience is " the perfect law of liberty,"—the whole revealed will of God, contained in the Scriptures; and not his own will, or the inventions of men.—Isa. viii. 20.

3. New obedience is performed in a *new manner*,—that is, the believer depends upon the strength of the covenant, seeing he has none of his own; he depends upon Christ for the acceptance both of himself and of what he does; and he has no dependence whatever upon his own works for righteousness before God.

4. New obedience is directed to a *new end*,—that is, what the believer does is not for the world, or for a name in the world, which is the end of those who know not God; but for the glory of God,—1 Cor. x. 31; and in subordination to this, for the best interests of himself and others.—Matt. v. 16.

We may here remark, that no one can yield this obedience until his nature be renewed or regenerated by the Holy Spirit; for the tree must first be made good, before its fruit can be good.

When obedience is of this kind, it is *universal* obedience, or it has respect to all God's commandments, although it is impossible to obey any one of them perfectly; it is *uniform* obedience,—that is, it is not confined to particular seasons, but performed at all times; it is *cheerful* obedience,—that is, it is not performed through constraint or through fear of punishment; it is obedience performed in *secret*, when no one sees us but God, as well as in public, when the eyes of others are upon us; and it is *inward* obedience, or the obedience of the *heart*, as well as the obedience of the life or of the outward conduct.

In order to a worthy receiving of the Lord's Supper, new obedience is absolutely necessary, because they who are in a state of nature, who are estranged from God, and whose conduct is the reverse of new obedience, can have no communion with a holy God in such a holy ordinance. And moreover, it is evident, that holiness is absolutely necessary to seeing God.—Heb. xii. 14.

Obs. 340.—*They who neglect the duty of self-examination, are in danger of communicating unworthily, and thus of eating and drinking judgment to themselves.*

Without self-examination, none can become acquainted with their state before God; they cannot know whether they have a right to approach the Lord's Table or not; they must remain ignorant of their wants, and how they may be supplied—of their sins, and therefore they will cleave to them—of their graces, and consequently they will show no desire for an increase of grace. They who come to the Lord's Table in such a state, must neces-

sarily eat and drink judgment to themselves,—that is, by eating and drinking unworthily, they do that which renders them obnoxious to the righteous judgment of God, to *temporal* judgments or afflictions in this world, and to *eternal* judgment or condemnation (if mercy prevent not) in the world to come.—1 Cor. xi. 30–32.

We may here observe, that besides the duty of self-examination, there are other things which are not to be neglected in our preparation for the Lord's Supper ; and these are, prayer to God for his presence and blessing, and for the assistance of his Spirit; reading such religious books as treat of the sufferings of Christ, and chiefly suitable portions of the Scriptures ; and devout meditation, in order to the exciting of our affections, and the drawing forth of our graces into lively exercise. The same danger may arise from the neglect of these things, that arises from the neglect of self-examination ; for they are all necessary to a worthy participation of this ordinance. But after all that we can do in this way, we must place no dependence on our preparation, but rely solely on the grace of God to work all our work in us and for us.

Obs. 341.—*Communicants should be properly engaged while at the Lord's Table.*

" When seated at the Lord's Table, and partaking of the sacramental elements, we should consider that we are not merely in the presence of our fellow-creatures, who may be imposed upon by the appearance of sanctity, but in the presence of Almighty God himself, who cannot be deceived, to whose eyes the inmost recesses of our hearts are open, and who hath declared, that 'the hope of the hypocrite shall perish.' We should therefore 'keep the feast, not with the leaven of malice and wickedness, but with the unleavened bread of *sincerity* and *truth*,'—1 Cor. v. 8; having a pious and spiritual frame of mind, as well as great decency of outward behaviour. We should study to banish the cares of the world, to repress every sinful and unworthy thought, and to devote our whole attention to the sacred service that is going on. We should rejoice that we are admitted to such a great privilege, and rejoice ' with trembling,' when we think how unworthy we are to enjoy it. We should meditate with the most ardent affection and gratitude on the character, and sufferings, and death of that gracious Redeemer, who said, ' Do this in remembrance of me.' We should have believing views of that great atoning sacrifice which he offered up for sin, and know and feel, that when we eat the bread and drink the wine, we assent in the most solemn manner to the merciful and holy covenant which he sealed with his blood. We should now surrender our souls and our bodies, our hearts and our lives, to him who 'loved us and gave himself for us.'—Gal. ii. 20. And we should resolve, over the memorials of his death, and in the strength of Divine grace, to 'glorify God in our bodies and in our spirits which are his,'—1 Cor. vi. 20; by denying ourselves to sinful gratifications; by 'perfecting holiness in the fear of the Lord,'—2 Cor. vii. 1 ; and by living, as much as lieth in us, in peace and charity with all mankind."

Obs. 342.—*Self-examination is necessary after partaking of the Lord's Supper, as well as before it.*

That self-examination is necessary after communicating, is evident from the following passages of Scripture :—1 Cor. xi. 31, 32; Gal. vi. 4 ; 2 John 8 ; John xvi. 31. , By this exercise we may know something concerning ourselves; how we have acted towards God, and how God has acted toward us. If we have communicated *unworthily,*—that is, if we have been unaffected with the exhibition of Christ crucified, if vain and worldly thoughts have engaged our attention, and if we have gone through the service as a mere form, more anxious to be approved in the sight of our fellow-creatures than in the sight of God ; we should search out the cause of our want of success; we should be deeply humbled on account of our guilt; we should confess and lament it before God, and apply anew to that blood which cleanseth from all sin; and we should resolve, through the grace of God, to be more diligent in our preparation for the time to come. If we have been enabled to communicate *worthily,*— that is, if we have been enabled devoutly to contemplate, by faith, Jesus Christ crucified, as the only ground of our hopes before God ; if we have been enabled to look on him whom we have pierced, and to mourn after a godly sort ; if we have been enabled in any degree to love him who first loved us and gave himself for us; if we have been enabled to love those who are dear to him for his sake, and to forgive our enemies because he hath forgiven us; and if we have been enabled to resolve, in the strength of Divine grace, to serve him with greater diligence for the time to come,—we ought to be thankful to him who is the author of all good, and ascribe our success to the grace of God alone, and not to anything in ourselves ; and we should endeavour to make grateful returns of love and obedience, by carefully performing our vows and keeping the covenant which we have renewed. But we must ever remember, that our most worthy communicating is accompanied with imperfection and defilement, and that, therefore, we must apply to Jesus Christ to wash us after Supper, otherwise we can have no part in him.

We may also consider at this time, if any sin has been subdued; if any lust has been mortified; if any resolution has been strengthened ; if any doubt has been resolved; if any fear has been dispelled; if any temptation has been removed ; if any enemy has been overcome ; if any want has been supplied ; if any light has been imparted ; if faith has been increased; if love has been inflamed; if hope has been animated; if the affections have been solemnised; in a word, if the Lord has manifested himself to us in another manner than he doth unto the world.

INFERENCES.

From this subject we learn,—1. The necessity of self-examination, in order to know whether or not we are in Christ. 2. That the Lord will be sanctified in them that draw near unto him. 3. That the state of the soul deserves our most serious attention. 4. That the ordinance of the Lord's Supper is designed only for holy persons—for those who are in covenant with God. 5. The necessity of obeying the injunction of Christ, "Do this in remembrance of me." 6. The danger of approaching this ordinance without preparation—or trusting in our preparation.

DIV. 3.—OF PRAYER AS A MEANS OF GRACE—UNDER WHICH ARE CONSIDERED THE NATURE OF PRAYER AND THE RULE OF DIRECTION AS GIVEN IN THE LORD'S PRAYER.

Of the Nature of Prayer.

Q. 98. What is Prayer?

Prayer is an offering up of our desires unto God, for things agreeable to his will, in the name of Christ, with confession of our sins, and thankful acknowledgment of his mercies.

ANALYSIS AND PROOFS.

We are here taught,—

1. That prayer is the offering up of our desires to God. Ps. lxii. 8.—"Ye people, pour out your heart before him."

2. That prayer must be offered up for those things only which are agreeable to the will of God. 1 John v. 14.—"If we ask any thing according to his will, he heareth us."

3. That prayer must be offered up in the name of Christ. John xvi. 23.—"Whatsoever ye shall ask the Father in my name, he will give it you."

4. That prayer must be offered up with confession of sin. Dan. ix.,4.—"I prayed unto the Lord my God, and made my confession."

5. That prayer must be offered up with thanksgiving. Phil. iv. 6.—"In everything, by prayer and supplication with thanksgiving, let your requests be made known unto God."

EXPLANATION.

Obs. 343.—*Prayer is the offering up of our desires to God.*

As prayer is a part of religious worship, the object whom all ought to worship, is the object to whom all ought to pray; and this object most certainly is *God*—God the Father, Son, and Holy Ghost.—Matt. iv. 10. God alone ought to be the object of prayer, because he alone can search the hearts and try the reins of the children of men; he alone is "the hearer of prayer," being everywhere present; and he alone can pardon sin, and fulfil the desires of all.—Ps. cxlv. 18, 19.

Prayer is here described as *an offering up of our desires to God;* and in this the very nature of prayer consists. When we address God, it must be in a manner very different from that in which we address our fellow-creatures. It will not do to command him; it will not do to demand of him; but we must *offer up* our desires to him, as the only way in which we may have our wants supplied. Petitions or supplications are here called *desires,* because there may be much speaking where there are no desires; and the words of the mouth, without the desires of the heart, are but empty sounds in the ears of a prayer-hearing God. And there is said to be *an offering up,* because prayers are spiritual sacrifices, which must be offered up to God alone.— 1 Pet. ii. 5; 2 Kings xvii. 36.

If we would have our prayers accepted in the sight of God, they must be offered up in an acceptable manner, which includes a variety of things. We must pray with an "awful apprehension of the Divine majesty" upon our minds; in a language which we understand,- 1 Cor. xiv. 15, 19; with a deep sense of our own unworthiness, and necessities, and wants,—Gen. xviii. 27, and xxxii. 10; Luke xv. 18, 19, and xviii. 13; with penitent, and thankful, and enlarged hearts,—Ps. li. 17; with faith,—Heb. xi. 6; Matt. xxi. 22; Mark xi. 24; James i. 6; with sincerity,— Ps. cxlv. 18; Jer. xxix. 13; with fervency,—James v. 16; with love,—1 Tim. ii. 8; by which we are to understand an earnest desire after God's presence with us, and an unfeigned delight in him as the only satisfying portion of the soul,—Ps. lxxiii. 25; Isa. xxv. 9; with perseverance,—Eph. vi. 18; Rom. xii. 12; Matt. xv. 22-28; and we must pray waiting upon God with humble submission to his will.—Mic. vii. 7; Matt. xxvi. 39.

We may here remark, that the *end* for which we pray to God. is not that we may inform him of our wants, for he knows them better than we ourselves do,—Ps. cxxxix. 4; not that we may alter his mind concerning us, or incline him to any thing which he was formerly unwilling to grant, for with him there is no variableness nor shadow of turning;—but we must pray to him, because he commands, and entreats, and encourages us to do so, that he may confer upon us what we may know and believe he is most willing to bestow.—2 Chron. vii. 14; Ps. cv. 4; Matt. vii. 7; Luke xviii. 1; Phil. iv. 6; Col. iv. 2; 1 Pet. i. 17; John v. 14.

Obs. 344.—*Prayer must be offered up for those things only which are agreeable to the will of God.*

We are not to pray for the fulfilling of any sinful desires.—James iv. 3. But we may and ought to pray to God only for those things which are agreeable to his will.—1 John v. 14, 15. We are not, however, to pray for all things which are agreeable to his *secret* will; for all things which come to pass, even the greatest sins, are agreeable to God's secret counsel and determination; but we may pray for all things which are agreeable to God's revealed will, or all those things which God hath promised to bestow; and these include all the spiritual and temporal mercies of which we stand in need.—John iii. 33; Matt. vi. 33; Ps. xxxiv. 10; Isa. xxxiii. 16. We must, however, prefer spiritual to temporal mercies in our prayers; for thus saith the Lord, "Seek ye *first* the kingdom of God and his righteousness, and all these things shall be added unto you."—Matt. vi. 33.

Obs. 345.—*Prayer must be offered up in the name of Christ, and in dependence on the assistance of the Holy Spirit.*

Our desires must be offered up to God *in the name of Jesus Christ.* This is not merely to mention the name of Christ in the conclusion or in any other part of our prayers; but it is to mention his name by faith, depending on him alone for access to God, and for acceptance and a gracious answer to our prayers.—Eph iii. 12.

The offering up of our desires to God in the name of Christ is absolutely necessary, because God is so holy and just, and righteous, and we are so unholy and sinful, and our prayers are at best mingled with so much imperfection and sin, that neither our persons nor our prayers can find acceptance with God, but through the merits and mediation of the Lord Jesus Christ.—Rev. viii. 3, 4.

We may here remark, that Jesus Christ is the only mediator in whose name we may approach unto God; for there is no one either in heaven or on earth who is appointed to this glorious work, or fit for it, but Jesus Christ: "There is one Mediator between God and men, the man Christ Jesus."—1 Tim. ii. 5. See also John xiv. 13, 14, xv. 16, and xvi. 23; Eph. v. 20; Col. iii. 17; Heb. xiii. 15.

Our desires must also be offered up to God in dependence upon the *assistance of the Holy Spirit.* This is absolutely necessary in order to our praying in a right and acceptable manner. It is the Spirit, the Comforter, who helpeth our infirmities, who teacheth us all things, and bringeth all things to our remembrance—our need, and the only way in which we may be supplied; and it is he also who bringeth to mind the encouraging promises, upon which we may rest in all our approaches to God; by which we may be assured, that if we ask not amiss, we shall not be sent empty away.—Rom. viii. 26, 27.

Obs. 346.—*Prayer must be offered up with confession of sin.*

Confession of our sins reminds us of our true condition, as sinners by nature and by practice. On this account it is a most necessary part of prayer; for, if we would pray for mercy, we cannot do it in a right manner, without acknowledging our true state—as ill-deserving and hell-deserving creatures—as utterly unworthy of the least mercy from the Lord. And it may be observed, that where there is a real sense of guilt, there will also be a most unfeigned confession of guilt.—Ezra ix.; Dan. ix.; Neh. ix.

In the faith that our iniquity shall be forgiven, we must confess our *original sin*, which is the source of all actual transgression,—Ps. li. 5; and also all our *actual sins*, both of omission and commission, which are past reckoning. We must confess our sins against God, against our neighbour, and against ourselves; our sins against both tables of the Divine law; our sins in thought, in word, and in deed; and the sin which most easily besets us, for every one has some sin to which he is particularly addicted. In a word, every sin, without exception, which we know to be sin; every sin, great or small; every sin, however unknown to all around, that is, known only to God and to ourselves,—must be ingenuously acknowledged; for without this we shall never see our unworthiness of the least mercy, when we would address God by prayer and supplication.

Confession of sin is absolutely necessary for the following reasons:—1. If we do not confess our sins, by which God is greatly dishonoured, and express our guilt, we cannot be said to justify him when he proceeds against us in a way of punishment. 2. If there is no confession of sin, there can be no mercy; for the promise is, " Whoso confesseth and forsaketh his sins, shall find mercy; but he that covereth his sin shall not prosper."—Prov. xxviii. 13. 3. The more humbled we are under a sense of sin, the more ready are we to receive Divine favours with heartfelt gratitude, and especially the unspeakable mercy of the pardon of sin.—Ps. xxxii. 5, 6.

When we confess our sins, we must consider the manner in which confession ought to be made; for every confession of sin is not acceptable to God. 1. To *confess sin and to love it*, is not genuine confession before God. The very idea of confession implies shame, and sorrow, and hatred; and it is only when these things accompany our confession, that we can have any hope of forgiveness.—Luke xviii. 13; Job xxxiv. 32. 2. To *confess sin and hide it,* is not genuine confession. This is done when some sins are acknowledged, but not all sins; when some sins are confessed, but not in all their aggravations; when some sins are confessed, but other sins palliated; or when some sins are confessed, but other sins justified.—Prov. xxviii. 13. 3. To *confess sin through constraint and not willingly*, is not genuine confession. Many things may occur to extort confession of sin on various occasions, but if confession is not most free and voluntary, it cannot be viewed as proceeding from a contrite heart and humbled soul.

Obs. 347.—*Prayer must be offered up with thankful acknowledgment of God's mercies.*

That *thanksgiving* is necessary, is evident from Phil. iv. 6; Ps. ciii., and cxvi. 17, and innumerable other passages of Scripture. *Mercy* respects the miserable; and as man has rendered himself miserable, he is the object of mercy; and the blessings which are necessary in order to his happiness, are called *mercies*. Hence, whatever gifts man receives, may remind him of his misery. The mercies which we receive are called *God's mercies*, because they come from God, who is "the Father of mercies," and who contrived the scheme of mercy; and they come to us as free gifts.—1 Tim. vi. 17.

The mercies for which we ought to be thankful, are either of a *spiritual* or of a *temporal* nature,—mercies which respect the life that now is, or the life which is to come. *Spiritual mercies* include every thing connected with the great salvation, from the gift of Jesus Christ himself to the least mercy of a spiritual nature (but no mercy is small) which comes to us in the channel of the covenant.—Eph. i. 3. *Temporal mercies* are those which we have received from the womb until now, both for ourselves and for others with whom we are connected, whether by nature, or grace, or gratitude. For all these we ought to be thankful. And although we are to be peculiarly thankful for mercies conferred upon ourselves, yet we ought to join with others in praising God for the mercies bestowed upon them; as they in like manner ought to do with us.—Ps. cxxxix. 14.

Thanksgiving to God for his mercies is absolutely necessary, for the following reasons:—1. That mercies may be blessed to us in the use of them; for we cannot expect a blessing to accompany them, while we have not a heart to acknowledge them. 2. Because it is a debt which we owe to God.—Hos. xiv. 2. 3. Because, if there is no acknowledgment of mercies received, it is the highway to prevent us from receiving more.—Isa. i. 15.

When we would engage in the exercise of thankfully acknowledging the innumerable and invaluable mercies which we receive from the Lord, it ought to be accompanied with the following things:—1. With *wonder*, that so much undeserved kindness should be conferred upon such ill-deserving creatures as we are, who are less than the least of all God's mercies. With *deep humility* of soul, that such mercies should be drawn from the treasures of heaven, and bestowed on us, who are utterly unworthy of the least favour from the Lord. And, 3. With *fervent desire* to lay them out to the best advantage, by which God may be glorified, and our brethren of mankind profited.

Obs. 348.—*Prayer has been commonly distinguished into secret, private, and public prayer.*

1. *Secret prayer* is the retirement of individuals for a time from all concern with others, that they may have an opportunity more freely of pouring out their hearts before God.—Matt. vi. 6, xiv. 23, and xxvi. 37–39. Under this kind is comprehended *ejaculatory prayer*, which is a secret and sudden lifting up of the desires to God, when our circumstances may be peculiar, of which we ourselves are the best judges. And we may be said to engage in this kind of prayer by a simple thought sent up to God, while there are no words expressed; or by words uttered in the mind, although the voice is not heard.—Neh. ii. 4; 1 Sam. i. 13.

2. *Private prayer* is prayer among some Christians, met for the purposes of mutual edification and of engaging in this exercise. Under this is included *family prayer*, which ought to be observed by every family,—Jer. x. 25; where we find recorded the dreadful doom of all those who neglect this duty. Under this also is included *social prayer*, by which we are to understand prayer among a few belonging to several families, who meet together from time to time, as a society, for spiritual edification, prayer, and spiritual conversation about the great things of God. This seems to be sanctioned by Mal. iii. 16, 17.

3. *Public prayer* is a part of the public worship of God, in which we join when we meet together, according to Divine appointment, in public assemblies; and when one, who is authorised to preach the gospel, is the mouth of all in offering up their desires to God for things agreeable to his will. And when we thus join in public prayer, it is the same as if we were individually offering up our desires to God; or, as if the desires which proceed from the mouth of the speaker were offered up by ourselves.

Obs. 349.—*It is possible to know that our prayers are heard and accepted.*

If it were impossible to come to the knowledge of our prayers being heard by " the Hearer of prayer," this exercise would in a great measure be useless, and we could receive little comfort from it. Two things may satisfy us on this subject,—viz., if we have been enabled to be importunate with God in prayer respecting any thing; and if, at the same time, we have attained to submission to the Divine will with regard to this very thing; then we may conclude that our prayer has been graciously heard. —2 Chron. xx. 12–19.

INFERENCES.

From this subject we learn,—1. That prayer is a suitable exercise for all; that it is a necessary duty; and that it is a great privilege. 2. From whom and through whom our mercies flow. 3. The necessity of faith in prayer. 4. That all prayer is not accepted; many prayers never reach the throne. 5. That we must be particular in the confession of sin. 6. That if prayer is not answered, it is our own fault. 7. That they who neglect this duty, oppose a known command. 8. That the danger of those who neglect family prayer is very great,—Jer. x. 25; where such are classed among heathens; and, consequently, they cannot be Christians but in profession. Indeed, they are worse than heathens, for even they were convinced of the necessity of this duty by the light of nature; seeing we read that every family had their household gods, to which they prayed, together with their children. But as family prayer is a very important part of family religion, and as it seems to be much neglected in the present day by those who call themselves Christians, we shall extend this inference a little. We say, then, that they who neglect this duty do not believe the Scriptures to be the Word of God. They may, indeed, acknowledge them to be so; but they do not firmly believe that they are the Word of God. For instance, they do not believe the passage formerly alluded to, viz., that God will "pour out his fury upon those families that call not upon his name;" otherwise why do they neglect this duty? But to reject part of the Scriptures, or those parts of them which are not agreeable to their natural inclinations, is the same as to reject the whole. The true Christian believes the whole Scripture to be the Word of God, notwithstanding that there are many parts of it which oppose his natural inclinations; and he endeavours, through the strength of Divine grace, to perform every commanded duty; and this he knows to be one, viz., family worship. But again, they who neglect this duty, live in a continual breach of the Fifth and Sixth Commandments of the moral law,—of the Fifth Commandment, which requires parents to instruct their children in the doctrines and duties of religion, and to pray with and for them; and of the Sixth Commandment, which not only forbids us to take away the natural life of ourselves or others, but also, according to its spiritual import, commands us to do what he can to promote the life of our own souls and of the souls of others. Surely, then, he must be a hard-hearted parent who does not do what he can to save the souls of his children, or, in other words, who does what he can to damn them; for we may readily believe, that he who neglects family religion will not be very anxious to keep his family from conforming themselves to the world,—that is, from following its maxims, customs, and amusements; the love of which and the love of God are utterly inconsistent. "Love not the world, neither the things that are in the world. If any man love the world, the love of the Father is not in him."—1 John ii. 15. He, then, who neglects the duty of family worship, has sure and infallible evidence that he has no real concern about the salvation either of his own soul or of the souls of his family. But further, they who call themselves Christians, while they neglect this duty, are guilty of very great hypocrisy. They pretend to worship God in public, when the eyes of their fellow-creatures are upon them; but when in private and secret, or in the presence of the heart-searching God alone, they neglect religion altogether—they bow not a knee to him who made them. Such have a name to live, but they are dead—spiritually dead; and if they do not consider their ways, and turn to the Lord and to their duty, they will in a short time be eternally dead. Let those, then, who neglect family religion, begin the performance of this duty, humbly depending on the grace of God, and ever remembering that none can be true Christians who neglect it. Although there is no express command for it in Scripture, yet we find that it was practised by the saints, which is equal to a command; and surely they who would be Christians, must imitate Christ, who did not neglect this duty, but prayed with his disciples, who were his family; and, moreover, it is, as formerly mentioned, a duty of mere natural religion, or a duty, the obligation of which is evident from the light of nature alone.

Of the Rule of Direction in Prayer.

Q. 99.—*What Rule hath God given for our Direction in Prayer?*

The whole Word of God is of use to direct us in prayer; but the special rule of direction is that form of prayer which Christ taught his disciples, commonly called "The Lord's Prayer."

ANALYSIS AND PROOFS.

We are here taught,—

1. That we need a rule to direct us in prayer. Rom. viii. 26. —"We know not what we should pray for as we ought."

2. That the whole Word of God is of use to direct us in prayer. 1 John v. 14.—"If we ask any thing according to his will, he heareth us." See also John xv. 7.

3. That the Lord's Prayer is the special rule given us for our direction in prayer. Matt. vi. 9.—"After this manner, therefore, pray ye: Our Father," &c.

EXPLANATION.

Obs. 350.— *We require a rule to direct us in prayer.*

That we *need to be directed* in prayer, appears evident, when we consider the following things:—

1. The nature of God. As God is far above the comprehension of creatures, and as it is only by the light which he himself imparts that he can be beheld; so we require a sure direction in prayer, when we would call upon his name. It is to him alone that we ought to make known our requests; but if we do not know him, we cannot glorify him in this respect.

2. The nature of man. Man is a guilty and condemned criminal; and, consequently, he ought to approach God with reverence. But he cannot do so with propriety without a rule of direction, seeing he is so ignorant of himself.

3. That we may greatly err respecting the matter of our prayers, and thus their success would be impeded. Had we no direction in prayer, we should be ready to pray for that which is included neither in the command nor in the promise, and our prayers would not be accepted.

4. That we may also greatly err with respect to the manner in which we ought to pray. Without a rule, we should certainly overlook what is most necessary to render our prayers an acceptable service; namely, the mediation of Jesus Christ, through which alone our prayers can be accepted, and the assistance of the Holy Spirit, whose office it is to help our infirmities, and to teach us to pray as we ought.

5. The danger to which we are exposed in obtaining a curse and not a blessing, if our prayers are not according to the will of God.

Hence, direction in prayer is most necessary; and we ought to bless the Lord, that he hath given us a rule of direction. But we must remember, that this rule of direction is only an *external* help, although fully sufficient as such. That we may pray acceptably, something more is absolutely necessary. Whatever *external* help we may have, we must have the *internal* help of the Holy Spirit, without which we cannot pray as we ought.— Rom. viii. 26. This internal help is also the gift of God—the blessing promised to his Church; and this promise is fulfilled in all the seed of Jacob, who pray in the Spirit, and who know that they cannot call Jesus *Lord* but by the Holy Ghost.

Obs. 351.—*The whole Word of God is of use to direct us in prayer.*

By the *whole Word of God*, we are to understand the whole of Divine revelation contained in the Scriptures of the Old and New Testaments, which God hath given us as a *general rule* of direction in prayer. By this we are informed that we ought to pray; by this we are furnished with every thing necessary for our help in prayer, at all times and upon all occasions, for ourselves and for others, in whatever circumstances we or they may be placed; by this we are furnished with all needful matter for prayer—for all the parts of prayer, and also with the most suitable and necessary directions respecting the manner in which we ought to pray; and by this also words are put into our mouths which ought to be used in prayer; so that we can be at no loss for want of just and proper expressions, which we may adopt, when we approach the throne of grace.

Obs. 352.—*The Lord's Prayer is the special rule given us for our direction in prayer.*

That *form of prayer* which is the *special rule* of our direction, when addressing the throne of grace, is called The Lord's Prayer, because it was dictated by our Lord Jesus Christ, in answer to this petition of his disciples: "Lord, teach us to pray, as John also taught his disciples."—Luke xi. 1. But, properly speaking, it is not the *Lord's Prayer*, because he could not use every part of it for himself. He could not make use of the fifth petition, "Forgive us our debts;" for he had no sin to be forgiven, being the Holy One of God—holy, harmless, undefiled, and separated from sinners.

That our Lord did not prescribe this prayer to be used by his people in all succeeding ages as a *form*, from which they were not to deviate, but only as a *pattern* of prayer, the various parts of which they might clothe in other language of Scripture, or in language suited to the peculiar circumstances in which they might find themselves placed, may be proved from various considerations:—1. This prayer does not *expressly* contain all the parts of prayer, although it may do so by inference. There is no direct mention made of confession of sin and thankful acknowledgment of mercies, nor of the name of Christ as Mediator, and of his sufferings and death, which must be considered as the foundation on which our prayers rest, and through which alone they can find acceptance. 2. This prayer cannot be used as a *form*, from which we must not deviate, because the evangelists, Matthew and Luke, who record it, differ in their mode of expression, which they would not surely have done, had Christ designed it only as a *form*. 3. We have several prayers in the New Testament, which were afterwards used by Christ and his apostles; but none of them are expressed in the language of this prayer, nor are they concluded with it; which is no mean argument against the necessity of adopting the very language or expressions of this prayer.—Acts i. 24, and iv. 24; Eph. i. 24; 1 Thess. iii. 11; Heb. xiii. 20; John xvii. But although we are not bound to use this prayer as a set form from which we are not to deviate, yet the words of it "may be used as a prayer" to God, equally with other Scriptures, provided it be done with understanding, faith, reverence, and the other graces which are necessary to the right and acceptable performance of the duty of prayer. And that it may be thus used, is evident from its being called "*that form of prayer which Christ taught his disciples.*"—Luke xi. 2.

This pattern of prayer consists of three parts,—a preface, six petitions, and a conclusion. The *preface* is, "Our Father who art in heaven;" the *conclusion* is, "For thine is the kingdom, and the power, and the glory for ever;" and the *petitions* compose the rest of it. In the first three petitions, we pray for the advancement of the honour of God; and in the last three, we pray for our own happiness. We are first to pray for the honour of God, to show that this is preferable to our happiness, and is the spring of the whole of it.—1 Cor. x. 31. And there is only one petition for temporal mercies, namely, the fourth, to show that we ought to be more earnest at the throne of grace for spiritual than for temporal mercies.

INFERENCES.

From this subject we learn,—1. The necessity of prayer. 2. The goodness of God in giving us direction in prayer. 3. That we ought to treasure up the Word of God. 4. The sin of those who neglect prayer, seeing such help is afforded. 5. That they who neglect it have no excuse.

Of the Preface to the Lord's Prayer.

Q. 100.—What doth the Preface of the Lord's Prayer teach us?

The preface of the Lord's Prayer [which is, "Our Father which art in heaven"] teacheth us to draw near to God with all holy reverence and confidence, as children to a father, able and ready to help us; and that we should pray with and for others.

ANALYSIS AND PROOFS.

We are here taught,—

1. That the preface to the Lord's Prayer is, "Our Father which art in heaven."—Matt. vi. 9.

2. That in prayer we must approach God with holy reverence. Heb. xii. 28.—"Let us have grace, whereby we may serve God acceptably with reverence and godly fear." See also Ps. cxlv. 19.

3. That in prayer we must approach God with holy confidence. Eph. iii. 12.—"In whom we have boldness and access with confidence."

4. That in prayer we must approach God as our Father. Rom. viii. 15.—"Ye have received the Spirit of adoption, whereby we cry, Abba, Father."

5. That in prayer we must approach God as being able to help

as. Eph. iii. 20.—" Unto him who is able to do exceeding abundantly above all that we ask or think."

6. That in prayer we must approach God as being willing to help us. Matt. vii. 11.—" How much more shall your Father who is in heaven give good things to them that ask him?"

7. That we must join with others in prayer. Acts xii. 12.—" Many were gathered together praying."

8. That we must pray for others. 1 Tim. ii. 1.—" I exhort, therefore, that first of all, supplications, prayers, intercessions, and giving of thanks be made for all men."

EXPLANATION.

Obs. 353.—*By the preface to the Lord's Prayer, " Our Father who art in heaven," we are taught, that we should draw near to God with all holy reverence and confidence, as children to a father able and willing to help us.*

The calling of God " *Father*," may show us how we ought to address the object of all religious worship. In praying to God, we ought to make mention of some of his names, titles, or attributes, in a suitableness to the nature of the exercise in which we engage. And when this is done in a reverential manner, it will prevent us from rushing into his presence without consideration, and without due conceptions of his infinite majesty.

God is the *Father* of all in the following respects:—1. He is the Father of all men by creation and preservation.—Mal. ii. 10; Acts xvii. 28; Numb. xvi. 22. 2. He may be considered as the Father of Church members by external covenant relation, when he favours them with the revelation of his will from heaven, sets his name among them, and offers himself to them. And this is the case with ourselves as a nation. 3. He is in a peculiar manner the Father of believers by regeneration and adoption. And hence they are said to be born of God, to be made partakers of a godlike nature, to receive the adoption of sons, and to be made partakers of all the privileges of his children.

When we call God " *Our Father*," it imports the faith which we express in him as standing in such a close and such an amiable relation. But it does not mean, that when we pray in secret, we must always say, *Our* Father, and not *my* Father; for we may appropriate God as our Father in particular, and say, *my Father;* thus claiming an individual relation to him.—Jer. iii. 4, 19; Ps. xviii. 1, 2, and lxxxix. 26.

From the expression, " *Our Father who art in heaven*," we are not to conclude, that the presence of God is included in *heaven;* for the heaven of heavens cannot contain him. He is every where present, and fills heaven and earth. But he may be said to be in *heaven*, because he is there in a peculiar manner, and there his glory is most fully displayed. This consideration should lead us to have exalted thoughts of the majesty of God who, although he is adored by all the hosts of heaven, yet condescends to regard us, the sinful children of men, who dwell upon the earth, his footstool.—1 Kings viii. 27.

This preface teaches us, that when we approach God, we must manifest the dispositions of children when they draw near their father. 1. By the expression, "Who art in heaven," we are taught to draw near to God *with all holy reverence*, because of the infinite distance between him and us, he being not our earthly father, but our Father who is in heaven.—Eccl. v. 2. By the expression, "Our Father," we are taught to draw near to God *with confidence* both of his ability and willingness to help us; and also with a filial affection of desire, love, and delight, as children to a father.—Rom. viii. 15; Eph. iii. 20; Matt. vii. 11. As it is through Christ alone that we can draw near to God, so it is through him alone that we can draw near with confidence.—Eph. iii. 12. This confidence we should have in the most unlimited degree; but we must avoid presumption, which is a spirit very different from that confidence which we are allowed to have in prayer towards our heavenly Father. True confidence disposes those who have it to repose an entire trust in God, as *able and willing to help them;* which persuasion flows from his all-sufficiency and his boundless liberality, as exhibited in the promises of the new covenant, which are all yea and amen in Christ.—Luke xi. 13; Ps. lxxxiv. 11; Phil. iv. 19.

We may further observe, that the spirit of this preface leads us to believe, that the saving knowledge of the Son of God and of his Spirit is absolutely necessary, before we can say aright, "Our Father who art in heaven."—John i. 12; Eph. ii. 18; Gal. iv. 6; Rom. viii. 26. It also teaches us, that none can call God "*Father*" in the highest sense, but such as are born again. If we are not the children of God by regeneration and adoption, it is impossible that we can call God "Father," or "Our Father in heaven," in the strictest sense; or that we can have any right to the privileges of his family.

But it may be here remarked, that although unregenerate men cannot call God their *Father* in the strictest sense, yet this is no reason why they should not pray. Prayer is a duty incumbent on all. It is a duty even of natural religion, and a duty, the neglect of which shall be signally punished.—Jer. x. 25. And although the Lord may have no respect to prayer, as it is a duty performed by the unregenerate,—for "without faith it is impossible to please God,"—yet he may have respect to it as his own ordinance; which surely is a reason why all should attempt the performance of duty. The neglect of prayer altogether is a sin of very great magnitude; it is even a greater sin than if it were performed without due order.

Obs. 354.—*By the preface to the Lord's Prayer.* "*Our Father* who art in heaven," we are taught that we should pray with and for others.

The expression, "*Our Father*," implies, that when we pray to God, we must not forget others; but that we must pray with them and for them. To pray *with* others, is to be the mouth of others to God, or to join with them in family or social worship. And to pray *for* others, is to express our concern about them, or our sympathy with them before God, as sincerely and ingenuously as we would do with respect to ourselves, if we were in the same circumstances.—Ps. xxxv. 13. We must express our sympathy with them, as exposed to similar trials and wants with ourselves, as children of the same Father, as partakers of the same nature, and as looking forward to the same inheritance.

There are various classes of persons for whom we must pray. Our desires must be offered up,—1. For the whole *Church of Christ* upon earth, that they may be all one in him, who is the glorious head of Zion; and that they may grow up into him in all things, till they all come in the unity of the faith, and of the knowledge of the Son of God, unto a perfect man, unto the measure of the stature of the fulness of Christ.—Eph. iv. 13. 2. For *kings* and *magistrates*, or for all in authority over us.—1 Tim. ii. 1-3. 3. For *ministers of the gospel.*—Rom. xv. 30. 4. For our *brethren*, by whom we are to understand both the members of the visible Church, and all our fellow-creatures.—1 John iv. 21. 5. For the *nation* to which we belong. 6. For the *place* in which our lot is cast. 7. For the *congregation* in which we statedly worship God.—Jer. xxix. 7. 8. For our near *relations*, or our kindred according to the flesh.—Job i. 5; 2 Kings vi. 17; Gen. xxiv. 12. 9. For our *enemies.*—Matt. v. 46, and vi. 12, 14, 15. And, 10. For those that shall live hereafter,—Ps. cii. 18, and John xvii. 20, where Christ prays for those that should afterwards believe on him.

INFERENCES.

From this subject we learn,—1. The happiness of those who have God as their Father. 2. The misery of all those who cannot call God their Father. 3. That there can be no acceptable prayer without faith. 4. That nevertheless it is the duty of all to obey the command of God in this respect. 5. That we are bound to pray with and for others. 6. The honour of the saints. 7. That all are not saints who appear to be so.

Of the First Petition in the Lord's Prayer.

Q. 101.—What do we pray for in the First Petition?

In the first petition, [which is, "Hallowed be thy name,"] we pray, that God would enable us and others to glorify him in all that whereby he maketh himself known; and that he would dispose all things to his own glory.

ANALYSIS AND PROOFS.

We are here taught,—
1. That the first petition in the Lord's Prayer is, "Hallowed be thy name."—Matt. vi. 9.
2. That of ourselves we are unable to glorify God. 2 Cor. iii. 5.—" Not that we are sufficient of ourselves to think any thing as of ourselves; but our sufficiency is of God."
3. That we should pray that God would enable us to glorify him. Ps. li. 15.—" O Lord, open thou my lips; and my mouth shall show forth thy praise."
4. That we should pray that God would enable others to glorify him. Ps. lxvii. 3.—" Let the people praise thee, O God; let all the people praise thee."
5. That we should pray that God would dispose all things to his own glory. John xii. 28.—" Father, glorify thy name."

EXPLANATION.

Obs. 355.—*By the first petition in the Lord's Prayer, "Hallowed be thy name," we are taught to pray, that God would enable us and others to glorify him in all things by which he maketh himself known.*

We may here observe, that this petition is with the utmost propriety placed first, because the name of God, and the honour and glory which belong to it, are most precious in his sight, and ought to be so in ours. If it is not our design above all things to hallow the name of God, we cannot use this prayer aright; nor can we, with any propriety, present unto God the other petitions.

By the *name* of God we are here to understand, every thing by which he hath made himself known to his creatures; such as his names, titles, attributes, ordinances, word, and works; and more particularly, by *name* we are here to understand *God himself;* for we sometimes find that *persons* are expressed by *names.* —Rev. iii. 4. And the reason why *name* is here put for God himself, may arise from the impossibility of finding a word which includes all that he is.

By *hallowing* the name of God we are to understand the *glorifying* or *sanctifying* of it. Lev. x. 3.—" I will be *sanctified* in them that come nigh me, and before all the people I will be *glorified.*" Hence, to *hallow* or sanctify, and to *glorify*, are expressions of similar import. When we pray, then, that the name of God may be *hallowed*, it is not to be understood, that it can be *made holy*, for it is infinitely holy; but the meaning of the petition is, that the holiness of his name may be *manifested or declared to be what it really is*—infinitely holy; that he would demonstrate this more and more to the world, that he may appear to be a God infinitely glorious, so as to excite the admiration and esteem which are most justly due to him.

This petition imports, that the name of God is hallowed by *himself*, and that it must be hallowed by the *creatures* which he hath made.

1. The name of God is hallowed by himself in the works of creation and providence, but especially in the work of redemption. God glorified himself in his manner of dealing with our first parents, before he gave any intimation of his mercy and grace in the promise of Jesus Christ; in the promise of a Saviour, in whom all the families of the earth were to be blessed; in selecting Abraham and his seed as his peculiar people; in causing the Saviour, according to the flesh, to descend from him; in the promises of the Messiah, which he made from time to time; in the actual appearance of Jesus Christ in this world in the fulness of time, as the fulfilment of prophecies and predictions from the beginning; in carrying him through the arduous undertaking of man's redemption on earth, and in his resurrection and exaltation; in sending the Spirit to carry on Christ's work on earth until his second coming; and in the means which he adopted for the propagation of the gospel throughout the world. And he glorifies himself still, by preserving it in the world, notwithstanding all opposition; and by what Jesus Christ is now doing in behalf of his people. In a word, God glorifies himself in every part of the work of redemption; in every step of the salvation of every sinner; in the manner of his conversion, illumination, justification, sanctification, increase of grace, and perseverance therein to the end, and final glorification; having redeemed him by the blood of the Lamb slain from the foundation of the world.

2. The name of God must be hallowed by his creatures. And this may be done in various ways:—(1.) We glorify the name of God in his *names, titles,* and *attributes,* when we think and speak of them with becoming reverence; when we acknowledge them to be inconceivably glorious; and when we set them before us, and study to exercise faith upon them, as all our own. (2.) We glorify the name of God in his *ordinances,* when we carefully wait upon God in them; when we desire communion with him in them; and when we improve them for our spiritual nourishment and growth in grace. (3.) We glorify the name of God in his *Word,* when we believe the Scriptures to be the record of God—the only revelation of his mind and will to mankind, in which the way of salvation is made known; and when we make it the rule of our faith and obedience. (4.) We glorify the name of God in the *work of creation,* when we consider the things which are made as the work of an infinitely wise and powerful being; and when we are led to acknowledge his eternal power and godhead, as manifested in them.—Rom. i. 20. (5.) We glorify the name of God in the *works of providence,* when

we have such a sense of his mercies as excites our gratitude and love; when we tremble at his judgments; and when we justify him in all his ways towards us.—Gen. xxxii. 10; Ps. cxix. 120. (6.) We glorify the name of God in the wondrous *plan of redemption*, when we receive and rest upon Christ alone for salvation, as he is offered to us in the gospel; when we renounce all our own righteousness; and when we are careful to maintain good works, that we may adorn the doctrine of God our Saviour in all things.

We pray that *others* may be *enabled to glorify God*, when we pray that the honour of his name may be maintained by them; that all nations may be turned from lying vanities to the service of the living God; that the earth may be full of the knowledge of the Lord as the waters cover the sea; and that God would send the gospel to those who have never yet heard the glad tidings of salvation through Jesus Christ, and that he would make it more successful where it is already.

The reason why we pray that ourselves and others may be *enabled* to glorify or hallow the name of God, is, because there is naturally in all an utter inability and a total want of disposition; so that we must be enabled and disposed to give to God the glory which is due unto his name.

Obs. 356.—*By the first petition in the Lord's Prayer, "Hallowed be thy name," we are taught to pray, that God would dispose all things to his own glory.*

The true meaning of this petition is not kept in view, unless we pray that God, to whom nothing is impossible, would display his glorious power in the removal of every thing by which his name is dishonoured, or which prevents his name from being sanctified as it ought to be; and that he would *dispose of all things to his own glory.*

God glorifies his name, in the disposals of his providence towards the *righteous* and the *wicked*, in the following manner:—

1. With respect to the *righteous;* God brings glory to himself from their *falls* and *backslidings*, when he overrules them in such a manner as thereby to make them more humble, and watchful, and circumspect for the future; as was the case with David and with the Apostle Peter. In this and various other ways, the Lord overrules the events in the lives of the saints for his own glory; while, at the same time, they all work together for good to them that love his blessed name.

2. With respect to the *wicked;* God disposes all things to his own glory, when he restrains his enemies and the enemies of his saints; when he vindicates his saints from the reproaches of the wicked, and enables them to endure these reproaches for his sake. by communicating to them grace suited to their needs and when

he delivers his Church from oppression and from persecution unto death.

INFERENCES.

From this subject we learn,—1. That the glory of God ought to be our habitual study. 2. That the Divine attributes are the comfort of the saints. 3. The necessity of glorifying God in his names, titles, attributes, ordinances, Word, and works. 4. The happiness of those who make the hallowing of the name of God their chief end. 5. The misery of all those who know not the name of God, and, consequently, who do not glorify or hallow it.

Of the Second Petition in the Lord's Prayer.

Q. 102.—What do we pray for in the Second Petition?

In the second petition, [which is, "Thy kingdom come,"] we pray, that Satan's kingdom may be destroyed; and that the kingdom of grace may be advanced, ourselves and others brought into it, and kept in it; and that the kingdom of glory may be hastened.

ANALYSIS AND PROOFS.

We are here taught,—

1. That the second petition in the Lord's Prayer is, "Thy kingdom come."—Matt. vi. 10.

2. That Satan has a kingdom in this world. John xiv. 30.—"The prince of this world cometh, and hath nothing in me."

3. That we should pray for the destruction of Satan's kingdom. Ps. lxviii. 1.—"Let God arise; let his enemies be scattered: let them also that hate him flee before him."

4. That God in Christ hath established a kingdom of grace in the world. Luke i. 33.—"He shall reign over the house of Jacob for ever; and of his kingdom there shall be no end."

5. That we should pray for the advancement of the kingdom of grace. Isa. lxii. 7.—"Give him no rest till he establish, and till he make Jerusalem a praise in the earth."

6. That we should pray that we ourselves may be brought into Christ's kingdom of grace. Luke xxiii. 42.—"Lord, remember me when thou comest into thy kingdom."

7. That we should pray that others may be brought into the kingdom of grace. Rom. x. 1.—"Brethren, my heart's desire and prayer to God for Israel is, that they may be saved."

8. That we should pray that God would keep us in his kingdom of grace. Ps. cxix. 117.—"Hold thou me up, and I shall be safe; and I will have respect to thy statutes continually."

9. That we should pray that God would keep others in his kingdom of grace. 1 Thess. v. 23.—"I pray God that your whole spirit, and soul, and body, be preserved blameless, unto the coming of our Lord Jesus Christ."

10. That there is approaching for the people of God a kingdom of glory. Rev. xxii. 5.—"There shall be no night there, and they need no candle, neither light of the sun; for the Lord God giveth them light; and they shall reign for ever and ever."

11. That we should pray that the kingdom of glory may be hastened. Rev. xxii. 20.—" He who testifieth these things saith, Surely I come quickly. Amen. Even so, come, Lord Jesus."

EXPLANATION.

Obs. 357.—*By the second petition in the Lord's Prayer, " Thy kingdom come," we are taught to pray, that God would more and more demonstrate his absolute power and dominion over all things.*

We may here observe that the *kingdom of God* may be considered as twofold :—

1. His *essential* or *general kingdom;* by which we are to understand that universal and absolute power and sovereignty which he exercises in heaven, on earth, and in hell, for the purposes of his glory.—Ps. ciii. 19. This kingdom embraces every thing which he hath made and every thing which he preserves, from the most glorious luminary in the heavens to the minutest particle that dances in the sunbeam, and from the meanest reptile upon earth to the highest archangel that stands in the presence of God.

2. His *special kingdom;* by which we are in general to understand that government and care which he exercises in and over his Church and people, as a society distinct and separated from the world.—Ps. lix. 13. This special kingdom may be viewed as twofold: the *kingdom of grace*, and the *kingdom of glory*. And it is this special kingdom that is chiefly intended in the second petition in the Lord's Prayer.

There is only one respect in which it is warrantable to pray for the coming of God's *essential* or *general kingdom*,—namely, that God would more and more demonstrate his absolute power and sovereignty over all things; and that it may be acknowledged by the children of men that Jehovah, the Most High, ruleth over all the earth.—Ps. lxxxiii. 18; Dan. iv. 17. This is the only meaning in which we can understand it; for we cannot warrantably pray, that God would exercise his universal dominion, which he cannot but do, being the creator and preserver of all things. We cannot pray that God would be an infinite sovereign, which he cannot but be. Nor can we pray that he would act agreeably to his nature, which he cannot but do.

Obs. 358.—*By the second petition in the Lord's Prayer, " Thy kingdom come," we are taught to pray, that the kingdom of Satan may be destroyed.*

The kingdom of Satan is the grand impediment in the way of the coming of Christ's kingdom. In order, then, to the advancement of the kingdom of grace, it is absolutely necessary that we should pray for the *destruction of Satan's kingdom*. And we do this when we pray that God would root out all idolatry, superstition, error, delusion, will-worship, ignorance, profaneness, and every other abomination from the earth; that Christ would bruise the serpent's head; that he would deliver the souls of men from his slavery; and that unbelievers may be brought to the acknowledgment of the truth as it is in Jesus, or to the obedience of the gospel.

In order to the destruction of Satan's kingdom, it is necessary to pray particularly for the following things:—We must pray for the destruction of *Antichrist* and *Mahomet*, the two great enemies of the kingdom of Christ. We must pray that the man of sin may be consumed with the breath of the Lord, and destroyed with the brightness of his coming; and that the false prophet may be destroyed to arise no more. We must also pray that the *Jews* may be converted and gathered to Shiloh, who is come, and whose is the kingdom and the glory; that their eyes may be opened when they read Moses and the Prophets; and that the veil which is upon their hearts may be taken away, that they may see and understand how much the gospel or Christian dispensation excelleth the Mosaic one in glory. And we must also pray that the divisions and differences among the professed friends of the kingdom of Christ may come to an end; for, while these things continue, it is impossible that his kingdom can come, even where his name is named.

Obs. 359.—*By the second petition in the Lord's Prayer,* " *Thy kingdom come," we are taught to pray, that the kingdom of grace may be advanced, by ourselves and others being brought into it.*

The *kingdom of grace*, in its most extensive meaning, is a kingdom which comprehends all those to whom the gospel is preached, or who are members of the visible Church. And although all such are not in Christ,—although tares are mingled with the wheat,—although godly and ungodly worship together yet all such are a people favoured by the Lord, in comparison with all those who have not the privilege of a preached gospel conferred upon them; and they all profess subjection to Christ as their king,—Ps. ii. 6; Eph. i. 22, 23. And although some have pretended supremacy over this kingdom, or over the visible Church, it is but a vile usurpation; for none, however great or holy, have a right to claim, as their prerogative, what belongs to *Him* whom God hath exalted with his own right hand. But, strictly speaking, the *kingdom of grace* is not so extensive: for, none are true subjects of this kingdom but believers in Christ,—they who have been made alive to God, and who have in very deed been brought from the kingdom of Satan into the kingdom of God's dear Son; they who are the subjects of grace, who have the kingdom of God within them, and in whom grace reigns from first to last unto eternal life.

We must pray that this kingdom of grace *may be advanced* more and more among men; that the earth may be full of the knowledge of the Lord, as the waters cover the sea; that many of Adam's guilty race may be converted by means of his instituted ordinances; that Christ may be rewarded by the justification of many plucked as brands from the burning; that the Father would more and more honour the Son, by the Spirit giving efficacy to the word of his grace; and that the promises respecting the gathering of the people to Shiloh may be accomplished, in order that the Redeemer may " see of the travail of his soul and be satisfied."

The kingdom of grace may be said to be *advanced*, when *ourselves and others are brought into it*, by the power of the Holy Spirit accompanying the means of salvation; and *kept in it* by continued emanations of grace out of the fulness of Christ, by which the principle of grace implanted in the heart is quickened, and strengthened, and preserved.—Ps. cx. 2, 3; Hos. xiv. 5. It is among the important works of God, to preserve his people in the faith, as well as to work it in them; to keep them from death, as well as to implant life; to keep them from falling, as well as to raise them up; and to preserve them by his power through faith unto salvation, as well as to bring them into a state of salvation by a Redeemer.

Obs. 360.—*By the second petition in the Lord's Prayer, " Thy kingdom come," we are taught to pray, that the kingdom of glory may be hastened.*

The *kingdom of glory* is that state of inconceivable happiness and bliss into which the saints are admitted at death; or rather, into which they shall be admitted at the resurrection, when both soul and body shall be for ever with the Lord. And it may be here remarked, that the kingdom of grace and the kingdom of glory are not so much two distinct kingdoms as different states of the same kingdom; the one existing in order to the other. The genuine subjects of the kingdom of grace are subjects also of the kingdom of glory; but while they remain in this world, they are not fully prepared for glory, although they are daily growing in meetness for it, through the various operations of the Holy Spirit.

We must pray that this *kingdom of glory may be hastened;* which implies,—1. That this kingdom is *not yet come*. Christ is not yet beheld with the crown which he shall wear; but the time is approaching when his glory shall break through every opposing obstacle, and when it shall appear to be the glory of the Father—glory, like himself, inconceivable and incomprehensible. 2. That it *shall come.* As certainly as Christ is now glorified, so certainly shall he come again the second time to be glorified in his saints, and to be admired in all them that believe. The evidence is too strong to admit of a doubt. The Father hath said it; the Son hath fought for the kingdom; and the work of the Holy Spirit upon the soul of every subject of this kingdom, proves that it shall come. 3. The fervent desires of the saints that the kingdom of glory may come. In it they themselves are exceedingly interested; but it is not merely or chiefly on this account that they fervently desire it, but on account of *him,* whose is the kingdom and the glory.

INFERENCES.

From this subject we learn,—1. That the gospel is a great privilege. 2. That all who are favoured with it are not in Christ. 3. The necessity of submitting to the sceptre of Christ. 4. The happiness of those who are subjects of the kingdom of grace. 5. The misery of those who are not the subjects of Christ's kingdom. 6. That the gospel has many enemies; but that all shall be taken out of the way. 7. That Christ has always a kingdom on earth —a seed to serve him. 8. The necessity of prayer for the coming of Christ's kingdom.

Of the Third Petition in the Lord's Prayer.

Q. 103.—What do we pray for in the Third Petition?

In the third petition, [which is, "Thy will be done in earth, as it is in heaven,"] we pray, that God, by his grace, would make us able and willing to know, obey, and submit to his will in all things, as the angels do in heaven.

ANALYSIS AND PROOFS.

We are here taught,—

1. That the third petition in the Lord's Prayer is, "Thy will be done on earth as it is in heaven."—Matt. vi. 10.

2. That of ourselves we are unable to know or to obey the will of God. 1 Cor. ii. 14.—"The natural man receiveth not the things of the Spirit of God; for they are foolishness unto him; neither can he know them, because they are spiritually discerned."

3. That God alone can make us able and willing to obey and submit to his will. Phil. ii. 13.—"It is God who worketh in you, both to will and to do of his good pleasure."

4. That we should pray that the will of God may be known and obeyed over all the earth. Ps. lxvii. 2.—"That thy way may be known upon earth, and thy saving health among all nations."

5. That we should pray that God would make us able and willing to know his will. Eph. i. 18.—" The eyes of your understanding being enlightened; that ye may know what is the hope of his calling, and what the riches of the glory of his in heritance in the saints."

6. That we should pray that God would make us able and willing to obey his will. Ps. cxix. 35.—" Make me to go in the path of thy commandments; for therein do I delight."

7. That we should pray that God would make us able and willing to submit to his will. Acts xxi. 14.—" The will of the Lord be done."

8. That we should obey the will of God in all things. Ps. cxix. 5, 6.—" O that my ways were directed to keep thy statutes! Then shall I not be ashamed, when I have respect unto all thy commandments."

9. That we should submit to the will of God in all things. 1 Sam. iii. 18.—" It is the Lord; let him do what seemeth him good."

10. That we should obey and submit to the will of God as the angels do in heaven. Ps. ciii. 20.—" Bless the Lord, ye his angels, that excel in strength, that do his commandments, hearkening to the voice of his word."

EXPLANATION.

Obs. 361.—*By the third petition in the Lord's Prayer*, " *Thy will be done on earth as it is in heaven,*" *we are taught to pray, that God, by his grace, would make us able and willing to know and obey his revealed will in all things.*

The *revealed or preceptive will of God* is that which is contained in the Scriptures of the Old and New Testaments; and it is comprehended in believing and obeying, or in faith and holiness; which is both the sum of his will, and the order in which it must be done.—John vi. 29; 1 Thess. iv. 3; Heb. xi. 6, and xii. 14; 1 John iii. 23. We may here observe, that it is chiefly the revealed will of God that we should pray may be done on earth; for the Lord himself will accomplish his secret will, or the things which he hath purposed.

With respect to the revealed will of God, we must pray, " That God, by his grace, would make us *able and willing to know and to obey it.*" And this we do, when we pray, that by his Spirit he would remove our natural blindness, and open our understanding, that we may understand the Scriptures; that he would incline us to keep up the practice of every commanded duty, in the strength of that grace which is secured in the promise, " I will cause you to walk in my statutes, and ye shall keep my judgments and do them,"—Ezek. xxxvi. 27; that obedience to the whole will of God may be as extensive as the revelation of this will; that it may be done where it is not done; and that the only boundaries may be the ends of the earth. And this implies the following things:—1. That the will of God is not done on earth as it is done in heaven. 2. An acknowledgment of weakness, blindness, indisposedness, and perverseness of heart; all which unite to prevent the will of God from being done.—Eph. i. 17, 18, and iii. 16; Matt. xxvi. 40, 41; Jer. xxxi. 18, &c. 3. An expression of grief of heart, that the will of God is not done on earth, either by ourselves or by others.—Ps. cxix. 136. 4. An ardent desire, that God would remove out of the way every obstacle to the doing of his will on earth as it is done in heaven.

We must pray that God would make us able and willing to know and obey his will, because we are naturally unable and unwilling to know and obey his revealed will.—1 Cor. ii. 14. All are prone to rebel against his will, although it is holy, and just, and good. And hence we must pray, that God would make us able and willing *by his grace;* for it is wholly of his free love and sovereign good pleasure that he worketh in us, both to will and to do. In vain does man think that he can know the will of God without the teaching of the Spirit, or that he can do it without that power which is promised from above.

Obs. 362.—*By the third petition in the Lord's Prayer, " Thy will be done on earth as it is in heaven," we are taught to pray, that God, by his grace, would make us able and willing to submit to his providential will in all things.*

The *providential or secret will of God*, is the rule of his own procedure; and it is exercised over all men and all things, from the least to the greatest, in every possible circumstance in which they may be placed.—Matt. vi. 25–34.

With respect to this providential or secret will of God, or, as it is sometimes called, his will of purpose, we must pray, " That God would, by his grace, make us *able and willing to submit to it.*" And this implies a full, and unqualified, and unreserved submission to the Divine procedure in all afflicting dispensations which may befal us in this world, seeing they all come from God, and are all ordered for our good; and likewise an improvement of merciful providences according to his Word.

We must pray that God would *make* us able and willing, *by his grace*, to submit to, and acquiesce in, his secret will when made known us, because we are naturally unable and unwilling to do so, and prone to quarrel with his providences towards us, although all just and good, and designed for our spiritual and eternal welfare.

Obs. 363.—*By the third petition in the Lord's Prayer, " Thy will be done on earth as it is in heaven," we are taught to pray, that God would make us able and willing to know, obey, and submit to his will in all things, as the angels do in heaven.*

We must pray that the will of God may be done on earth *as it is done in heaven*. This expression may be viewed either with reference to the visible heavens and the works of God which we behold, or with reference to those exalted spirits called angels, who constantly fulfil all his pleasure.

1. With reference to the *heavenly bodies*. As man is frequently sent to the beasts of the field, to the fishes of the sea, and to the fowls of the air for instruction, and also to many of the works of God in nature, that he may see how obedient all things are to *him* who gave them existence; so we may here view him as sent for the same end to the sun, the moon, and the stars, and to all the host of heaven, which have kept an invariable motion for almost six thousand years, serving the Lord and bringing glory to his wonderful name; and among which, from the greatest to the least, and from the nearest to the most distant, nothing takes place but what is appointed by Him who made them. A valuable example set before us all! But,

2. With reference to the *angels in heaven;* in which light the explanation given above principally views the text. If, then, we ourselves would do the will of God, and wish others to do it, we must pray that we and they may be enabled to imitate the holy angels, who perform the will of the Most High with humility,—Isa. vi. 2; Mic. vi. 8; with cheerfulness,—Ps. ciii. 20, and c. 2; with faithfulness,—Isa. xxxviii. 3; with diligence and zeal,—Ps. cxix. 4, 5, and xix. 5; Rom. xii. 11; universally, —Ps. ciii. 21, and cxix. 6; most readily,—Isa. vi. 2; Ps. cxix. 60; constantly,—Ps. cxix. 112; and with sincerity,—Ps. cxix. 80.

INFERENCES.

From this subject we learn.—1. That it is the duty of all to study the revealed will of God, and to submit to his providential will. 2. The danger of disobedience. 3. The necessity of the grace of God to enable us to understand and to do his revealed will, and to submit to his providential will. 4. That it is the duty of all to send the revealed will of God to all those who have not yet received it; seeing it is inconsistent to pray that his will may be done, without endeavouring, at the same time, to make t known to those who are ignorant of it.

Of the Fourth Petition in the Lord's Prayer.

Q. 104.—What do we pray for in the Fourth Petition?

In the fourth petition, [which is, "Give us this day our daily bread,"] we pray, that of God's free gift we may receive a competent portion of the good things of this life, and enjoy his blessing with them.

ANALYSIS AND PROOFS.

We are here taught,—

1. That the fourth petition in the Lord's Prayer is, "Give us this day our daily bread."—Matt. vi. 11.
2. That temporal good things may be made the subject of prayer. Gen. xxviii. 20.—" If God will be with me, and will keep me in this way that I go, and will give me bread to eat and raiment to put on—."
3. That every good thing which we enjoy is undeserved by us, and is a free gift from God. Gen. xxxii. 10.—" I am not worthy of the least of all the mercies, and of all the truth, which thou hast showed unto thy servant."
4. That we are to seek only what may be necessary for the present day, and not to be over-anxious for the future. Matt. vi. 34.—" Take no thought for (or be not over-anxious about) the morrow; for the morrow shall take thought for the things of itself. Sufficient unto the day is the evil thereof."
5. That we are to ask for such a portion of the good things of life, as God in his wisdom sees to be best for us. Prov. xxx. 8. —" Give me neither poverty nor riches; feed me with food convenient for me."
6. That we must ask God's blessing on what we receive, which alone makes temporal good things valuable. Prov. x. 22.—" The blessing of the Lord maketh rich, and he addeth no sorrow with it."

EXPLANATION.

Obs. 364.—*By the fourth petition in the Lord's Prayer, " Give us this day our daily bread," we are taught to pray, that, of God's free gift, we may receive a competent portion of the good things of this life.*

We may here observe, that *spiritual mercies* are not at all intended by bread in this petition. Jesus Christ, indeed, calls himself the *bread of life* which came down from heaven; but for this we pray in the second petition. If we consider how perfect this prayer is, we shall see that the good things of this life must be included; for it would be absurd to imagine, that Christ, who knows that his people require these things, should have given them no place in this directory. And as it is but short, we cannot suppose that he would have spoken of spiritual mercies in every petition. We find that the other petitions are full of them; and we may well believe that he has appropriated the fourth solely to temporal mercies.

By *bread*, then, we are here to understand *all the necessaries and conveniences of life*. And bread may be particularly specified, because it is the most common support of life; because it is the most necessary; because it is called the *staff* of bread,—Isa. iii. 1: because by it both the rich and the poor are maintained:

and because it is found to be that kind of provision which, of all others, is least loathed by mankind in general.

This petition, "Give us this day our daily bread," naturally implies the following things:—

1. That all mankind depend upon God for the support of life, and for all its comforts and conveniences. Were not this the case, there would be no propriety whatever in presenting to God this petition; for we do not generally ask any thing from those on whom we have no dependence, or who we think have nothing to bestow.

2. That it is a lawful request to pray for bread. And although the bread that perisheth may appear a trifle, when compared with that which endureth to everlasting life; yet, while we are in the body, it is a most necessary concern of ours, to which we ought to give due attention. Spiritual things claim our first and chief attention; but temporal things ought not to be neglected; for without them we could neither glorify God, nor be of much advantage to our fellow-creatures. And hence we must deem this a lawful request.

3. That it is a lawful request to pray for bread, not only for ourselves, but also for others,—" Give *us* bread." And seeing that we are allowed to extend our request for others, as well as to request for ourselves, we should not in this respect withhold more than is meet—we should not withhold our brother's due; but we should prove that we love our neighbour as ourselves, and that it is our desire that others, as well as ourselves, may be happy.

4. That whatever we enjoy in this world to make life comfortable and happy, we should seek to have such a right to it as that it may be called *ours*. "Give us *our* bread."

5. That we are not at liberty to ask riches from God. "Give us our *daily* bread." And although there are saints who are very rich in this world's goods, yet it is not in consequence of their prayers; for no saint can, consistently with his character, pray for riches. But we may pray as Agur did, "Give me neither poverty nor riches; feed me with food convenient for me."—Prov. xxx. 8.

6. That it is unlawful to indulge anxiety about futurity. "Give us *this day* our daily bread."—Matt. vi. 34. We are here taught to go daily unto God in prayer for what is necessary for us, that, by using the means which he hath appointed, we may show that we continually depend upon him for what is needful for the body.

7. That our bread—our daily bread—the comforts and conveniences of life, are all the *gift of God;* and that to him we must look for all. "*Give* us this day our daily bread." And although men obtain their bread by industry and diligence, yet it is God who " giveth power to get wealth," and who blesseth the labour of the hands. Having forfeited life and every enjoyment with

it in Adam, whatever we now enjoy is the unmerited gift of the Most High.

We may here remark the difference between prayer for *spiritual*, and prayer for *temporal* good things. With respect to *spiritual* good things, there is no restriction; or the desires of the believer may be as large as he will. Let them be as extensive as the covenant, this is only what is promised—what he has reason to expect—and what he shall assuredly receive. But with respect to things of a *temporal* nature, we must restrict our desires, and pray only for such things as are for the honour of God and our own good. Whatever we ask of a temporal nature, it must be with a desire that God may be glorified ; or, in other words, temporal good things must be asked for spiritual purposes,—Prov. xxx. 7-9 ; 1 Sam. i. ; James iv. 3.

Obs. 365.—*By the fourth petition in the Lord's Prayer, " Give us this day our daily bread," we are taught to pray, that we may enjoy God's blessing along with the good things of life.*

In order that we may have the comfortable use of what we enjoy, it is necessary that we should pray for *the blessing of God* along with it. Without this, there will always be a worm at the root,—without this, our hopes shall never be realized, whatever we promise ourselves,—and without this, outward comforts cannot answer the end which they are designed to serve, and for which they are used.

We may here observe the difference with respect to the *manner* in which the *righteous* and the *wicked* hold their outward enjoyments. The title which the wicked have to outward enjoyments is only a *common* right, there being nothing in it to show that they are the Lord's ; whereas the right which believers have is a *special* right—a title founded upon the covenant, or it is a spiritual right which they have to daily bread. The wicked have their portion in this life; whereas godliness hath the promise, not only of this life, but also of that which is to come. The wicked have nothing but outward enjoyments ; they want the blessing of the Lord on their basket and their store ; whereas the righteous have his blessing along with what they enjoy; and this makes their comforts doubly valuable.

INFERENCES.

From this subject we learn,—1. That the Lord is mindful of all in this life, as well as hereafter. 2. That we ought to be grateful for present mercies. 3. That the Lord hath not left himself without witness, in giving us rain from heaven and fruitful seasons, filling our hearts with food and gladness. 4. That we ought to correspond with him daily in private and in secret. 5. That the Lord can make up to his own people the want of much in this world. 6. That we have more than we deserve.

7. That they who possess much of this world's goods, and do not what they can for the advancement of God's glory in the world, by sending the "Bread of Life" to those who want it, are none of God's people.

Of the Fifth Petition in the Lord's Prayer.

Q. 105.—What do we pray for in the Fifth Petition?

In the fifth petition, [which is, "And forgive us our debts as we forgive our debtors,"] we pray that God, for Christ's sake, would freely pardon all our sins; which we are the rather encouraged to ask, because by his grace we are enabled from the heart to forgive others.

ANALYSIS AND PROOFS.

We are here taught,—
1. That the fifth petition in the Lord's Prayer is, "And forgive us our debts as we forgive our debtors."—Matt. vi. 12.
2. That we should pray for the pardon of sin. Hos. xiv. 2.—"Take away all iniquity, and receive us graciously." See also Ps. li. 1.
3. That pardon of sin is to be expected only through Jesus Christ. Eph. i. 7.—"In whom we have redemption through his blood, the forgiveness of sins, according to the riches of his grace."
4. That we must forgive others. Col. iii. 13.—"Forbearing one another, and forgiving one another."
5. That God alone can enable us from the heart to forgive others. Gal. v. 22, 23.—"The fruit of the Spirit is love, joy, peace, long-suffering, gentleness, goodness, faith, meekness, temperance; against such there is no law."
6. That our being enabled to forgive others, encourages us to ask forgiveness for ourselves. Luke xi. 4.—"Forgive us our sins; for we also forgive every one that is indebted to us."
7. That unless we forgive others, we ourselves shall not be forgiven. Matt. xviii. 35.—"So likewise shall my heavenly Father do also unto you, if ye from your hearts forgive not every one his brother their trespasses." See also Matt. vi. 14, 15.

EXPLANATION.

Obs. 366.—*By the fifth petition in the Lord's Prayer, "And forgive us our debts as we forgive our debtors," we are taught to pray, that God, for Christ's sake, would freely pardon all our sins.*

We may here remark, that this petition is connected with the former by the particle *and*, to show that, however large a portion, and whatever share of the comforts and conveniences of life may be conferred, daily bread cannot of itself constitute a real good; and it is only when such outward comforts are connected with the pardon of sin, that they can be deemed a good really desirable.

By *debts* we are here to understand *sins*.—Luke xi. 4. Every sin is a debt, and every sinner is a debtor. Now, if sin be viewed as a debt, it consists in withholding from God what is most justly his due, viz., honour and love; for which we owe him an equivalent, or the reparation of his injured glory. If, then, by *debts* we are to understand *sins*, they must mean original and actual sin—sins of omission and commission; on account of which we owe the debt of satisfaction to the justice of God; for, saith the Scripture, " The wages of sin is death." But we not only owe the debt of *satisfaction* as transgressors, but we also owe the debt of *obedience* to the law as a covenant. Every sinner, then, is a debtor, owing more than he can possibly pay.

The nature of the debt of sin may be seen from the following things:—1. Sin is a debt which no man can pay. Every sinner is, as it were, drowned in debt to the law and justice of God; and all, without exception, would have perished in consequence of this, had not a Surety been provided, every way able to answer the demands of the creditor. 2. Sin is debt which the sinner endeavours in various ways to diminish; not, indeed, by paying what he owes, but by persuading himself that his debt is not what it really is. 3. Sin is a debt which is continually increasing. And whatever means the sinner may adopt to liquidate his debt, it will be found to multiply, until all be freely forgiven for Christ's sake—until all be cancelled by the blood of Christ. Hence we read of sinners " treasuring up to themselves wrath against the day of wrath."—Rom. ii. 5. 4. Sin is a debt which excites hatred to God. Sinners do not love God, and they cannot bear the idea of being brought to give an account. 5. Sin is a debt which is most fairly stated in the book of God; and a debt which shall be exacted to the last farthing. 6. Sin is a debt for which the Lord will soon prosecute the sinner. As God hath expressed his love towards his insolvent debtors to such a high degree, as to have provided a Surety himself; so, if sinners will not employ this Surety to liquidate their debt, in order that they may go free, it is but just that he should pursue and cast them into prison; from which they shall not come until they shall have paid the last farthing,—which shall never come to pass. And hence, 7. Sin is a debt of the worst kind, seeing we ourselves have nothing to pay. We can neither give to God what we have taken away, nor can we give an equivalent for it. And hence we do not pray that we may *pay* our debts, but we pray that they *may be forgiven.*

If by *debts* we are to understand *sins*, then by *our debts* (" Forgive us *our* debts ") we are to understand *our sins*—all the sins that can be laid to our charge in any way whatever. Every sin in thought, word, and action; sin original and actual; sins of omission and commission; secret sins, as well as those committed at noonday; sins of infirmity, as well as wilful sins; sins of childhood and youth, as well as sins committed in riper years; sins against God, against our neighbour, and against ourselves;—in a word, every sin with which the Lord can charge us, may be justly considered as *our debts*.

The *forgiveness of debts*, which we are here taught to pray for, is the *removal of guilt*, which lays the sinner under an obligation to suffer the punishment due to his sins. Or, it is an *acquittal* from the guilt and punishment of sin, which must be a blessing of inconceivable value; and to be allowed to pray for this mercy, must be the highest privilege conferred upon us, seeing all are condemned, and are by nature the children of wrath.

The spring or fountain in God, from which the pardon of sin flows, is his own *gracious nature* and *sovereign good-will*.—Exod. xxxiii. 19. But it is obvious from Revelation, that it is *only for Christ's sake* that the guilty can be pardoned. And when we speak of pardon "for Christ's sake," it means that God vents his pardoning mercy and grace only through the obedience and satisfaction of Christ, apprehended and applied by faith.—Rom. iii. 25. And without respect to his obedience and satisfaction, sin cannot be pardoned; for, although God is merciful, his mercy can find its way to the sinner only through the atonement or propitiation. Justice must be satisfied, and without shedding of blood there is no remission.—Heb. ix. 22. However precious and necessary a blessing pardon of sin is, it is vain to expect it through any other medium; and it will be found, that they who do not see that it is through the righteousness of Christ alone that God is just, and the justifier of him that believeth in Jesus, are not very serious in their desires after forgiveness.—Acts v. 31.

The mercy of pardon extends to *all sins*.—Ps. ciii. 3. Whatever be their nature, whatever their number, whatever their aggravations, there is mercy enough in a reconciled God to forgive all; and there is merit enough in Christ to obtain the pardon of all,—efficacy enough in his blood to cleanse from all sin.—Ps. cxxx. 4, 7, 8; 1 John i. 7.

That which adds much to the mercy of forgiveness, is the *freeness* of it. "We pray that God would *freely* pardon all our sins." If pardon of sin were not free, we could never be pardoned; for we have nothing with which we could purchase our discharge. It is the glory of God *freely to forgive* the greatest debt, and he would spurn at the idea of receiving anything for it. Pardon is freely given, and it must be freely received; for if it is not freely received, it is not received at all.

But here it may be asked, How can God be said to pardon *all* our sins *freely*, when he does not pardon *one* sin but on account of the finished righteousness of Jesus Christ? To this we answer, that, although Christ obtained the pardon of sin *by merit*, yet it comes to us *freely through him*. It is *of debt* to *him*, but *of grace* to *us*. When God accepted of Christ as the sinner's surety, it was an act of rich, and free, and sovereign grace; and when he accepted of his work and labour of love, or when he was well pleased for his righteousness' sake, it was an act of the same nature.—Eph. i. 7.

Obs. 367.—*By the fifth petition in the Lord's Prayer,* "*And forgive us our debts as we forgive our debtors,*" *we are taught, that our being enabled, by the grace of God, heartily to forgive others, is an encouragement to ask forgiveness for ourselves.*

The argument by which this petition is enforced, is, "*As we forgive our debtors;*" or, as it is expressed in the explanation of the text, " Because, by God's grace, we are enabled from the heart to forgive others." But it must ever be remembered, that we are not to view our forgiveness of others, however hearty, as a *motive* to prevail with God to forgive us; for this is not the ground upon which we are to ask forgiveness; but we are to view it merely as an *encouragement* to us to believe that our sins are forgiven, when we find in ourselves a readiness from the heart to forgive others who may have injured or offended us.— Matt. vi. 14, 15.

By our *debtors* we are to understand all those who may have cursed us, hated us, despitefully used us, or said all manner of evil against us falsely; in a word, our debtors are all those who may have sinned against us or injured us in any respect, whether by word or deed, whether in our reputation, our family, our relations, or our substance,—Matt. v. 44, where Christ informs us who are our debtors.

The indispensable duty of all who would be forgiven of God, is to *forgive their debtors*. And this we may be said to do, when, notwithstanding all that they have done to us, we discover no spirit of revenge; when we entertain no hatred or malice against them; when we strive against the very thoughts of revenge, which belongeth to God alone; when we forbear to hurt our enemies in any way, although we have it in our power to do so in various ways; when we love them, and wish well to them, and are ready to do them good at all times, as if nothing had been done by them; when we do not rejoice, but grieve at their calamities; and when we pray for them, and desire reconciliation with them, and relieve their wants when it is in our power to do so. All this is certainly included in the command of our Saviour. —Matt. v. 44-48.

With respect to the *manner* in which we are to forgive our debtors, we observe, that we must forgive them in the same manner that God forgives us. And, 1. God forgives us with the *utmost good will;* and so must we forgive our debtors. We must not say that we forgive, while there is still in the heart enmity against those who may have wronged us. 2. God forgives *all sin;* and if we would have the evidence in ourselves, that our sins are forgiven, we must not forgive some, and not forgive other offences done to us; but we must do to others as we wish God to do to us. 3. God forgives sin *frequently;* he multiplies to pardon; and so should we do to others. We must forgive our brother, not only seven times, but seventy times seven, —that is, an indefinite number of times, or always.—Matt. xviii. 21, 22.

But we cannot thus forgive others *of ourselves*. Such a disposition is found in none naturally; and hence we are informed, that it is *by Divine grace* that we are *enabled* from the heart to forgive others. There is in all men a natural disposition to harbour in the heart hatred and malice on account of personal injuries, and to revenge them if possible, and as far as possible; and, consequently, this forgiveness which is required of us must come *from the heart*. And we are not only to forgive them in a *negative* way,—that is, by laying aside all resentment against them; but we must forgive them in a *positive* way, that is, by doing them all the offices of kindness which it is in our power to do, as if they had never injured us at all in any way. It is evident that, all things being considered, this is one of the most difficult practical lessons to be learned in Christianity; human nature recoils at the injunction. But there is no alternative: Divine authority is laid upon us; and in Divine strength we can do all things.

When we pray, "Forgive us our debts *as* we forgive our debtors," we must not intend by it to state a comparison between God's forgiveness of us, and our forgiveness of others. This is by no means implied in the particle *as;* for there is no proportion at all between the one and the other; but, on the contrary, an infinite disproportion. The injuries which others do, or can do to us, are but few and small when compared with the innumerable and aggravated crimes with which we are chargeable against God.—Matt. xviii. 24, &c. The meaning, then, of the words, "*As* we forgive our debtors," is, that we ought to *take encouragement* to hope that God will forgive us our daily sins, from this confidence in ourselves, that we are enabled from the heart to forgive others their offences or trespasses.—Matt. vi. 14 15.

The following things may be proposed as *motives* to persuade us to forgive others:—1. The example of Jesus Christ should influence all his followers to forgiveness.—1 Pet. ii. 23; Luke xxiii. 34. 2. The example of the saints should influence us to this.—Gen. l. 15–21; Exod. xv. and xvii.; 2 Kings vi.

Acts vii. 60. 3. The danger of an implacable and unmerciful disposition should influence to this. A revengeful temper prevents those who indulge it from profiting by the means of grace; for, even in the presence of God, it will be contriving methods of vengeance congenial to itself. The very service of such is abomination in the sight of God; for they do not worship God in a state of peace with all men; and they are destitute of that charity which is the bond of perfection. 4. To forgive is the best way to overcome an enemy.—Rom. xii. 20, 21; Prov. xxv. 21, 22; 1 Sam. xxiv. 16, 17. 5. God hath inseparably connected our forgiveness of others with his forgiveness of us.—Matt. vi. 14, 15. 6. As an unforgiving spirit bespeaks one a stranger to vital godliness; so a forgiving spirit is a very great evidence of a gracious change being wrought in the heart, although there may be some naturally of a more forgiving spirit than others. 7. There is none so like the devil as a man of revenge. Revenge is his delight; and they who delight in revenge, delight in him. 8. They who are of a bitter and revengeful disposition, must either omit this prayer altogether, or be guilty of the highest presumption.

INFERENCES.

From this subject we learn,—1. That there are none without sin; and that none can pay this debt. 2. The necessity of an interest in Jesus Christ, who is the sinner's surety, and who has paid the debt due to God's law and justice. 3. The necessity of confessing and forsaking our sins. 4. That forgiveness is a precious blessing. 5. The necessity of avoiding sin, which is a debt that we cannot pay. 6. The danger of those whose sin is not pardoned. 7. The inconsistency of those who pray for forgiveness, but do not forgive. 8. That it is incumbent upon all to forgive others. 9. That forgiveness of others is an evidence of forgiveness to ourselves.

Of the Sixth Petition in the Lord's Prayer.

Q. 106.—What do we pray for in the Sixth Petition?

In the sixth petition, [which is, " And lead us not into temptation, but deliver us from evil,"] we pray, that God would either keep us from being tempted to sin, or support and deliver us when we are tempted.

ANALYSIS AND PROOFS.

We are here taught,—
1. That the sixth petition in the Lord's Prayer is, " And lead us not into temptation, but deliver us from evil."—Matt. vi. 13.
2. That we should pray that God, if consistent with his will, would keep us from being tempted to sin. Matt. xxvi. 41.—

"Watch and pray, that ye enter not into temptation." See also 2 Chron. xxxii. 31.

3. That we should pray for support under temptation. Ps. cxix. 133.—"Let not any iniquity have dominion over me." See also 1 Cor. x. 13.

4. That we should pray for deliverance from temptation. 2 Cor. xii. 8.—"For this thing I besought the Lord thrice, that it might depart from me." See also 1 Cor. x. 13.

EXPLANATION.

Obs. 368.—*By the sixth petition in the Lord's Prayer*, "*And lead us not into temptation, but deliver us from evil,*" *we are taught to pray, that God would keep us from being tempted to sin.*

While the believer is in this world, he is not free from tribulation in it, although his sins are pardoned. And hence the connection of this petition with the former by the particle *and*, may remind him that he must always be on his guard; and that he must cleave to the Lord for ever, if he would obtain victory over temptations.

This petition necessarily presupposes that God may, for the best ends, so order things, as that his people may be assaulted and foiled, and for a season led captive by temptations.—2 Chron. xxxii. 31.

The word *temptation* may be taken either in a good or in a bad sense. When it is taken in a good sense, it means only a *trial*, which God may design to make of any one, that he may be proved; and this not so much with reference to himself as to his saints. God himself perfectly knows what is in man; but he may try his people that they themselves may know what is in them. And thus God tempted or tried Abraham.—Gen. xxii. But strictly speaking, this is not the meaning of *temptation* in this place; it being most commonly taken in a bad sense; and accordingly it signifies *an enticing to sin*, some means being used to draw into it. In this respect God tempts no man. James i. 13, 14.—"Let not any man say, when he is tempted, I am tempted of God; for God cannot be tempted with evil, neither tempteth he any man; but every man is tempted, when he is drawn away of his own lust and enticed."

All temptations to sin spring or take their rise from three grand sources, viz., Satan, the world, and the flesh. These are ever ready most powerfully to draw us aside and to ensnare us. —1 Chron. xxi.; Luke xxi. 34; James i. 14. And even after we are in a renewed state, we are in danger of being drawn aside by these enemies, in consequence of remaining corruption, on which and by which they operate, through weakness and want of watchfulness. On these accounts, we are both subject to temptations, and prone to expose ourselves to them.—Gal. v. 17. And considering the nature, strength, and subtlety of these enemies, we are of ourselves unable to resist them; nay, we are naturally unwilling to do so,—unwilling to recover ourselves out of them, and to improve them as we ought.—Rom. vii. 23, &c.; 1 Chron. xxi. 1, &c.

The first source from which temptations take their rise, is *Satan;* hence called *the tempter*, by way of eminence,—Matt. iv. 3; and this, too, with the utmost propriety, on account of his strong and violent instigation and solicitation to sin.—Luke xxii. 3; Acts v. 3. Satan began to tempt so early as in Paradise, where he succeeded too well; and ever since he has been making assaults upon all ranks of men; for he goeth about as a roaring lion, seeking whom he may devour.—1 Pet. v. 8.

We may here observe, that Satan cannot *force* any to comply with his temptations. Were this the case, his temptations would be irresistible,—which we are assured they are not. The saints are exhorted to " resist the devil, and he will flee from them;" and they have been actually enabled by grace to do so.—James iv. 7; 2 Cor. xii. 8, 9.

But, notwithstanding this, there arises *uncommon danger* from his temptations. And this will be evident, when we consider his character. And,—1. He is a most *malicious* tempter. He desires nothing less than the everlasting ruin of mankind; and hence he is called the destroyer. 2. He is a most *unwearied* tempter.—1 Pet. v. 8. He is perpetually going up and down through the earth, lion-like, lurking for his prey; and contriving numberless base stratagems by which he may ensnare the sons of men. 3. He is a most *powerful* tempter. This is evident from the names by which he is known; such as, a strong man, the god of this world, the prince of the power of the air, the prince of this world, and the great red dragon. He is a most *cunning* and *subtle* tempter. There are various expressions in Scripture which prove this; such as the fiery darts of the wicked one, the wiles of the devil,—Eph. vi.; the devices of Satan,—2 Cor. ii. 11; and the depths of Satan.—Rev. ii. 24.

The cunning of Satan discovers itself in the following respects: —1. In the choice of those *seasons of temptation* which are peculiarly fitted for his purpose. This is evident from the case of our first parents, and also from that of Christ.—Gen. iii.; Matt. iv. 2. In choosing the *fittest instruments* for conducting his temptations. Thus he made use of Job's wife in tempting him, of Peter in tempting Jesus, and of Judas in betraying him. He also makes use of bad men, of great men, and of men of talents, to carry on his temptations. 3. In choosing, not only the fittest instruments for carrying on his temptations, but also the *fittest persons* as *objects* of temptation. Thus he easily works upon persons given to melancholy, or idleness, or pride,—2 Sam. xxiv. 2: and the history of Haman in the Book of Esther. The ignorant, also, and those who believe not, become an easy prey to him. 4. In tempting men by those things which are in themselves lawful, but which become a snare to them.—Ps. lxix. 22. 5. In leaving the objects of his temptations for a season, having been unsuccessful at first.—Luke iv. 13, and xi. 24. 6. In the way in which he represents Christianity,—namely, in the most unfavourable light. In order that men may be kept from embracing it, and that those who have embraced it may give it up, he represents it as the most melancholy thing in the world. 7. In exciting men to broach false doctrines, and doctrines which are agreeable to the flesh; and in exciting others to embrace them instead of the truth.—Jude 4; 2 Pet. ii. 1. 8. In presenting himself as a *friend*, when he would carry on his malicious designs. Thus he appeared as a friend to Eve and to Christ.—Gen. iii. 4, 5; Matt. iv. 2, 3. 9. In tempting men to *delay repentance;* and to believe that, although they sin, they can break off their sins by repentance. This is a depth of Satan, and one of his most dangerous wiles. This is a temptation in which men readily acquiesce, and to which he has not much to do to persuade them. The devil goes upon the principle, that it is easy to repent, and that the sinner can repent if he will, and when he will. But although the sinner can forsake God, yet he cannot return unto him of himself; for repentance is the *gift of God.* 10. In endeavouring to destroy *faith.* He aims chiefly at this grace of the Spirit in believers, because it is by faith that the believer stands, and overcomes, and resists him; and although he cannot wholly destroy it, yet he may greatly shake and weaken it. 11. In throwing obstacles in the way of the saints, when they would be found in the way of commanded duty,—1 Thess. ii. 18, where we are informed, that the Apostle Paul, having purposed to visit the Thessalonians, was prevented from executing his intention by Satan, who carved out work for him by exciting divisions in other places. He likewise tempts people to neglect self-examination, meditation on the Word of God, and prayer; and various other duties. 12. In withdrawing the minds of men from attention to the procedure of God in providence; and from attending to his providences towards themselves in particular. And, 13. It may be added, that the cunning of Satan appears in tempting men to fight duels, and to lay violent hands upon themselves. These are some of the wiles, devices, depths, and fiery darts of the wicked one; and hence we see the necessity of this petition, "Lead us not into temptation."

But it may be here asked, Is Satan to be blamed for all these temptations? Is it not possible to ascribe to him more than we ought? And do not many temptations arise from the heart of man himself, which ought not to be laid to Satan's charge? This is evident. But to distinguish between those temptations which come from Satan, and those which come from the heart of man, is not an easy matter. It may, however, be remarked,—1. That those temptations which spring up suddenly in the heart (and hence called fiery *darts*), may be considered as the production of Satan; whereas those which arise in the heart of man, are not of such sudden growth, as they require time for deliberation, that the thing in view may not miscarry. 2. That the motions which arise in the heart of man, are found not to alarm so much as those which come from Satan. 3. That the motions which arise in the heart, are cherished and fostered; whereas those that come from Satan are abhorred. And hence his temptations are called *fiery darts*.

Another source of temptation, is the things of the *world;* and these comprehend both its *good* things and its *evil* things. 1. The *good* things of the world which give rise to temptations, are those things which are deemed good by *men;* such as riches, honours, pleasures, preferments, &c. But it is only when these things are abused, by being trusted to or rested in, or when they are perverted to base purposes, that they become a snare and destruction to the soul.—1 Tim. vi. 9; 2 Tim. iv. 10; Matt. xiii. 22. 2. The *evil* things of the world which give rise to temptations, are all the outward troubles and afflictions which befal us, and to which we are exposed; such as poverty, persecution, reproach, sickness, &c. And these prove temptations, either when they are despised, or when we faint under the rod.—Heb. xii. 5.

A third source from which temptations take their rise, is the *flesh*, by which we are to understand our corrupt and depraved nature. And upon reflection, this will be found to be the most dangerous enemy with which we have to do, being *within.* And it is the spring of temptation, inasmuch as it entices to sin, and is the inlet to temptations from Satan and from the world.— James i. 14.

In whatever way we are to understand the expression, " Lead us not into temptation," it is evident, that God cannot be the author of sin. If temptation be taken in a good sense for *trial*, as in the case of Abraham, he may be said to " lead us into temptation," or to *try* us; and against such trials we dare not pray absolutely. But if temptation be taken in a bad sense, then God cannot be said to *tempt* any man; "but every man is tempted, when he is drawn away of his own lust, and enticed."—James i. 14. God, however, may be said to *lead into temptation*, when, in the course of his providence, men are placed in certain circumstances, from which their hearts may take occasion to sin: and such circumstances are so various that they cannot be named. He may also be said to *lead into temptation*, when he permits his people to fall into sin, or when he permits Satan and his agents to tempt them to the commission of sin.—Compare 2 Sam. xxiv. 1, with 1 Chron. xxi. 1. But although the procedure of God be such in his providence, yet his holiness remains untainted, and his character pure in every respect; for it is easy for him to bring glory to his name, and good to his people, out of such temptations. Thus were checked the pride of King Hezekiah (Isa. xxxix.), and the self-confidence of the Apostle Peter. Here, however, we may remark, that in Scripture language, the word *lead* is equivalent to *leave* or *abandon*; and thus the petition might be rendered, "Leave or abandon us not to temptation." The original word sometimes denotes no more than to *permit* or not to hinder. This form of expression is frequently used in Scripture. Thus in Mark v. 12, the expression *send us*, means no more than *suffer us to go*. The word has the same meaning in the following passages.—Gen. xxiv. 54, 56, 59; 2 Thess. ii. 11.

Obs. 369.—*By the sixth petition in the Lord's Prayer, "And lead us not into temptation, but deliver us from evil," we are taught to pray, that God would support and deliver us when we are tempted.*

By *evil* in this petition, "Deliver us from evil," we may understand,—1. The *evil of sin;* which is doubtless the greatest evil that can be named or conceived; seeing it is the cause of every other evil in which we can be involved in this world or the next; for, were there no sin, there would be no evil in any thing whatever. 2. The *evil of temptation;* which is everything that is calculated to draw into sin; and from which we may pray that we may be kept, or supported and delivered when we are tempted.

But we may here mention some of the *particular evils*, from which we may pray that we may be delivered. We may lawfully pray to God for deliverance,—1. From *temporal evils*, so far as it is for the glory of God, and our own best interests both here and hereafter. 2. From the *evil of our own heart*, which is called "an evil heart of unbelief,"—Heb. iii. 12, and which is the origin of all the sin that is in the world; for, were there not an evil heart within, the devil and the world from without would make no impression so as to destroy. 3. From the *evil of Satan*, who is called *the evil one*,—Matt. xiii. 19, and whose constant employment is, to go to and fro through the earth, seeking whom he may devour. And, 4. From the *evil of the world* which is called an *evil world*.—Gal. i. 4.

The petition, "Deliver us from evil," does not imply, that the saints shall wholly escape the evils to which they are exposed in the present state of existence; for, although they may in the providence of God, be exempted from dangerous evils, so as that occasions of sin may not be presented to them; yet they cannot flee from themselves,—from that corruption which is within them, and which is inseparable from them in this world. There is, however, no inconsistency between the impossibility of a total exemption from evil, and their desire of deliverance; for this is exactly consonant to their circumstances in providence

But although this prayer does not import a total deliverance from evil, while in this life, yet it certainly amounts to something with which the saints are well pleased, and by which they are encouraged to hope that to their utmost wishes this petition shall soon be granted. Its true import, then, is clearly expressed in the explanation here given of the text, viz., " *That God would keep us from being tempted to sin, or support and deliver us when we are tempted.*" By this mode of expression, the saints leave themselves wholly in the hand of their God, that he may do with them what seemeth good in his sight, from a real conviction that all things shall work together for their good both here and hereafter.—Rom. viii. 28.

The great end which we should have in view in offering up this petition, is, that our *sanctification and salvation may be perfected;* that Satan may be overcome; and that we may be fully freed from sin, and temptation, and every evil whatever. And there must be a firm persuasion that God can deliver us from all evil, and that he alone can do it; for without faith, neither this nor any other petition can be offered up with acceptance.--Heb. xi. 6.

INFERENCES.

From this subject we learn,—1. That this is a world of danger to which we are always exposed. 2. That God may try us for his own glory and for our good. 3. The duty and necessity of self-knowledge. 4. The necessity of faith to overcome the devil, the world, and the flesh. 5. The necessity of watchfulness and prayer. 6. That God may justly lead us or allow us to enter into temptation, for sinning against him. 7. That temptation is eventually for good to the saints.—Rom. viii. 28. 8. That of ourselves we are utterly unable to withstand temptation; and, consequently, the absolute necessity of dependence upon the Spirit of God.

Of the Conclusion of the Lord's Prayer.

Q. 107.—𝔚𝔥𝔞𝔱 𝔡𝔬𝔱𝔥 𝔱𝔥𝔢 𝔒𝔬𝔫𝔠𝔩𝔲𝔰𝔦𝔬𝔫 𝔬𝔣 𝔱𝔥𝔢 𝔏𝔬𝔯𝔡'𝔰 𝔓𝔯𝔞𝔶𝔢𝔯 𝔱𝔢𝔞𝔠𝔥 𝔲𝔰?

The conclusion of the Lord's Prayer, [which is, " For thine is the kingdom, and the power, and the glory, for ever. Amen,"] teacheth us to take our encouragement in prayer from God only ; and in our prayers to praise him, ascribing kingdom, power, and glory to him ; and in testimony of our desire and assurance to be heard. we say, Amen..

ANALYSIS AND PROOFS.

We are here taught,—

1. That the conclusion of the Lord's Prayer is, "For thine is the kingdom, and the power, and the glory, for ever. Amen."—Matt. vi. 13.

2. That we should take our encouragement in prayer from God only. Dan. ix. 18.—"We do not present our supplications before thee for our righteousness, but for thy great mercies."

3. That in our prayers we should join thanksgiving and praise. 1 Chron. xxix. 10.—"David blessed the Lord before all the congregation; and David said, Blessed be thou, Lord God of Israel, our Father, for ever and ever." See also Phil. iv. 6.

4. That in our prayers we should ascribe the kingdom or universal dominion to God. 1 Chron. xxix. 11.—"All that is in the heaven and the earth is thine; thine is the kingdom, O Lord; and thou art exalted as head above all."

5. That in our prayers we should ascribe all power and glory unto God. 1 Chron. xxix. 11.—"Thine, O Lord, is the greatness, and the power, and the glory, and the victory, and the majesty."

6. That in prayer we should earnestly desire that God would hear us. Dan. ix. 19.—"O Lord, hear; O Lord, forgive; O Lord, hearken and do; defer not, for thine own sake, O my God."

7. That we should pray with a hope and an humble assurance that God will hear us. Heb. x. 22.—"Let us draw near with a true heart, in full assurance of faith."

8. That our prayers should be concluded with an "Amen." Ps. cvi. 48.—"Let all the people say, Amen."

EXPLANATION.

Obs. 370.—*By the conclusion of the Lord's Prayer, "For thine is the kingdom, and the power, and the glory, for ever," we are taught, that we should take our encouragement in prayer from God alone.*

The conclusion of the Lord's Prayer teaches us to enforce our petitions with arguments.—Rom. xv. 30. And this idea arises from the connection of the conclusion with the petitions by the particle *for;* which shows, that what follows may be used as arguments in prayer to God. It is the same as if it had been said, "Give us this day our daily bread,—for thine is the kingdom: Forgive us our debts,—for thine is the power and the glory," &c. There are many examples in Scripture of the saints enforcing their prayers by arguments. See Exod. xxxii. 11-13,—where Moses urges his request with peculiar arguments; Dan. ix. 4-19,—where Daniel urges his requests with arguments no less strong, although of a different nature; 2 Chron. xiv. 11,—

how Asa urges his petition; Matt. xv. 22,—how the Syrophenician woman multiplied her arguments, that she might succeed, if t all possible; for it appears that she was determined to be heard; Job xxiii. 4,—where Job says, that he would fill his mouth with arguments; and many other examples of this kind are to be found in Scripture. The very nature of prayer shows, that if we obtain its true spirit, we must urge, and plead, and enforce our petitions with suitable arguments; seeing that prayer is a transacting with God about matters of eternal importance, in which all are most intimately concerned. A cold and lifeless form of expression, and an indifferent mode of uttering our requests, have no influence with God; for he delights not in mere lip service, but in earnestness, and fervour, and importunity, and enlarged desires after him, as if we would not come away from his throne unheard and unanswered.

But although we are to enforce our petitions by arguments, yet we must remember that no arguments whatever can *move*, o1 *persuade*, or *prevail with God*, to bestow on us what we desire, or what he does not see proper to bestow, although we ourselves may deem it necessary. God perfectly knoweth what our circumstances are; he knoweth also what is necessary for us; and what he will bestow upon us he hath determined in his own mind, and no arguments whatever can alter his purpose; for with him there is no variableness nor shadow of turning. The great design, then, of enforcing our petitions with arguments is, not to affect God, but to *affect ourselves;* to quicken our faith and encourage our hope, that we shall receive what is necessary for us out of the fulness of the covenant, in God's own time and way. —Dan. ix. 18. What is necessary to increase our faith and fervency in prayer, it is certainly our duty to attend to; and what is calculated to do so, becomes highly necessary. The effect of every argument, then, rests with *ourselves*, and not with God; although, according to the order of the covenant, this is called " prevailing in prayer," when we fill our mouth with arguments, and when our prayers are answered; and hence it is said, that " the effectual fervent prayer of a righteous man availeth much." —James v. 16.

Every argument urged in prayer must be taken *from God alone;* for, if God is the only object of prayer, and if from him every answer must come, it becomes us to take every encouragement in prayer from him alone. It is vain for any to plead their own worthiness, or the worthiness of any other creature,—Dan ix. 19; where Daniel takes his arguments for being heard entirely from his God. And there is certainly a sufficiency in God for everything that is needful in this respect; and consequently, there can be no necessity for having recourse to any thing besides him as an argument to enforce our requests.

Again: Every argument that is taken from God, or every en

couragement in prayer, must be derived from the display of the harmony of his attributes in a finished salvation,—Ps. lxxxv. 10; where we learn, that all the perfections and excellencies of the Divine nature harmoniously agree in conferring all promised blessings on sinners of mankind, on account of the meritorious obedience and satisfaction of Christ, imputed to them, and received by faith alone. See also 1 Cor. iii. 21-23; where God is discovered in so many gracious ways, that every one of them constitutes a most suitable plea in prayer, according to our respective circumstances. And when all is the believer's, it becomes an inexhaustible fountain of argument, which must be truly acceptable to God, when drawn from himself,—from that character which he sustains, as revealed in his Son, in whom alone he is "the Hearer of prayer."

But it may be here asked, Do we not find the saints (as David, Ps. xxv. 11) urging as an argument with God in prayer, the *greatness of their sin?* To this we answer in the affirmative; but the force of the plea rests with God himself, whose name is magnified by the pardon of great sin. In the passage alluded to, David's prayer is, "Pardon mine iniquity, for it is great;" but the argument rests with God; "For thy name's sake, O Lord." And it is the same as if he had said, "O Lord, pardon mine iniquity, that thy name may be magnified." By this confession David the more affected his own mind, which is a great point gained in prayer. The greatness, then, of our misery, the number of our sins, and our need, may be urged in prayer; but we must ever have respect to God himself, and keep in view his glorious attributes, which are glorified in hearing and in answering prayer through Jesus Christ, in whom he is ever well pleased.

Obs. 371.—*By the conclusion of the Lord's Prayer, " For thine is the kingdom, and the power, and the glory, for ever," we are taught, that in our prayers we should praise God, by ascribing kingdom, power, and glory to him.*

The conclusion of the Lord's Prayer teaches us to *praise* God in our prayers. And it may be here observed, that this form or pattern of prayer both begins and ends with praise, which should be the case with all our prayers. When we begin to pray, we should have exalted thoughts of God, which is praising him; and when we conclude, we should also have exalted thoughts of him, that when we leave the throne of grace for the time, we may carry along with us suitable ideas of the Divine majesty. By the first, we shall be fitted to worship him reverently; and by the last, we shall be the more guarded against sin. In these ways we praise God; and in every part of worship we praise him, and in prayer we do so eminently, when we exercise the grace of *faith;* for he deems himself highly honoured by every exercise of this grace.—Heb. xi.

We must praise God in our prayers, by *ascribing to him the kingdom, and the power, and the glory.* By these we are to understand,—1. His *eternal sovereignty* in the kingdom of nature and the kingdom of grace; in both of which he hath an opportunity of discovering his eternal sovereignty. 2. His *omnipotence;* by which we are to understand, not only the *authority* by which he *may* do what he will in his kingdom, but also the *ability* by which he *can* do it. And considering the nature and extent of the kingdom of God, it is necessary that power should belong to him; for without this his sovereignty could not be maintained—his kingdom could not be governed. 3. His *glorious excellency;* which is the end that he proposes to himself in the government of his kingdom and in the exercise of his power. And, accordingly, whatever he doth, whatever he hath made, and whatever he wills, is for his own pleasure, and shall redound to his glory. Isa. xlviii. 11.

We *ascribe the kingdom to God,* when we behold him swaying the sceptre over universal nature, guiding the helm of providence, and steering his people to the haven of everlasting rest in his own time and way; acquiescing in all things respecting ourselves and others, when we acknowledge that he who made us has a right to govern us, and to be served and obeyed by us; when we study to give him the glory due unto his name; when we confess that all things are in his hands, and that he can do what he will with all his creatures; when we ascribe equity and justice to him in all his ways, and maintain that he can do no wrong to any; when we ascribe to him the most unlimited power; and when we affirm that he alone ought to reign as universal king.

We *ascribe the power to God,* when we ascribe to him omnipotence and all power in heaven and on earth; when we acknowledge that he can fulfil all his purposes, that none can oppose his designs, and that he can bestow or withhold what seemeth good unto him; when we acknowledge that he can give effect to his word, however much it may oppose the will of the creatures; when we confess that nothing is too hard for him—that what appears impossible to angels and men is easy to God; and when we acknowledge that there are everywhere in his extensive dominions traces of his almighty power, which is necessary to govern the creatures which he hath made, and the whole system of the universe.

We *ascribe the glory to God,* when we acknowledge that he is possessed of every excellence which can render him glorious in the eyes of angels and of men; when we confess that the praise and honour of every thing that is great and excellent, or that has a tendency to raise our esteem and admiration, are due to him; when we acknowledge that there is none so worthy as the Lord; and when we allow that he alone ought to be praised by angels and by men. It may be here remarked, that in this place, *glory* has a particular reference to what God does in his kingdom, and to the exercise of his power in it; from which glory redounds to God, and shall redound to him throughout the endless ages of eternity.

In prayer, we may take *encouragement* from the kingdom, power, and glory of God in the following respects :—1. From the *kingdom* of God we may take this encouragement in prayer, that we shall want nothing that is good for us, either as his creatures or as his children.—Matt. vii. 11. 2. From the *power* of God we may take this encouragement in prayer, that no difficulty whatever shall hinder or prevent the accomplishment of his promises.—Rom. iv. 21; Eph. iii. 20. 3. From the *glory* of God we may take this encouragement in prayer, that the accomplishment of his glorious purposes, and the performance of his gracious promises, shall redound to his praise and glory.—Ps. xlv. 7.

That this encouragement may be as great as possible, *eternity* is ascribed to the kingdom, and power, and glory of God: "For thine is the kingdom, and the power, and the glory, *for ever.*" These we must ascribe to God through eternity; and in this respect God differs from all earthly kings and potentates whatever. However long in duration their kingdom, and power, and glory may be, it is but a moment when compared with the duration of *him*, whose kingdom is an everlasting kingdom, whose power is for ever, and whose glory shall be proclaimed through all eternity.

Obs. 372.—*By the addition of " Amen" to the conclusion of the Lord's Prayer, we are taught that we should add Amen to our prayers, in testimony of our desire and assurance to be heard.*

Amen is a Hebrew word; in which language it signifies *true, faithful, certain.* Among the Jews it was used to affirm anything; and in the New Testament we find it frequently adopted by our Saviour. When thus used by him, it is rendered *verily* in our translation.—John iii. 3, 5. The promises of the covenant are said to be *Amen* in Christ,—that is, they are all *certain,* and *sure,* and shall be accomplished.—2 Cor. i. 20. And Jesus Christ himself is called *the Amen,* the faithful and true witness.—Rev iii. 14. At the end of a creed it means, *so it is,* implying a belief of the doctrines contained in it ; and at the end of a prayer it means, *so let it be,* or *so it shall be.*

We are here informed, that we should conclude all our prayers with Amen, *in testimony of our desire and assurance to be heard*

1. We conclude our prayers with Amen, *in testimony of our desire to be heard,* when by faith we are emboldened to plead with God, that he would answer our prayers and fulfil our requests. And in this view it signifies, *so be it,* or *so let it be.*—2 Chron. xx. 6, 11; Rev. xxii. 20.

2. We conclude our prayers with Amen, *in testimony of our assurance that we shall be heard,* when by faith we are embol-

dened to rest upon God, and to trust in him, that he will assuredly answer our prayers, and fulfil our requests, or the desires of our heart. And in this view it signifies, *so it shall be.*—2 Chron. xiv. 11.

Amen is here to be considered in both these significations. Surely the sincere Christian, in his approaches to God, desires to be heard; and in faith he assures himself that he shall be heard in the Lord's own time and way. There cannot be a desire of any promised blessing in faith, but there must be some measure of assurance that the blessing shall be bestowed when the Lord will. In the very nature of faith there must be assurance, more or less; for it is a relying upon the *veracity* of God; and "faithful is he who hath promised." This is certainly a firm foundation for the faith of every believer in the Lord Jesus Christ.

INFERENCES.

From this subject we learn,—1. That we should enforce our prayers by arguments, seeing in them we transact with God concerning matters of eternal importance. 2. That arguments are to be used in prayer, not that we may move, or persuade, or prevail with God, but that we ourselves may be affected. 3. That every argument urged in prayer must be taken from God alone. 4. That every encouragement in prayer must be derived from the display of the harmony of the Divine attributes in the work of redemption. 5. That in prayer we should praise God, by ascribing to him the kingdom, and the power, and the glory. 6. That we must add Amen to our prayers, not as a warning that our prayers are finished (as too many suppose, who are ignorant of the meaning of the word), but in testimony of our desire to be heard by the "Hearer of prayer," and also in testimony of our assurance that we shall be heard in the Lord's own time and way.

INDEX.

Adam, all mankind sinned in, 69.
Adoption, nature of, 132; effect of, 133, 134.
Adultery forbidden, 234.
Assurance of Faith, evidences of, 276-280.
Atheism forbidden, 175.
Atonement, by whom made, 95; for whom, 96; effects of, 97.

Baptism, nature of, 308-10; how to be administered, 310; designs of, 311; efficacy of, 312; necessity of its observance, 313; duty of Christians respecting, ib.; to whom not to be administered, 315; right of infants of believing parents to, 315-19; not to be administered more than once, 319; naming of child no part of, ib.; none but immediate parents may present child for, ib.

Chastity required, 222.
Christ, the Lord Jesus, the only Redeemer, 83; eternal Son of God, 84; became man, 85; both God and man, ib.; will continue so for ever, 86; took to himself a true body and a reasonable soul, 87; conceived by the power of the Holy Ghost, ib.; born of the Virgin Mary, 88; born without sin, ib.; prophet, priest, and king, 89-91; must be received by faith in all his offices, 91; reveals will of God by his Word and Spirit, 92; and for his people's salvation, 93; the only priest that can take away sin, 94; offered himself in sacrifice to God, 95; but "once," ib.; for the elect only, 96; to satisfy divine justice, 97; and to reconcile sinners to God, ib.; he maketh continual intercession, ib.; is a king, 100; has two kingdoms, 101; his mediatorial kingdom, ib.; his acts as a king, 102; he humbleth himself, 104-6; submitted to death, was buried, and continued under the power of death for a time, 106; was exalted by his resurrection and ascension, 107-10; will judge the world, 110; purchased redemption for his people, 113; must be received as offered in the gospel, 270-2; his body partaken of by faith in the Lord's Supper, 327.
——'s imputed righteousness received by faith, 128; redounds to God's glory, 131.
Commandment, First, what required in, 173-4; forbidden in, 175-7; expression "before Me" in, 178.
—————— Second, what required in, 179-81; forbidden in, 182-3; reasons annexed to, 184-6.
—————— Third, what required in, 187-91; forbidden in, 192-3; reason annexed to, 194-5.
—————— Fourth, expressed in peculiar manner, 197; what required in, 197-8; binding in all ages, 199; what forbidden in, 208-9; reasons annexed to, 210-11.
—————— Fifth, general scope of, 213; what required in, 215-19; forbidden in, 221-4; promise in, 225; promise limited, 226.
—————— Sixth, what required in, 227-8; forbidden in, 229.

Commandment, Seventh, what required in, 233; forbidden in, 234 reasons why forbidden, 235.
——————— Eighth, what required in, 236-8; forbidden in, 239-41
——————— Ninth, what required in, 242-3; forbidden in, 244-7.
——————— Tenth, what required in, 248-9: forbidden in, 250-3.
Commandments of God, none able, since the fall, perfectly to keep, 254; are daily broken, 256.
——————— Ten, how given, 162; what summarily comprehended in, 163; rules necessary for proper understanding of, 165; first and principal subject of, 166; second subject of, 167; reasons for keeping, 169-70.
Coveteousness forbidden, 250.
Creation, the, 52.

Decrees of God, 48; have various properties, 49; object whatever comes to pass, ib.; for God's own glory, 50; doctrine of calculated for good, ib.; not the rule of our conduct, ib.; executed in creation and providence, 51.
Death, by the fall, 74; state of believers at, 147; after, 147-8; of unbelievers after, 148.

Election, 76; purpose of from eternity, 77; what result of, ib.
Effectual Calling, believers united to Christ in, 116; the work of the Spirit, 118; the Spirit convinces of sin and misery in, 119; enlightens the mind in, ib.; renews the will in, 120; persuades and enables to embrace Christ in, ib.

Faith, foundation of obedience, 28; unites the believer to Christ, 115; definition of, 266-8; the end of, 268-70; the gift of God, 273; how to distinguish if true, 274-5; consciousness principal but not only evidence of, 276-80; other evidence of, 281.
Father, the, is God, 45.
Free Will, our First Parents created with, 62; will to good lost by fall, 63; will renewed in effectual calling, 120.

God, glorifying and enjoying of, 21; rule of direction for, 23; existence of, 30; titles of, ib.; a Spirit, 31; perfections of, ib.; infinite, 32; unchangeable, 33; eternal, ib.; infinitely wise, 34; powerful ib.; holy, 35; just, 36; good and merciful, 37; true and faithful, 38; but one, 40; living and true, ib.; wrath and curse of, how escaped, 263.
Godhead, persons in, 42; only three persons in, 43; incommunicable properties of, 44.
Grace, covenant of, 78; parties to, 79; condition of, 80; promise in, 81; administration of committed to Christ, 81: design of, 82.

Hell, pains of, 75; are eternal, ib.
Holy Ghost, is God, 45; sin against, description of it, 121.
Holy Spirit, influence of, 118-20.
Husbands and wives, duties of, 215, 222.

Idolatry forbidden, 175, 182.

Judgment, Last, proof of, 111; Christ judge at, 112; acknowledgment of believers at, 151; condition of the wicked at, 152.
Justification and sanctification, difference between, 124.
——————— an act of free and unmerited grace, 125; righteousness of Christ imputed in, 126; believers' sins pardoned in, 127; grounds of acceptance in, ib.

INDEX.

Law of God, want of conformity to, 64; transgression of, ib.
Laws of God, natural and positive, 156.
Lord's Prayer, preface to, teaches how to draw near to God, 351; that we should pray with and for others, 353.
—— First petition in, teaches to pray that all may glorify God, 354-5; that God would dispose all things to his own glory, 356.
—— Second petition in, teaches to pray that God would more and more demonstrate his power, &c., 358; that Satan's kingdom may be destroyed, ib.; that the kingdom of grace may be advanced, 359; that the kingdom of glory may be hastened, 360.
—— Third petition in, teaches to pray that God would enable us to know and obey his will, 362; to submit to his providential will, 363; as the angels do in heaven, 364.
—— Fourth petition in, teaches to pray for a competent portion of the good things of this life, 365-6; that we may enjoy God's blessing with them, 367.
—— Fifth petition in, teaches to pray that God, for Christ's sake, would freely pardon all our sins, 368-71; that our being enabled to forgive others, is an encouragement to ask forgiveness for ourselves, 371.
—— Sixth petition in, teaches to pray that God would keep us from being tempted to sin, 374-8; that he would support and deliver us when tempted, 378-9.
—— Conclusion of, teaches us to take our encouragement in prayer from God alone, 380-2; that we should ascribe kingdom, power, and glory to Him, 382-4; that we should add " Amen," 384-5.
Lord's Supper, various names of, 321; elements in celebration of, 322-3; sacramental actions in, 324; design of, 325; worthy receivers of, and what they partake in, 346; consequences of worthily partaking, 328; ordinance of, not a sacrifice for sin, 329; self-examination required before partaking, 330-31; self-examination respecting knowledge, 332; faith, 333; repentance, 334; love, 335; new obedience, 336; danger of neglecting self-examination, 337; how communicants should be engaged while partaking of, 338; self-examination necessary after partaking of, 339.
Lying forbidden, 244.

Magistrate and subject, duties of, 219, 224.
Man, creation of, end of, in reference to God, 20; to himself, 21; male and female, 55; after the image of God, 55; with dominion over the creatures, 55.
—— Fall of, 65; by eating the forbidden fruit, 66; occasion of, ib.; what it involves, ib.; aggravation of, 67; consequences of, 70-4.
Master and servants, duties of, 217, 223.
Means of grace, outward and ordinary, 287; special, 238; to whom made effectual, 289.
Ministers and people, duties of, 218.
Moral law, the first given to man, 156; nature of, 157; what cannot be obtained by it, ib.; viewed in three forms, 158; to whom of use, 160; what laws besides given of old, 161.
Murder forbidden, 230.

Oaths, lawfulness of, 189-90.
Obedience required of God by man, 153; rule of, 154; nature of, ib.

Parents and children, duties of, 215, 223.
—— First, left to freedom of will, 62; fall of, 63.
Perseverance of saints 145.

Prayer, nature of, 340-1; for what to be made, 442; in whose name, ib.; offered up with confession of sin, 343; with thankful acknowledgment of God's mercies, 344; into what commonly distinguished, 345; rule of direction in, needed, 347; whole word of God of use to direct us, 348; Lord's Prayer special rule, 349.
Prayers, possible to know ours are accepted, 345.
Profanity forbidden, 192.
Providence, 56; what consists in, 57; objects of, ib.; character of, ib.; what distinguished into, 58.

Redemption, purchased by Christ, 113; must be applied to believers, ib.; is effectually applied by the Holy Spirit, ib.; applied to sinners by the Spirit working faith in them, 115; benefits of in this life, 123; additional benefits of, 140-5; benefits of at death, 147; after death, 148; at the resurrection, 150-2; benefits of, how communicated, 264, 289.
Repentance, what distinguished into, 283; how wrought when true, 284; springs of, ib.; what it consists of, 285-6.

Sabbath, institution of, 202; change of, 202-4; how to be sanctified, 205; how spent, 206.
Sacraments, nature of, 301; what consist of, 302; end or design of, ib.; what means of, 298; virtue of, ib.; how rendered effectual, 299; of the Old Testament, 303-5; of the New, 306; none but two appointed by Christ, ib.
Salvation through Christ, tendency of doctrine, 130.
———— purchased, how conveyed, 262; offer and promise of, 272.
Sanctification, a work of free grace, 136; effect of, 136-8.
Scriptures the Word of God, 23; only rule, 24; perfect rule, 25; written in Hebrew and Greek, ib.; principally teach what to believe of God, 27; what duty God requires of man, ib.
"Sincere obedience" not substituted for "perfect obedience," 129.
Sin, original, 71; consists in, 72; nature of, ib.; what every sin deserves, 259-61.
Sins, some more heinous in themselves than others, 257; some on account of aggravations, ib.
Son, the, is God, 45.
Stations and relations, various, 213.
Superiors, inferiors, and equals, duties of, 213, 221.

Theft forbidden, 239.
Trinity, belief in, necessary to salvation, 46.

Union of Christ and believers real, &c., 116.

Word of God, reading and preaching of the, 291-4; how becomes effectual to salvation, 295-7; of use to direct in prayer, 348.
Works, Covenant of, 59; parties of, ib.; condition of, 60; reward promised in, ib.; penalty of, 61; made with Adam and his posterity, 68.
World, Creation of the, from nothing, 52; by the word of God's power 53; in six days, ib.; very good, 54; for God's own glory, ib.
Worship of God, 185-6.

THE END.

OPINIONS OF THE PRESS.

"This is a posthumous work of a townsman, who was cut off at an early age, from the promise of a life of distinguished usefulness. It is the fruit of his exertions to qualify himself for the office of the sacred ministry—exertions pushed so far beyond the limits of physical capability, as to bring the laborious student to a premature grave. Mr Paterson died in 1828, in the 25th year of his age. The present work was left by him in a state of entire preparation for the press, but various circumstances have delayed its publication. The manuscript was submitted to several distinguished ministers, who expressed their opinions of it in terms of the most unqualified approbation. By one of them its merits were considered so great, that he declared he could not suggest the change of a single word. Its acknowledged excellence, and prospective utility as a help to the study of the doctrines and duties of religion, so admirably set forth in the Shorter Catechism, induced the publisher to give it to the world. We have no doubt that the expectations formed of its success will be fully realized; and earnestly recommend it as a masterly illustration of an accredited repository of the doctrines of the Church."—*Aberdeen Journal, Sept.* 8, 1841.

"Mr Paterson's manner in the treatment of each question is, to give, first, the *analysis* and *proofs*, then the *explanation*, and, thirdly, the *inferences*. For perfect clearness of statement, and for copiousness of matter, joined to conciseness of language, he is not easily to be surpassed. We have the greatest pleasure in commending the work to the favourable notice of our readers as a singularly admirable and practicable compend of the Scripture system, and can very confidently predict its speedy and certain popularity."—*Witness, Sept.* 4, 1841.

" We less regret our delay in bringing this work under the attention of our readers, as we have had frequent occasion to refer to its pages for private use, and the favourable opinion we were at first led to form of its design and execution has thereby been greatly enhanced. There is a maturity of mind displayed throughout the work far beyond the years of its promising and lamented author; and while it will be found of great advantage to the young, and eminently so to the Sabbath-school teacher, the most experienced Christian will find in its pages much to instruct and edify. The success that has attended the author's labours is just another proof of the inexhaustible resources of that wonderful compendium of revealed religion, the Shorter Catechism. The author's plan is, to give an analysis and scriptural proofs of each answer in the Catechism; then to explain it more at large by references to other corresponding passages of Scripture; and finally to give the practical inferences. The whole evidences great research, care, and labour. It is thoroughly scriptural, and altogether the best help to the study of the Catechism we have ever seen. We strongly recommend it to the attention of Sabbath-school teachers, and to the Christian public at large."—*Scottish Guardian, Nov.* 12, 1841.

" Several commentaries on the Shorter Catechism have been written, with the view of explaining the various doctrines and duties briefly stated. None of them seem to be more comprehensive or useful than Mr Paterson's work. The laborious and minute division of subjects adopted by the author renders it highly efficient for the use of Sabbath-school teachers and heads of families. To the former class especially we scarcely know a better assistant, and they should carefully peruse its contents. It is a legacy to the world by one whose few years were marked by many proofs of his genius, and of whose after-life high hopes were formed by those who knew him best. These expectations have been blighted by his early death; but not until, in this single work, he had done more for the world's good than many men who plod out their three score and ten or fourscore years, in professions for its advancement. ..... We cannot take extracts from a volume of this nature, which is in itself an elaborate dissection of another and a well-known work. But we may again commend it to clergymen, to schoolmasters, to Sabbath-school teachers, to heads of families, and to all who are anxious to acquire a minute guide in the development of those great doctrines of which the Shorter Catechism treats. If we knew what other steps we could adopt to advance its circulation, they would be cheerfully adopted, in the conviction that we were thus doing some service to the interests of religion."—*Aberdeen Banner.*

"This is such a work as we have long considered a desideratum. It is a very judicious and admirable exposition of the Shorter Catechism. It analyzes each question with much clearness and accuracy; presents a good summary of Scripture proofs; states and elucidates the doctrine held forth, and deduces appropriate inferences. It truly contains much in little space, giving the substance of some large *bodies of divinity*, in a neat portable volume. Our readers will indeed find, on inspection, that its excellence far exceeds our feeble recommendation. Parents, ministers, and others engaged in the religious instruction of youth, will receive from it valuable assistance; and we are unacquainted with any book of the same size that is better fitted to impart to students a correct and practical view of the theology of the Bible."—*Covenanter Nov.* 1841.

"Many high encomiums have been pronounced upon this volume, yet we are satisfied they are well merited. It is elaborate, yet luminous and well arranged, and forms an admirable system of theology. As a guide to the Sabbath-school teacher, a companion to the student of divinity, or a help to the youthful pastor in his weekly classes, it is worthy of the highest praise."—*Christian Journal.*

"Paterson's Catechism is indeed a 'concise,' but very judicious system of theology, showing an accurate and extensive acquaintance with divine truth, and displaying extraordinary power of analysis and arrangement. We would recommend it especially to Sabbath-school teachers, as fitted to afford them ample assistance in explaining the Shorter Catechism to their scholars, and in enforcing its doctrines and duties."—*United Secession Magazine, Feb.,* 1842.

"A truly excellent system of theology, compiled with much care and pains, and fitted to be useful, if kept, as all human systems ought to be, in its proper place, and not allowed to displace, or usurp equality with, the oracles of eternal truth." —*Presbyterian Review, April,* 1842.

"We can speak in commendation of this work from long and intimate acquaintance with its contents; and we can have no hesitation in pointing it out to Sabbath-school teachers especially, as beyond comparison the best work for their purpose we have ever seen. The more we have become acquainted with it, the more have we felt the opinion of it confirmed which we gave some years ago, in noticing the first edition. Having often recommended it privately, we have great pleasure in once more having an opportunity of testifying to its excellency to all who may be desirous of possessing, whether for public or private use, a complete systematic analysis of the Shorter Catechism. . . . . It is the BEST aid to the study of the best of human productions, because it is most *like* the Catechism, which derives all its excellence from being so like the Bible."—*Scottish Guardian, October* 1, 1844.

"We need scarcely say that we have the greatest pleasure in recommending a work of such singular excellence, and of so much practical utility, especially to heads of families and Sabbath-school teachers."—*Fife Sentinel.*

"It is without the slightest hesitation we affirm, that this work will be found, on examination, superior to all former attempts made at analytically disclosing the beauties of our admirable Catechism. . . . . To Sabbath-school teachers, parents, and guardians, we most earnestly invite their attention to an examination of the work for themselves, confident that they will thank us for directing their attention to it."—*Western Watchman.*

"This is a work of great value and merit, and we willingly recommend it to Sabbath-school teachers, parents, and others engaged in the instruction of youth, as a manual of much practical utility, and well adapted to afford them the most valuable assistance in acquiring a correct and comprehensive knowledge of the doctrines of the Holy Scriptures."—*Dumfries Standard.*

"This little work really is what it professes to be. . . . . It is encumbered with no surplus words, or long useless disquisitions. It is plain, explicit, and practical, and admirably adapted to the anxious inquirer, whose concern it is to get at the truth, rather than to burden his mind with a crude mass of theological erudition. It is an excellent hand-book for teachers and heads of families."—*Border Watch.*

"It is indeed 'a system of theology,' brief, yet comprehensive, including, in one small volume, matter which *might have been* expanded into many great ones. Considering that the author was so young a man (he died in his 25th year), we cannot but admire the soundness of judgment, as well as the mental vigour and industrious research which almost every page exhibits."—*Watchman.*

"The merits of this excellent work are sufficiently attested by the fact of its having reached a second edition, within a comparatively short period. It must prove a lasting monument of the industry and intelligence of the pious and amiable author, who was removed at an early age from a sphere in which, had life been spared, he gave abundant promise of proving eminently useful."—*Aberdeen Journal.*

"This is the second edition of a truly admirable work, forming a complete manual of theology. It is well adapted for Sabbath-school teachers, and all who are engaged in teaching the young. The Shorter Catechism stands unrivalled as a compend of sound theology; and every contribution towards the exposition and illustration of the great truths which it inculcates, merits an extensive circulation."—*Banner of Ulster.*

"This work is all that it professes to be—*A Concise System of Theology.* It is minute and comprehensive, and discovers on the part of its author, who was only 25 years of age when he died, talent of no mean order, maturity of judgment, extensive and accurate acquaintance with Scripture doctrine, and great industry in the study of divine things. It fills up with the hand of a master, and, considering his youth, in a way that awakens our astonishment, the inimitable outline of Scripture truth embodied in the Shorter Catechism."—*Scottish Presbyterian.*

"Of the numerous works we possess or have read on the 'Shorter Catechism,' excellent although many of them are, we know not one superior to the volume before us. The young man who shall sit down and thoroughly master it, will be no ordinary theologian. In this superficial age, in this day of unsettled opinion, it is most cheering to see fresh editions of this invaluable system of genuine scriptural theology. The plan is, perhaps, the best that can be adopted. Of each question there is first the 'analysis and proofs,' next the 'explanation,' and lastly the 'inferences.' The whole forms a rich compendium, deserving the most extensive circulation."—*Christian Witness.*

www.ingramcontent.com/pod-product-compliance
Lightning Source LLC
Chambersburg PA
CBHW051249300426
44114CB00011B/947